Identity: a reader

The Identity Reader

This Reader provides some of the set readings for a 16 week module (D853 *Identity in Question*) which is offered by The Open University Masters Programme in the Social Sciences.

The Open University Masters Programme in the Social Sciences

The MA/MSc Programme enables students to select from a range of modules to create a programme to Suit their own professional or personal development. Students can choose from a range of social science modules to obtain an MA in the Social Sciences, or may choose to specialize in a particular subject area by studying modules in one of the offered study lines. D853 *Identity in Question* is one of the modules for the MA in Cultural and Media Studies.

OU Supported Learning

The Open University's unique, supported ('distance') learning Masters Programme in the Social Sciences is designed to facilitate engagement at an advanced level with the concepts, approaches, theories and techniques associated with a number of academic areas of study. The Social Sciences Masters Programme provides great flexibility. Students study in their own environments, in their own time, anywhere in the European Union. They receive specially prepared course materials, benefit from structured tutorial support throughout all the coursework and assessment assignments, and have the chance to work with other students.

How to apply

If you would like to register for this programme, or simply find out more information, please write for the Masters Programme in the Social Sciences Prospectus to The Open University, Course Reservations Centre, PO Box 625, Milton Keynes, MK7 6ZW, UK (Telephone +44 (0)1908 858585) E-mail: ces-gen@nen.ac.uk)

Identity: a reader

edited by
Paul du Gay, Jessica Evans
and Peter Redman

Identity

SAGE Publications
London • Thousand Oaks • New Delhi

in association with
The Open University

First published 2000

Reprinted 2002, 2003.

SAGE Publications Ltd
6 Bonhill Street
London EC2A 4PU

SAGE Publications Inc.
2455 Teller Road
Thousand Oaks, California 91320

SAGE Publications India Pvt Ltd
32, M-Block Market
Greater Kailash – I
New Delhi 110 048

British Library Cataloguing in Publication data

A catalogue record for this book is available
from the British Library

ISBN 0 7619 6915 2
ISBN 0 7619 6916 0 (pbk)

Library of Congress catalog record available

Text and cover design: Barker/Hilsdon
Typeset by Mayhew Typesetting, Rhayader, Powys
Printed in Great Britain by The Cromwell Press Ltd,
Trowbridge, Wiltshire

Contents

Notes on contributors

Louis Althusser (1918–1990) was a French philosopher known for his theoretical reformulations of classic Marxism. His memoirs, *The Future Lasts a Long Time* (1993), were published after his suicide. He is the author of *Lenin and Philosophy and Other Essays* (1972), *For Marx* (1977) and *Philosophy and the Spontaneous Philosophy of the Scientists* (1989).

Jessica Benjamin is a practising psychoanalyst in New York City, and is on the faculty of New York University Postdoctoral Psychology Program in Psychoanalysis and the New School for Social Research Program in Psychoanalytic Studies. Among other works, she is the author of *The Bonds of Love: Psychoanalysis, Feminism and the Problem of Domination* (1988) and *Like Subjects, Love Objects: Essays on Recognition and Sexual Difference* (1995).

Emile Benveniste (1902–1976) was born in Cairo and studied linguistics at the Sorbonne as a student of Saussure. He became a professor of linguistics at the Collège de France. He had a significant impact on the development of structural linguistic thought espoused by theorists like Lacan, Kristeva and Barthes. His books include *Problems in General Linguistics* (1971) and *Indo-European Language and Society* (1973).

Homi K. Bhabha is Professor of Art History and of English in the Department of Art History at the University of Chicago. He researches in the areas of colonial and post-colonial theory, cosmopolitanism, nineteenth- and twentieth-century British and other English-language literatures. His books include *Nation and Narration* (1990), *The Location of Culture* (1994) and *Anish Kapoor* (1998).

Pierre Bourdieu is Professor of Sociology at the Collège de France and Director of Studies at the Ecole Pratique des Hautes Etudes en Sciences Sociales. He is the author of numerous works in anthropology, sociological theory, the sociology of education and the sociology of culture. His publications include *Outline of a Theory of Practice* (1977), *The Logic of Practice* (1990), *The Field of Cultural Production* (1993) and *Acts of Resistance: Against the Tyranny of the Market* (1998).

Judith Butler is Maxine Elliot Professor in the Departments of Rhetoric and Comparative Literature at the University of California at Berkeley. She has published extensively in philosophy, feminist and queer theory. Her books include *Gender Trouble* (1990), *Bodies that Matter* (1993), *The Psychic Life of Power* (1997) and *Excitable Speech* (1997).

Ian Craib is Professor of Sociology at the University of Essex and a group-analytic psychotherapist. He is the author of a number of works in sociology, social theory and psychoanalysis, including *The Importance of Disappointment* (1994) and *Experiencing Identity* (1998).

Jacques Derrida is Director of Studies at the Ecole Pratique des Hautes Etudes en Sciences Sociales and holds a visiting appointment at the University of California, Irvine. He founded the International College of Philosophy in Paris and the International Group for Research into the Teaching of Philosophy. His published work includes *Speech and Phenomena* (1973), *Writing and Difference* (1978), *Margins of Philosophy* (1983) and, more recently, *Specters of Marx* (1994) and *Politics of Friendship* (1997).

Norbert Elias (1897–1990) studied philosophy and medicine at Breslau, and sociology at Heidelberg, and was then assistant to Karl Mannheim at Frankfurt (1929–33). In exile in England, he eventually became Reader in Sociology at the University of Leicester, and briefly professor at the University of Ghana. He is the author of numerous articles and books, including *The Civilizing Process* (2 vols, 1939/1978), *The Court Society* (1983) and *Involvement and Detachment* (1987).

Frantz Fanon (1926–1961) was born in Martinique and studied medicine and psychiatry in France. A hospital assignment in Algeria led to his becoming a spokesman for Algeria during the rising against the French. He was a leading contributor to anti-colonial revolutionary thought. His writing includes *Black Skins, White Masks* (1952) and *The Wretched of the Earth* (1961).

Michel Foucault (1926–1984) was Professor of the History of Systems of Thought at the Collège de France and one of the most celebrated and controversial intellectuals of the twentieth century. His many books include the three-volume *The History of Sexuality* (1979–86), *Madness and Civilisation* (1961), *The Order of Things* (1966), *The Archaeology of Knowledge* (1969) and *Discipline and Punish* (1975).

Anthony Giddens is Director of the London School of Economics and Political Science. His research interests embrace politics, sociology, social theory and the nature of social democracy. His numerous books include *Modernity and Self-identity* (1990), *Beyond Left and Right* (1994) and, more recently, *The Third Way* (1998).

Pierre Hadot is Professeur Honoraire at the Collège de France. His writings on philosophical thought and method include *Plotinus or the Simplicity of Vision* (1994), *Philosophy as a Way of Life* (1995) and *The Inner Citadel* (1998).

Stuart Hall is Emeritus Professor at The Open University and Visiting Professor at Goldsmiths College, London. A leading figure of the intellectual left, he has written extensively on politics, race and culture. Some of these writings are collected in *The Hard Road to Renewal* (1988). He is editor or co-editor of numerous collections, including *Culture, Media and Language* (1980), *Questions of Cultural Identity* (1996), *Representation* (1997) and *Visual Culture: a reader* (1999).

Melanie Klein (1882–1960) was born in Vienna but settled in Britain. She was a psychoanalytic practitioner in the Freudian school but her work with children led to the development of a theoretical and clinical approach which was at odds with orthodox Freudianism. Her approach was based on innovative therapeutic techniques in the treatment of children. Her writings include *The Psycho-analysis of Children* (1932) and *Narrative of a Child Analysis* (1961).

Julia Kristeva is a psychoanalytic practitioner and member of the faculty of the University of Paris VII as well as Visiting Professor at Columbia University. She has combined insights from various disciplines, including philosophy, linguistics, psychoanalysis and literary theory, to develop her own critical method. She has written many articles and contributed to an array of edited collections. Her books include *Essays in Semiotics* (1971), *Strangers to Ourselves* (1988), *Nations without Nationalism* (1993) with L.S. Roudiez, and *Proust: Questions of Identity* (1998).

Jacques Lacan (1901–1981) was briefly President of the Société Pyschoanaly- tique de Paris, but after disputes with the society he led a breakaway faction which became L'École Freudienne de Paris. He was a central figure in the development of contemporary psychoanalytic and structuralist thought. A selection of Lacan's seminars from the 1950s and early 1960s was published as *Ecrits: a Selection* (1966/1977) Further seminars are now widely available in translation.

Christopher Lasch (1932–1994) was Watson Professor of History at the University of Rochester. A renowned historian and social critic, he is the author of a number of books exploring late twentieth-century culture and politics in the United States, including *The Agony of the American Left* (1969), *The Culture of Narcissism* (1979), *The Minimal Self* (1984) and *The Revolt of the Elites and the Betrayal of Democracy* (1994).

Thomas H. Marshall (1893–1982) was Professor of Sociology at the London School of Economics. He is best known for his work on the nature of citizenship. He is the author of *Social Policy in the Twentieth Century* (1965), *Class, Citizenship and Social Development* (1977) and *The Right to Welfare and Other Essays* (1981).

Marcel Mauss (1872–1950) was Professor of Primitive Religion at the Ecole Pratique des Hautes Etudes and taught at the Collège de France. His major intellectual contribution was to theories of human classification and gift exchange based on his anthropological studies of the peoples of Melanesia, Polynesia and North America. He is the author of a number of books, including *The Gift* (1976) and *Sociology and Psychology* (1979).

Isabel Menzies Lyth is a member of the British Psychoanalytic Society and combines part-time private practice with consultancy and academic research. A leading exponent of the socio-psychoanalytic perspective, she is the author of a number of important articles and essays, some of which are collected in

Containing Anxiety in Institutions (1988) and *The Dynamics of the Social* (1989).

Amélie Oksenberg Rorty is Director of the Program in the History of Ideas at Brandeis University and teaches philosophy at the Harvard Graduate School of Education. She is the author of *Mind in Action: Essays in the Philosophy of Mind* (1988) and has edited many anthologies, including *The Identities of Persons* (1976).

Jacqueline Rose is Professor of English at Queen Mary and Westfield College, London. She is widely known for her work on female sexuality and Lacanian theory. She is the author of *Sexuality in the Field of Vision* (1986), *The Case of Peter Pan: Or, the Impossibility of Children's Fiction* (1992) and *Why War? Psychoanalysis and the Return to Melanie Klein* (1993). She co-edited *Feminine Sexuality: Jacques Lacan and the école freudienne* with Juliet Mitchell in 1982.

Nikolas Rose is Professor of Sociology at Goldsmiths College, London. He is the author of a number of studies of the social and conceptual history of the human sciences, including *Governing the Soul* (1990), *Inventing Ourselves* (1996) and, most recently, *The Powers of Freedom: Reframing Political Thought* (1999).

Michael Rustin is Professor of Sociology at the University of East London and also teaches at the Tavistock Clinic. He publishes in the areas of psychoanalysis, politics and culture and is the author of *The Good Society and the Inner World* (1991).

Kaja Silverman is Professor of Rhetoric at the University of California at Berkeley. She is the author of a number of books and articles, including *The Subject of Semiotics* (1983) and *Male Subjectivity at the Margins* (1992).

Max Weber (1864–1920) held professorships at the universities of Freiberg, Heidelberg and Munich. He is generally regarded as a founder of modern social science. His best-known works are *The Protestant Ethic and the Spirit of Capitalism* (1904–5, trans. 1930) and *Economy and Society* (2 vols, 1978).

Donald W. Winnicott (1896–1971) began his career as a paediatrician but became increasingly involved in psychoanalysis as a pioneer of what became known as the object relations perspective. He made a lasting contribution to both theory and clinical practice. A prolific writer throughout his career, his many books include *The Child, the Family and the Outside World* (1964), *Playing and Reality* (1971), *Through Paediatrics to Psycho-Analysis* (1975) and *The Maturational Process and the Facilitating Environment* (1965).

Acknowledgements

The authors and publishers wish to thank the following for permission to use copyright material.

Sage Publications Ltd for 'Who needs Identity?' from *Questions of Cultural Identity*, Stuart Hall and Paul du Gay, 1996; 'What's Happening to Mourning?' from *Experiencing Identity* by Ian Craib, 1998; and 'Genealogies of Subjectification' by Nikolas Rose from *Questions of Cultural Identity*, Stuart Hall and Paul du Gay, 1996.

Monthly Review Press for 'Ideology Interpellates Individuals as Subjects' from 'Ideology and Ideological State Apparatuses' in *Lenin Philosophy and Other Essays*, Louis Althusser.

Editions Gallimard for 'Subjectivity in language' from *Problems in General Linguistics*, Emile Benveniste, 1966.

W.W. Norton & Company for 'The Narcisstistic Personality of Our Time', from *The Culture of Narcissism: American life in an age of diminishing expectations* by Christopher Lasch. Copyright © 1991 by Christopher Lasch; 'The Narcisstistic Personality of Our Time', from *The Culture of Narcissism: American life in an age of diminishing expectations* by Christopher Lasch. Copyright © 1991 by Christopher Lasch; and Taylor and Francis and W.W. Norton & Company Inc. for 'The Mirror Stage' by Jaques Lacan, translated by Alan Sheridan, from *Ecrits: a Selection by Jaques Lacan*, translated by Alan Sheridan. Copyright © 1966 by Editions du Seuil. English translation copyright © 1977 by Tavistock Publications.

Verso for 'Feminine Sexuality: Jacques Lacan and the *ecole freudienne*' from *Sexuality in the Field of Vision*, 1986; and 'Psychoanalysis, Racism and Anti-Racism' from *The Good Society and the Inner World*, Michael Rustin, 1991.

Columbia University Press for 'Revolution in Poetic Language' by Julia Kristeva from *Literary Theory: An Anthology* edited by J. Rivkin and M. Ryan, (1984).

Oxford University Press for 'Suture: The Cinematic Model' by Kaja Silverman from *The Subject of Semiotics*, 1983.

Columbia University Press for 'Differance' by Jacques Derrida from *A Derrida Reader*, edited by Peggy Kamuf and Jean-Francoise Lyotard, 1991.

Professor Bhabha for 'Interrogating Identity' by H.K. Bhabha, from *Anatomy of Racism* edited by D.T. Goldberg.

Penguin Books Ltd., Editions Gallimard and Georges Borchardt Inc. for 'Domain' by Michel Foucault from *The History of Sexuality* (New York: Random House, 1978). Originally published in French as *La Volonté de savior*. Copyright © 1976 by Les Editions Minuit.

Taylor and Francis, Inc./Routledge, Inc., http://www.routledge-ny.com for 'Critically Queer' from *Bodies That Matter*, Judith Butler, 1993.

Random House Group Ltd. for 'Notes on Some Schizoid Mechanisms', by Melanie Klein from The *Complete Writing of Melanie Klein* edited by J. Mitchell, 1986.

Taylor and Francis Books Ltd. and The Winnicott Trust for 'Mirror Role of Mother and Family in Child Development' and 'Transnational Objects and Transnational Phenomena', from *Playing and Reality*, D.W. Winnicott, 1971.

Free Association Books, London, England (1998) for 'The Functioning of the Social Systems as a Defence Against Anxiety' by Isabel Menzies Lyth from *Containing Anxiety in Institutions, Selected Essays, Volume 1*. © Isabel Menzies Lyth 1980.

Editions du Seuil for 'The Negro and Psychopathology' from *Black Skins, White Masks*, the English translation of *Peau Noirse, Masques Blancs* by Frantz Fanon © Editions du Seuil, 1971.

Pantheon Books, a division of Random House Inc. for 'The Oedipal Riddle' from *The Bonds of Love* by Jessica Benjamin. Copyright © 1988 by Jessica Benjamin.

Blackwell Publishers for 'Homo Clausus and the Civilizing Process' from *The Civilizing Process* by Norbert Elias, 1978; and Stanford University Press and Blackwell Publishers for 'The Trajectory of the Self' from *Modernity and Self Identity* by Anthony Giddens, 1991.

Pierre Bourdieu, Wendy Leeds-Hurwitz and Yves Winkin for 'The Biographical Illusion' by Pierre Bourdieu (translated by Yves Winkin and Wendy Leeds-Hurwitz) from *Working Papers and Proceedings of the Centre for Psychosocial Studies*.

Cambridge University Press and Blackwell Publishers for 'A Category of the Human Mind: the notion of "person"; the notion of "self"' by Marcel Mauss (translated by W.D. Halls) from M. Carrithers et al., *The Category of the Person* originally published in the *Journal of the Royal Anthropological Institute*: 1–25 1985.

Cambridge University Press for 'The Profession and Vocation of Politics' by Max Weber from *Weber Political Writings*, edited by P. Lassman and R. Spiers (1994).

Penguin Books Ltd. for 'Introduction' from 'The Use of Pleasure' in *The History of Sexuality Volume 1* by Michel Foucault, translated by Robert Huxley (Viking 1986, first published in France as *L'Usage des Plaisirs* by Editions Gallimard. Copyright © Editions Gallimard, 1984. Translations copyright Random House Inc. 1985.

Etudes Auguestiennes for 'Reflections on the Idea of the "Cultivation of the Self"' from *Philosophy as a Way of Life* by Pierre Hadot.

Beacon Press for 'Persons and Personae' from *Mind In Action* by Amélie Oskenberg Rorty. Copyright © 1988 Amilie Oskenberg Rorty.

ACKNOWLEDGEMENTS

General introduction
Paul du Gay, Jessica Evans and Peter Redman

In recent years questions of 'identity' have attained a remarkable centrality within the human and social sciences. In the field of politics and international relations, for example, the 'identity' of the modern nation-state as an ostensibly sovereign entity has been called into question in the light of a perceived intensification in patterns of global interconnectedness. Similarly, in various forms of sociological analysis, the dominance of 'class' as the 'master identity' of the social – that category through which all other social identities are to be mediated – has been challenged by the growth of various new social movements: 'feminisms', black struggles and the ecological movement to name but a few of the most obvious candidates. Although the term 'identity' takes on different connotations depending upon the context within which it is deployed, one thing at least appears relatively clear, 'identity' has achieved its contemporary centrality both theoretically and substantively because that to which it is held to refer – whether the 'it' in question is, for example, the category 'man', 'black', 'work', 'nation' or 'community' – is regarded in some sense as being more contingent, fragile and incomplete and thus more amenable to reconstitution than was previously thought possible.

The very scope and diversity of contemporary debates about identity suggest that anyone hoping to produce the definitive 'Identity' Reader is likely to be involved in a somewhat immodest, and probably impossible, task. However, once it is recognized that the term 'identity' often provides only simple cover for a plethora of very particular and perhaps non-transferable debates, the task of providing an 'Identity' Reader becomes slightly less daunting (although by no means unproblematic). Rather than attempt to map 'the' field, the compiler can, instead, track specific themes, debates or positions. *Identity: a reader* opts for this latter, more modest route. Its main focus is on a highly influential set of theoretical debates concerning the status of the 'subject', the 'individual' and the 'person'. One consistent theme in this otherwise diverse corpus is the powerful challenge it offers to the metaphysics associated with the concept of the person as an individual subject, understood here as a given entity, the author of its own acts and centred in a unitary, reflexive and directive consciousness. The critique of the integral, self-sustaining subject assumed to lie at the heart of post-Cartesian Western metaphysics has been comprehensively advanced in philosophy, for example, while the question of subjectivity and its relation to 'the unconscious' has been developed within the discourses of psychoanalytically inflected cultural studies and feminism. However, while there appears to be considerable interdisciplinary agreement concerning the fictional status of the claim that, ontologically speaking, human beings are 'free agents', directed by a sovereign and integral consciousness, there is also extensive and intensive controversy about how 'identity' should be conceptualized in the wake of the various anti-foundational critiques to which it has been subject.

Identity: a reader attempts to introduce three distinct and influential responses to this question. The first of these we have termed the 'subject-of-language' approach. As the chapters in Part I illustrate, this approach is far from uniform, drawing upon a heterogeneous if overlapping body of predominantly francophone theory, including structural linguistics, Althusserian Marxism, Lacanian psychoanalysis, elements of the project of deconstruction and Foucauldian-inspired 'discourse' theory. Nevertheless, it is reasonable to view these diverse strands as working together to form a recognizable theoretical trajectory within contemporary cultural studies of identity. Distinguishing features of the approach include the idea that identities are constituted through the reiterative power of discourse to produce that which it also names and regulates; that identities are constituted in and through 'difference' and that, as a result, they are inherently 'dislocated' (that is, dependent upon an 'outside' that both denies them and provides the conditions of their possibility); and that 'subjects' are 'interpellated' by or 'sutured' to the subject positions made available in discourse through the operation of the unconscious.

The readings in Parts II and III take issue, in their very different ways, with many of the key assumptions of the 'subject-of-language approach' (as well as with one another, obviously). Part II interrogates the picture of psychoanalysis that emerges from the 'subject-of-language' approach and suggests that its conception of the subject is of a rather abstract creature, removed from the actual experiences of suffering (whether it be 'everyday' or 'uncommon unhappiness') arising from the messy conflicts and ambivalences of unconscious life. In the subject-of-language approach, it is suggested, formal mechanisms – of language and its modes of signification – take precedence over any affective content. As a result, the individual-as-subject is divided through a generalized and pervasive cultural code dominated by a universalizing 'name of the father'. Ultimately, it is argued, this too tightly conceived relationship between the symbolic social order and subjectivity leads to an omission of the dimension of feelings, the defences of the unconscious and the dynamics of intersubjectivity, and to an almost metaphysical preoccupation with difference and sameness. Part II, then, presents a number of classic readings mostly from the Kleinian and object-relations 'British school' of clinically based psycho-analytic literature which serve not only to highlight the specificity of psychoanalytic concepts but to illustrate their workings 'in action' within particular institutional and social settings. One of the key purposes of Part II, in its relationship to Part I, is to indicate some of the crucial differences governing the rationale of clinically based psychoanalytic concepts and the more philosophically inflected 'subject-of-language' appropriation and deployment of psychoanalytic theory. It also indicates some of the problems of explanatory reach that arise from the importation of psychoanalytic ideas both into the more generalized arena of cultural and social theory, and into other areas, such as self-improvement texts and the counselling industry. At stake here are the very definitions of different psychoanalytic traditions: their aims and applications, and the idiom in which they are expressed – in short, their varying normative aspects.

One of the central and continuing developments within the 'subject-of-language' approach has been a sustained attempt to draw together into one analytical framework insights from theoretical practices that are often regarded as inherently antithetical to one another: Foucauldian analyses of 'subjectification' and Lacanian psychoanalysis. This attempt, visible most recently, perhaps, in forms of 'post-Marxist' critique (Laclau and Mouffe, 1985; Laclau, 1990) and in the work of certain 'corporeal' feminists (Butler, 1990, 1993), functions as something like a nodal point connecting Part I with Part III.

Part III registers a distinct scepticism towards the possibility of a *rapprochement* between 'psychoanalysis' and 'genealogy' as complementary and compatible modes of theorizing 'identity' and human habitus. However, in so doing, it also attempts to offer some explanation as to why these two projects have sometimes failed to be recognized as different. One possible reason for this concerns the manner in which psychoanalytically informed 'subject-of-language' theories of identity have come to be seen as expressible in Foucauldian genealogical terms, despite the fact that these very terms aim at dispensing with psychoanalysis as a method of explanation as well as with theories of representation. Indeed, psychoanalytic and genealogical approaches could be said to operate with rather different assumptions concerning what Cousins and Hussain (1984: 254–6) refer to as the relative depth and thickness of 'human material'. Psychoanalytic thinkers tend to operate with a relatively 'thick' view of human material. They elaborate a psychical apparatus whose primary process entails an unconscious whose effects have to be inferred from interpretation. From a psychoanalytic perspective, there is necessarily, not contingently, a complex layering and interpenetration of conflicting elements derived both from the 'inner' history of the individual and from his or her 'external' social environment.

By contrast, genealogies of subjectification require or presuppose only a weak, minimal or 'thin' conception of the human material on which history operates. Genealogists are primarily interested in the 'diversity of strategies and tactics of subjectification that have taken place and been deployed in diverse practices at different moments and in relation to different classifications and differentiations of persons' (Nikolas Rose on p. 311). For advocates of such an approach, accepting the 'depth' of psychoanalytic concepts would require the adoption of an historically specific understanding of the human being, one emerging at the end of the nineteenth century, as the basis of an investigation of the historicity of being human. This would go against the grain of a genealogy of subjectification, where the representation of human beings as interiorizied and psychologized entities is treated as an historical instance and not as a given.

Part III of the book, then, contains a range of classic and contemporary readings which are all, though in somewhat different ways, focused upon the social relations, techniques and forms of training and practice through which human beings have acquired definite capacities and attributes for social existence as particular sorts of person. This shift of focus involves a distinct movement away from (and problematization of) the concerns and assumptions of both the 'subject-of-language' approach to 'subjectivity' contained in Part I, and the psychoanalytic accounts of 'identification' outlined in Part II, and towards a 'thin', historically and contextually informed understanding of the limited and specific forms of personhood that individuals acquire in their passage through social institutions. The readings in Part III, then, argue for a less philosophical and more technical, less universal and more contextualized approach to questions of 'identity'. With this particularizing and contextualizing emphasis comes recognition of the historical contingency and plurality of personae and the necessity of not abstracting the properties of particular forms of personhood from the specific cultural milieux in which they are formed. As one of its advocates has argued, 'the contextual approach . . . emphasises description rather than reconstruction' and prefers 'to leave empirically charged questions open for further investigation, rather than to cover unknown territory with theories that inherit or import theoretical constructs originally introduced for quite different purposes, in quite different contexts' (Rorty, 1988: 14).

The aim of this Reader is not to advocate any one of these particular 'lines' concerning the vexed question of 'identity' but to provide a vehicle for others, all of whom have lines to offer. At the very least, the Reader attempts to set up a framework which, even if necessarily simplified at times, provides a coherent sense of the differences between, and limits of, these three controversial but highly significant approaches. By letting the various protagonists and critics speak in their own words, this collection seeks to provide a more vivid impression of the theoretical and methodological issues at stake in these debates than is usually possible in even the most accomplished of detached commentaries. In conjunction with wider reading, this collection will, we hope, provide a pointer to some of the possibilities and pitfalls of attempting to think within and without the limits of contemporary perspectives on the question of 'identity'.

References

Butler, J. (1990) *Gender Trouble*. London: Routledge.
Butler, J. (1993) *Bodies that Matter*. London: Routledge.
Cousins, M. and Hussain, A. (1984) *Michel Foucault*. Basingstoke: Macmillan.
Laclau, E. (1990) *New Reflections on the Revolution of our Time*. London: Verso.
Laclau, E. and Mouffe, C. (1985) *Hegemony and Socialist Strategy*. London: Verso.
Rorty, A.O. (1988) *Mind in Action: Essays in the Philosophy of Mind*. Boston: Beacon Press.

THE SUBJECT OF LANGUAGE, IDEOLOGY AND DISCOURSE

Introduction
Peter Redman

Part I introduces what has undoubtedly proved to be one of the most fertile if provocative intellectual projects of the past thirty years: the elaboration, in English-speaking cultural studies and related fields, of what we have chosen to call the 'subject-of-language' approach to identity. As argued in the General Introduction to this volume, this 'subject-of-language' approach is far from uniform, drawing on a heterogeneous if overlapping body of mainly French theory, including structural linguistics and speech-act theory, Althusserian Marxism, Lacanian psychoanalysis, and elements of the philosophy of deconstruction and Foucauldian discourse theory. Nevertheless, it is feasible to view these various strands as forming a recognizable tendency within English-speaking cultural studies of identity. The readings that follow aim to provide a preliminary introduction to this 'subject-of-language' approach to identity production. The section begins with Stuart Hall's overview, 'Who needs "identity"?' In this, Hall maps the development of the 'subject-of-language' approach, from Althusser's 'Ideological state apparatuses' essay in the 1970s to Judith Butler's work on gender performativity in the 1990s. In the process, Hall indexes a number of characteristic themes or 'moves' in the 'subject-of-language' argument. Most obviously, he foregrounds the argument, central to structuralist accounts of identity, that there is no 'essential', 'true' or pre-social self but that, instead, identities are constituted or 'performatively' enacted in and through the subject positions made available in language and wider cultural codes. Equally, he stresses the claim, derived from Saussurian linguistics and Derridean deconstruction, that identities are constructed through difference and are in consequence inherently unstable, divided and haunted by the liminal presence of those 'Others' from whom they seek to distinguish themselves. Finally, Hall's essay draws our attention to the Lacanian claim that the subject 'finds itself' in or is 'sutured' to the subject positions made available in language and wider cultural codes through the operation of the unconscious.

However, as well as exploring the development and implications of these arguments, Hall also signals a number of major tensions that run through the 'subject-of-language' tradition. For example, he draws our attention to the ways in which psychoanalysis, contrary to the version of it which appears in the 'subject-of-language' approach, may employ a notion of 'identificatory capacities' or other pre-social 'human material' that is always already present. Needless to say, this brings into question the more extreme anti-essentialist claims of the structuralist paradigm, an issue that is explored further in the readings in Part II of this volume.

Equally, Hall foregrounds a major fault-line dividing Foucauldian work from the linguistic and Lacanian orientations of the 'subject-of-language' approach. As Hall argues, despite the influence of aspects of Foucauldian theory on the approach, Foucault himself did not use the terminology of signifying practices or of psychoanalysis to describe identity production. For Foucault, the subject is constituted purely in the discursive practices of 'disciplinary' regimes and the iterative performance of 'technologies of the self'. The implications of this critique are, of course, further developed in Part III of this volume. Hall, however, closes his review with a discussion of Judith Butler's work on gender performativity, arguing that this provides a potential *rapprochement* between Foucauldian discourse theory and psychoanalysis, one in which Foucauldian insights are reclaimed for a broader 'subject-of-language' project.

Hall's opening chapter having set the scene, the subsequent chapters in Part I go on to illustrate and explore the origins and development of the 'subject-of-language' approach to identity in English-speaking cultural studies and related fields of enquiry. Chapters 2–4 introduce a number of 'foundational' texts, beginning with Althusser's germinal 'Ideological state apparatuses' essay, written in 1969. Appearing in English translation in 1971, this essay was to become a central resource in cultural studies' theorization of identity production. The extract (Chapter 2) focuses on Althusser's third main thesis: that 'ideology interpellates [i.e. "hails" or "recruits"] individuals as subjects'. In elaborating this claim, Althusser advances the classic structuralist argument that 'all ideology has the function (which defines it) of "constituting" concrete individuals as subjects' (p. 31), and develops a Lacanian-inspired account of 'interpellation' as the means by which individuals are 'recruited' to the subject positions made available in 'ideology'.

Chapters 3 and 4 contain two earlier texts whose arguments helped shape Althusser's position and which underpin the wider 'subject-of-language' approach to identity. Chapter 3, Emile Benveniste's 'Subjectivity in language', first published in 1958, is one of the major statements on identity formation by a structural linguist; it is echoed in later works such as Barthes's (1986/1968) famous essay 'The death of the author'. Benveniste's essay clearly signals the shift away from a notion of identity as the property of a purposeful human agent to a notion of the subject as an effect of language. Chapter 4 is Jacques Lacan's 'The mirror stage as formative of the function of the I', first published in 1949 from a conference paper originally given in 1936. This contains a very early Lacanian formulation of the preliminary sense of identity but one that was to remain central to his subsequent work. In this chapter, Lacan describes the process by which the infant 'still sunk in his motor incapacity and nursling dependence' *misrecognizes* itself in its mirror image (p. 45). The point of immediate relevance to our current discussion is that this process is said to be one in which the subject is constituted 'from the outside'. In Lacan's words, the mirror-image 'situates the agency of the ego, before its social determination, in a *fictional* direction' (p. 45, emphasis added). Thus, for Lacan, identity is not something that is always already present within the subject but comes into being 'from the place of the Other' (following the mirror phase, from the place of language and wider cultural codes). It is, thereby, from its very earliest stages, a fictional construct.

Having established some of the positions underpinning the 'subject-of-language' approach to identity, the remaining chapters in Part I explore a number of intellectual and political sites in which the approach has been subsequently elaborated and critiqued, beginning with psychoanalytic feminism. Chapter 5 is an edited version of 'Feminine sexuality: Jacques Lacan and the *école freudienne*' by Jacqueline Rose. First published in 1982, the chapter provides both a comprehensive introduction to key aspects of Lacanian thought and an analysis of their relevance to feminist theory. In particular, Rose discusses the potential of Lacanian theory to provide an account of gender acquisition that is both social and psychological, arguing that Lacan's work serves to underline the constant 'failure' of gender identities in the face of unconscious desire ('*jouissance*'). For Rose, Lacan's analysis of the 'unfinished' (and unfinishable) nature of identity indicates a potential site of women's resistance to patriarchy.

Chapter 6 is also located in the terrain of feminist psychoanalytic theory but offers an alternative account from that available in Rose's Lacanian reading of the development of sexual differences. Julia Kristeva's 'Revolution in poetic language', first published in 1974, has been a major resource in feminist attempts to think outside the Lacanian framework. In the extract provided in Chapter 6, Kristeva outlines her theory of the '*chora*' as a state existing prior to the subject's constitution in language and wider cultural codes and intimately connected to the child's experience of the mother's body. For Kristeva, the '*chora*' provides an alternative site of subjectivity, one that is profoundly disruptive of the patriarchal relations and subject positions made available in language.

Chapter 7 introduces a second area in which, during the 1970s and early 1980s, the 'subject-of-language' approach to identity was developed: film theory. During this time, the British film studies journal, *Screen*, played a major role in theorizing cinema as an apparatus for the production of subjectivities. Central to this was the concept of 'suture', which is introduced in Chapter 7 by Kaja Silverman's overview from her 1983 commentary, *The Subject of Semiotics*. Focusing on the 'shot/reverse shot' convention of mainstream narrative cinema, the chapter explores 'suture' as the process through which unconscious dynamics motivate the individual's 'stitching into' or 'articulation' with the subject positions made available in language and wider cultural codes.

Chapter 8 moves away from a psychoanalytic orientation, focusing instead on the place of deconstruction in the 'subject-of-language' approach to identity. The chapter, first published in 1972, focuses on Derrida's famous term, '*différance*'. The concept of *différance* foregrounds both the centrality of difference to meaning production and the endless slippage or 'deferral' of meaning in language. This argument has unsettling implications for our conception of identity. First and foremost, *différance* suggests that identities are not fixed, for example, in biology or a shared history and do not, in consequence, cohere round a characteristic and defining 'core' or 'centre'. Instead, the concept of *différance* suggests that identities take their meaning from signifying practices: that is, from relations of difference internal to language and other cultural codes. This suggests that identities take their definition only from that which they are not, implying, for example, that the identity of the supposedly 'civilized European' is constructed in relation to a range of 'different' others: the 'barbaric' African, the 'exotic' Oriental' and so on. Disturbingly, this forces us to think of these differential identities as inherently unstable. From the perspective of *différance*, the identity of the 'civilized' European is constantly haunted by the liminal presence of the 'black' and 'Oriental' others against which it defines itself and into which it continually threatens to collapse.

Chapter 9, an extract from Homi Bhabha's influential essay, 'Interrogating identity: the post-colonial prerogative' uses the lens of the post-colonial experience to explore the concept of a 'self' that is absent from and endlessly deferred in language. Bhabha cites two poetic descriptions of the migrant's experience of 'invisibility'. This sense of invisibility, he suggests, can be read as dramatizing the absence of the subject from language. Just as the stereotypes of colonial representation do not provide the migrant with a secure position from which she or he can speak of a 'self', so there is no 'authentic' position rooted in black experience, just more representations. However, Bhabha argues that this 'absence' also serves to undermine the colonial gaze. The impossibility of ever 'seeing' this 'invisible' or 'absent' object of the colonial gaze (a black subject fully present in language) constantly thwarts the attempt to fix a 'white' identity in terms of its difference from a black Other.

Finally, Chapters 10 and 11 turn to 'queer' theory as a further area where the 'subject-of-language' approach has been elaborated. Chapter 10 provides a brief extract from what is now regarded as one of the 'founding' texts of 'queer' theory, the Introduction to Michel Foucault's *History of Sexuality*, first published in 1976. As has been already indicated, Foucault is an important although contradictory figure in the 'subject-of-language' project. His analysis of the historical construction of subjects (such as the 'homosexual') chimes with the anti-essentialism of structuralist theory. Equally, his rejection of class and economic reductionism in favour of a dispersed conception of 'discursive' relations of power was central to cultural studies' retreat from Marxist theory in the late 1970s and 1980s and the replacement of a theory of ideology by a theory of discourse (see Foucault, 1980; Barrett, 1991). Foucault's discussion of sexuality as a 'strategy' that is productive of specific subjects (for example, the 'hysterical' woman and the 'homosexual') and which is not reducible to a 'stubborn [biological] drive' or to the demands of a capitalist economy index these various moves. However, as indicated earlier, Foucault himself was opposed to the primarily linguistic and psychoanalytic orientation of the 'subject-of-language' model.

As previously indicated, Judith Butler's, 'Critically queer', the final chapter in this section, provides one possible route out of the theoretical differences between a Foucauldian or 'genealogical' approach and the psychoanalytic/semiotic approach of the 'subject-of-language' model. Butler's argument focuses on the notion of gender 'performativity', a concept borrowed from J.L. Austin's speech-act theory (Austin, 1962) via Derrida's deconstructive reading of this (Derrida, 1982). Performativity refers to the process by which discourse produces that which it names. Thus, for Butler, the midwife's cry, 'It's a girl!' is not a description of a state inscribed in nature but a 'performative act', a practice of 'girling' that ascribes gendered meaning to particular bodies. The notion of performativity can be linked to Foucauldian concepts such as 'technologies of the self' (discussed in Part III). In particular, it emphasizes the ways in which identity is enacted through iterative practices. However, unlike Foucault, Butler has no qualms about combining this approach with psychoanalytic insights, arguing in the same vein as theorists of 'suture' that performatively enacted subject positions cannot be understood except in relation to what is excluded from those subject positions, namely the unconscious. In the extract that appears in Chapter 11, Butler explores this argument in relation to 'heterosexual melancholy': the notion that the performance of, for example, heterosexual masculinity always contains within it, and thereby preserves, a 'lost' homosexual identification. Of course, whether Butler's arguments truly bring about the long-awaited *rapprochement* between psychoanalysis and discourse theory remains a matter of debate, a debate that is taken up in Parts II and III of this volume.

Acknowledgements

I would like to thank Adrian Kear, Emma Parker, Mark J. Smith, Deborah Lynn Steinberg and Kath Woodward for their help and advice in the preparation of Part I of this volume.

References

Austin, J. (1962) *How to do Things with Words*. Oxford: Clarendon Press.
Barrett, M. (1991) *The Politics of Truth*. Cambridge: Polity Press.
Barthes, R. (1986/1968) 'The death of the author', in *The Rustle of Language*. Oxford: Blackwell.
Derrida, J. (1982) 'Signature, event, context', in *Margins of Philosophy*, trans. A. Bass. Chicago: University of Chicago Press.
Foucault, M. (1980) 'Truth and power', in C. Gordon (ed.), *Power/Knowledge: Selected Interviews and Other Writings 1972–77*. Brighton: Harvester Wheatsheaf.

Who needs 'identity'?   **Stuart Hall**

There has been a veritable discursive explosion in recent years around the concept of 'identity', at the same moment as it has been subjected to a searching critique. How is this paradoxical development to be explained? And where does it leave us with respect to the concept? The deconstruction has been conducted within a variety of disciplinary areas, all of them, in one way or another, critical of the notion of an integral, originary and unified identity. The critique of the self-sustaining subject at the centre of post-Cartesian western metaphysics has been comprehensively advanced in philosophy. The question of subjectivity and its unconscious processes of formation has been developed within the discourse of a psychoanalytically influenced feminism and cultural criticism. The endlessly performative self has been advanced in celebratory variants of postmodernism. Within the anti-essentialist critique of ethnic, racial and national conceptions of cultural identity and the 'politics of location' some adventurous theoretical conceptions have been sketched in their most grounded forms. What, then, is the need for a further debate about 'identity'? Who needs it?

There are two ways of responding to the question. The first is to

This chapter is taken from 'Introduction: who needs identity?', in *Questions of Cultural Identity*, eds S. Hall and P. du Gay (London, Sage, 1996), pp. 1–17.

observe something distinctive about the deconstructive critique to which many of these essentialist concepts have been subjected. Unlike those forms of critique which aim to supplant inadequate concepts with 'truer' ones, or which aspire to the production of positive knowledge, the deconstructive approach puts key concepts 'under erasure'. This indicates that they are no longer serviceable – 'good to think with' – in their originary and unreconstructed form. But since they have not been superseded dialectically, and there are no other, entirely different concepts with which to replace them, there is nothing to do but to continue to think with them – albeit now in their detotalized or deconstructed forms, and no longer operating within the paradigm in which they were originally generated (cf. Hall, 1995). The line which cancels them, paradoxically, permits them to go on being read. Derrida has described this approach as thinking at the limit, as thinking in the interval, a sort of double writing. 'By means of this double, and precisely stratified, dislodged and dislodging writing, we must also mark the interval between inversion, which brings low what was high, and the irruptive emergence of a new "concept", a concept that can no longer be and never could be, included in the previous regime' (Derrida, 1981). Identity is such a concept – operating 'under erasure' in the interval between reversal and emergence; an idea which cannot be thought in the old way, but without which certain key questions cannot be thought at all.

A second kind of answer requires us to note where, in relation to what set of problems, does the *irreducibility* of the concept, identity, emerge? I think the answer here lies in its centrality to the question of agency and politics. By politics, I mean both the significance in modern forms of political movement of the signifier 'identity', its pivotal relationship to a politics of location – but also the manifest difficulties and instabilities which have characteristically affected all contemporary forms of 'identity politics'. By 'agency', I express no desire whatsoever to return to an unmediated and transparent notion of the subject or identity as the centred author of social practice, or to restore an approach which 'places its own point of view at the origin of all historicity – which, in short, leads to a transcendental consciousness' (Foucault, 1970: xiv). I agree with Foucault that what we require here is 'not a theory of the knowing subject, but rather a theory of discursive practice'. However, I believe that what this decentring requires – as the evolution of Foucault's work clearly shows – is not an abandonment or abolition of 'the subject' but a reconceptualization – thinking it in its new, displaced or decentred position within the paradigm. It seems to be in the attempt to rearticulate the relationship between subjects and discursive practices that the question of identity recurs – or rather, if one prefers to stress the process of subjectification to discursive practices, and the politics of exclusion which all such subjectification appears to entail, the question of *identification*.

Identification turns out to be one of the least well-understood concepts – almost as tricky as, though preferable to, 'identity' itself; and certainly no guarantee against the conceptual difficulties which have beset the latter. It is drawing meanings from both the discursive and the psychoanalytic repertoire, without being limited to either. This semantic field is too complex to unravel here, but it is useful at least to establish its relevance to the task in hand indicatively. In common sense language, identification is constructed on the back of a recognition of some common origin or shared characteristics with another person or group, or with an ideal, and with the natural closure of solidarity and allegiance established on this foundation. In contrast with the 'naturalism' of this definition, the discursive approach sees identification as a construction, a process never completed – always 'in process'. It is not determined in the sense that it can always be 'won' or

WHO NEEDS 'IDENTITY'?

'lost', sustained or abandoned. Though not without its determinate conditions of existence, including the material and symbolic resources required to sustain it, identification is in the end conditional, lodged in contingency. Once secured, it does not obliterate difference. The total merging it suggests is, in fact, a fantasy of incorporation. [. . .] Identification is, then, a process of articulation, a suturing, an over-determination not a subsumption. There is always 'too much' or 'too little' – an over-determination or a lack, but never a proper fit, a totality. Like all signifying practices, it is subject to the 'play' of *différance*. It obeys the logic of more-than-one. And since as a process it operates across difference, it entails discursive work, the binding and marking of symbolic boundaries, the production of 'frontier-effects'. It requires what is left outside, its constitutive outside, to consolidate the process.

[. . .]

[. . .] The concept of identity deployed here is therefore not an essentialist, but a strategic and positional one. That is to say, directly contrary to what appears to be its settled semantic career, this concept of identity does *not* signal that stable core of the self, unfolding from beginning to end through all the vicissitudes of history without change; the bit of the self which remains always-already 'the same', identical to itself across time. Nor – if we translate this essentializing conception to the stage of cultural identity – is it that 'collective or true self hiding inside the many other, more superficial or artificially imposed "selves" which a people with a shared history and ancestry hold in common' (Hall, 1990) and which can stabilize, fix or guarantee an unchanging 'oneness' or cultural belongingness underlying all the other superficial differences. It accepts that identities are never unified and, in late modern times, increasingly fragmented and fractured; never singular but multiply constructed across different, often intersecting and antagonistic, discourses, practices and positions. They are subject to a radical historicization, and are constantly in the process of change and transformation. [. . .]

Precisely because identities are constructed within, not outside, discourse, we need to understand them as produced in specific historical and institutional sites within specific discursive formations and practices, by specific enunciative strategies. Moreover, they emerge within the play of specific modalities of power, and thus are more the product of the marking of difference and exclusion, than they are the sign of an identical, naturally constituted unity – an 'identity' in its traditional meaning (that is, an all-inclusive sameness, seamless, without internal differentiation).

Above all, and directly contrary to the form in which they are constantly invoked, identities are constructed through, not outside, difference. This entails the radically disturbing recognition that it is only through the relation to the Other, the relation to what it is not, to precisely what it lacks, to what has been called its *constitutive outside* that the 'positive' meaning of any term – and thus its 'identity' – can be constructed (Derrida, 1981; Laclau, 1990; Butler, 1993). Throughout their careers, identities can function as points of identification and attachment only *because* of their capacity to exclude, to leave out, to render 'outside', abjected. Every identity has at its 'margin', an excess, something more. The unity, the internal homogeneity, which the term identity treats as foundational is not a natural, but a constructed form of closure, every identity naming as its necessary, even if silenced and unspoken other, that which it 'lacks'. Laclau (1990: 33) argues powerfully and persuasively that 'the constitution of a social identity is an act of power' since,

> If . . . an objectivity manages to partially affirm itself it is only by repressing that which threatens it. Derrida has shown how an identity's constitution is always based on excluding something and establishing a violent hierarchy between the two resultant poles – man/woman, etc. What is peculiar to the second term is thus reduced to the function of an accident as opposed to the essentiality of the first. It is the same with the black–white relationship, in which white, of course, is equivalent to 'human being'. 'Woman' and 'black' are thus 'marks' (i.e. marked terms) in contrast to the unmarked terms of 'man' and 'white'.

So the 'unities' which identities proclaim are, in fact, constructed within the play of power and exclusion, and are the result, not of a natural and inevitable or primordial totality but of the naturalized, over-determined process of 'closure' (Hall, 1992; Bhabha, 1994).

If 'identities' can only be read against the grain – that is to say, specifically *not* as that which fixes the play of difference in a point of origin and stability, but as that which is constructed in or through *différance* and is constantly destabilized by what it leaves out, then how can we understand its meaning and how can we theorize its emergence? Avtar Brah (1992), in her important article on 'Difference, diversity and differentiation', raises an important series of questions which these new ways of conceptualizing identity have posed:

> Fanon notwithstanding, much work is yet to be undertaken on the subject of how the racialized 'other' is constituted in the psychic domain. How is post-colonial gendered and racialized subjectivity to be analyzed? Does the privileging of 'sexual difference' and early childhood in psychoanalysis limit its explanatory value in helping us to understand the psychic dimensions of social phenomena such as racism? How do the 'symbolic order' and the social order articulate in the formation of the subject? In other words, how is the link between social and psychic reality to be theorized?' (Brah, 1992: 142)

What follows is an attempt to begin to respond to this critical but troubling set of questions.

In some recent work on this topic, I have made an appropriation of the term identity which is certainly not widely shared and may not be well understood. I use 'identity' to refer to the meeting point, the point of *suture*, between, on the one hand, the discourses and practices which attempt to 'interpellate', speak to us or hail us into place as the social subjects of particular discourses, and on the other hand, the processes which produce subjectivities, which construct us as subjects which can be 'spoken'. Identities are thus points of temporary attachment to the subject positions which discursive practices construct for us (see Hall, 1995). They are the result of a successful articulation or 'chaining' of the subject into the flow of the discourse, what Stephen Heath, in his path-breaking essay on 'Suture' called 'an intersection' (1981: 106). 'A theory of ideology must begin not from the subject but as an account of suturing effects, the effecting of the join of the subject in structures of meaning.' Identities are, as it were, the positions which the subject is obliged to take up while always 'knowing' (the language of consciousness here betrays us) that they are representations, that representation is always constructed across a 'lack', across a division, from the place of the Other, and thus can never be adequate – identical – to the subject processes which are invested in them. The notion that an effective suturing of the subject to a subject-position requires, not only that the subject is 'hailed', but that the subject invests in the position, means that suturing has to be thought of as an *articulation*, rather than a one-sided process, and that in turn places *identification*, if not identities, firmly on the theoretical agenda.

The references to the term which describes the hailing of the subject by discourse – interpellation – remind us that this debate has a significant and uncompleted pre-history in the arguments sparked off by Althusser's 'Ideological state apparatuses' essay (1971). This essay introduced the notion of interpellation, and the speculary structure of ideology in an attempt to circumvent the economism and reductionism of the classical Marxist theory of ideology, and to bring together within one explanatory framework both the materialist function of ideology in reproducing the social relations of production (Marxism) and (through its borrowings from Lacan) the symbolic function of ideology in the constitution of subjects. Michele Barrett, in her recent discussion of this debate, has gone a con-siderable way to demonstrating 'the profoundly divided and contradictory nature of the argument Althusser was beginning to make' (Barrett, 1991: 96; see also Hall, 1985: 102: 'The two sides of the difficult problem of ideology were fractured in that essay and, ever since, have been assigned to different poles'). Nevertheless, the ISAs essay, as it came to be known, has turned out to be a highly significant, even if not successful, moment in the debate. Jacqueline Rose, for example, has argued in *Sexuality in the Field of Vision* (1986) that 'the question of identity – how it is constituted and maintained – is therefore the central issue through which psychoanalysis enters the political field.'

> This is one reason why Lacanian psychoanalysis came into English intellec-tual life, via Althusser's concept of ideology, through the two paths of

feminism and the analysis of film (a fact often used to discredit all three). Feminism because the issue of how individuals recognize themselves as male or female, the demand that they do so, seems to stand in such fundamental relation to the forms of inequality and subordination which it is feminism's objective to change. Film because its power as an ideological apparatus rests on the mechanisms of identification and sexual fantasy which we all seem to participate in, but which – outside the cinema – are for the most part only ever admitted on the couch. If ideology is effective, it is because it works at the most rudimentary levels of psychic identity and the drives. (Rose, 1986: 5)

However, if we are not to fall directly from an economistic reductionism into a psychoanalytic one, we need to add that, if ideology is effective, it is because it works at *both* 'the rudimentary levels of psychic identity and the drives' *and* at the level of the discursive formation and practices which constitute the social field; and that it is in the articulation of these mutually constitutive but not identical fields that the real conceptual problems lie. The term identity – which arises precisely at the point of intersection between them – is thus the site of the difficulty. It is worth adding that we are unlikely ever to be able to square up these two constituents as equivalents – the unconscious itself acting as the bar or cut between them which makes it 'the site of a perpetual postponement or deferral of equivalence' (Hall, 1995: 65) but which cannot, for that reason, be given up.

Heath's essay (1981) reminds us that it was Michael Pêcheux who tried to develop an account of discourse within the Althusserian perspective, and who, in effect, registered the unbridgeable gap between the first and the second halves of Althusser's essay in terms of 'the heavy absence of a conceptual articulation elaborated between *ideology* and the *unconscious*' (quoted in Heath, 1981: 106). Pêcheux tried 'to describe with reference to the mechanisms of the setting in position of its subjects' (Heath, 1981: 101–2), using the Foucauldian notion of discursive formation as that which 'determines what can and must be said'. As Heath put Pêcheux's argument:

Individuals are constituted as subjects through the discursive formation, a process of subjection in which [drawing on Althusser's loan from Lacan concerning the specular character of the constitution of subjectivity] the individual is identified as subject to the discursive formation in a structure of misrecognition (the subject thus presented as the source of the meanings of which it is an effect). Interpellation names the mechanism of this structure of misrecognition, effectively the term of the subject in the discursive and the ideological, the point of their correspondence. (Heath, 1981: 101–2).

Such 'correspondence', however, remained troublingly unresolved. Interpellation, through it continues to be used as a general way of describing the 'summoning into place' of the subject, was subjected to Hirst's famous

WHO NEEDS 'IDENTITY'?

critique. It depended, Hirst argued, on a recognition which, in effect, the subject would have been required to have the capacity to perform *before* it had been constituted, within discourse, as a subject. 'This something which is not a subject must already have the faculties necessary to support the recognition that will constitute it as a subject' (Hirst, 1979: 65). This argument has proved very persuasive to many of Althusser's subsequent readers, in effect bringing the whole field of investigation to an untimely halt.

The critique was certainly a formidable one, but the halting of all further inquiry at this point may turn out to have been premature. Hirst's critique was effective in showing that all the mechanisms which constituted the subject in discourse as an interpellation (through the specularly structure of misrecognition modelled on the Lacanian mirror phase) were in danger of presupposing an already constituted subject. However, since no one proposed to renounce the idea of the subject as constituted in discourse as an effect, it still remained to be shown by what mechanism which was not vulnerable to the charge of presupposition this constitution could be achieved. The problem was postponed, not resolved. Some of the difficulties, at least, seemed to arise from accepting too much at face value, and without qualification, Lacan's somewhat sensationalist proposition that *everything* constitutive of the subject not only happens through this mechanism of the resolution of the Oedipal crisis, but happens in the same moment. The 'resolution' of the Oedipal crisis, in the over-condensed language of the Lacanian hot-gospellers, *was* identical with, and occurred through the equivalent mechanism as, the submission to the Law of the Father, the consolidation of sexual difference, the entry into language, the formation of the unconscious as well – after Althusser – as the recruitment into the patriarchal ideologies of late capitalist western societies! The more complex notion of a subject-in-process is lost in these polemical conden-sations and hypothetically aligned equivalences. (Is the subject racialized, nationalized and constituted as a late-liberal entrepreneurial subject in this moment too?)

Hirst, too, seems to have assumed what Michele Barrett calls 'Althusser's Lacan'. However, as he puts it, 'the complex and hazardous process of formation of a human adult from "a small animal" does not necessarily correspond to Althusser's mechanism of ideology . . . *unless the Child* . . . remains in Lacan's mirror phase, or unless we fill the child's cradle with anthropological assumptions' (Hirst, 1979: 67). His response to this is somewhat perfunctory. 'I have no quarrel with Children, and I do not wish to pronounce them blind, deaf or dumb, merely to deny that they possess the capacities of *philosophical* subjects, that they have the attri-butes of "knowing" subjects independent of their formation and training as social beings.' What is at issue here is the capacity for self-recognition. But it is an unwarrantable assumption to make, that 'recognition' is a purely cognitive let alone 'philosophical' attribute, and unlikely that it should appear in the child at one fell swoop, in a before/after fashion. The stakes here seem, unaccountably, to have been pitched very high indeed. It hardly requires us to endow the individual 'small animal' with the full philosophical apparatus to account for why it may have the capacity to 'misrecognize' itself in the look from the place of the other which is all we require to set the passage between the Imaginary and the Symbolic in motion in Lacan's terms. After all, following Freud, the basic cathexing of the zones of bodily activity and the apparatus of sensation, pleasure and pain must be already 'in play' in however embryonic a form in order for any relation of any kind to be established with the external world. There is already a relation to a source of pleasure – the relation to the Mother in the Imaginary – so there must be already something which is capable of 'recognizing' what pleasure is. Lacan himself noted in his essay on 'The mirror stage' (Lacan, 1977a) that 'The child, at an age when he is for a time, however short, outdone by the chimpanzee in instrumental intelligence, can nevertheless already recognize as such his own image in a mirror' [see this volume, p. 44]. What is more, the critique seems to be pitched in a rather binary, before/after, either/or logical form. The mirror stage is not the *beginning* of something, but the *interruption* – the loss, the lack, the division – which initiates the process that 'founds' the sexually differentiated subject (and the unconscious) and this depends not alone on the instantaneous formation of some internal cognitive capacity, but on the dislocating rupture of the look from the place of the Other. For Lacan, however, this is already a fantasy – the very image which places the child divides its identity into two. Furthermore, that moment only has meaning in relation to the supporting presence and the look of the mother who guarantees its reality for the child. Peter Osborne (1995: 257) notes that in *The Field of the Other* Lacan (1977b) describes the 'parent holding him up before the mirror', with the child looking towards the Mother for confirmation, the child seeing her as a 'reference point . . . not his ego ideal but his ideal ego'. This argument, Osborne suggests, 'exploits the indeterminacy inherent in the discrepancy between the temporality of Lacan's description of the child's encounter with its bodily image in the mirror as a "stage" and the punctuality of his depiction of it as a scene, the dramatic point of which is restricted to the relations between two "characters" alone: the child and its bodily image'. However, as Osborne says, either it represents a critical addition to the 'mirror stage' argument – in which case, why is it not developed? Or it introduces a different logic whose implications remain unaddressed in Lacan's subsequent work.

The notion that nothing of the subject is there until the Oedipal drama is an exaggerated reading of Lacan. The assertion that subjectivity is not fully constituted until the Oedipal crisis has been 'resolved' does not require a blank screen, *tabula rasa*, or a before/after conception of the subject, initiated by a sort of *coup de théâtre*, even if – as Hirst rightly noted – it leaves unsettled the problematic relationship between 'the individual' and the subject. (What is the individual 'small animal' that is not yet a subject?)

One could add that Lacan's is only one of the many accounts of the formation of subjectivity which takes account of unconscious psychic processes and the relation to the other, and the debate may look different now that the 'Lacanian deluge' is somewhat receding and in the absence of the early powerful impulsion in that direction which we were given by Althusser's text. In his thoughtful recent discussion of the Hegelian origins of this concept of 'recognition' referred to above, Peter Osborne has criticized Lacan for 'the way in which the child's relation to the image is absolutized by being abstracted from the context of its relations to others (particularly, the mother)', while being made ontologically constitutive of 'the symbolic matrix in which the I is precipitated in a primordial form . . .' and considers several other variants (Kristeva, Jessica Benjamin, Laplanche) which are not so confined within the alienated misrecognition of the Lacanian scenario. These are useful pointers beyond the impasse in which this discussion, in the wake of 'Althusser's Lacan', has left us, with the threads of the psychic and the discursive spinning loose in our hands.

Foucault, I would argue, also approaches the impasse with which Hirst's critique of Althusser leaves us, but so to speak from the opposite direction. Ruthlessly attacking 'the great myth of inferiority', and driven both by his critique of humanism and the philosophy of consciousness and by his negative reading of psychoanalysis, Foucault also undertakes a radical historicization of the category of the subject. The subject is produced 'as an effect' through and within discourse, within specific discursive formations, and has no existence, and certainly no transcendental continuity or identity from one subject position to another. In his 'archaeological' work (*Madness and Civilization, The Birth of the Clinic, The Order of Things, The Archaeology of Knowledge*), discourses construct subject positions through their rules of formation and 'modalities of enunciation'. Powerfully compelling and original as these works are, the criticism levelled against them in this respect at least seems justified. They offer a formal account of the construction of subject positions within discourse while revealing little about why it is that certain individuals occupy some subject positions rather than others. By neglecting to analyse how the social positions of individuals interact with the construction of certain 'empty' discursive subject positions, Foucault reinscribes an antinomy between subject positions and the individuals who occupy them. Thus his archaeology provides a critical, but one-dimensional, formal account of the subject of discourse. Discursive subject positions become *a priori* categories which individuals seem to occupy in an unproblematic fashion (McNay, 1994: 76–7). McNay cites Brown and Cousins's key observation that Foucault tends here to elide 'subject positions of a statement with individual capacities to fill them' (Brown and Cousins, 1980: 272) – thus coming up against the very difficulty which Althusser failed to resolve, by a different route.

The critical shift in Foucault's work from an archaeological to a genealogical method does many things to render more concrete the somewhat 'empty formalism' of the earlier work, especially in the powerful ways in which power, which was missing from the more formal account of discourse, is now centrally reintroduced and the exciting possibilities opened up by Foucault's discussion of the double-sided character of subjection/ subjectification (*assujettisement*). Moreover, the centring of questions of power, and the notion that discourse itself is a regulative and regulated formation, entry into which is 'determined by and constitutive of the power relations that permeate the social realm' (McNay, 1994: 87), brings Foucault's conception of the discursive formation closer to some of the classical questions which Althusser tried to address through the concept of 'ideology' – shorn, of course, of its class reductionism, economistic and truth-claiming overtones.

In the area of the theorization of the subject and identity, however, certain problems remain. One implication of the new conceptions of power elaborated in this body of work is the radical 'deconstruction' of the body, the last residue or hiding place of 'Man', and its 'reconstruction' in terms of its historical, genealogical and discursive formations. The body is con-structed by, shaped and reshaped by, the intersection of a series of disciplinary discursive practices. Genealogy's task, Foucault proclaims, 'is to expose the body totally imprinted by history and the processes of history's destruction of the body' (1984: 63). While we can accept this, with its radically 'constructivist' implications (the body becomes infinitely malleable and contingent), I am not sure we can or ought to go as far as his proposition that 'Nothing in man – not even his body – is sufficiently stable to serve as a basis for self-recognition or for understanding other men.' This is not because the body *is* such a stable and true referent for self-understanding, but because, though this may be a 'misrecognition', it is precisely how the body has served *to function as the signifier of the condensation of subjectivities in the individual* and this function cannot simply be dismissed because, as Foucault effectively shows, it is not true.

Further, my own feeling is that, despite Foucault's disclaimers, his invocation of *the body* as the point of application of a variety of discip-linary practices tends to lend this theory of disciplinary regulation a sort of 'displaced or misplaced concreteness' – a residual materiality – and in this way operates discursively to 'resolve' or appear to resolve the unspecified relationship between the subject, the individual and the body. To put it crudely, it pins back together or 'sutures' those things which the theory of the discursive production of subjects, if taken to its limits, would irretrievably fracture and disperse. I think 'the body' has acquired a totemic value in post-Foucauldian work precisely because of this talismanic status. It is almost the only trace we have left in Foucault's work of a 'transcendental signifier'.

The more well-established critique, however, has to do with the problem which Foucault encounters with theorizing resistance within the theory of power he deploys in *Discipline and Punish* (1977) and *The History of Sexuality* (1981): the entirely self-policing conception of the subject which emerges from the disciplinary, confessional and pastoral modalities of power discussed there, and the absence of any attention to what might in any way interrupt, prevent or disturb the smooth insertion of individuals into the subject positions constructed by these discourses. The submission of the body through 'the soul' to the normalizing regimes of truth constitutes a powerful way of rethinking the body's so-called 'materiality' (which has been productively taken up by Nikolas Rose, and the 'governmentality' school, as well as, in a different mode, by Judith Butler in *Bodies That Matter* (1993). But it is hard not to take Foucault's own formulation seriously, with all the difficulties it brings in its train: namely, that the subjects which are constructed in this way are 'docile bodies'. There is no theorized account of how or why bodies should not always-for-ever turn up, in place, at the right time (exactly the point from which the classical Marxist theory of ideology started to unravel, and the very difficulty which Althusser reinscribed when he normatively defined the function of ideology as 'to reproduce the social relations of production'). Furthermore, there is no theorization of the psychic mechanism or interior processes by which these automatic 'interpellations' might be produced, or – more significantly – fail or be resisted or negotiated. Powerful and productive as this work undoubtedly is, then, it remains the case that here 'Foucault steps too easily from describing disciplinary power as a *tendency* within modern forms of social control, to positing disciplinary power as a fully installed monolithic force which saturates all social relations. This leads to an overestimation of the efficacy of disciplinary power and to an impoverished understanding of the individual which cannot account for experiences that fall outside the realm of the "docile" body' (McNay, 1994: 104).

That this became obvious to Foucault, even if it is still refused as a critique by many of his followers, is apparent from the further and distinctive shift in his work marked by the later (and incomplete) volumes of his so-called 'History of Sexuality' (*The Use of Pleasure*, 1987; *The Care of the Self*, 1988, and, as far as we can gather, the unpublished – and from the point of view of the critique just passed, the critical – volume on 'The Perversions'). For here, without moving very far from his insightful work on the productive character of normative regulation (no subjects outside the law, as Judith Butler puts it), he tacitly recognizes that it is not enough for the law to summon, discipline, produce and regulate, but there must also be the corresponding production of a response (and thus the capacity and apparatus of subjectivity) from the side of the subject. In the critical introduction to *The Use of Pleasure* Foucault lists what by now we would expect of his work – 'the correlation between fields of knowledge, types of normativity and forms of subjectivity in particular cultures' – but now critically adds

> the practices by which individuals were led to focus attention on themselves,
> to decipher, recognize and acknowledge themselves as subjects of desire,

bringing into play between themselves and themselves a certain relationship that allows them to discover, in desire, the truth of their being, be it natural or fallen. In short, with this genealogy, the idea was to investigate how individuals were led to practice, on themselves and on others, a hermeneutics of desire. (Foucault, 1987: 5)

Foucault describes this – correctly, in our view – as 'a third shift, in order to analyze what is termed "the subject". It seemed appropriate to look for the forms and modalities of the relation to self by which the individual constitutes and recognizes himself *qua* subject.' Foucault, of course, would not commit anything so vulgar as actually to deploy the term 'identity', but I think, with 'the relation to self' and the constitution and recognition of 'himself *qua* subject', we are approaching something of the territory which, in the terms established earlier, belongs to the problematic of 'identity'.

This is not the place to trace through the many productive insights which flow from Foucault's analysis of the truth-games, the elaboration of ethical work, of the regimes of self-regulation and self-fashioning, of the 'technologies of the self' involved in the constitution of the desiring subject. There is certainly no single switch to 'agency', to intention and volition, here (though there are, very centrally, the practices of freedom which prevent this subject from ever being simply a docile sexualized body).

But there is the *production* of self as an object in the world, the practices of self-constitution, recognition and reflection, the relation to the rule, alongside the scrupulous attention to normative regulation, and the constraints of the rules without which no 'subjectification' is produced. This is a significant advance, since it addresses for the first time in Foucault's major work the existence of some interior landscape of the subject, some interior mechanisms of assent to the rule, as well as its objectively disciplining force, which saves the account from the 'behaviourism' and objectivism which threaten certain parts of *Discipline and Punish*. Often, in this work, the ethics and practices of the self are most fully described by Foucault as an 'aesthetics of existence', a deliberate stylization of daily life; and its technologies are most effectively demonstrated in the practices of self-production, in specific modes of conduct, in what we have come from later work to recognize as a kind of *performativity*.

What I think we can see here, then, is Foucault being pushed, by the scrupulous rigour of his own thinking, through a series of conceptual shifts at different stages in his work, towards a recognition that, since the decentring of the subject is not the destruction of the subject, and since the 'centring' of discursive practice cannot work without the constitution of subjects, the theoretical work cannot be fully accomplished without complementing the account of discursive and disciplinary regulation with an account of the practices of subjective self-constitution. It has never been enough – in Marx, in Althusser, in Foucault – to elaborate a theory of how individuals are summoned into place in the discursive structures. It has always, also, required an account of how subjects are constituted; and, in this work, Foucault has gone a considerable way in showing this, in reference to historically specific discursive practices, normative self-regulation and technologies of the self. The question which remains is whether we also require to, as it were, close the gap between the two: that is to say, a theory of what the mechanisms are by which individuals as subjects identify (or do not identify) with the 'positions' to which they are summoned; as well as how they fashion, stylize, produce and 'perform' these positions, and why they never do so completely, for once and all time, and some never do, or are in a constant, agonistic process of struggling with, resisting, negotiating and accommodating the normative or regulative rules with which they confront and regulate themselves. In short, what remains is the requirement to think this relation of subject to discursive formations *as an articulation* (all articulations are properly relations of 'no necessary correspondence', i.e. founded on that contingency which 'reactivates the historical'; cf. Laclau, 1990: 35).

It is therefore all the more fascinating that, when finally Foucault *does* make the move in this direction (in work which was then tragically cut short), he was prevented, of course, from going to one of the principal sources of thinking about this neglected aspect – namely, psychoanalysis; prevented from moving in that direction by his own critique of it as simply another network of disciplinary power relations. What he produces instead is a discursive *phenomenology* of the subject (drawing perhaps on earlier sources and influences whose importance for him have been somewhat underplayed) and a genealogy of the *technologies of the self*. But it is a phenomenology which is in danger of being overwhelmed by an over-emphasis on intentionality – precisely because it cannot engage with *the unconscious*. For good or ill, that door was already foreclosed.

Fortunately it has not remained so. In *Gender Trouble* (1990) and more especially in *Bodies That Matter* (1993), Judith Butler has taken up, through her concern with 'the discursive limits of "sex"' and with the politics of feminism, the complex transactions between the subject, the body and identity, through the drawing together in one analytic framework insights drawn from a Foucauldian and a psychoanalytic perspective. Adopting the position that the subject is discursively constructed and that there is no subject before or outside the law, Butler develops a rigorously argued case that

> sex is, from the start, normative; it is what Foucault has called a 'regulatory ideal'. In this sense, then, sex not only functions as a norm, but is part of a regulatory practice that produces (through the repetition or iteration of a norm which is without origin) the bodies it governs, that is, whose regulatory force is made clear as a kind of productive power, the power to produce – demarcate, circulate, differentiate – the bodies it controls . . . 'sex' is an ideal construct which is forcibly materialized through time. (Butler, 1993:1)

Materialization here is rethought as an effect of power. The view that the subject is produced in the course of its materialization is strongly grounded in a performative theory of language and the subject, but performativity is shorn of its associations with volition, choice and intentionality and (against some of the misreadings of *Gender Trouble*) re-read 'not as the act by which a subject brings into being what she/he names but rather as that reiterative power of discourse to produce the phenomena that it regulates and constrains' (Butler, 1993: 2).

The decisive shift, from the viewpoint of the argument being developed here, however, is 'a linking of this process of "assuming" a sex with the question of *identification*, and with the discursive means by which the heterosexual imperative enables certain sexed identifications and forecloses and/or disavows other identifications' (Butler, 1993: 5). This centring of the question of identification, together with the problematic of the subject which 'assumes a sex', opens up a critical and reflexive dialogue in Butler's work between Foucault and psychoanalysis which is enormously productive. It is true that Butler does not provide an elaborate theoretical meta-argument for the way the two perspectives, or the relation between the discursive and the psychic, are 'thought' together in her text beyond a suggestive indication: 'There may be a way to subject psychoanalysis to a Foucauldian redescription even as Foucault himself refused that possibility.' At any rate

> this text accepts as a point of departure Foucault's notion that regulatory power produces the subjects it controls, that power is not only imposed externally but works as the regulatory and normative means by which subjects are formed. The return to psychoanalysis, then, is guided by the question of how certain regulatory norms form a 'sexed' subject in terms that establish the indistinguishability of psychic and bodily formation. (Butler, 1993: 23)

However, Butler's relevance to the argument is made all the more pertinent because it is developed in the context of the discussion of gender and sexuality, framed by feminism, and so is directly recurrent both to the questions of identity and identity politics, and to the questions which Avtar Brah's work posed earlier about the paradigmatic function of sexual difference in relation to other axes of exclusion. Here Butler makes a powerful case that all identities operate through exclusion, through the discursive construction of a constitutive outside and the production of abjected and marginalized subjects, apparently outside the field of the symbolic, the representable – 'the production of an "outside", a domain of intelligible effects' (Butler, 1993: 22) – which then returns to trouble and unsettle the foreclosures which we prematurely call 'identities'. She deploys this argument with effect in relation to the sexualizing and the racializing of the subject – an argument which requires to be developed if the constitution of subjects in and through the normalizing regulatory effects of racial discourse is to acquire the theoretical development hitherto reserved for gender and sexuality (though, of course, her most well-worked example is in relation to the production of these forms of sexual abjection and lived unintelligibility usually 'normalized' as pathological or perverse).

As James Souter (1995) has pointed out, 'Butler's internal critique of feminist identity politics and its foundationalist premises questions the adequacy of a representational politics whose basis is the presumed universality and unity of its subject – a seamless category of women.' Paradoxically, as in all other identities treated politically in a foundational manner, this identity 'is based on excluding "different" women . . . and by normatively prioritizing heterosexual relations as the basis for feminist politics'. This 'unity', Souter (1995) argues, is a 'fictive unity', 'produced and restrained by the very structures of power through which emancipation is sought'. Significantly, however, as Souter also argues, this does *not* lead Butler to argue that all notions of identity should therefore be abandoned because they are theoretically flawed. Indeed, she takes the speculary structure of identification as a critical part of her argument. But she acknowledges that such an argument *does* suggest 'the necessary limits of identity politics'.

> In this sense, identifications belong to the imaginary; they are phantasmatic efforts of alignment, loyalty, ambiguous and cross-corporeal cohabitations, they unsettle the I; they are the sedimentation of the 'we' in the constitution of any I, the structuring present of alterity in the very formulation of the I. Identifications are never fully and finally made; they are incessantly reconstituted, and, as such, are subject to the volatile logic of iterability. They are that which is constantly marshalled, consolidated, retrenched, contested and, on occasion, compelled to give way. (Butler, 1993: 105)

The effort, now, to think the question of the distinctiveness of the logic within which the racialized and ethnicized body is constituted discursively, through the regulatory normative ideal of a 'compulsive Eurocentrism' (for want of a different word), cannot be simply grafted on to the arguments briefly sketched above. But they have received an enormous and original impetus from this tangled and unconcluded argument, which demonstrates beyond the shadow of a doubt that the question, and the theorization, of identity is a matter of considerable political significance, and is only likely to be advanced when both the necessity and the 'impossibility' of identities, and the suturing of the psychic and the discursive in their constitution, are fully and unambiguously acknowledged.

References

Althusser, L. (1971) *Lenin and Philosophy and Other Essays*. London: New Left Books.
Barrett, M. (1991) *The Politics of Truth*. Cambridge: Polity Press.

Bhabha, H. (1994) 'The Other question', in *The Location of Culture*. London: Routledge pp. 66–84.

Brah, A. (1992) 'Difference, diversity and differentiation', in J. Donald and A. Rattansi (eds), *Race, Culture and Difference*. London: Sage pp. 126–45.

Brown, B. and Cousins, M. (1980) 'The linguistic fault', *Economy and Society*, 9 (3) pp. 251–78.

Butler, J. (1990) *Gender Trouble*. London: Routledge.

Butler, J. (1993) *Bodies That Matter*. London: Routledge.

Derrida, J. (1981) *Positions*. Chicago: University of Chicago Press.

Foucault, M. (1970) *The Order of Things*. London: Tavistock.

Foucault, M. (1972) *The Archaeology of Knowledge*. London: Tavistock.

Foucault, M. (1977) *Discipline and Punish*. Harmondsworth: Penguin.

Foucault, M. (1981) *The History of Sexuality, Volume 1*. Harmondsworth: Penguin.

Foucault, M. (1984) 'Nietzsche, genealogy, history', in P. Rabinow (ed.), *The Foucault Reader*. Harmondsworth: Penguin.

Foucault, M. (1987) *The Use of Pleasure*. Harmondsworth: Penguin.

Foucault, M. (1988) *The Care of the Self*. Harmondsworth: Penguin.

Hall, S. (1985) 'Signification, representation and ideology: Althusser and the post-structuralist debates', *Critical Studies in Mass Communication*, 2 (2) pp. 91–114.

Hall, S. (1990) 'Cultural identity and diaspora', in J. Rutherford (ed.), *Identity*. London: Lawrence & Wishart pp. 222–37.

Hall, S. (1992) 'Cultural identity in question', in S. Hall, D. Held and T. McGrew (eds), *Modernity and its Futures*. Cambridge: Polity Press pp. 273–316.

Hall, S. (1995) 'Fantasy, identity, politics', in E. Carter, J. Donald and J. Squires (eds), *Cultural Remix: Theories of Politics and the Popular*. London: Lawrence & Wishart pp. 63–9.

Heath, S. (1981) *Question of Cinema*. Basingstoke: Macmillan.

Hirst, P. (1979) *On Law and Ideology*. Basingstoke: Macmillan.

Laclau, E. (1990) *New Reflections on the Revolution of our Time*. London: Verso.

Lacan, J. (1977a) *Ecrits*. London: Tavistock.

Lacan, J. (1977b) *The Four Fundamental Concepts of Psychoanalysis*. London: Hogarth Press.

McNay, L. (1994) *Foucault: Critical Introduction*. Cambridge: Polity Press.

Osborne, P. (1995) *The Politics of Time*. London: Verso.

Rose, J. (1986) *Sexuality in the Field of Vision*. London: Verso.

Souter, J. (1995) 'From *Gender Trouble* to *Bodies That Matter*', unpublished manuscript.

2

Ideology interpellates individuals as subjects
Louis Althusser

This chapter, written in 1969, is an extract from 'Ideology and ideological state apparatuses', in *Lenin and Philosophy and Other Essays.* (London, New Left Books, 1971), pp. 170–86.

[. . .] I can now come to my central thesis [. . .]: there is no ideology except by the subject and for subjects. Meaning, there is no ideology except for concrete subjects, and this destination for ideology is only made possible by the subject: meaning, *by the category of the subject* and its functioning.

By this I mean that, even if it only appears under this name (the subject) with the rise of bourgeois ideology, above all with the rise of legal ideology,[1] the category of the subject (which may function under other names: e.g., as the soul in Plato, as God, etc.) is the constitutive category of all ideology, whatever its determination (regional or class) and whatever its historical date – since ideology has no history.

I say: the category of the subject is constitutive of all ideology, but at the same time and immediately I add that *the category of the subject is only constitutive of all ideology insofar as all ideology has the function (which defines it) of 'constituting' concrete individuals as subjects.* In the interaction of this double constitution exists the functioning of all ideology, ideology being nothing but its functioning in the material forms of existence of that functioning.

In order to grasp what follows, it is essential to realize that both he who is writing these lines and the reader who reads them are themselves subjects, and therefore ideological subjects (a tautological proposition), i.e. that the author and the reader of these lines both live 'spontaneously' or 'naturally' in ideology in the sense in which I have said that 'man is an ideological animal by nature'.

That the author, insofar as he writes the lines of a discourse which claims to be scientific, is completely absent as a 'subject' from 'his' scientific discourse (for all scientific discourse is by definition a subject-less discourse, there is no 'Subject of science' expect in an ideology of science) is a different question which I shall leave on one side for the moment.

As St Paul admirably put it, it is in the 'Logos', meaning in ideology, that we 'live, move and have our being'. It follows that, for you and for me, the category of the subject is a primary 'obviousness' (obviousnesses are always primary): it is clear that you and I are subjects (free, ethical, etc . . .). Like all obviousnesses, including those that make a word, 'name a thing' or 'have a meaning' (therefore including the obviousness of the 'transparency' of language), the 'obviousness' that you and I are subjects – and that that does not cause any problems – is an ideological effect, the elementary ideological effect.[2] It is indeed a peculiarity of ideology that it imposes (without appearing to do so, since these are 'obviousnesses') obviousnesses as obviousnesses, which we cannot *fail to recognize* and before which we have the inevitable and natural reaction of crying out (aloud or in the 'still, small voice of conscience'): 'That's obvious! That's right! That's true!'

At work in this reaction is the ideological *recognition* function which is one of the two functions of ideology as such (its inverse being the function of *misrecognition – méconnaissance*).

To take a highly 'concrete' example, we all have friends who, when they knock on our door and we ask, through the door, the question 'Who's there?', answer (since 'it's obvious') 'It's me.' And we recognize that 'it is him', or 'her'. We open the door, and 'it's true, it really was she who was there.' To take another example, when we recognize somebody of our (previous) acquaintance ((*re*)-*connaissance*) in the street, we show him that we have recognized him (and have recognized that he has recognized us) by saying to him 'Hello, my friend', and shaking his hand (a material ritual practice of ideological recognition in everyday life – in France, at least; elsewhere, there are other rituals).

In this preliminary remark and these concrete illustrations, I only wish to point out that you and I are *always already* subjects, and as such constantly practice the rituals of ideological recognition, which guarantee for us that we are indeed concrete, individual, distinguishable and (naturally) irreplaceable subjects. The writing I am currently executing and the reading you are currently[3] performing are also in this respect rituals of ideological recognition, including the 'obviousness' with which the 'truth' or 'error' of my reflections may impose itself on you.

But to recognize that we are subjects and that we function in the practical rituals of the most elementary everyday life (the hand-shake, the fact of calling you by your name, the fact of knowing, even if I do not know what it is, that you 'have' a name of your own, which means that you are recognized as a unique subject, etc.) – this recognition only gives us the 'consciousness' of our incessant (eternal) practice of ideological recognition – its consciousness, i.e. its *recognition* – but in no sense does it give us the (scientific) *knowledge* of the mechanism of this recognition. Now it is this knowledge that we have to reach, if you will, while speaking in ideology, and from within ideology we have to outline a discourse which tries to break with ideology, in order to dare to be the beginning of a scientific (i.e. subjectless) discourse on ideology.

Thus in order to represent why the category of the 'subject' is constitutive of ideology, which only exists by constituting concrete subjects as subjects, I shall employ a special mode of exposition: 'concrete' enough to be recognized, but abstract enough to be thinkable and thought, giving rise to a knowledge.

As a first formulation I shall say: *all ideology hails or interpellates concrete individuals as concrete subjects*, by the functioning of the category of the subject.

This is a proposition which entails that we distinguish for the moment between concrete individuals on the one hand and concrete subjects on the other, although at this level concrete subjects only exist insofar as they are supported by a concrete individual.

I shall then suggest that ideology 'acts' or 'functions' in such a way that it 'recruits' subjects among the individuals (it recruits them all), or 'transforms' the individuals into subjects (it transforms them all) by that very precise operation which I have called *interpellation* or hailing, and which can be imagined along the lines of the most commonplace everyday police (or other) hailing: 'Hey, you there!'[4]

Assuming that the theoretical scene I have imagined takes place in the street, the hailed individual will turn round. By this mere one-hundred-and-eighty-degree physical conversion, he becomes a *subject*. Why? Because he has recognized that the hail was 'really' addressed to him, and that 'it was *really him* who was hailed' (and not someone else). Experience shows that the practical telecommunication of hailings is such that they hardly ever miss their man: verbal call or whistle, the one hailed always recognizes that it is really him who is being hailed. And yet it is a strange phenomenon, and one which cannot be explained solely by 'guilt feelings', despite the large numbers who 'have something on their consciences'.

Naturally for the convenience and clarity of my little theoretical theatre I have had to present things in the form of a sequence, with a before and an after, and thus in the form of a temporal succession. There are individuals walking along. Somewhere (usually behind them) the hail rings out: 'Hey, you there!' One individual (nine times out of ten it is the right one) turns round, believing/suspecting/knowing that it is for him, i.e. recognizing that 'it really is he' who is meant by the hailing. But in reality these things happen without any succession. The existence of ideology and the hailing or interpellation of individuals as subjects are one and the same thing.

I might add: what thus seems to take place outside ideology (to be precise, in the street), in reality takes place in ideology. What really takes place in ideology seems therefore to take place outside it. That is why those who are in ideology believe themselves by definition outside ideology: one of the effects of ideology is the practical *denegation* of the ideological character of ideology by ideology: ideology never says, 'I am ideological.' It is necessary to be outside ideology, i.e. in scientific knowledge, to be able to say: I am in ideology (a quite exceptional case) or (the general case): I was in ideology. As is well known, the accusation of being in ideology only applies to others, never to oneself [. . .]. Which amounts to saying that ideology *has no outside* (for itself), but at the same time *that it is nothing but outside* (for science and reality).

[. . .]

Thus ideology hails or interpellates individuals as subjects. As ideology is eternal, I must now suppress the temporal form in which I have presented the functioning of ideology, and say: ideology has always-already interpellated individuals as subjects, which amounts to making it clear that individuals are always-already interpellated by ideology as subjects, which necessarily leads us to one last proposition: *individuals are always-already subjects*. Hence individuals are 'abstract' with respect to the subjects which they always-already are. This proposition might seem paradoxical.

That an individual is always-already a subject, even before he is born, is nevertheless the plain reality, accessible to everyone and not a paradox at all. Freud shows that individuals are always 'abstract' with respect to the subjects they always-already are, simply by noting the ideological ritual that surrounds the expectation of a 'birth', that 'happy event'. Everyone knows how much and in what way an unborn child is expected. Which amounts to saying, very prosaically, if we agree to drop the 'sentiments', i.e. the forms of family ideology (paternal/maternal/conjugal/fraternal) in which the unborn child is expected: it is certain in advance that it will bear its Father's Name, and will therefore have an identity and be irreplaceable. Before its birth, the child is therefore always-already a subject, appointed as a subject in and by the specific familial ideological configuration in which it is 'expected' once it has been conceived. I hardly need add that this familial ideological configuration is, in its uniqueness, highly structured, and that it is in this implacable and more or less 'pathological' (presupposing that any meaning can be assigned to that term) structure that the former subject-to-be will have to 'find' 'its' place, i.e. 'become' the sexual subject (boy or girl) which it already is in advance. [. . .]

Let me go one step further. What I shall now turn my attention to is the way the 'actors' in this *mise-en-scène* of interpellation, and their respective roles, are reflected in the very structure of all ideology.

An example: the Christian religious ideology

As the formal structure of all ideology is always the same, I shall restrict my analysis to a single example, one accessible to everyone, that of religious ideology, with the proviso that the same demonstration can be produced for ethical, legal, political, aesthetic ideology, etc.

Let us therefore consider the Christian religious ideology. I shall use a rhetorical figure and 'make it speak', i.e. collect into a fictional discourse what it 'says' not only in its two Testaments, its Theologians, Sermons, but also in its practices, its rituals, its ceremonies and its sacraments. The Christian religious ideology says something like this:

It says: I address myself to you, a human individual called Peter (every individual is called by his name, in the passive sense, it is never he who provides his own name), in order to tell you that God exists and that you are answerable to Him. It adds: God addresses himself to you through my voice (Scripture having collected the Word of God, Tradition having transmitted it, Papal Infallibility fixing it for ever on 'nice' points). It says: this is who you are: you are Peter! This is your origin, you were created by God for all eternity, although you were born in the 1920th year of Our Lord! This is your place in the world! This is what you must do! By these means, if you observe the 'law of love' you will be saved, you, Peter, and will become part of the Glorious Body of Christ! Etc. . . .

Now this is quite a familiar and banal discourse, but at the same time quite a surprising one.

Surprising because if we consider that religious ideology is indeed addressed to individuals,[5] in order to 'transform them into subjects', by interpellating the individual, Peter, in order to make him a subject, free to obey or disobey the appeal, i.e. God's commandments; if it calls these individuals by their names, thus recognizing that they are always-already interpellated as subjects with a personal identity (to the extent that Pascal's Christ says: 'It is for you that I have shed this drop of my blood!'); if it interpellates them in such a way that the subject responds: '*Yes; it really is me!*'; if it obtains from them the *recognition* that they really do occupy the place it designates for them as theirs in the world, a fixed residence: 'It really is me, I am here, a worker, a boss or a soldier!' in this vale of tears; if it obtains from them the recognition of a destination (eternal life or damnation) according to the respect or contempt they show to 'God's Commandments', Law become Love; – if everything does happen in this way (in the practices of the well-known rituals of baptism, confirmation, communion, confession and extreme unction, etc. . . .), we should note that all this 'procedure' to set up Christian religious subjects is dominated by a strange phenomenon: the fact that there can only be such a multitude of possible religious subjects on the absolute condition that there is a Unique, Absolute, *Other Subject*, i.e. God.

It is convenient to designate this new and remarkable Subject by writing Subject with a capital S to distinguish it from ordinary subjects, with a small s.

It then emerges that the interpellation of individuals as subjects presupposes the 'existence' of a Unique and central Other Subject, in whose Name the religious ideology interpellates all individuals as subjects. All this is clearly[6] written in what is rightly called the Scriptures. 'And it came to pass at that time that God the Lord (Yahweh) spoke to Moses in the cloud. And the Lord cried to Moses, "Moses!" And Moses replied "It is (really) I! I am Moses thy servant, speak and I shall listen!" And the Lord spoke to Moses and said to him, "*I am that I am.*"'

God thus defines himself as the Subject *par excellence*, he who is through himself and for himself ('I am that I am'), and he who interpellates his subject, the individual subjected to him by his very interpellation, i.e. the individual named Moses. And Moses, interpellated – called by his Name, having recognized that it 'really' was he who was called by God, recognizes that he is a subject, a subject *of* God, a subject subjected to God, *a subject through the Subject and subjected to the Subject*. The proof: he obeys him, and makes his people obey God's Commandments.

God is thus the Subject, and Moses and the innumerable subjects of God's people, the Subject's interlocutors–interpellates: his *mirrors*, his *reflections*. Were not men made *in the image* of God? As all theological reflection proves, whereas He 'could' perfectly well have done without men, God needs them, the Subject needs the subjects, just as men need God, the subjects need the Subject. Better: God needs men, the great Subject needs subjects, even in the terrible inversion of his image in them (when the subjects wallow in debauchery, i.e. sin).

Better: God duplicates himself and sends his Son to the Earth, as a mere subject 'forsaken' by him (the long complaint of the Garden of Olives which ends in the Crucifixion), subject but Subject, man but God, to do what prepares the way for the final Redemption, the Resurrection of Christ. God thus needs to 'make himself' a man, the Subject needs to become a subject, as if to show empirically, visibly to the eye, tangibly to the hands (see St Thomas) of the subjects, that, if they are subjects, subjected to the Subject, that is solely in order that finally, on Judgement Day, they will re-enter the Lord's Bosom, like Christ, i.e. re-enter the Subject.[7]

Let us decipher into theoretical language this wonderful necessity for the duplication of *the Subject into subjects* and of *the Subject itself into a subject–Subject*.

We observe that the structure of all ideology, interpellating individuals as subjects in the name of a Unique and Absolute Subject is *speculary*, i.e. a mirror-structure, and *doubly* speculary: this mirror duplication is constitutive of ideology and ensures its functioning. Which means that all ideology is *centred*, that the Absolute Subject occupies the unique place of the Centre, and interpellates around it the infinity of individuals into subjects in a double mirror-connexion such that it *subjects* the subjects to the Subject, while giving them in the Subject in which each subject can contemplate its own image (present and future) the *guarantee* that this really concerns them and Him, and that since everything takes place in the Family (the Holy Family: the Family is in essence Holy), 'God will *recognize* his own in it', i.e. those who have recognized God, and have recognized themselves in Him, will be saved.

Let me summarize what we have discovered about ideology in general.

The duplicate mirror-structure of ideology ensures simultaneously:

1   The interpellation of 'individuals' as subjects.

2   Their subjection to the Subject.

3   The mutual recognition of subjects and Subject, the subjects' recognition of each other, and finally the subject's recognition of himself.[8]

4   The absolute guarantee that everything really is so, and that on condition that the subjects recognize what they are and behave accordingly, everything will be all right: Amen – 'So be it.'

Result: caught in this quadruple system of interpellation as subjects, of subjection to the Subject, of universal recognition and of absolute guarantee, the subjects 'work', they 'work by themselves' in the vast majority of cases, with the exception of the 'bad subjects' who on occasion provoke the intervention of one of the detachments of the (repressive) State apparatus. But the vast majority of (good) subjects work all right 'all by themselves', i.e. by ideology (whose concrete forms are realized in the Ideological State Apparatuses). They are inserted into practices governed by the rituals of the ISAs. They 'recognize' the existing state of affairs (*das Bestehende*), that 'it really is true that it is so and not otherwise', and that they must be obedient to God, to their conscience, to the priest, to de Gaulle, to the boss, to the engineer, that thou shalt 'love thy neighbour as thyself', etc. Their concrete, material behaviour is simply the inscription in life of the admirable words of the prayer: '*Amen – So be it.*'

Yes, the subjects 'work by themselves'. The whole mystery of this effect lies in the first two moments of the quadruple system I have just discussed, or, if you prefer, in the ambiguity of the term *subject*. In the ordinary use of the term, subject in fact means: (1) a free subjectivity, a centre of initiatives, author of and responsible for its actions; (2) a subjected being, who submits to a higher authority, and is therefore stripped of all freedom except that of freely accepting his submission. This last note gives us the meaning of this ambiguity, which is merely a reflection of the effect which produces it: the individual *is interpellated as a (free) subject in order that he shall submit freely to the commandments of the Subject, i.e. in order that he shall (freely) accept his subjection*, i.e. in order that he shall make the gestures and actions of his subjection 'all by himself'. *There are no subjects except by and for their subjection.* That is why they 'work all by themselves'.

'*So be it! . . .*' This phrase which registers the effect to be obtained proves that it is not 'naturally' so ('naturally': outside the prayer, i.e. outside the ideological intervention). This phrase proves that it *has* to be so if things are to be what they must be, and let us let the words slip: if the reproduction of the relations of production is to be assured, even in the processes of production and circulation, every day, in the 'consciousness', i.e. in the attitudes of the individual-subjects occupying the posts which the sociotechnical division of labour assigns to them in production, exploitation, repression, ideologization, scientific practice, etc. Indeed, what is really in question in this mechanism of the mirror recognition of the Subject and of the individuals interpellated as subjects, and of the guarantee given by the Subject to the subjects if they freely accept their subjection to the Subject's 'commandments'? The reality in question in this mechanism, the reality which is necessarily *ignored* (*méconnue*) in the very forms of recognition (ideology = misrecognition/ignorance) is indeed, in the last resort, the reproduction of the relations of production and of the relations deriving from them. [. . .]

Notes

1 Which borrowed the legal category of 'subject in law' to make an ideological notion: man is by nature a subject.

2 Linguists and those who appeal to linguistics for various purposes often run up against difficulties which arise because they ignore the action of the ideological effects in all discourses – including even scientific discourses.

3 NB: this double 'currently' is one more proof of the fact that ideology is 'eternal', since these two 'currently's are separated by an indefinite interval; I am writing these lines on 6 April 1969, you may read them at any subsequent time.

4 Hailing as an everyday practice subject to a precise ritual takes a quite 'special' form in the policeman's practice of 'hailing' which concerns the hailing of 'suspects'.

5 Although we know that the individual is always-already a subject, we go on using this term, convenient because of the contrasting effect it produces.

6 I am quoting in a combined way, not to the letter but 'in spirit and truth'.

7 The dogma of the Trinity is precisely the theory of the duplication of the Subject (the Father) into a subject (the Son) and of their mirror-connexion (the Holy Spirit).

8 Hegel is (unknowingly) an admirable 'theoretician' of ideology insofar as he is a 'theoretician' of Universal Recognition who unfortunately ends up in the ideology of Absolute Knowledge. Feuerbach is an astonishing 'theoretician' of the mirror-connexion, who unfortunately ends up in the ideology of the Human Essence. To find the material with which to construct a theory of the guarantee, we must turn to Spinoza.

3

Subjectivity in language   **Emile Benveniste**

This chapter, which
was first published
in *Journal de
psychologie*, 55
(July–September,
1958), is taken from
*Problems in General
Linguistics* (Florida,
University of Miami
Press, 1971),
pp. 223–7.

If language is, as they say, the instrument of communication, to what
does it owe this property? The question may cause surprise, as does
everything that seems to challenge an obvious fact, but it is sometimes
useful to require proof of the obvious. Two answers come to mind. The
one would be that language is *in fact* employed as the instrument of
communication, probably because men have not found a better or more
effective way in which to communicate. This amounts to stating what
one wishes to understand. One might also think of replying that language
has such qualities as make it suited to serve as an instrument; it lends
itself to transmitting what I entrust to it – an order, a question, an
announcement – and it elicits from the interlocutor a behavior which is
adequate each time. Developing a more technical aspect of this idea, one
might add that the behavior of language admits of a behaviorist
description, in terms of stimulus and response, from which one might
draw conclusions as to the intermediary and instrumental nature of
language. But is it really language of which we are speaking here? Are we
not confusing it with discourse? If we posit that discourse is language put
into action, and necessarily between partners, we show amidst the confusion, that we are begging the question, since the nature of this 'instrument' is explained by its situation as an 'instrument.' As for the role of
transmission that language plays, one should not fail to observe, on the
one hand, that this role can devolve upon nonlinguistic means – gestures
and mimicry – and, on the other hand, that, in speaking here of an
'instrument,' we are letting ourselves be deceived by certain processes of
transmission which in human societies without exception come after
language and imitate its functioning. All systems of signals, rudimentary
or complex, are in this situation.

In fact, the comparison of language to an instrument – and it should necessarily be a material instrument for the comparison to even be comprehensible – must fill us with mistrust, as should every simplistic notion about language. To speak of an instrument is to put man and nature in opposition. The pick, the arrow, and the wheel are not in nature. They are fabrications. Language is in the nature of man, and he did not fabricate it. We are always inclined to that naïve concept of a primordial period in which a complete man discovered another one, equally complete, and between the two of them language was worked out little by little. This is pure fiction. We can never get back to man separated from language and we shall never see him inventing it. We shall never get back to man reduced to himself and exercising his wits to conceive of the existence of another. It is a speaking man whom we find in the world, a man speaking to another man, and language provides the very definition of man.

All the characteristics of language, its immaterial nature, its symbolic functioning, its articulated arrangement, the fact that it has *content*, are in themselves enough to render suspect this comparison of language to an instrument, which tends to dissociate the property of language from man. Certainly in everyday practice the give and take of speaking suggests an exchange, hence a 'thing' which we exchange, and speaking seems thus to assume an instrumental or vehicular function which we are quick to hypostasize as an 'object.' But, once again, this role belongs to the individual act of speech.

Once this function is seen as belonging to the act of speech, it may be asked what predisposition accounts for the fact that the act of speech should have it. In order for speech to be the vehicle of 'communication,' it must be so enabled by language, of which it is only the actualization. Indeed, it is in language that we must search for the condition of this aptitude. It seems to us that it resides in a property of language barely visible under the evidence that conceals it, which only sketchily can we yet characterize.

It is in and through language that man constitutes himself as a *subject*, because language alone establishes the concept of 'ego' in reality, in *its* reality which is that of the being.

The 'subjectivity' we are discussing here is the capacity of the speaker to posit himself as 'subject.' It is defined not by the feeling which everyone experiences of being himself (this feeling, to the degree that it can be taken note of, is only a reflection) but as the psychic unity that transcends the totality of the actual experiences it assembles and that makes the permanence of the consciousness. Now we hold that that 'subjectivity,' whether it is placed in phenomenology or in psychology, as one may wish, is only the emergence in the being of a fundamental property of language. 'Ego' is he who *says* 'ego.' That is where we see the foundation of 'subjectivity,' which is determined by the linguistic status of 'person.'

Consciousness of self is only possible if it is experienced by contrast. I use I only when I am speaking to someone who will be a *you* in my address. It is this condition of dialogue that is constitutive of *person*, for it implies that reciprocally *I* becomes *you* in the address of the one who in his turn designates himself as *I*. Here we see a principle whose consequences are to spread out in all directions. Language is possible only because each speaker sets himself up as a *subject* by referring to himself as *I* in his discourse. Because of this, *I* posits another person, the one who, being, as he is, completely exterior to 'me,' becomes my echo to whom I say *you* and who says *you* to me. This polarity of persons is the fundamental condition in language, of which the process of communication, in which we share, is only a mere pragmatic consequence. It is a polarity, moreover, very peculiar in itself, as it offers a type of opposition whose equivalent is encountered nowhere else outside of language. This polarity does not mean either equality or symmetry: 'ego' always has a position of transcendence with regard to *you*. Nevertheless, neither of the terms can be conceived of without the other; they are complementary, although according to an 'interior/exterior' opposition, and, at the same time, they are reversible. If we seek a parallel to this, we will not find it. The condition of man in language is unique.

And so the old antinomies of 'I' and 'the other,' of the individual and society, fall. It is a duality which it is illegitimate and erroneous to reduce to a single primordial term, whether this unique term be the 'I,' which must be established in the individual's own consciousness in order to become accessible to that of the fellow human being, or whether it be, on the contrary, society, which as a totality would preexist the individual and from which the individual could only be disengaged gradually, in proportion to his acquisition of self-consciousness. It is in a dialectic reality that will incorporate the two terms and define them by mutual relationship that the linguistic basis of subjectivity is discovered.

But must this basis be linguistic? By what right does language establish the basis of subjectivity?

As a matter of fact, language is responsible for it in all its parts. Language is marked so deeply by the expression of subjectivity that one might ask if it could still function and be called language if it were constructed otherwise. We are of course talking of language in general, not simply of particular languages. But the concordant facts of particular languages give evidence for language. We shall give only a few of the most obvious examples.

The very terms we are using here, *I* and *you*, are not to be taken as figures but as linguistic forms indicating 'person.' It is a remarkable fact – but who would notice it, since it is so familiar? – that the 'personal pronouns' are never missing from among the signs of a language, no matter what its type, epoch, or region may be. A language without the expression of person cannot be imagined. It can only happen that in certain languages, under certain circumstances, these 'pronouns' are deliberately omitted; this is the case in most of the Far Eastern societies, in which a convention of politeness imposes the use of periphrases or of special forms between certain groups of individuals in order to replace the direct personal references. But these usages only serve to underline the value of the avoided forms; it is the implicit existence of these pronouns that gives social and cultural value to the substitutes imposed by class relationships.

Now these pronouns are distinguished from all other designations a language articulates in that *they do not refer to a concept or to an individual*.

There is no concept 'I' that incorporates all the *I*s that are uttered at every moment in the mouths of all speakers, in the sense that there is a concept 'tree' to which all the individual uses of *tree* refer. The 'I,' then, does not denominate any lexical entity. Could it then be said that *I* refers to a particular individual? If that were the case, a permanent contradiction would be admitted into language, and anarchy into its use. How could the same term refer indifferently to any individual whatsoever and still at the same time identify him in his individuality? We are in the presence of a class of words, the 'personal pronouns,' that escape the status of all the other signs of language. Then, what does *I* refer to? To something very peculiar which is exclusively linguistic: *I* refers to the act of individual discourse in which it is pronounced, and by this it designates the speaker. It is a term that cannot be identified except in what we have called elsewhere an instance of discourse and that has only a momentary reference. The reality to which it refers is the reality of the discourse. It is in the instance of discourse in which *I* designates the speaker that the speaker proclaims himself as the 'subject.' And so it is literally true that the basis of sub-jectivity is in the exercise of language. If one really thinks about it, one will see that there is no other objective testimony to the identity of the subject except that which he himself thus gives about himself.

Language is so organized that it permits each speaker to *appropriate to himself* an entire language by designating himself as *I*.

The personal pronouns provide the first step in this bringing out of subjectivity in language. Other classes of pronouns that share the same status depend in their turn upon these pronouns. These other classes are the indicators of *deixis*, the demonstratives, adverbs, and adjectives, which organize the spatial and temporal relationships around the 'subject' taken as referent: 'this, here, now,' and their numerous correlatives, 'that, yesterday, last year, tomorrow,' etc. They have in common the feature of being defined only with respect to the instances of discourse in which they occur, that is, in dependence upon the *I* which is proclaimed in the discourse.

It is easy to see that the domain of subjectivity is further expanded and must take over the expression of temporality. No matter what the type of language, there is everywhere to be observed a certain linguistic organ-ization of the notion of time. It matters little whether this notion is marked in the inflection of the verb or by words of other classes (particles, adverbs, lexical variations, etc.); that is a matter of formal structure. In one way or another, a language always makes a distinction of 'tenses'; whether it be a past and a future, separated by a 'present,' as in French [or English], or, as in various Amerindian languages, of a preterite-present opposed to a future, or a present-future distinguished from a past, these distinctions being in their turn capable of depending on variations of aspect, etc. But the line of separation is always a reference to the 'present.' Now this 'present' in its turn has only a linguistic fact as temporal reference: the coincidence of the event described with the instance of discourse that describes it. The temporal referent of the present can only be internal to the discourse. The *Dictionnaire générale* defines the 'present' as '*le temps du verbe qui exprime le temps où l'on est.*' But let us beware of this; there is no other criterion and no other expression by which to indicate 'the time at which one *is*' except to take it as 'the time at which one *is speaking.*' This is the eternally 'present' moment, although it never relates to the same events of an 'objective' chronology because it is determined for each speaker by each of the instances of discourse related to it. Linguistic time is *self-referential.* Ultimately, human temporality with all its linguistic apparatus reveals the subjectivity inherent in the very using of language.

Language is accordingly the possibility of subjectivity because it always contains the linguistic forms appropriate to the expression of subjectivity, and discourse provokes the emergence of subjectivity because it consists of discrete instances. In some way language puts forth 'empty' forms which each speaker, in the exercise of discourse, appropriates to himself and which he relates to his 'person,' at the same time defining himself as *I* and a partner as *you.* The instance of discourse is thus constitutive of all the coordinates that define the subject and of which we have briefly pointed out only the most obvious. [. . .]

The mirror stage **Jacques Lacan**

This chapter was
delivered at the
16th International
Congress of
Psychoanalysis, held
in Zurich on 17 July
1949, as 'The mirror
stage as formative
of the function of
the I as revealed in
psychoanalytic
experience'. It is
based on an earlier
paper given to the
Fourteenth
International
Psychoanalytical
Congress at
Marienbad in 1936.
The chapter is taken
from Écrits: a
Selection (London,
Routledge, 1989),
pp. 1–7.

The conception of the mirror stage that I introduced at our last congress, thirteen years ago, has since become more or less established in the practice of the French group. However, I think it worthwhile to bring it again to your attention, especially today, for the light it sheds on the formation of the *I* as we experience it in psychoanalysis. It is an experience that leads us to oppose any philosophy directly issuing from the *Cogito*.

Some of you may recall that this conception originated in a feature of human behaviour illuminated by a fact of comparative psychology. The child, at an age when he is for a time, however short, outdone by the chimpanzee in instrumental intelligence, can nevertheless already recognize as such his own image in a mirror. This recognition is indicated in the illuminative mimicry of the *Aha-Erlebnis*, which Köhler sees as the expression of situational apperception, an essential stage of the act of intelligence.

This act, far from exhausting itself, as in the case of the monkey, once the image has been mastered and found empty, immediately rebounds in the case of the child in a series of gestures in which he experiences in play the relation between the movements assumed in the image and the reflected environment, and between this virtual complex and the reality it redupli-cates – the child's own body, and the persons and things, around him.

This event can take place, as we have known since Baldwin, from the age of six months, and its repetition has often made me reflect upon the startling spectacle of the infant in front of the mirror. Unable as yet to walk, or even to stand up, and held tightly as he is by some support, human or artificial (what, in France, we call a '*trotte-bébé*'), he never-theless overcomes, in a flutter of jubilant activity, the obstructions of his support and, fixing his attitude in a slightly leaning-forward position, in order to hold it in his gaze, brings back an instantaneous aspect of the image.

For me, this activity retains the meaning I have given it up to the age of eighteen months. This meaning discloses a libidinal dynamism, which has hitherto remained problematic, as well as an ontological structure of the human world that accords with my reflections on paranoiac knowledge.

We have only to understand the mirror stage *as an identification*, in the full sense that analysis gives to the term: namely, the transformation that takes place in the subject when he assumes an image – whose predestination to this phase-effect is sufficiently indicated by the use, in analytic theory, of the ancient term *imago*.

This jubilant assumption of his specular image by the child at the *infans* stage, still sunk in his motor incapacity and nursling dependence, would seem to exhibit in an exemplary situation the symbolic matrix in which the *I* is precipitated in a primordial form, before it is objectified in the dialectic of identification with the other, and before language restores to it, in the universal, its function as subject.

This form would have to be called the Ideal-I,[1] if we wished to incorporate it into our usual register, in the sense that it will also be the source of secondary identifications, under which term I would place the functions of libidinal normalization. But the important point is that this form situates the agency of the ego, before its social determination, in a fictional direction, which will always remain irreducible for the individual alone, or rather, which will only rejoin the coming-into-being (*le devenir*) of the subject asymptotically, whatever the success of the dialectical syntheses by which he must resolve as *I* his discordance with his own reality.

The fact is that the total form of the body by which the subject anticipates in a mirage the maturation of his power is given to him only as *Gestalt*, that is to say, in an exteriority in which this form is certainly more constituent than constituted, but in which it appears to him above all in a contrasting size (*un relief de stature*) that fixes it and in a symmetry that inverts it, in contrast with the turbulent movements that the subject feels are animating him. Thus, this *Gestalt* – whose pregnancy should be regarded as bound up with the species, though its motor style remains scarcely recognizable – by these two aspects of its appearance, symbolizes the mental permanence of the *I*, at the same time as it pre-figures its alienating destination; it is still pregnant with the corre-spondences that unite the *I* with the statue in which man projects himself, with the phantoms that dominate him, or with the automaton in which, in an ambiguous relation, the world of his own making tends to find completion.

Indeed, for the *imagos* – whose veiled faces it is our privilege to see in outline in our daily experience and in the penumbra of symbolic efficacity[2] – the mirror-image would seem to be the threshold of the visible world, if we go by the mirror disposition that the *imago of one's own body* presents in hallucinations or dreams, whether it concerns its individual features, or even its infirmities, or its object-projections; or if we observe the role of the mirror apparatus in the appearances of the *double*, in which psychical realities, however heterogeneous, are manifested.

That a *Gestalt* should be capable of formative effects in the organism is attested by a piece of biological experimentation that is itself so alien to the idea of psychical causality that it cannot bring itself to formulate its results in these terms. It nevertheless recognizes that it is a necessary condition for the maturation of the gonad of the female pigeon that it should see another member of its species, of either sex; so sufficient in itself is this condition that the desired effect may be obtained merely by placing the individual within reach of the field of reflection of a mirror. Similarly, in the case of the migratory locust, the transition within a generation from the solitary to the gregarious form can be obtained by exposing the individual, at a certain stage, to the exclusively visual action of a similar image, provided it is animated by movements of a style sufficiently close to that characteristic of the species. Such facts are inscribed in an order of homeomorphic identification that would itself fall within the larger question of the meaning of beauty as both formative and erogenic.

But the facts of mimicry are no less instructive when conceived as cases of heteromorphic identification, in as much as they raise the problem of the signification of space for the living organism – psychological concepts hardly seem less appropriate for shedding light on these matters than ridiculous attempts to reduce them to the supposedly supreme law of adaptation. We have only to recall how Roger Caillois (who was then very young, and still fresh from his breach with the sociological school in which he was trained) illuminated the subject by using the term *'legendary psychasthenia'* to classify morphological mimicry as an obsession with space in its derealizing effect.

I have myself shown in the social dialectic that structures human knowledge as paranoiac[3] why human knowledge has greater autonomy than animal knowledge in relation to the field of force of desire, but also why human knowledge is determined in that 'little reality' (*ce peu de réalité*), which the Surrealists, in their restless way, saw as its limitation. These reflections lead me to recognize in the spatial captation manifested in the mirror stage, even before the social dialectic, the effect in man of an organic insufficiency in his natural reality – in so far as any meaning can be given to the word 'nature'.

I am led, therefore, to regard the function of the mirror stage as a particular case of the function of the *imago*, which is to establish a relation between the organism and its reality – or, as they say, between the *Innenwelt* and the *Umwelt*.

In man, however, this relation to nature is altered by a certain dehiscence at the heart of the organism, a primordial Discord betrayed by the signs of uneasiness and motor unco-ordination of the neo-natal months. The objective notion of the anatomical incompleteness of the pyramidal system and likewise the presence of certain humoral residues of the maternal organism confirm the view I have formulated as the fact of a real *specific prematurity of birth* in man.

It is worth noting, incidentally, that this is a fact recognized as such by embryologists, by the term *foetalization*, which determines the prevalence of the so-called superior apparatus of the neurax, and especially of the cortex, which psycho-surgical operations lead us to regard as the intra-organic mirror.

This development is experienced as a temporal dialectic that decisively projects the formation of the individual into history. The *mirror stage* is a drama whose internal thrust is precipitated from insufficiency to anticipation – and which manufactures for the subject, caught up in the lure of spatial identification, the succession of phantasies that extends from a fragmented body-image to a form of its totality that I shall call orthopaedic – and, lastly, to the assumption of the armour of an alienating identity, which will mark with its rigid structure the subject's entire mental development. Thus, to break out of the circle of the *Innenwelt* into the *Umwelt* generates the inexhaustible quadrature of the ego's verifications.

This fragmented body – which term I have also introduced into our system of theoretical references – usually manifests itself in dreams when the movement of the analysis encounters a certain level of aggressive disintegration in the individual. It then appears in the form of disjointed limbs, or of those organs represented in exoscopy, growing wings and taking up arms for intestinal persecutions – the very same that the visionary Hieronymus Bosch has fixed, for all time, in painting, in their ascent from the fifteenth century to the imaginary zenith of modern man. But this form is even tangibly revealed at the organic level, in the lines of 'fragilization' that define the anatomy of phantasy, as exhibited in the schizoid and spasmodic symptoms of hysteria.

Correlatively, the formation of the *I* is symbolized in dreams by a fortress, or a stadium – its inner arena and enclosure, surrounded by marshes and rubbish-tips, dividing it into two opposed fields of contest where the subject flounders in quest of the lofty, remote inner castle whose form (sometimes juxtaposed in the same scenario) symbolizes the id in a quite startling way. Similarly, on the mental plane, we find realized the structures of fortified works, the metaphor of which arises spontaneously, as if issuing from the symptoms themselves, to designate the mechanisms of obsessional neurosis – inversion, isolation, reduplication, cancellation and displacement.

But if we were to build on these subjective givens alone – however little we free them from the condition of experience that makes us see them as partaking of the nature of a linguistic technique – our theoretical attempts would remain exposed to the charge of projecting themselves into the unthinkable of an absolute subject. This is why I have sought in the present hypothesis, grounded in a conjunction of objective data, the guiding grid for a *method of symbolic reduction*.

It establishes in the *defences of the ego* a genetic order, in accordance with the wish formulated by Miss Anna Freud, in the first part of her great work, and situates (as against a frequently expressed prejudice) hysterical repression and its returns at a more archaic stage than obsessional inversion and its isolating processes, and the latter in turn as preliminary to paranoic alienation, which dates from the deflection of the specular *I* into the social *I*.

This moment in which the mirror stage comes to an end inaugurates, by the identification with the *imago* of the counterpart and the drama of primordial jealousy (so well brought out by the school of Charlotte Bühler in the phenomenon of infantile *transitivism*), the dialectic that will henceforth link the *I* to socially elaborated situations.

It is this moment that decisively tips the whole of human knowledge into mediatization through the desire of the other, constitutes its objects in an abstract equivalence by the co-operation of others, and turns the *I* into that apparatus for which every instinctual thrust constitutes a danger, even though it should correspond to a natural maturation – the very normalization of this maturation being henceforth dependent, in man, on a cultural mediation as exemplified, in the case of the sexual object, by the Oedipus complex.

In the light of this conception, the term primary narcissism, by which analytic doctrine designates the libidinal investment characteristic of that moment, reveals in those who invented it the most profound awareness of semantic latencies. But it also throws light on the dynamic opposition between this libido and the sexual libido, which the first analysts tried to define when they invoked destructive and, indeed, death instincts, in order to explain the evident connection between the narcissistic libido and the alienating function of the *I*, the aggressivity it releases in any relation to the other, even in a relation involving the most Samaritan of aid.

In fact, they were encountering that existential negativity whose reality is so vigorously proclaimed by the contemporary philosophy of being and nothingness.

But unfortunately that philosophy grasps negativity only within the limits of a self-sufficiency of consciousness, which, as one of its premises, links to the *méconnaissances* that constitute the ego, the illusion of autonomy to which it entrusts itself. This flight of fancy, for all that it draws, to an unusual extent, on borrowings from psychoanalytic experience, culminates in the pretention of providing an existential psychoanalysis.

At the culmination of the historical effort of a society to refuse to recognize that it has any function other than the utilitarian one, and in the anxiety of the individual confronting the 'concentrational'[4] form of the social bond that seems to arise to crown this effort, existentialism must be judged by the explanations it gives of the subjective impasses that have indeed resulted from it; a freedom that is never more authentic than when it is within the walls of a prison; a demand for commitment, expressing the impotence of a pure consciousness to master any situation; a voyeuristic–sadistic idealization of the sexual relation; a personality that realizes itself only in suicide; a consciousness of the other that can be satisfied only by Hegelian murder.

These propositions are opposed by all our experience, in so far as it teaches us not to regard the ego as centred on the *perception–consciousness system*, or as organized by the 'reality principle' – a principle that is the expression of a scientific prejudice most hostile to the dialectic of knowledge. Our experience shows that we should start instead from the *function of méconnaissance* that characterizes the ego in all its structures, so markedly articulated by Miss Anna Freud. For, if the *Verneinung* represents the patent form of that function, its effects will, for the most part, remain latent, so long as they are not illuminated by some light reflected on to the level of fatality, which is where the id manifests itself.

We can thus understand the inertia characteristic of the formations of the *I*, and find there the most extensive definition of neurosis – just as the captation of the subject by the situation gives us the most general formula for madness, not only the madness that lies behind the walls of asylums, but also the madness that deafens the world with its sound and fury.

The sufferings of neurosis and psychosis are for us a schooling in the passions of the soul, just as the beam of the psychoanalytic scales, when we calculate the tilt of its threat to entire communities, provides us with an indication of the deadening of the passions in society.

At this junction of nature and culture, so persistently examined by modern anthropology, psychoanalysis alone recognizes this knot of imaginary servitude that love must always undo again, or sever.

For such a task, we place no trust in altruistic feeling, we who lay bare the aggressivity that underlies the activity of the philanthropist, the idealist, the pedagogue, and even the reformer.

In the recourse of subject to subject that we preserve, psychoanalysis may accompany the patient to the ecstatic limit of the '*Thou art that*', in which is revealed to him the cipher of his mortal destiny, but it is not in our mere power as practitioners to bring him to that point where the real journey begins.

Notes

1   Throughout this [chapter] I leave in its peculiarity the translation I have adopted for Freud's *Ideal-Ich* [i.e. '*je-idéal*'], without further comment, other than to say that I have not maintained it since.

2   Cf. Claude Lévi-Strauss, *Structural Anthropology* (New York, Basic Books, 1963), ch. 10.

3   Cf. Jacques Lacan, 'Aggressivity in Psychoanalysis', *Écrits: a Selection* (London, Routledge, 1989), p. 8, and 'Propos sur la causalité psychique', *Écrits* (Paris, Seuil, 1966), p. 180.

4   *Translator's note*: 'Concentrationnaire', an adjective coined after World War II (this [chapter] was written in 1949) to describe the life of the concentration camp. In the hands of certain writers it became, by extension, applicable to many aspects of 'modern' life.

5

Feminine sexuality   **Jacqueline Rose**

[. . .] Re-opening the debate on feminine sexuality must start [. . .] with the link between sexuality and the unconscious. No account of Lacan's work which attempts to separate the two can make sense. For Lacan, the unconscious undermines the subject from any position of certainty, from any relation of knowledge to his or her psychic processes and history, and *simultaneously* reveals the fictional nature of the sexual category to which every human subject is none the less assigned. In Lacan's account, sexual identity operates as a law – it is something enjoined on the subject. For him, the fact that individuals must line up according to an opposition (having or not having the phallus) makes that clear. But it is the constant difficulty, or even impossibility, of that process which Lacan emphasised. Exposure of that difficulty within psychoanalysis and for feminism is, therefore, part of one and the same project.

This chapter was first written as part of the Introduction to *Feminine Sexuality: Jacques Lacan and the école freudienne*, edited by Juliet Mitchell and Jacqueline Rose (London, Macmillan, 1982). The extract reproduced here is taken from *Sexuality in the Field of Vision* (London, Verso, 1986), pp. 49–81.

I

[. . .] Lacan's account of subjectivity was always developed with reference to the idea of a fiction. Thus, in the 1930s he introduced the concept of the 'mirror stage,'[1] which took the child's mirror image as the model and basis for its future identifications. This image is a fiction because it conceals, or freezes, the infant's lack of motor co-ordination and the fragmentation of its drives. But it is salutary for the child, since it gives it the first sense of a coherent identity in which it can recognise itself. For Lacan, however, this is already a fantasy – the very image which places the child divides its identity into two. Furthermore, that moment only has meaning in relation to the presence and the look of the mother who guarantees its reality for the child. The mother does not (as in D.W. Winnicott's account)[2] mirror the child to itself; she grants an image *to* the child, which her presence instantly deflects. [. . .] The mirror image is central to Lacan's account of subjectivity, because its apparent smoothness and totality is a myth. The image in which we first recognise ourselves is a *misrecognition*. Lacan is careful to stress, however, that his point is not restricted to the field of the visible alone: 'the idea of the mirror should be understood as an object which reflects – not just the visible, but also what is heard, touched and willed by the child.'[3]

[. . .]

For Lacan the subject is constituted through language – the mirror image represents the moment when the subject is located in an order outside itself to which it will henceforth refer. The subject is the subject *of* speech (Lacan's '*parle-être*'), and subject *to* that order. But if there is division in the image. [. . .] there is equally loss, and difficulty, in the word. Language can only operate by designating an object in its absence. Lacan takes this further, and states that symbolisation turns on the object *as* absence. He gives as his reference Freud's early account of the child's hallucinatory cathexis of the object for which it cries, and his later description in *Beyond the Pleasure Principle* of the child's symbolisation of the absent mother in play.[4] In the first example, the child hallucinates the object it desires; in the second, it throws a cotton reel out of its cot in order to symbolise the absence and the presence of the mother. Symbolisation starts, therefore, when the child gets its first sense that something could be missing; words stand for objects, because they only have to be spoken at the moment when the first object is lost. For Lacan, the subject can only operate within language by constantly repeating that moment of fundamental and irreducible division. The subject is therefore constituted in language *as* this division or splitting (Freud's *Ichspaltung*, or splitting of the ego).

Lacan termed the order of language the symbolic, that of the ego and its identifications the imaginary (the stress, therefore, is quite deliberately on symbol and image, the idea of something which 'stands in'). [. . .]

Lacan's account of childhood then follows his basic premise that identity is constructed in language, but only at a cost. Identity shifts, and language speaks the loss which lay behind that first moment of symbolisation. When the child asks something of its mother, that loss will persist over and above anything which she can possibly give, or say, in reply. Demand always 'bears on something other than the satisfaction which it calls for',[5] and each time the demand of the child is answered by the satisfaction of its needs, so this 'something other' is relegated to the place of its original impossibility. Lacan terms this 'desire'. It can be defined as the 'remainder' of the subject, something which is always left over, but which has no content as such. Desire functions much as the zero unit in the numerical chain – its place is both constitutive *and* empty.

The concept of desire is crucial to Lacan's account of sexuality. He considered that the failure to grasp its implications leads inevitably to a reduction of sexuality back into the order of a need (something, therefore, which could be satisfied). Against this, he quoted Freud's statement: 'we must reckon with the possibility that something in the nature of the sexual instinct itself is unfavourable to the realisation of complete satisfaction.'[6]

At the same time 'identity' and 'wholeness' remain precisely at the level of fantasy. Subjects in language persist in their belief that somewhere there is a point of certainty, of knowledge and of truth. When the subject addresses its demand outside itself to another, this other becomes the fantasied place of just such a knowledge or certainty. Lacan calls this the Other – the site of language to which the speaking subject necessarily refers. The Other appears to hold the 'truth' of the subject and the power to make good its loss. But this is the ultimate fantasy. Language is the place where meaning circulates – the meaning of each linguistic unit can only be established by reference to another, and it is arbitrarily fixed. Lacan, therefore, draws from Saussure's concept of the arbitrary nature of the linguistic sign – introduced in his *Course in General Linguistics* – the implication that there can be no final guarantee or securing of language. There is, Lacan writes, 'no Other of the Other', and anyone who claims to take up this place is an imposter (the Master and/or psychotic).

Sexuality belongs in this area of instability played out in the register of demand and desire, each sex coming to stand, mythically and exclusively, for that which could satisfy and complete the other. It is when the categories 'male' and 'female' are seen to represent an absolute and complementary division that they fall prey to a mystification in which the difficulty of sexuality instantly disappears: 'to disguise this gap by relying on the virtue of the "genital" to resolve it through the maturation of tenderness . . . however piously intended, is nonetheless a fraud.'[7] Lacan therefore argued that psychoanalysis should not try to produce 'male' and 'female' as complementary entities, sure of each other and of their own identity, but should expose the fantasy on which this notion rests.

There is a tendency, when arguing for the pre-given nature of sexual difference, for the specificity of male and female drives, to lose sight of the more radical aspects of Freud's work on sexuality – his insistence on the disjunction between the sexual object and the sexual aim, his difficult challenge to the concept of perversion, and his demand that heterosexual object-choice be explained and not assumed.[8] For Lacan, the 'vicissitudes' of the instinct ('instinct' was the original English translation for the German word *trieb*) cannot be understood as a deviation, accident or defence on the path to a normal heterosexuality which would ideally be secured. Rather the term 'vicissitude' indicates a fundamental difficulty inherent in human sexuality, which can be seen in the very concept of the drive.

The concept of the drive is crucial to the discussion of sexuality because of the relative ease with which it can be used to collapse psychoanalysis into biology, the dimension from which, for Lacan, it most urgently needed to be retrieved. He rejected the idea of a gradual 'maturation' of the drive, with its associated emphasis on genital identity (the 'virtue' of the genital) because of the way it implies a quasi-biological sequence of sexual life. Instead he stressed the resistance of the drive to any biological definition.

The drive is not the instinct precisely because it cannot be reduced to the order of need (Freud defined it as an internal stimulus only to distinguish it immediately from hunger and thirst). The drive is divisible into pressure, source, object and aim; and it challenges any straightforward concept of satisfaction – the drive can be sublimated and Freud described its object as 'indifferent'. What matters, therefore, is not what the drive *achieves*, but its *process*. For Lacan, that process reveals all the difficulty which characterises the subject's relationship to the Other. In his account, the drive is something in the nature of an appeal, or searching out, which always goes beyond the actual relationships on which it turns. [. . .] The drive touches on an area of excess (it is 'too much'). Lacan calls this *jouissance* (literally 'orgasm', but used by Lacan to refer to something more than pleasure which can easily tip into its opposite).

[. . .]

The structure of the drive and what Lacan calls the 'nodal point' of desire are the two concepts in his work as a whole which undermine a normative account of human sexuality [. . .].

By focusing on what he calls the symbolic order, Lacan was doing no more than taking to its logical conclusion Freud's preoccupation with an 'historic event' in the determination of human subjectivity (the myth of the primal horde). But for Lacan this is not some mythical moment of our past; it is the present order in which every individual subject must take up her or his place. [. . .] As was the case with Freud, the concept of castration came into Lacan's account of sexuality as the direct effect of this emphasis. [. . .] The concept of castration was central to Lacan because of the reference which it always contains to paternal law.

Addressing Melanie Klein, Lacan makes it clear that the argument for a reintroduction of the concept of desire into the definition of human sexuality is a return to, and a reformulation of, the law and the place of the father as it was originally defined by Freud ('a dimension . . . increasingly evaded since Freud'):[9]

> Melanie Klein describes the relationship to the mother as a mirrored relationship: the maternal body becomes the receptacle of the drives which the child projects onto it, drives motivated by aggression born of a fundamental disappointment. This is to neglect the fact that the outside is given for the subject as the place where the desire of the Other is situated, and where he or she will encounter the third term, the father.[10]

Lacan argued, therefore, for a return to the concept of the father, but this concept is now defined in relation to that of desire. What matters is that the relationship of the child to the mother is not simply based on 'frustration and satisfaction' ('the notion of frustration (which was never employed by Freud)'),[11] but on the recognition of her desire. The mother is refused to the child in so far as a prohibition falls on the child's desire to be what the mother desires (not the same, note, as a desire to possess or enjoy the mother in the sense normally understood):

> What we meet as an accident in the child's development is linked to the fact that the child does not find himself or herself alone in front of the mother, and that the phallus forbids the child the satisfaction of his or her own desire, which is the desire to be the exclusive desire of the mother.[12]

The duality of the relation between mother and child must be broken [. . .]. In Lacan's account, the phallus stands for that moment of rupture. It refers mother and child to the dimension of the symbolic which is figured by the father's place. The mother is taken to desire the phallus not because she contains it (Klein), but precisely because she does not. The phallus therefore belongs somewhere else; it breaks the two-term relation and initiates the order of exchange. For Lacan, it takes on this value as a function of the androcentric nature of the symbolic order itself [. . .]. But its status is in itself false, and must be recognised by the child as such. Castration means first of all this – that the child's desire for the mother does not refer *to* her but *beyond* her, to an object, the phallus, whose status is first imaginary (the object presumed to satisfy her desire) and then symbolic (recognition that desire cannot be satisfied).

The place of the phallus in the account, therefore, follows from Lacan's return to the position and law of the father, but this concept has been reformulated in relation to that of desire. [. . .] [Lacan insists] that the father stands for a place and a function which is not reducible to the presence or absence of the real father as such:

> To speak of the Name of the Father is by no means the same thing as invoking paternal deficiency (which is often done). We know today that an Oedipus complex can be constituted perfectly well even if the father is not there, while originally it was the excessive presence of the father which was held responsible for all dramas. But it is not in an environmental perspective that the answer to these questions can be found. So as to make the link between the Name of the Father, in so far as he can at times be missing, and the father whose effective presence is not always necessary for him not to be missing, I will introduce the expression *paternal metaphor*.[13]

[. . .]

Thus when Lacan calls for a return to the place of the father he is crucially distinguishing himself from any sociological conception of role. The father is a function and refers to a law, the place outside the imaginary dyad and against which it breaks. To make of him a referent is to fall into an ideological trap: the 'prejudice which falsifies the conception of the Oedipus complex from the start, by making it define as natural, rather than normative, the predominance of the paternal figure'.[14]

There is, therefore, no assumption about the ways in which the places come to be fulfilled (it is this very assumption which is questioned). This is why, in talking of the genetic link between the mother and child, Lacan could refer to the 'vast social connivance' which *makes* of her the 'privileged site of prohibitions'.[15] And why Safouan, in an article on the function of the real father, recognises that it is the intervention of the third term which counts, and that nothing of itself requires that this should be embodied by the father as such.[16] Lacan's position should be read against two alternative emphases – on the actual behaviour of the mother alone (adequacy and inadequacy), and on a literally present or absent father (his idealisation and/or deficiency).

The concept of the phallus and the castration complex can only be understood in terms of this reference to prohibition and the law, just as rejection of these concepts tends to lose sight of this reference. The phallus needs to be placed on the axis of desire before it can be understood, or questioned, as the differential mark of sexual identification (boy or girl, having or not having the phallus). By breaking the imaginary dyad, the phallus represents a moment of division (Lacan calls this the subject's 'lack-in-being') which re-enacts the fundamental splitting of subjectivity itself. And by jarring against any naturalist account of sexuality ('phallocentrism . . . strictly impossible to deduce from any pre-established harmony of the said psyche to the nature it expresses'),[17] the phallus relegates sexuality to a strictly other dimension – the order of the symbolic outside of which, for Lacan, sexuality cannot be understood. The importance of the phallus is that its status in the development of human sexuality is something which nature *cannot* account for.

When Lacan is reproached with phallocentrism at the level of his theory, what is most often missed is that the subject's entry into the symbolic order is equally an exposure of the value of the phallus itself. The subject has to recognise that there is desire, or lack in the place of the Other, that there is no ultimate certainty or truth, and that the status of the phallus is a fraud (this is, for Lacan, the meaning of castration). The phallus can only take up its place by indicating the precariousness of any identity assumed by the subject on the basis of its token. Thus the phallus stands for that moment when prohibition must function, in the sense of whom may be assigned to whom in the triangle made up of mother, father and child, but at that same moment it signals to the subject that 'having' only functions at the price of a loss and 'being' as an effect of division. Only if this is dropped from the account can the phallus be taken to represent an unproblematic assertion of male privilege, or else lead to reformulations intended to guarantee the continuity of sexual development for both sexes (Jones).

It is that very continuity which is challenged in Lacan's account. The concept of the phallus and the castration complex testify above all to the problematic nature of the subject's insertion into his or her sexual identity [. . .].

The subject then takes up his or her identity with reference to the phallus, but that identity is thereby designated symbolic (it is something enjoined on the subject). Lacan inverts Saussure's formula for the linguistic sign (the opposition between signifier and signified), giving primacy to the signifier over that which it signifies (or rather creates in that act of signification). For it is essential to his argument that sexual difference is a legislative divide which creates and reproduces its categories. Thus Lacan replaces Saussure's model for the arbitrary nature of the linguistic sign:

TREE

[. . .] with this model:[18]

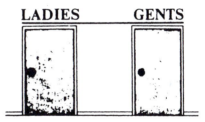

'Any speaking being whatever' must line up on one or other side of the divide.[19]

Sexual difference is then assigned according to whether individual subjects do or do not possess the phallus, which means not that anatomical difference *is* sexual difference (the one as strictly deducible from the other), but that anatomical difference comes to *figure* sexual difference, that is, it becomes the sole representative of what that difference is allowed to be. It thus covers over the complexity of the child's early sexual life with a crude opposition in which that very complexity is refused or repressed. The phallus thus indicates the reduction of difference to an instance of visible perception, a *seeming* value.

Freud gave the moment when the boy and girl child saw that they were different the status of a trauma in which the girl is seen to be lacking (the objections often start here). But something can only be *seen* to be missing according to a pre-existing hierarchy of values ('there is nothing missing in the real').[20] What counts is not the perception but its already assigned meaning – the moment therefore belongs in the symbolic. And if Lacan states that the symbolic usage of the phallus stems from its visibility (something for which he was often criticised), it is only in so far as the order of the visible, the apparent, the seeming is the object of his attack. In fact he constantly refused any crude identification of the phallus with the order of the visible or real ('one might say that this signifier is chosen as what stands out as most easily seized upon in the real of sexual copulation'),[21] and he referred it instead to that function of 'veiling' in which he locates the fundamental duplicity of the linguistic sign: 'All these propositions merely veil over the fact that the phallus can only play its role as veiled, that is, as in itself the sign of the latency with which everything signifiable is struck as soon as it is raised to the function of signifier'.[22]

Meaning is only ever erected, it is set up and fixed. The phallus symbolises the effects of the signifier in that having no value in itself, it can represent that to which value *accrues*.

Lacan's statements on language need to be taken in two directions – towards the fixing of meaning itself (that which is enjoined on the subject), and away from that very fixing to the point of its constant slippage, the risk or vanishing-point which it always contains (the unconscious). Sexuality is placed on both these dimensions at once. The difficulty is to hold these two emphases together – sexuality in the symbolic (an ordering), sexuality as that which constantly fails. Once the relationship between these two aspects of psychoanalysis can be seen, then the terms in which feminine sexuality can be described undergo a radical shift. The concept of the symbolic states that the woman's sexuality is inseparable from the representations through which it is produced ('images and symbols *for* the woman cannot be isolated from images and symbols *of* the woman . . . it is the representation of sexuality which conditions how it comes into play'),[23] but those very representations will reveal the splitting through which they are constituted as such. The question of what a woman is in this account always stalls on the crucial acknowledgement that there is absolutely no guarantee that she *is* at all [. . .]. But if she takes up her place according to the process described, then her sexuality will betray, necessarily, the impasses of its history.

[. . .]

II

Three points emerge from what has been described so far:

1   Anatomy is what figures in the account: 'for me "anatomy is not destiny", but that does not mean that anatomy does not figure',[24] but it *only figures* (it is a sham).

2   The phallus stands at its own expense and any male privilege erected upon it is an imposture: 'what might be called a man, the male speaking being, strictly disappears as an effect of discourse . . . by being inscribed within it solely as castration'.[25]

3   Woman is not inferior, she is *subjected*:

> That the woman should be inscribed in an order of exchange of which she is the object, is what makes for the fundamentally conflictual, and, I would say, insoluble, character of her position: the symbolic order literally submits her, it transcends her . . . There is for her something insurmountable, something unacceptable, in the fact of being placed as an object in a symbolic order to which, at the same time, she is subjected just as much as the man.[26]

It is the strength of the concept of the symbolic that it systematically repudiates any account of sexuality which assumes the pre-given nature of sexual difference – the polemic within psychoanalysis and the challenge to any such 'nature' by feminism appear at their closest here. But a problem remains. Lacan's use of the symbolic at this stage relied heavily on Lévi-Strauss's notion of kinship in which women are defined as objects of exchange. As such it is open to the same objections as Lévi-Strauss's account in that it presupposes the subordination which it is intended to explain.[27] Thus while at first glance these remarks by Lacan seem most critical of the order described, they are in another sense complicit with that order and any argument constructed on their basis is likely to be circular.[28]

I think it is crucial that at the point where Lacan made these remarks he had a concept of full speech, of access to the symbolic order whose subjective equivalent is a successful linguistic exchange.[29] But his work underwent a shift, which totally undercut any such conception of language as mediation, in favour of an increasing stress on its fundamental division, and the effects of that division on the level of sexuality itself.

'There is no sexual relation' – this became the emphasis of his account. 'There is no sexual relation' because the unconscious divides subjects to and from each other, and because it is the myth of that relation which acts as a barrier against the division, setting up a unity through which this division is persistently disavowed. [. . .]

In the earlier texts, the unity was assigned to the imaginary, the symbolic was at least potentially its break. In the later texts, Lacan located the fantasy of 'sameness' within language and the sexual relation at one and the same time. 'There is no sexual relation' because subjects relate through what makes sense in *lalangue*.[30] This 'making sense' is a supplement, a making good of the lack of subjectivity and language, of the subject *in* language, against which lack it is set. Psychoanalysis states meaning to be sexual but it has left behind any notion of a repressed sexuality which it would somehow allow to speak. Meaning can only be described as sexual by taking the limits of meaning into account, for meaning in itself operates *at* the limit, the limits of its own failing: 'Meaning indicates the direction in which it fails'.[31] The stress, therefore, is on the constant failing within language and sexuality, which meaning attempts to supplement or conceal: 'Everything implied by the analytic engagement with human behaviour indicates not that meaning reflects the sexual but that it makes up for it.'[32] Sexuality is the vanishing-point of meaning. Love, on the other hand, belongs to the *Lust-Ich* or pleasure-ego which disguises that failing in the reflection of like to like (love as the ultimate form of self-recognition).

We could say that Lacan has taken the relationship between the unconscious and sexuality and has pushed it to its furthest extreme, producing an account of sexuality solely in terms of its divisions – the division *of* the subject, division *between* subjects (as opposed to relation). [. . .] The challenge to the unity of the subject, its seeming coherence, is then addressed to the discourse of sexuality itself: 'instead of one signifier we need to interrogate, we should interrogate the signifier One.'[33] Thus there is no longer imaginary 'unity' and then symbolic difference or exchange, but rather an indictment of the symbolic for the imaginary unity which its most persistent myths continue to promote.

Within this process, woman is constructed as an absolute category (excluded and elevated at one and the same time), a category which serves to guarantee that unity on the side of the man. The man places the woman at the basis of his fantasy, or constitutes fantasy through the woman. Lacan moved away, therefore, from the idea of a problematic but socially assured process of exchange (women as objects) to the construction of woman as a category within language (woman as *the* object, the fantasy of her definition). What is now exposed in the account is 'a carrying over onto the woman of the difficulty inherent in sexuality' itself.[34]

[. . .]

In the later texts, the central term is the *object small a* [*objet a*], Lacan's formula for the lost object which underpins symbolisation, cause of and 'stand in' for desire. What the man relates to is this object and the 'whole of his realisation in the sexual relation comes down to fantasy'.[35] As the place onto which lack is projected, and through which it is simultaneously disavowed, woman is a 'symptom' for the man.

Defined as such, reduced to being nothing other than this fantasmatic place, the woman does not exist. Lacan's statement 'The woman does not exist' is, therefore, the corollary of his accusation, or charge, against sexual fantasy. It means, not that women do not exist, but that her status as an absolute category and guarantor of fantasy (exactly *The* woman) is false (The). Lacan sees courtly love as the elevation of the woman into the place where her absence or inaccessibility stands in for male lack ('For the man, whose lady was entirely, in the most servile sense of the term, his female subject, courtly love is the only way of coming off elegantly from the absence of sexual relation),[36] just as he sees her denigration as the precondition for man's belief in his own soul ('For the soul to come into being, she, the woman, is differentiated from it . . . called woman and defamed').[37] In relation to the man, woman comes to stand for both difference and loss: 'On the one hand, the woman becomes, or is produced, precisely as what he is not, that is, sexual difference, and on the other, as what he has to renounce, that is, *jouissance*.'[38]

Within the phallic definition, the woman is constituted as 'not all', in so far as the phallic function rests on an exception (the 'not') which is assigned to her. Woman is excluded *by* the nature of words, meaning that the definition poses her as exclusion. Note that this is not the same thing as saying that woman is excluded *from* the nature of words, a misreading which leads to the recasting of the whole problem in terms of woman's place outside language, the idea that women might have of themselves an entirely different speech.

For Lacan, men and women are only ever in language ('Men and women are signifiers bound to the common usage of language').[39] All speaking beings must line themselves up on one side or the other of this division, but anyone can cross over and inscribe themselves on the opposite side from that to which they are anatomically destined.[40] It is, we could say, an either/or situation, but one whose fantasmatic nature was endlessly reiterated by Lacan: 'these are not positions able to satify us, so much so that we can state the unconscious to be defined by the fact that it has a much clearer idea of what is going on than the truth that man is not woman.'[41]

The woman, therefore, is *not*, because she is defined purely against the man (she is the negative of that definition – 'man is *not* woman'), and because this very definition is designated fantasy, a set which may well be empty. If woman is 'not all', writes Lacan, then 'she' can hardly refer to all women.

As negative to the man, woman becomes a total object of fantasy (or an object of total fantasy), elevated into the place of the Other and made to stand for its truth. [. . .] The *object a*, cause of desire and support of male fantasy, gets transposed onto the image of the woman as Other who then acts as its guarantee. The absolute 'Otherness' of the woman, therefore, serves to secure for the man his own self-knowledge and truth. Remember that for Lacan there can be no such guarantee – there is no 'Other of the Other'. His rejection of the category 'Woman', therefore, belonged to his assault on any unqualified belief in the Other as such: 'This ~~The~~ of the woman] crossed through . . . relates to the signifier O when it is crossed through [Ø]'.[42]

Increasingly this led Lacan to challenge the notions of 'knowledge' and 'belief', and the myths on which they necessarily rely. All Lacan's statements against belief in the woman, against her status as knowing, problematic as they are, can only be understood as part of this constant undercutting of the terms on which they rest. In the later writing, Lacan continually returns to the 'subject supposed to know', the claim of a subject to know (the claim to know oneself as subject), and the different forms of discourse which can be organised around this position.[43] 'Knowing' is only ever such a claim, just as 'belief' rests entirely on the supposition of what is false. To believe in The Woman is simply a way of closing off the division or uncertainty which also underpins conviction as such. And when Lacan says that women do not know, while at one level he relegates women outside, and against the very mastery of his own statement, he was also recognising the binding, or restricting, of the parameters of knowledge itself ('masculine knowledge irredeemably an erring').[44]

The Other crossed through [Ø] stands against this knowledge as the place of division where meaning falters, where it slips and shifts. It is the place of *signifiance*, Lacan's term for this very movement in language against, or away from, the positions of coherence which language simultaneously constructs. The Other therefore stands against the phallus – its pretence to meaning and false consistency. It is from the Other that the phallus seeks authority and is refused.

The woman belongs on the side of the Other in this second sense, for in so far as *jouissance* is defined as phallic so she might be said to belong somewhere else. The woman is implicated, of necessity, in phallic sexuality, but at the same time it is 'elsewhere that she upholds the question of her own *jouissance*',[45] that is, the question of her status as desiring subject. Lacan designates this *jouissance* supplementary so as to avoid any notion of complement, of woman as a complement to man's phallic nature (which is precisely the fantasy). But it is also a recognition of the 'something more', the 'more than *jouissance*',[46] which Lacan locates in the Freudian concept of repetition – what escapes or is left over from the phallic function, and exceeds it. Woman is, therefore, placed *beyond* (beyond the phallus). That 'beyond' refers at once to her total mystification as absolute Other (and hence nothing other than other), and to a *question*, the question of her own *jouissance*, of her greater or lesser access to the residue of the dialectic to which she is constantly subjected. The problem is that once the notion of 'woman' has been so relentlessly exposed as a fantasy, then any such question becomes an almost impossible one to pose.

Lacan's reference to woman as Other needs, therefore, to be seen as an attempt to hold apart two moments which are in constant danger of collapsing into each other – that which assigns woman to the negative place of its own (phallic) system, and that which asks the question as to whether women might, as a very effect of that assignation, break against and beyond that system itself. For Lacan, that break is always within language, it is the break of the subject *in* language. The concept of *jouissance* (what escapes in sexuality) and the concept of *signifiance* (what shifts within language) are inseparable.

[. . .]

Towards the end of his work, Lacan talked of woman's 'anti-phallic' nature as leaving her open to that 'which of the unconscious cannot be spoken' (a reference to women analysts in which we can recognise, ironically, the echo of Freud's conviction that they would have access to a different stratum of psychic life).[47] In relation to the earlier texts we could say that woman no longer masquerades, she *defaults*: 'the *jouissance* of the woman does not go without saying, that is, without the saying of truth', whereas for the man 'his *jouissance* suffices which is precisely why he understands nothing'.[48] There is a risk, here, of giving back to the woman a status as truth (the very mythology denounced). But for Lacan, this 'truth' of the unconscious is only ever that moment of fundamental division through which the subject entered into language and sexuality, and the constant failing of position within both.

This is the force of Lacan's account – his insistence that femininity can only be understood in terms of its construction, an insistence which produced in reply the same reinstatement of women, the same argument for *her* sexual nature as was seen in the 1920s and 1930s in response to Freud. This time the question of symbolisation, which was latent in the earlier debate, has been at the centre of that response. This is all the more clear in that the specificity of feminine sexuality in the more recent discussion[49] has explicitly become the issue of women's relationship to language. In so far as it is the order of language which structures sexuality around the male term, or the privileging of that term which shows sexuality to be constructed within language, so this raises the issue of women's relationship to that language and that sexuality simultaneously. The question of the body of the girl child (what she may or may not know of that body) as posed in the earlier debate, becomes the question of the woman's body as language (what, of that body, can achieve symbolisation). The objective is to retrieve the woman from the dominance of the phallic term and from language at one and the same time. What this means is that femininity is assigned to a point of origin prior to the mark of symbolic difference and the law. The privileged relationship of women to that origin gives them access to an archaic form of expressivity outside the circuit of linguistic exchange.

This point of origin is the maternal body, an undifferentiated space, and yet one in which the girl child recognises herself. The girl then has to suppress or devalue that fullness of recognition in order to line up within the order of the phallic term. In the argument for a primordial femininity, it is clear that the relation between the mother and child is conceived of as dyadic and simply reflective (one to one – the girl child fully *knows* herself in the mother) which once again precludes the concept of desire. Feminine specificity is, therefore, predicated directly onto the concept of an unmediated and unproblematic relation to origin.

The positions taken up have not been identical, but they have a shared stress on the specificity of the feminine drives, a stress which was at the basis of the earlier response to Freud. They take a number of their concepts directly from that debate (the concept of concentric feminine drives in Montrelay comes directly from Jones and Klein). But the effects of the position are different. Thus whereas for Jones, for example, those drives ideally anticipated and ensured the heterosexual identity of the girl child, now those same drives put at risk her access to any object at all (Montrelay)[50] or else they secure the woman to herself and, through that, to other women (Irigaray). Women are *returned*, therefore, in the account and to each other – against the phallic term but also against the loss of origin which Lacan's account is seen to imply. It is therefore a refusal of division which gives the woman access to a different stratum of language, where words and things are not differentiated, and the real of the maternal body threatens or holds off woman's access to prohibition and the law.

There is a strength in this account, which has been recognised by feminism. At its most forceful it expresses a protest engendered by the very cogency of what Freud and then Lacan describe (it is the *effect* of that description).[51] And something of its position was certainly present in Lacan's earlier texts ('feminine sexuality . . . as the effort of a *jouissance* wrapped in its own contiguity').[52] But Lacan came back to this response in the later texts, which can therefore be seen as a sort of reply, much as Freud's 1931 and 1933 papers on femininity addressed some of the criticisms which he had received.

For Lacan, as we have seen, there is no pre-discursive reality ('How return, other than by means of a special discourse, to a pre-discursive reality?'),[53] no place prior to the law which is available and can be retrieved. And there is no feminine outside language. First, because the unconscious severs the subject from any unmediated relation to the body as such ('there is nothing in the unconscious which accords with the body'),[54] and secondly because the 'feminine' is constituted as a division in language, a division which produces the feminine as its negative term. If woman is defined as other it is because the definition produces her as other, and not because she has another essence. Lacan does not refuse difference ('if there was no difference how could I say there was no sexual relation'),[55] but for him what is to be questioned is the seeming 'consistency' of that difference – of the body or anything else – the division it enjoins, the definitions of the woman it produces.

For Lacan, to say that difference is 'phallic' difference is to expose the symbolic and arbitrary nature of its division as such. It is crucial – and it is something which can be seen even more clearly in the response to the later texts on femininity – that refusal of the phallic term brings with it an attempt to reconstitute a form of subjectivity free of division, and hence a refusal of the notion of symbolisation itself. If the status of the phallus is to be challenged, it cannot, therefore, be directly from the feminine body but must be by means of a different symbolic term (in which case the relation to the body is immediately thrown into crisis), or else by an entirely different logic altogether (in which case one is no longer in the order of symbolisation at all).

The demands against Lacan therefore collapse two different levels of objection – that the body should be mediated by language and that the privileged term of that mediation be male. The fact that refusal of the phallus turns out once again to be a refusal of the symbolic does not close, but leaves open as still unanswered, the question as to why that necessary symbolisation and the privileged status of the phallus appear as inter-dependent in the structuring and securing (never secure) of human subjectivity.

There is, therefore, no question of denying here that Lacan was implicated in the phallocentrism he described, just as his own utterance constantly rejoins the mastery which he sought to undermine. The question of the unconscious and of sexuality, the movement towards and against them, operated at exactly this level of his own speech. But for Lacan they function as the question of that speech, and cannot be referred back to a body outside language, a place to which the 'feminine', and through that, women, might escape. In the response to Lacan, therefore, the 'feminine' has returned as it did in the 1920s and 1930s in reply to Freud, but this time with the added meaning of a resistance to a phallic organisation of sexuality which is recognised as such. The 'feminine' stands for a refusal of that organisation, its ordering, its identity. For Lacan, on the other hand, interrogating that same organisation undermines any absolute definition of the 'feminine' at all.

Psychoanalysis does not produce that definition. It gives an account of how that definition is produced. While the objection to its dominant term must be recognised, it cannot be answered by an account which returns to a concept of the feminine as pre-given, nor by a mandatory appeal to an androcentrism in the symbolic which the phallus would simply reflect. The former relegates women outside language and history, the latter simply subordinates them to both.

Lacan's writing gives an account of how the status of the phallus in human sexuality enjoins on the woman a definition in which she is simul-taneously symptom and myth. As long as we continue to feel the effects of that definition we cannot afford to ignore this description of the funda-mental imposture which sustains it.

Notes

1   Jacques Lacan, 'Le stade du miroir comme formateur de la fonction du Je' (1936), *Écrits* (Paris, Seuil, 1996); translated as 'The mirror stage as formative of the function of the I', *Écrits: a Selection* (London, Routledge, 1989).

2   D.W. Winnicott, 'Mirror-role of mother and family in child development' (1967) *Playing and Reality* (London, Penguin, 1971).

3   Jacques Lacan, 'Cure psychanalytique à l'aide de la poupée fleur', *Revue française de la psychanalyse* 4 (October–December 1949), p. 567.

4   Sigmund Freud, *Project for a Scientific Psychology* (1895), in *The Standard Edition of the Works of Sigmund Freud*, ed. James Strachey (London, Hogarth Press and the Institute of Psychoanalysis, 1953), volume 1, p. 319; *Beyond the Pleasure Principle*, ibid., volume 18, pp. 14–17, 283–7.

5   Jacques Lacan, 'La signification du phallus' (1958), *Écrits* ('The meaning of the phallus', *Feminine Sexuality: Jacques Lacan and the école freudienne*, ed. J. Mitchell and J. Rose (London, 1982), p. 80).

6   Sigmund Freud, 'On the universal tendency to debasement in the sphere of love' (1912), *Standard Edition*, volume 11, pp. 188–9; The Penguin Freud Library, On Sexuality: Three Essays on the theory of sexuality and other works, ed. Angela Richards, Trans. James Strachey (London, Penguin, 1991), volume 7, p. 258.

7   Lacan, 'The meaning of the phallus', p. 81.

8   Freud, *Three Essays on the Theory of Sexuality* (1905), *Standard Edition*, volume 7, pp. 144–6; Penguin Freud, volume 7, p. 57n.

9   Jacques Lacan, 'La phase phallique et la portée subjective du complexe de castration', *Scilicet* 1 (1968) ('The phallic phase and the subjective import of the castration complex', *Feminine Sexuality*, p. 117. *Scilicet* was the review published in Lacan's series, *Le champ freudien*, at Editions du Seuil in Paris; apart from those by Lacan, the articles in the first issues were unsigned).

10   Jacques Lacan, 'Les formations de l'inconscient', *Bulletin de Psychologie*, 2 (1957–8), p. 13.

11   Lacan, 'The meaning of the phallus', p. 80.

12   Lacan, 'Les formations de l'inconscient', p. 14.

13   Ibid., p. 8.

14   Jacques Lacan, 'Intervention on transference', *Feminine Sexuality*, p. 69.

15   Jacques Lacan, *Le séminaire XVII: L'envers de la psychanalyse* (1969–70), 6, p. 10 (unpublished seminar references to week and page of the typescript).

16   Moustapha Safouan, 'Is the Oedipus complex universal?' (trans. Ben Brewster from chapter 7 of *Etudes sur l'oedipe*, Paris, 1974), *m/f*, 5–6 (1981), p. 127.

17   Jacques Lacan, 'D'une question préliminaire à tout traitement possible de la psychose' (1955–6), *Écrits* ('On a question preliminary to any possible treatment of psychosis', *Écrits: a Selection*, p. 198).

18   Jacques Lacan, 'L'instance de la lettre dans l'inconscient ou la raison depuis Freud' (1957), *Écrits* ('The agency of the letter in the unconscious or reason since Freud' *Écrits: a Selection*, p. 151).

19   Jacques Lacan, 'Une lettre d'âmour', *Le séminaire XX: Encore* (1972–3) (Paris, 1975) ('A love letter', *Feminine Sexuality*, p. 150).

20   Lacan, 'The phallic phase', p. 113.

21   Lacan, 'The meaning of the phallus', p. 82.

22   Ibid., p. 82.

23   Jacques Lacan, 'Guiding remarks', p. 90.

24   Moustapha Safouan, *La sexualité féminine dans la doctrine freudienne* (Paris: Seuil, 1976), p. 131.

25   Lacan, *L'envers de la psychanalyse*, 12, p. 4.

26   Jacques Lacan, *Le séminaire II: Le moi dans la théorie de Freud et dans la technique de la psychanalyse* (1954–5) (Paris, 1978), pp. 304–5 (trans. Sylvana Tomaselli, *The Ego in Freud's Theory and in the Technique of Psychoanalysis* (Cambridge, 1987).

27   See Elizabeth Cowie, 'Woman as sign', *m/f*, 1 (1978) pp. 49–63.

28   Cf., for example, Gayle Rubin, 'The traffic in women', in Rayna M. Reiter (ed.), *Towards an Anthropology of Women* (New York, 1975), which describes psychoanalysis as a 'theory about the reproduction of Kinship', losing sight, again, of the concept of the unconscious and the whole problem of sexual identity, reducing the relations described to a quite literal set of acts of exchange.

29   Jacques Lacan, 'Fonction et champ de la parole et du langage en psychanalyse', *Écrits* ('The function and field of speech and language in psychoanalysis' in *Écrits: a Selection* pp. 30–113 Trans. A. Sheridan) (London: Routledge, 1989).

30   Lacan's term for Saussure's *langue* (language) from the latter's distinction between *langue* (the formal organisation of language) and *parole* (speech), the individual utterance. Lacan's term displaces this opposition in so far as, for him, the organisation of language can only be understood in terms of the subject's relationship to it. *Lalangue* indicates that part of language which reflects the laws of unconscious processes, but whose effects go beyond that reflection, and escape the grasp of the

subject (*Le séminaire XX: Encore* (1972–3), ed. Jacques-Alain Miller, Paris: Seuil, 1975. pp. 126–7).

31 Lacan, 'A love letter', p. 150.

32 Jacques Lacan, *Le séminaire XXI: Les non-dupes errent* (1973–4) (unpublished typescript), 15, p. 9.

33 Lacan, *Encore*, p. 23.

34 Lacan, 'The phallic phase', p. 118.

35 Lacan, A love letter, p. 157.

36 Jacques Lacan, 'Dieu et la jouissance de La femme', *Encore* ('God and the jouissance of The woman', *Feminine Sexuality*, p. 141).

37 Lacan, 'A love letter', p. 156.

38 Jacques Lacan, *Le séminaire XVIII: D'un discours quine sera pas semblant* (1970–1), 6, pp. 9–10; see also Otto Fenichel, in a paper to which Lacan often referred, on the refusal of difference which underpins the girl = phallus equation frequently located as a male fantasy: 'the differentness of woman is denied in both cases; in the one case, in the attempt to repress women altogether, in the other, in denying their individuality' (Otto Fenichel, 'The symbolic equation: girl = phallus', *Psychoanalytic Quarterly*, 18(3) (1949), p. 13).

39 Lacan, *Encore*, p. 36.

40 Note how this simultaneously shifts the concept of bisexuality – not an undifferentiated sexual nature prior to symbolic difference (Freud's earlier sense), but the availability to all subjects of both positions in relation to that difference itself.

41 Lacan, *Les non-dupes errent*, 6, p. 9.

42 Ibid., p. 151.

43 Much of the difficulty of Lacan's work stemmed from his attempt to subvert that position from within his own utterance, to rejoin the place of 'non-knowledge' which he designated the unconscious, by the constant slippage or escape of his speech, and thereby to undercut the very mastery which his own position as speaker (master and analyst) necessarily constructs. In fact one can carry out the same operation on the statement 'I do not know' as Lacan performed on the utterance 'I am lying' [. . .] – for, if I do not know, then how come I know enough to know that I do not know and if I do know that I do not know, then it is not true that I do not know. Lacan was undoubtedly trapped in this paradox of his own utterance.

44 Lacan, *Les non-dupes errent*, 6, p. 11.

45 Lacan, 'The phallic phase', p. 121.

46 At times *jouissance* is opposed to the idea of pleasure as the site of this excess, but where *jouissance* is defined as phallic, Lacan introduces the concept of the supplement ('more than') with which to oppose it.

47 Jacques Lacan, *Ornicar?*, 20–1 (Summer 1980), p. 12. (*Ornicar?* is the periodical of the Department of Psychoanalysis, under Lacan's direction up to 1981, at the University of Paris VIII at Vincennes.) At the time of writing Lacan had just dissolved his school in Paris, rejoining in the utterance through which he represented that act – 'Je père-sévère' ('I persevere' – the pun is on 'per' and 'père' (father)) – the whole problem of mastery and paternity which has cut across the institutional history of his work. From the early stand against a context which he (and others) considered authoritarian, and the cancellation, as its effect, of his seminar on the Name of the Father in 1953, to the question of mastery and transference which lay behind the further break in 1964, and which so clearly surfaces in the dissolution here. It has been the endless paradox of Lacan's position that he has provided the most systematic critique of forms of identification and transference which, by dint of this very fact, he has come most totally to represent. That a number of women analysts (cf. note 49 [. . .]) have found their position in relation to this to be an impossible one, only confirms the close relation between the question of feminine sexuality and the institutional divisions and difficulties of psychoanalysis itself.

48 Lacan, *Les non-dupes errent*, 7, p. 16.

49   In this last section I will be referring predominantly to the work of Michèle Montrelay and Luce Irigaray, the former a member of Lacan's school prior to its dissolution in January 1980 when she dissociated herself from him, the latter working within his school up to 1974 when she was dismissed from the newly reorganised department of psychoanalysis at the University of Paris VIII (Vincennes) on publication of her book, *Speculum de l'autre femme*. Both are practising psychoanalysts. Montrelay takes up the Freud–Jones controversy specifically in terms of women's access to language in her article 'Recherches sur la féminité' (*Critique*, 26 1970, trans. Parveen Adams, 'Inquiry into femininity'). Irigaray's book *Speculum* contained a critique of Freud's papers on femininity; her later *Ce sexe qui n'en est pas un* (Paris, 1977, trans. Catherine Porter, *This Sex Which Is Not One*, Ithaca, 1985) contains a chapter ('Cosi fan tutti') directly addressed to Lacan's *Encore*.

50   Montrelay attempts to resolve the 'Freud–Jones' controversy by making the two different accounts of femininity equal to *stages* in the girl's psychosexual development, femininity being defined as the passage from a concentric psychic economy to one in which symbolic castration has come into play. Access to symbolisation depends on the transition, and it is where it fails that the woman remains bound to a primordial cathexis of language as the undifferentiated maternal body. Montrelay should, therefore, be crucially distinguished from Irigaray at this point, since for her such a failure is precipitant of anxiety and is in no sense a concept of femininity which she is intending to promote.

51   Note too the easy slippage from Irigaray's title *Ce sexe qui n'en est pas un*, 'This sex which isn't one', to Lacan's formula: 'This sex which isn't *one*.'

52   Lacan, 'Guiding remarks', p. 97.

53   Lacan, *Encore*, p. 33.

54   Jacques Lacan, 'Seminar of 21 January, 1975', p. 165.

55   Lacan, *Les non-dupes errent*, 4, p. 18.

6

Revolution in poetic language   **Julia Kristeva**

[I]t seems possible to perceive a signifying practice which, although produced in language, is only intelligible *through* it. By exploding the phonetic, lexical, and syntactic object of linguistics, this practice [. . .] escapes the attempted hold of all anthropomorphic sciences. [. . .] Ultimately, it exhausts the ever tenacious ideological institutions and apparatuses, thereby demonstrating the limits of formalist and psycho-analytic devices.[1] This signifying practice – a particular type of modern literature – attests to a 'crisis' of social structures and their ideological, coercive, and necrophilic manifestations [. . .] With Lautréamont, Mallarmé, Joyce, and Artaud, to name only a few, this crisis represents a new phenomenon. For the capitalist mode of production produces and marginalizes, but simultaneously exploits for its own regeneration, one of the most spectacular shatterings of discourse. By exploding the subject and his ideological limits, this phenomenon has a triple effect, and raises three sets of questions:

This chapter, originally published in 1974, is taken from *Literary Theory: an Anthology*, eds J. Rivkin and M. Ryan (Oxford, Blackwell, 1998), pp. 451–63.

1   Because of its specific isolation within the discursive totality of our time, this shattering of discourse reveals that linguistic changes constitute changes in the *status of the subject* – his relation to the body, to others, and to objects; it also reveals that normalized language is just one of the ways of articulating the signifying process that encompasses the body, the material referent, and language itself. How are these strata linked? What is their interrelation within signifying practice?

2   The shattering further reveals that the capitalist mode of production, having attained a highly developed means of production through

science and technology, no longer need remain strictly within linguistic and ideological *norms*, but can also integrate their *process qua process*. As art, this shattering can display the productive basis of subjective and ideological signifying formations – a foundation that primitive societies call 'sacred' and modernity has rejected as 'schizophrenia.' What is the extent of this integration? Under what conditions does it become indispensable, censured, repressed, or marginal?

3   Finally, in the history of signifying systems and notably that of the arts, religion, and rites, there emerge, in retrospect, fragmentary phenomena which have been kept in the background or rapidly integrated into more communal signifying systems but point to the very process of *signifiance* [the primordial signifying practice]. Magic, shamanism, esoterism, the carnival, and 'incomprehensible' poetry all underscore the limits of socially useful discourse and attest to what it represses: the *process* that exceeds the subject and his communicative structures. But at what historical moment does social exchange tolerate or necessitate the manifestation of the signifying process in its 'poetic' or 'esoteric' form? Under what conditions does this 'esoterism,' in displacing the boundaries of socially established signifying practices, correspond to socioeconomic change, and, ultimately, even to revolution? And under what conditions does it remain a blind alley, a harmless bonus offered by a social order which uses this 'esoterism' to expand, become flexible, and thrive?

[. . .]

What we call *signifiance*, then, is precisely this unlimited and unbounded generating process, this unceasing operation of the instinctual drives toward, in, and through language; toward, in, and through the exchange system and its protagonists – the subject and his institutions. This heterogeneous process, neither anarchic, fragmented foundation nor schizophrenic blockage, is a structuring and destructuring *practice*, a passage to the outer *boundaries* of the subject and society. Then – and only then – can it be *jouissance* and revolution [. . .].

The semiotic *chora* ordering the drives

We understand the term 'semiotic' in its Greek sense [. . .], distinctive mark, trace, index, precursory sign, proof, engraved or written sign, imprint, figuration. This etymological reminder would be a mere archaeological embellishment (and an unconvincing one at that, since the term ultimately encompasses such disparate meanings), were it not for the fact that the preponderant etymological use of the word, the one that implies a *distinctiveness*, allows us to connect it to a precise modality in the signifying process. This modality is the one Freudian psychoanalysis points to in postulating not only the *facilitation* and the structuring *disposition* of instinctual drives, but also the so-called *primary processes* which displace and condense both energies and their inscription. Discrete quantities of energy move through the body of the subject who is not yet constituted as such and, in the course of his development, they are arranged according to the various constraints imposed on this body – always already involved in a semiotic process – by family and social structures. In this way the instinctual drives, which are 'energy' charges as well as 'psychical' marks, articulate what we call a *chora*: a nonexpressive totality formed by the drives and their stases in a motility that is as full of movement as it is regulated.

We borrow the term *chora*[2] from Plato's *Timaeus* to denote an essentially mobile and extremely provisional articulation constituted by movements and their ephemeral stases. [. . .] Although our theoretical description of the *chora* is itself part of the discourse of representation that offers it as evidence, the *chora* as rupture and articulations (rhythm), precedes evidence, verisimilitude, spatiality, and temporality. Our discourse – all discourse – moves with and against the *chora* in the sense that it simultaneously depends upon and refuses it. Although the *chora* can be designated and regulated, it can never be definitively posited: as a result, one can situate the *chora* and, if necessary, lend it a topology, but one can never give it axiomatic form.[3]

The *chora* is not yet a position that represents something for someone (i.e., it is not a sign); nor is it a position that represents someone for another position (i.e., it is not yet a signifier either); it is, however, generated in order to attain to this signifying position. Neither model nor copy, the *chora* precedes and underlies figuration and thus specularization, and is analogous only to vocal or kinetic rhythm. [. . .] The theory of the subject proposed by the theory of the unconscious will allow us to read in this rhythmic space, which has no thesis and no position, the process by which *signifiance* is constituted. Plato himself leads us to such a process when he calls this receptacle or *chora* nourishing and maternal,[4] not yet unified in an ordered whole because deity is absent from it. Though deprived of unity, identity, or deity, the *chora* is nevertheless subject to a regulating process [*règlementation*], which is different from that of symbolic law but nevertheless effectuates discontinuities by temporarily articulating them and then starting over, again and again.

The *chora* is a modality of *signifiance* in which the linguistic sign is not yet articulated as the absence of an object and as the distinction between real and symbolic. We emphasize the regulated aspect of the *chora*: its vocal and gestural organization is subject to what we shall call an objective *ordering* [*ordonnancement*], which is dictated by natural or sociohistorical constraints such as the biological difference between the sexes or family structure. We may therefore posit that social organization, always already symbolic, imprints its constraint in a mediated form which organizes the *chora* not according to a *law* (a term we reserve for the symbolic) but through an *ordering*.[5] What is this mediation?

According to a number of psycholinguists, 'concrete operations' precede the acquisition of language, and organize preverbal semiotic space according to logical categories, which are thereby shown to precede or transcend language. From their research we shall retain not the principle of an operational state[6] but that of a preverbal functional state that governs the connections between the body (in the process of constituting itself as a body proper), objects, and the protagonists of family structure.[7] But we shall distinguish this functioning from symbolic operations that depend on language as a sign system – whether the language [*langue*] is vocalized or gestural (as with deaf-mutes). The kinetic functional stage of the *semiotic* precedes the establishment of the sign; it is not, therefore, cognitive in the sense of being assumed by a knowing, already constituted subject. The genesis of the *functions*[8] organizing the semiotic process can be accurately elucidated only within a theory of the subject that does not reduce the subject to one of understanding, but instead opens up within the subject this other scene of pre-symbolic functions. The Kleinian theory expanding upon Freud's positions on the drives will momentarily serve as a guide.

Drives involve pre-Oedipal semiotic functions and energy discharges that connect and orient the body to the mother. We must emphasize that 'drives' are always already ambiguous, simultaneously assimilating and destructive; this dualism, which has been represented as a tetrad[9] or as a double helix, as in the configuration of the DNA and RNA molecule,[10] makes the semiotized body a place of permanent scission. The oral and anal drives, both of which are oriented and structured around the mother's body,[11] dominate this sensorimotor organization. The mother's body is therefore what mediates the symbolic law organizing social relations and becomes the ordering principle of the semiotic *chora*,[12] which is on the path of destruction, aggressivity, and death. For although drives have been described as disunited or contradictory structures, simultaneously 'positive' and 'negative,' this doubling is said to generate a dominant 'destructive wave' that is the drive's most characteristic trait: Freud notes that the most instinctual drive is the death drive.[13] In this way, the term 'drive' denotes waves of attack against stases, which are themselves constituted by the repetition of these charges; together, charges and stases lead to no identity (not even that of the 'body proper') that could be seen as a result of their functioning. This is to say that the semiotic *chora* is no more than the place where the subject is both generated and negated, the place where his unity succumbs before the process of charges and stases that produce him. We shall call this process of charges and stases a negativity to distinguish it from negation, which is the act of a judging subject.

Checked by the constraints of biological and social structures, the drive charge thus undergoes stases. Drive facilitation, temporarily arrested, marks *discontinuities* in what may be called the various material supports [*matériaux*] susceptible to semiotization: voice, gesture, colors. Phonic (later phonemic), kinetic, or chromatic units and differences are the marks of these stases in the drives. Connections or functions are thereby established between these discrete marks which are based on drives and articulated according to their resemblance or opposition, either by slippage or by condensation. Here we find the principles of metonymy and metaphor indissociable from the drive economy underlying them.

Although we recognize the vital role played by the processes of displacement and condensation in the organization of the semiotic, we must also add to these processes the relations (eventually representable as topological spaces) that connect the zones of the fragmented body to each other and also to 'external' 'objects' and 'subjects,' which are not yet constituted as such. This type of relation makes it possible to specify the semiotic as a psychosomatic modality of the signifying process; in other words, not a symbolic modality but one articulating (in the largest sense of the word) a continuum: the connections between the (glottal and anal) sphincters in (rhythmic and intonational) vocal modulations, or those between the sphincters and family protagonists, for example.

All these various processes and relations, anterior to sign and syntax, have just been identified from a genetic perspective as previous and necessary to the acquisition of language, but not identical to language. Theory can 'situate' such processes and relations diachronically within the process of the constitution of the subject precisely because *they function synchronically within the signifying process of the subject himself*, i.e., the subject of *cogitatio*. Only in dream logic, however, have they attracted attention, and only in certain signifying practices, such as the text, do they dominate the signifying process.

It may be hypothesized that certain semiotic articulations are transmitted through the biological code or physiological 'memory' and thus form the inborn bases of the symbolic function. Indeed, one branch of generative linguistics asserts the principle of innate language universals. As it will become apparent in what follows, however, the *symbolic* – and therefore syntax and all linguistic categories – is a social effect of the relation to the other, established through the objective constraints of biological (including sexual) differences and concrete, historical family structures. Genetic programmings are necessarily semiotic: they include the primary processes such as displacement and condensation, absorption and repulsion, rejection and stasis, all of which function as innate preconditions, 'memorizable' by the species, for language acquisition.

Mallarmé calls attention to the semiotic rhythm within language when he speaks of 'The Mystery in Literature' ['Le Mystère dans les lettres']; indifferent to language, enigmatic and feminine, this space underlying the written is rhythmic, unfettered, irreducible to its intelligible verbal translation; it is musical, anterior to judgment, but restrained by a single guarantee: syntax. [. . .]

Notes

1. *Translator's note*: 'Device' is Kristeva's own choice for the translation of 'dispositif': something devised or constructed for a particular purpose.

2. The term '*chora*' has recently been criticized for its ontological essence by Jacques Derrida, *Positions*, trans. and annotated by Alan Bass (Chicago, University of Chicago Press, 1981), pp. 75 and 106, n. 39.

3. Plato emphasizes that the receptacle (ὑποδοχεῖον), which is also called space (χώρα) *vis-à-vis* reason, is necessary but not divine since it is unstable, uncertain, ever changing and becoming; it is even unnameable, improbable, bastard: 'Space, which is everlasting, not admitting destruction, providing a situation for all things that come into being, but itself apprehended without the senses by a sort of bastard reasoning, and hardly an object of belief. This, indeed, is that which we look upon as in a dream and say that anything that is must needs be in some place and occupy some room . . .' (*Timaeus*, trans. Francis M. Cornford, 52a–b). Is the receptacle a 'thing' or a mode of language? Plato's hesitation between the two gives the receptacle an even more uncertain status. It is one of the elements that antedate not only the *universe* but also *names* and even *syllables*. 'We speak . . . positing them as original principles, elements (as it were, letters) of the universe; whereas one who has ever so little intelligence should not rank them in this analog even so low as syllables' (ibid., 48b). 'It is hard to say, with respect to any one of these which we ought to call really water rather than fire, or indeed which we should call by any given name rather than by all the names together or by each severally, so as to use language in a sound and trustworthy way . . . Since, then, in this way no one of these things ever makes its appearance as the *same* thing, which of them can we steadfastly affirm to be this – whatever it may be – and not something else, without blushing for ourselves? It cannot be done' (ibid., 49b–d).

4. The Platonic space or receptacle is a mother and wet nurse: 'Indeed we may fittingly compare the Recipient to a mother, the model to a father, and the nature that arises between them to their offspring' (ibid., 50d); 'Now the wet nurse of Becoming was made watery and fiery, received the characters of earth and air, and was qualified by all the other affections that go with these . . .' (ibid., 52d); translation modified).

5. 'Law,' which derives etymologically from *lex*, necessarily implies the act of judgment whose role in safeguarding society was first developed by the Roman law courts. 'Ordering,' on the other hand, is closer to the series 'rule,' 'norm' (from the Greek, meaning 'discerning' [adj.], 'carpenter's square' [noun]), etc. which implies a numerical or geometrical necessity; on normativity in linguistics, see Alain Rey, 'Usages, jugements et préscriptions linguistiques,' *Langue Française* (16 December 1972), p. 5. But the temporary ordering of the *chora* is not yet even a rule: the arsenal of geometry is posterior to the *chora*'s motility; it fixes the *chora* in place and reduces it.

6. Operations are, rather, an act of the subject of understanding. [*Translator's note*: Hans G. Furth, in *Piaget and Knowledge: Theoretical Foundations* (Englewood Cliffs, NJ, Prentice-Hall, 1969), offers the following definition of 'concrete operations': 'Characteristic of the first stage of operational intelligence. A concrete operation implies underlying general systems or groupings such as classification, seriation, number. Its applicability is limited to objects considered as real (concrete)', p. 260.]

7. Piaget stresses that the roots of sensorimotor operations precede language and that the acquisition of thought is due to the symbolic function, which, for him, is a notion separate from that of language *per se*. See Jean Piaget, 'Language and symbolic operations,' in Furth, *Piaget and Knowledge*, pp. 121–30.

8. By 'function' we mean a dependent variable determined each time the independent variables with which it is associated are determined. For our purposes, a function is what links stases within the process of semiotic facilitation.

9. Such a position has been formulated by Lipot Szondi, *Experimental Diagnostic of Drives*, trans. Gertrude Aull (New York, Grune and Stratton, 1952).

10 See James D. Watson, *The Double Helix: Personal Account of the Discovery of the Structure of DNA* (London, Weidenfeld and Nicolson, 1968).

11 Throughout her writings, Melanie Klein emphasizes the 'pre-Oedipal' phase, i.e., a period of the subject's development that precedes the 'discovery' of castration and the positing of the superego, which itself is subject to (paternal) Law. The processes she describes for this phase correspond, *but on a genetic level*, to what we call the semiotic, as opposed to the symbolic, which underlies and conditions the semiotic. Significantly, these pre-Oedipal processes are organized through projection onto the mother's body for girls as well as for boys: 'at this stage of development children of both sexes believe that it is the body of their mother which contains all that is desirable, especially their father's penis' (*The Psycho-analysis of Children*, trans. Alix Strachey (London, Hogarth Press, 1932), p. 269). Our own view of this stage is as follows: Without 'believing' or 'desiring' any 'object' whatsoever, the subject is in the process of constituting himself *vis-à-vis* a non-object. He is in the process of separating from this non-object so as to make that non-object 'one' and posit himself as 'other'; the mother's body is the not-yet-one that the believing and desiring subject will imagine as a 'receptacle.'

12 As for what situates the mother in symbolic space, we find the phallus again (see Jacques Lacan, 'La Relation d'objet et les structures freudiennes,' *Bulletin de Psychologie* (April, 1957), pp. 426–30), represented by the mother's father, i.e., the subject's maternal grandfather (see Marie-Claire Boons, 'Le Meurtre du Père chez Freud,' *L'Inconscient*, 5 (January–March, 1968) pp. 101–29).

13 Though disputed and inconsistent, the Freudian theory of drives is of interest here because of the predominance Freud gives to the death drive in both 'living matter' and the 'human being.' The death drive is transversal to identity and tends to disperse narcissisms whose constitution ensures the link between structures and, by extension, life. But at the same time and conversely, narcissism and pleasure are only temporary positions from which the death drive blazes new paths [*se fraye de nouveaux passages*]. Narcissism and pleasure are therefore inveiglings and realizations of the death drive. The semiotic *chora*, converting drive discharges into stases, can be thought of both as a delaying of the death drive and as a possible realization of this drive, which tends to return to a homeostatic state. This hypothesis is consistent with the following remark: 'at the beginning of mental life,' writes Freud, 'the struggle for pleasure was far more intense than later but not so unrestricted it had to submit to frequent interruptions' (*Beyond the Pleasure Principle*, in *The Standard Edition of the Works of Sigmund Freud*, ed. James Strachey (London, Hogarth Press and the Institute of Psychoanalysis, 1953), volume 18, p. 63).

7

Suture: the cinematic model   **Kaja Silverman**

[. . .] The concept of suture attempts to account for the means by which subjects emerge within discourse. [. . .] [A]lthough that concept has been most intensely theorized in relation to cinematic texts, its initial formulation comes from Jacques-Alain Miller, one of Lacan's disciples. We will look briefly at that formulation before turning to the cinematic one.

Miller defines suture as that moment when the subject inserts itself into the symbolic register in the guise of a signifier, and in so doing gains meaning at the expense of being. In 'Suture (elements of the logic of the signifier),' he writes:

> Suture names the relation of the subject to the chain of its discourse . . . it figures there as the element which is lacking, in the form of a stand-in. For, while there lacking, it is not purely and simply absent. Suture, by extension – the general relation of lack to the structure of which it is an element, inasmuch as it implies the position of a taking-the-place-of.[1]

Miller's account of suture locates the emphasis in orthodox Lacanian places; the key terms in his definition of it are 'lack' and 'absence.' Indeed, as Miller describes it, suture closely resembles the subject's inauguration into language, illustrated by Lacan with the '*fort*'/'*da*' game. A given signifier (a pronoun, a personal name) grants the subject access to the symbolic order, but alienates it not only from its own needs but from its drives. That signifier stands in for the absent subject (i.e. absent in being) whose lack it can never stop signifying.

The French theoretician Jean-Pierre Oudart subsequently transported the concept of suture into film studies, where it has been used to probe the precise nature of cinematic signification – to answer the frequently

This chapter is taken from *The Subject of Semiotics* (New York, Oxford University Press, 1983), pp. 199–215.

pondered questions 'what is the cinematic equivalent for language in the literary text?' and 'What is cinematic syntax?' These formal speculations have not pre-empted those about subjectivity but have been integrated into them. The theory of suture has been rendered more complex with each new statement about it, so that it now embraces a set of assumptions not only about cinematic signification, but about the viewing subject and the operations of ideology. [. . .]

Suture: the cinematic model

Theoreticians of cinematic suture agree that films are articulated and the viewing subject spoken by means of interlocking shots. They are thus in fundamental accord with Noel Burch's remark that 'Although camera movements, entrances into and exits from frame, composition and so on can all function as devices aiding in the organization of the film object . . . the shot transition [remains] the basic element [of that organization].'[2] Shot relationships are seen as the equivalent of syntactic ones in linguistic discourse, as the agency whereby meaning emerges and a subject-position is constructed for the viewer.

However, some theoreticians conceptualize those relationships differently from others. Whereas Oudart and Dayan find the shot/reverse shot formation to be virtually synonymous with the operations of suture, Heath suggests that it is only one element in a much larger system, and emphasizes features of the editing process which are common to all shot transitions. We will begin by discussing the shot/reverse shot formation, and then extend the theory of suture in the directions indicated by Heath.

The shot/reverse shot formation is a cinematic set in which the second shot shows the field from which the first shot is assumed to have been taken. The logic of this set is closely tied to certain 'rules' of cinematic expression, in particular the 180° rule, which dictates that the camera not cover more than 180° in a single shot. This stricture means that the camera always leaves unexplored the other 180° of an implicit circle – the half of the circle which it in fact occupies. The 180° rule is predicated on the assumption that a complete camera revolution would be 'unrealistic,' defining a space larger than the 'naked eye' would normally cover. Thus it derives from the imperative that the camera deny its own existence as much as possible, fostering the illusion that what is shown has an autonomous existence, independent of any technological interference, or any coercive gaze.

However, the viewing subject, unable to sustain for long its belief in the autonomy of the cinematic image, demands to know whose gaze controls what it sees. The shot/reverse shot formation is calculated to answer that question in such a manner that the cinematic illusion remains intact: Shot 1 shows a space which may or may not contain a human figure (e.g. the wall of a building, a view of the ocean, a room full of people), being careful not to violate the 180° rule. Shot 2 locates a spectator in the other 180° of the same circular field, thereby implying that the preceding shot was seen through the eyes of a figure in the cinematic narrative (this paradigm may be reversed). As a result, the level of enunciation remains veiled from the viewing subject's scrutiny, which is entirely absorbed within the level of the fiction; the subject of the speech seems to be the speaking subject, or to state it differently, the gaze which directs our look seems to belong to a fictional character rather than to the camera.

Theoretically, the filmmaker would be obliged to achieve an exact match between the two parts of the shot/reverse shot formation (i.e. shot 1 would delineate precisely half of a circle, and shot 2 the other half; moreover, in shot 1 the camera would take up a position identical with that of the spectator in shot 2). In practice, however, such precision is rarely observed. A simple display of a fictional character looking in shot 2 usually proves sufficient to maintain the illusion that shot 1 visually 'belongs' to that character. The camera may even adopt an oblique position, slightly to one side of the actor, rather than directly facing him or her.

Filmmakers are generally no more literal with shot 1 of the shot/ reverse shot formation. Often we are shown the shoulders or head of the character through whose eyes we are ostensibly looking. In fact, mathematical exactitude provides a much less successful approximation of 'reality' than does the loose application of the shot/reverse shot convention.

In 'Notes on suture' Stephen Heath cautions against too restrictive an identification of suture with the shot/reverse shot formation, which statistical studies have shown to be symptomatic of only about one-third of the shots in a classical Hollywood film.[3] Actually, the suture argument relies much less centrally on the notion of syntagmatic progression, and the question of whether it is achieved through the shot/reverse shot formation or by some other means, than on the process of cinematic signification, and its relationship to the viewing subject.

Consequently, the shot/reverse shot formation derives its real importance and interest for many of the theoreticians of suture because it demonstrates so lucidly the way in which cinema operates to reduplicate the history of the subject. The viewer of the cinematic spectacle experiences shot 1 as an imaginary plenitude, unbounded by any gaze, and unmarked by difference. Shot 1 is thus the site of a *jouissance* akin to that of the mirror stage prior to the child's discovery of its separation from the ideal image which it has discovered in the reflecting glass.

However, almost immediately the viewing subject becomes aware of the limitations on what it sees – aware, that is, of an absent field. At this point shot 1 becomes a signifier of that absent field, and *jouissance* gives way to unpleasure. Daniel Dayan offers a very clear summary of this transition in 'The tutor code of classical cinema':

> When the viewer discovers the frame – the first step in reading the film – the triumph of his former *possession* of the image fades out. The viewer discovers

that the camera is hiding things, and therefore distrusts it and the frame itself which he now understands to be arbitrary. He wonders why the frame is what it is. This radically transforms his mode of participation – the unreal space between characters and/or objects is no longer perceived as pleasurable. It is now the space which separates the camera from the characters. The latter have lost their quality of presence. The spectator discovers that his possession of space was only partial, illusory. He feels dispossessed of what he is prevented from seeing. He discovers that he is only authorized to see what happens to be in the axis of the gaze of another spectator, who is ghostly or absent.[4]

Jean-Pierre Oudart refers to the spectator who occupies the missing field as the 'Absent One.' The Absent One, also known as the Other, has all the attributes of the mythically potent symbolic father: potency, knowledge, transcendental vision, self-sufficiency, and discursive power. It is of course the speaking subject of the cinematic text, a subject which as we have already indicated finds its locus in a cluster of technological apparatuses (the camera, the tape-recorder, etc.). [. . .]

The speaking subject has everything which the viewing subject, suddenly cognizant of the limitations on its vision, understands itself to be lacking. This sense of lack inspires in that subject the desire for 'something else,' a desire to see more.

However, it is equally important that the presence of the speaking subject be hidden from the viewer. Oudart insists that the classic film text must at all costs conceal from the viewing subject the passivity of that subject's position, and this necessitates denying the fact that there is any reality outside of the fiction.

The shot/reverse shot formation is ideally suited for this dual purpose, since it alerts the spectator to that other field whose absence is experienced as unpleasurable while at the same time linking it to the gaze of a fictional character. Thus a gaze within the fiction serves to conceal the controlling gaze outside the fiction; a benign other steps in and obscures the presence of the coercive and castrating Other. In other words, the subject of the speech passes itself off as the speaking subject.

For Oudart, cinematic signification depends entirely upon the moment of unpleasure in which the viewing subject perceives that it is lacking something, i.e. that there is an absent field. Only then, with the disruption of imaginary plenitude, does the shot become a signifier, speaking first and foremost of that thing about which the Lacanian signifier never stops speaking: castration. A complex signifying chain is introduced in place of the lack which can never be made good, suturing over the wound of castration with narrative. However, it is only by inflicting the wound to begin with that the viewing subject can be made to want the restorative of meaning and narrative.

Stephen Heath emphasizes the process of negation which occurs concurrently with a film's positive assertions – its structuring absences and losses. In 'Narrative space,' he writes:

Film is the production not just of a negation but equally, simultaneously, of a negativity, the excessive foundation of the process itself, of the very movement of the spectator as subject in the film; which movement is stopped in the negation and its centring positions, the constant phasing in of subject vision ('this but not that' as the sense of the image in flow).[5]

The unseen apparatuses of enunciation represent one of these structuring losses, but there are others which are equally important. The classic cinematic organization depends upon the subject's willingness to become absent to itself by permitting a fictional character to 'stand in' for it, or by allowing a particular point of view to define what it sees. The operation of suture is successful at the moment that the viewing subject says, 'Yes, that's me,' or 'That's what I see.'

Equally important to the cinematic organization are the operations of cutting and excluding. It is not merely that the camera is incapable of showing us everything at once, but that it does not wish to do so. We must be shown only enough to know that there is more, and to want that 'more' to be disclosed. A prime agency of disclosure is the cut, which divides one shot from the next. The cut guarantees that both the preceding and the subsequent shots will function as structuring absences to the present shot. These absences make possible a signifying ensemble, convert one shot into a signifier of the next one, and the signified of the preceding one.

Thus cinematic coherence and plenitude emerge through multiple cuts and negations. Each image is defined through its differences from those that surround it syntagmatically and those it paradigmatically implies ('this but not that'), as well as through its denial of any discourse but its own. Each positive cinematic assertion represents an imaginary conversion of a whole series of negative ones. This castrating coherence, this definition of a discursive position for the viewing subject which necessitates not only its loss of being, but the repudiation of alternative discourses, is one of the chief aims of the system of suture.

Most classic cinematic texts go to great lengths to cover over these 'cuts.' Hitchcock's *Psycho*, on the other hand, deliberately exposes the negations upon which filmic plenitude is predicated. It unabashedly foregrounds the voyeuristic dimensions of the cinematic experience, making constant references to the speaking subject, and forcing the viewer into oblique and uncomfortable positions both *vis-à-vis* the cinematic apparatuses and the spectacle which they produce.

Psycho not only ruptures the Oedipal formation which provides the basis of the present symbolic order, but declines to put it back together at the end. The final shot of Norman/mother, which conspicuously lacks a reverse shot, makes clear that the coherence of that order proceeds from the institution of sexual difference, and the denial of bi-sexuality.

Finally, *Psycho* obliges the viewing subject to make abrupt shifts in identification. These identifications are often in binary opposition to each other; thus the viewing subject finds itself inscribed into the cinematic discourse at one juncture as victim, and at the next juncture as victimizer. These abrupt shifts would seem to thwart the process of identification, as would all the other strategies just enumerated. However, quite the reverse holds true. The more intense the threat of castration and loss, the more intense the viewing subject's desire for narrative closure.

Psycho's opening few shots take in the exterior of a group of city buildings, without a single reverse shot to anchor that spectacle to a fictional gaze. The transition from urban skyline to the interior of a hotel room is achieved by means of a trick shot: the camera appears to penetrate the space left at the bottom of a window whose venetian blind is three-quarters closed. The viewing subject is made acutely aware of the impossibility of this shot – not just the technical but the 'moral' impossibility, since the shot in question effects a startling breach of privacy.

Our sense of intruding is accentuated by the first shot inside the hotel room, which shows us a woman (Marion), still in bed, and her lover (Sam) standing beside the bed, half-undressed, with a towel in his hands. His face is cropped by the frame, so that he preserves a certain anonymity denied to Marion, who will be the object of numerous coercive gazes during the film. From the very outset, the viewer is not permitted to forget that he or she participates in that visual coercion.

Marion and Sam exchange a series of embraces before leaving the hotel room. Their love-making is interrupted by a discussion about Sam's marital status, and the strain imposed by their clandestine meetings. Marion expresses an intense desire to have their relationship 'normalized' – to be inserted through marriage into an acceptable discursive position. Sam comments bitterly on the economic obstacles in the way of such a union. Later in the same day when Marion is entrusted with $40,000 which is intended to buy someone else's marital bliss, and when the man who gives it to her announces that he never carries more money than he can afford to lose, Marion decides to achieve her culturally induced ambitions through culturally taboo means.

The sequence which follows is an extremely interesting one in terms of suture. In the first shot of that scene Marion stands in the doorway of her bedroom closet, her right side toward the camera, wearing a black brassière and half-slip. A bed separates the camera from her, and in the left far corner there is a vanity-table and mirror. Suddenly the camera moves backward to reveal a corner of the bed not previously exposed, on which lies the envelope of stolen money. It zooms in on the money, then pans to the left and provides a close-up of an open suitcase, full of clothing. During all of this time, Marion is facing the closet, unable to see what we see.

There is a cut to Marion, who turns and looks toward the bed. Once again the camera pulls back to reveal the packet of money. In the next shot, Marion adjusts her hair and clothes in front of the vanity-table and mirror. She turns to look at the bed, and we are given a reverse shot of the stolen envelope. This particular shot/reverse shot formation is repeated.

Finally, Marion sits down on the bed, puts the money in her purse, picks up the suitcase, and leaves.

This sequence achieves a number of things: it establishes the fascination of the money, not only for Marion but for us (we can't help looking at it, even when Marion's back is turned). It delimits a claustral transactional area, an area from which all mediating objects (i.e. the bed) are eventually removed, from which Marion can no longer emerge. The film resorts more and more obsessively to shot/reverse shots in the following episodes, suggesting Marion's absolute entrapment within the position of a thief. Finally, it associates the money with a transcendental gaze, a gaze which exceeds Marion's, and that can see her without ever being seen – one which knows her better than she knows herself.

The privileged object in the shot/reverse shot formations which punctuate the second half of this episode is the packet of money, not Marion. Indeed, the entire spatial field is defined in relation to that spot on the bed where the $40,000 lies; positioned in front of it, we look for a long time at the contents of the room before its human inhabitant ever casts a significant glance at anything. By privileging the point of view of an inanimate object, Hitchcock makes us acutely aware of what Oudart would call the 'Absent One' – i.e. of the speaking subject. Our relationship with the camera remains unmediated, 'unsoftened' by the intervention of a human gaze.

Far from attempting to erase our perception of the cinematic apparatus, the film exploits it, playing on the viewing subject's own paranoia and guilt. We enjoy our visual superiority to Marion, but at the same time we understand that the gaze of the camera – that gaze in which we participate – exceeds us, threatening not only Marion but anyone exposed to the film's spectacle.

It would appear that the system of suture cannot be too closely identified with that shot/reverse shot formation in which the function of looking is firmly associated with a fictional character, since by violating that convention Hitchcock throws a much wider net over his audience. He thereby forces the viewing subject to take up residence not only within one of the film's discursive positions (that of victim), but a second (that of sadistic and legalistic voyeur). The whole operation of suture can be made *more* rather than less irresistible when the field of the speaking subject is continually implied. Two other episodes in *Psycho* demonstrate the same point.

The earlier of these inscribes the law into the fictional level of the film through the figure of a highway patrolman. An opening long-shot shows Marion's car pulled over to the side of a deserted road. A police car pulls into frame and parks behind it. In the next shot the patrolman climbs out of his car, walks over to the driver's side of Marion's automobile, and looks through the window. A third shot shows us what he sees – a sleeping Marion. A succession of almost identical shot/reverse shot formations follow, by means of which the superiority of the legal point of view is dramatized. The patrolman knocks on Marion's window and at last she wakes up. We are now provided with a shot/reverse shot exchange between the two characters, but although Marion does in fact look back at the person who has intruded upon her, his eyes are concealed by a pair of dark glasses.

The policeman interrogates Marion about her reasons for sleeping in her car, and she explains that she pulled over because of fatigue. She asks: 'Have I broken a law?' The conversation is as oblique as the exchange of looks – rather than answering her question, the patrolman asks: 'Is there anything wrong?' His question is neither casual nor solicitous; it is a threat, backed up by a series of quick shot/reverse shots which expose Marion yet further to the scrutiny of a law which it seems impossible to evade, and impossible to decipher.

The police officer asks to see Marion's license. Again the question is far from innocent; 'license' has as broadly existential a meaning as the word 'wrong' in the earlier question. After she gives him her driver's license, the patrolman walks around to the front of the car to write down the license plate number. We see him through the windshield, still protected by his dark glasses from any personal recognition. The reverse shot discloses not Marion, but the license plate which seems to speak for her with greater authority, and to do so through a legal discourse which renders her even more passive.

The policeman permits Marion to resume her journey, but he tails her for several miles. Her paranoia during this period is conveyed through a group of alternating frontal shots of her driving, and reverse shots of her rear-view mirror. The patrol car is clearly visible in both – Marion is now doubly inscribed.

Several sequences later, as Marion continues on her journey in the rain and darkness, the voices of her boss, of the man whose money she has stolen, and of a female friend are superimposed on the sound track, speaking about Marion and defining her even more fully. This device is the acoustic equivalent of all those shots which we have seen, but which Marion has been unable to see because her back was turned, because she was looking in another direction, or because she was asleep. It serves, like those shots, to reinforce the viewing subject's consciousness of an Other whose transcendent and castrating gaze can never be returned, and which always sees one thing: guilt.

The famous shower sequence not only further disassociates the film's spectacle from any of its characters but suggests how much larger the system of suture is than any shot formation. The scene begins with Marion undressing in a motel bedroom, watched through a peep-hole by Norman, her eventual killer. She goes into the bathroom and flushes down the torn pieces of paper on which she has just taken stock of her financial situation (she has decided to return the stolen money, and wants to calculate how much of it she has spent). Marion then closes the bathroom door, effectively eliminating the possibility of Norman or anyone else within the fiction watching her while she showers. Once again the camera insists on the primacy of its own point of view.

Marion steps inside the bath, and we see her outline through the half-transparent curtain. Then, in a shot which parallels the earlier one in which we seem to slip through the bottom of the hotel window, we penetrate the curtain and find ourselves inside the shower with Marion. The film flaunts these trick shots, as if to suggest the futility of resisting the gaze of the speaking subject.

There are nine shots inside the shower before Marion's killer attacks. They are remarkable for their brevity, and for their violation of the 30° rule (the rule that at least 30° of space must separate the position of the camera in one shot from that which follows it in order to justify the intervening cut). Some of the theoreticians of suture argue that the narrative text attempts to conceal its discontinuities and ruptures, but the shower sequence repeatedly draws our attention to the fact of the cinematic cut. This episode also includes a number of obtrusive and disorienting shots – shots taken from the point of view of the shower head at which Marion looks. When the stabbing begins, there is a cinematic cut with almost every thrust of the knife. The implied equation is too striking to ignore: the cinematic machine is lethal; it too murders and dissects. The shower sequence would seem to validate Heath's point that the coherence and plenitude of narrative film are created through negation and loss.

We have no choice but to identify with Marion in the shower, to insert ourselves into the position of the wayward subject who has strayed from the highway of cultural acceptability, but who now wants to make amends. The vulnerability of her naked and surprisingly small body leaves us without anything to deflect that transaction. Marion's encounter with the warm water inside the shower not only suggests a ritual purification, but a contact so basic and primitive as to break down even such dividing lines as class or sexual difference. Finally, the whole process of identification is formally insisted upon by the brevity of the shots; the point of view shifts constantly within the extremely confined space of the shower, making Marion the only stable object, that thing to which we necessarily cling.

That identification is not even disrupted when the cutting activity is mirrored at the level of the fiction, and a bleeding, stumbling Marion struggles to avoid the next knife wound. It is sustained up until the moment when Marion is definitively dead, an inanimate eye now closed to all visual exchanges. At this point we find ourselves in the equally appalling position of the gaze which has negotiated Marion's murder, and the shading of the corners of the frame so as to stimulate the perspective of a peep-hole insists that we acknowledge our own voyeuristic implication.

Relief comes with the resumption of narrative, a resumption which is effected through a tracking shot from the bathroom into the bedroom.

That tracking shot comes to rest first upon the packet of money, then upon an open window through which Norman's house can be seen, and finally upon the figure of Norman himself, running toward the motel. When Norman emerges from his house, adjacent to the motel, the full extent of our complicity becomes evident, since we then realize that for the past five or ten minutes we have shared not his point of view, but that of a more potent and castrating Other. But the envelope of money rescues us from too prolonged a consideration of that fact.

The $40,000 assures us that there is more to follow, and that even though we have just lost our heroine, and our own discursive position, we can afford to finance others. What sutures us at this juncture is the fear of being cut off from narrative. Our investment in the fiction is made manifest through the packet of money which provides an imaginary bridge from Marion to the next protagonist.

Psycho is relentless in its treatment of the viewing subject, forcing upon it next an identification with Norman, who with sober face and professional skill disposes of the now affect-less body of Marion, cleans the motel room, and sinks the incriminating car in quicksand. Marion is subsequently replaced in the narrative by her look-alike sister, and Norman's schizophrenia dramatizes the same vacillation from the position of victim to that of victimizer which the viewing subject is obliged to make in the shower sequence and elsewhere. *Psycho* runs through a whole series of culturally overdetermined narratives, showing the same cool willingness to substitute one for another that it adopts with its characters. Moreover, the manifest context of these narratives yields all too quickly to the latent, undergoing in the process a disquieting vulgarization. We understand perfectly the bourgeois inspiration of Marion's marital dreams, and the spuriousness of the redemptive scenario she hopes to enact by returning the money. Similarly, Norman's Oedipal crisis is played more as farce than melodrama, replete with stuffed birds and hackneyed quarrels in which he plays both parts.

The film terrorizes the viewing subject, refusing ever to let it off the hook. That hook is the system of suture, which is held up to our scrutiny even as we find ourselves thoroughly ensnared by it. What *Psycho* obliges us to understand is that we want suture so badly that we'll take it at any price, even with the fullest knowledge of what it entails – passive insertions into pre-existing discursive positions (both mythically potent and mythically impotent); threatened losses and false recoveries; and subordination to the castrating gaze of a symbolic Other.

In fact, the more the operations of enunciation are revealed to the viewing subject, the more tenacious is its desire for the comfort and closure of narrative – the more anxious it will be to seek refuge within the film's fiction. In so doing, the viewing subject submits to cinematic signification, permits itself to be spoken by the film's discourse. For the theoreticians of suture, the viewing subject thereby re-enacts its entry into the symbolic order. [. . .]

Notes

1   Jacques-Alain Miller, 'Suture (elements of the logic of the signifier)', *Screen*, 18(4) (1977–8), pp. 25–6.

2   Noel Burch, *Theory of Film Practice*, trans. Helen R. Lane (New York, Praeger, 1973), p. 12.

3   Stephen Heath, 'Notes on suture', *Screen*, 18(2) (1977–8), pp. 65–6.

4   Daniel Daya, 'The tutor code of classical cinema', in *Movies and Methods*, ed. Bill Nichols (Berkeley, CA, University of California Press, 1976), p. 448.

5   Stephen Heath, 'Narrative space', *Screen*, 17(3) (1976), p. 107.

Différance **Jacques Derrida**

This chapter, first
published in 1972
from a lecture given
to the Société
française de
philosophie in
1968, is taken from
*A Derrida Reader:
Between the Blinds*,
ed. P. Kampuf
(Brighton, Harvester
Wheatsheaf, 1991),
pp. 60–67. It was
translated by Alan
Bass.

[. . .] *Différance* as temporization, *différance* as spacing. How are they to
be joined?

Let us start, since we are already there, from the problematic of the
sign and of writing. The sign is usually said to be put in the place of the
thing itself, the present thing, 'thing' here standing equally for meaning or
referent. The sign represents the present in its absence. It takes the place of
the present. When we cannot grasp or show the thing, state the present, the
being-present, when the present cannot be presented, we signify, we go
through the detour of the sign. We take or give signs. We signal. The sign,
in this sense, is deferred presence. Whether we are concerned with the
verbal or the written sign, with the monetary sign, or with electoral delegation and political representation, the circulation of signs defers the
moment in which we can encounter the thing itself, make it ours, consume
or expend it, touch it, see it, intuit its presence. What I am describing here
in order to define it is the classically determined structure of the sign in all
the banality of its characteristics – signification as the *différance* of temporization. And this structure presupposes that the sign, which defers
presence, is conceivable only on the *basis* of the presence that it defers and
moving toward the deferred presence that it aims to reappropriate.
According to this classical semiology, the substitution of the sign for the
thing itself is both *secondary* and *provisional*: secondary due to an original
and lost presence from which the sign thus derives; provisional as concerns
this final and missing presence toward which the sign in this sense is a
movement of mediation.

In attempting to put into question these traits of the provisional
secondariness of the substitute, one would come to see something like
an originary *différance*; but one could no longer call it originary or final in

87

the extent to which the values of origin, archi-, *telos*, *eskhaton*, etc. have always denoted presence – *ousia*, *parousia*.[1] To put into question the secondary and provisional characteristics of the sign, to oppose to them an 'originary' *différance*, therefore would have two consequences.

1   One could no longer include *différance* in the concept of the sign, which always has meant the representation of a presence, and has been constituted in a system (thought or language) governed by and moving toward presence.

2   And thereby one puts into question the authority of presence, or of its simple symmetrical opposite, absence, or lack. Thus one questions the limit that has always constrained us, still constrains us – as inhabitants of a language and a system of thought – to formulate the meaning of Being in general as presence or absence, in the categories of being or beingness *(ousia)*. [. . .]

But first let us remain within the semiological problematic in order to see *différance* as temporization and *différance* as spacing conjoined. Most of the semiological or linguistic researches that dominate the field of thought today, whether due to their own results or to the regulatory model that they find themselves acknowledging everywhere, refer genealogically to Saussure (correctly or incorrectly) as their common inaugurator. Now Saussure first of all is the thinker who put the *arbitrary character* of the sign and the *differential character* of the sign at the very foundation of general semiology, particularly linguistics. And, as we know, these two motifs – arbitrary and differential – are inseparable in his view. There can be arbitrariness only because the system of signs is constituted solely by the differences in terms, and not by their plenitude. The elements of signification function not through the compact force of their nuclei but rather through the network of oppositions that distinguishes them and then relates them one to another. 'Arbitrary and differential,' says Saussure, 'are two correlative characteristics.'

Now this principle of difference, as the condition for signification, affects the *totality* of the sign, that is, the sign as both signified and signifier. The signified is the concept, the ideal meaning; and the signifier is what Saussure calls the 'image,' the 'psychical imprint' of a material, physical – for example, acoustical – phenomenon. We do not have to go into all the problems posed by these definitions here. Let us cite Saussure only at the point which interests us:

> The conceptual side of value is made up solely of relations and differences with respect to the other terms of language, and the same can be said of its material side . . . Everything that has been said up to this point boils down to this: in language there are only differences. Even more important, a difference

generally implies positive terms between which the difference is set up; but in language there are only differences *without positive terms*. Whether we take the signified or the signifier, language has neither ideas nor sounds that existed before the linguistic system, but only conceptual and phonic differences that have issued from the system. The idea or phonic substance that a sign contains is of less importance than the other signs that surround it.[2]

The first consequence to be drawn from this is that the signified concept is never present in and of itself, in a sufficient presence that would refer only to itself. Essentially and lawfully, every concept is inscribed in a chain or in a system within which it refers to the other, to other concepts, by means of the systematic play of differences. Such a play, *différance*, is thus no longer simply a concept, but rather the possibility of conceptuality, of a conceptual process and system in general. [. . .]

[. . .]

In a language, in the *system* of language, there are only differences. Therefore a taxonomical operation can undertake the systematic, statistical, and classificatory inventory of a language. But, on the one hand, these differences *play*: in language, in speech too, and in the exchange between language and speech. On the other hand, these differences are themselves *effects*. They have not fallen from the sky fully formed, and are no more inscribed in a *topos noētos*, than they are prescribed in the gray matter of the brain. [. . .]

What is written as *différance*, then, will be the playing movement that 'produces' – by means of something that is not simply an activity – these differences, these effects of difference. This does not mean that the *différance* that produces differences is somehow before them, in a simple and unmodified – in-different – present. *Différance* is the nonfull, non-simple, structured and differentiating origin of differences. Thus, the name origin no longer suits it.

Since language, which Saussure says is a classification, has not fallen from the sky, its differences have been produced, are produced effects, but they are effects which do not find their cause in a subject or a substance, in a thing in general, a being that is somewhere present, thereby eluding the play of *différance*. If such a presence were implied in the concept of cause in general, in the most classical fashion, we then would have to speak of an effect without a cause, which very quickly would lead to speaking of no effect at all. I have attempted to indicate a way out of the closure of this framework via the 'trace,' which is no more an effect than it has a cause, but which in and of itself, outside its text, is not sufficient to operate the necessary transgression.

Since there is no presence before and outside semiological difference, what Saussure has written about language can be extended to the sign in general: 'Language is necessary in order for speech to be intelligible and to produce all of its effects; but the latter is necessary in order for language to be established; historically, the fact of speech always comes first.'[3]

Retaining at least the framework, if not the content, of this requirement formulated by Saussure, we will designate as *différance* the movement according to which language, or any code, any system of referral in general, is constituted 'historically' as a weave of differences. 'Is constituted,' 'is produced,' 'is created,' 'movement,' 'historically,' etc., necessarily being understood beyond the metaphysical language in which they are retained, along with all their implications. We ought to demonstrate why concepts like *production*, constitution, and history remain in complicity with what is at issue here. But this would take me too far today – toward the theory of the representation of the 'circle' in which we appear to be enclosed – and I utilize such concepts, like many others, only for their strategic convenience and in order to undertake their deconstruction at the currently most decisive point. In any event, it will be understood, by means of the circle in which we appear to be engaged, that as it is written here, *différance* is no more static than it is genetic, no more structural than historical. [. . .]

Let us go on. It is because of *différance* that the movement of signification is possible only if each so-called present element, each element appearing on the scene of presence, is related to something other than itself, thereby keeping within itself the mark of the past element, and already letting itself be vitiated by the mark of its relation to the future element, this trace being related no less to what is called the future than to what is called the past, and constituting what is called the present by means of this very relation to what it is not: what it absolutely is not, not even a past or a future as a modified present. An interval must separate the present from what it is not in order for the present to be itself, but this interval that constitutes it as present must, by the same token, divide the present in and of itself, thereby also dividing, along with the present, everything that is thought on the basis of the present, that is, in our metaphysical language, every being, and singularly substance or the subject. In constituting itself, in dividing itself dynamically, this interval is what might be called *spacing*, the becoming-space of time or the becoming-time of space (*temporization*). And it is this constitution of the present, as an 'originary' and irreducibly nonsimple (and therefore, *stricto sensu* nonoriginary) synthesis of marks, or traces of retentions and protentions (to reproduce analogically and provisionally a phenomenological and transcendental language that soon will reveal itself to be inadequate), that I propose to call archi-writing, archi-trace, or *différance*, which (is) (simultaneously) spacing (and) temporization.

[. . .] Differences, thus, are 'produced' – deferred – by *différance*. But *what* defers or *who* defers? In other words, *what is différance*? With this question we reach another level and another resource of our problematic.

What differs? Who differs? What is *différance*?

If we answered these questions before examining them as questions, before turning them back on themselves, and before suspecting their very form, including what seems most natural and necessary about them, we would immediately fall back into what we have just disengaged ourselves from. In effect, if we accepted the form of the question, in its meaning and its syntax ('What is?' 'Who is?' 'Who is it that?'), we would have to conclude that *différance* has been derived, has happened, is to be mastered and governed on the basis of the point of a present being, which itself could be some thing, a form, a state, a power in the world to which all kinds of names might be given, a *what*, or a present being as a *subject*, a *who*. And in this last case, notably, one would conclude implicitly that this present being, for example a being present to itself, as consciousness, eventually would come to defer or to differ: whether by delaying and turning away from the fulfillment of a 'need' or a 'desire,' or by differing from itself. But in neither of these cases would such a present being be 'constituted' by this *différance*.

Now if we refer, once again, to semiological difference, of what does Saussure, in particular, remind us? That 'language [which only consists of differences] is not a function of the speaking subject.' This implies that the subject (in its identity with itself, or eventually in its consciousness of its identity with itself, its self-consciousness) is inscribed in language, is a 'function' of language, becomes a *speaking* subject only by making its speech conform – even in so-called creation, or in so-called transgression – to the system of the rules of language as a system of differences, or at very least by conforming to the general law of *différance*, or by adhering to the principle of language that Saussure says is 'spoken language minus speech.' 'Language is necessary for the spoken word to be intelligible and so that it can produce all of its effects.'[4]

If, by hypothesis, we maintain that the opposition of speech to language is absolutely rigorous, then *différance* would be not only the play of differences with language but also the relation of speech to language, the detour through which I must pass in order to speak, the silent promise I must make; and this is equally valid for semiology in general, governing all the relations of usage to schemata, of message to code, etc. (Elsewhere I have attempted to suggest that this *différance* in language, and in the relation of speech and language, forbids the essential dissociation of speech and language that Saussure, at another level of his discourse, traditionally wished to delineate. The practice of a language or of a code supposing a play of forms without a determined and invariable substance, and also supposing in the practice of this play a retention and protention of differences, a spacing and a temporization, a play of traces – all this must be a kind of writing before the letter, an archi-writing without a present origin, without archi-. Whence the regular erasure of the archi-, and the transformation of general semiology into grammatology, this latter executing a critical labor on everything within semiology, including the central concept of the sign, that maintained metaphysical presuppositions incompatible with the motif of *différance*.

One might be tempted by an objection: certainly the subject becomes a *speaking* subject only in its commerce with the system of linguistic differences; or yet, the subject becomes a *signifying* (signifying in general, by means of speech or any other sign) subject only by inscribing itself in the system of differences. Certainly in this sense the speaking or signifying subject could not be present to itself, as speaking or signifying, without the play of linguistic or semiological *différance*. But can one not conceive of a presence, and of a presence to itself of the subject before speech or signs, a presence to itself of the subject in a silent and intuitive consciousness?

Such a question therefore supposes that, prior to the sign and outside it, excluding any trace and any *différance*, something like consciousness is possible. And that consciousness, before distributing its signs in space and in the world, can gather itself into its presence. But what is consciousness? What does *consciousness* mean? Most often, in the very form of meaning, in all its modifications, consciousness offers itself to thought only as self-presence, as the perception of self in presence. And what holds for consciousness holds here for so-called subjective existence in general. Just as the category of the subject cannot be, and never has been, thought without the reference to presence as *hupokeimenon* or as *ousia*, etc., so the subject as consciousness has never manifested itself except as self-presence. The privilege granted to consciousness therefore signifies the privilege granted to the present [. . .].

This privilege is the ether of metaphysics, the element of our thought that is caught in the language of metaphysics. One can delimit such a closure today only by soliciting[5] the value of presence that Heidegger has shown to be the ontotheological determination of Being; and in thus soliciting the value of presence, by means of an interrogation whose status must be completely exceptional, we are also examining the absolute privilege of this form or epoch of presence in general that is consciousness as meaning[6] in self-presence.

Thus one comes to posit presence – and specifically consciousness, the being beside itself of consciousness – no longer as the absolutely central form of Being but as a 'determination' and as an 'effect.' A determination or an effect within a system which is no longer that of presence but of *différance*, a system that no longer tolerates the opposition of activity and passivity, nor that of cause and effect, or of indetermination and determination, etc., such that in designating consciousness as an effect or a determination, one continues – for strategic reasons that can be more or less lucidly deliberated and systematically calculated – to operate according to the lexicon of that which one is delimiting. [. . .]

Notes

1   *Translator's note*: ousia and parousia imply presence as both origin and end, the founding principle (*arkhé-*) as that toward which one moves (*telos, eskhaton*).

2   Ferdinand de Saussure, *Course in General Linguistics*, trans. Wade Baskin (New York, Philosophical Library, 1959), pp. 117–18, 120.

3   Ibid., p. 18.

4   Ibid., p. 37.

5   *Translator's note*: the French *solliciter*, as the English *solicit*, derives from an Old Latin expression meaning to shake the whole, to make something tremble in its entirety. Derrida comments on this later, but is already using 'to solicit' in this sense here.

6   *Translator's note*: 'meaning' here is the weak translation of *vouloir-dire*, which has a strong sense of willing (*voluntas*) to say, putting the attempt to mean in conjunction with speech, a crucial conjunction for Derrida.

Interrogating identity: The Post Colonial Prerogative
Homi K. Bhabha

[. . .] Listen to my friend, the Bombay poet Adil Jussawalla, writing of the 'missing person' that haunts the identity of the postcolonial bourgeoisie:

> No Satan
> warmed in the electric coils of his creatures
> or Gunga Din
> will make him come before you.
> To see an invisible man or a missing person,
> trust no Eng. Lit. That
> puffs him up, narrows his eyes,
> scratches him fangs. Caliban
> is still not IT.
> But faintly pencilled
> behind a shirt, . . .
> Savage of no sensational paint,
> fangs cancelled.[1]

As that voice falters listen to its echo in the verse of a black woman, descendant of slaves, writing of the diaspora:

> We arrived in the Northern Hemisphere
> when summer was set in its way
> running from the flames that lit the sky
> over the Plantation.
> We were a straggle bunch of immigrants
> in a lily white landscape.
> . . .

This chapter is taken from 'Interrogating identity: the postcolonial prerogative', in *Anatomy of Racism*, ed. D.T. Goldberg (Minneapolis, University of Minnesota Press, 1990), pp. 188–209.

One day I learnt,
a secret art,
Invisible-Ness, it was called.
I think it worked
as even now you look
but never see me . . .
Only my eyes will remain to haunt,
and to turn your dreams
to chaos.[2]

As these images fade, and the empty eyes endlessly hold their menacing gaze, listen finally to Edward Said's attempt to historicize their chaos of identity:

One aspect of the electronic, postmodern world is that there has been a reinforcement of the stereotypes by which the Orient is viewed . . . If the world has become immediately accessible to a Western citizen living in the electronic age, the Orient too has drawn nearer to him, and is now less a myth perhaps than a place criss-crossed by Western, especially American interests.[3]

I have begun with these postcolonial portraits because they seize on the vanishing point of two familiar traditions in the discourse of identity: the philosophical tradition of identity as the process of self-reflection in the mirror of (human) nature; and the anthropological view of the difference of human identity as located in the division of Nature/Culture. In the postcolonial text the problem of identity returns as a persistent questioning of the frame, the space of representation, where the image – missing person, invisible eye, Oriental stereotype – is confronted with its difference, its Other. This is neither the glassy essence of Nature, to use Richard Rorty's image, nor the leaden voice of 'ideological interpellation,' as Louis Althusser suggests.

What is so graphically enacted in the moment of colonial identification is the splitting of the subject in its historical place of utterance: 'No Satan / or Gunga / Din will make him come before you / To see an invisible man or a missing person, / trust no Eng. Lit.' What these repeated negations of identity dramatize, in their elision of the seeing eye that must contemplate what is missing or invisible, is the impossibility of claiming an origin for the Self (or Other) within a tradition of representation that conceives of identity as the satisfaction of a totalizing, plenitudinous object of vision. By disrupting the stability of the ego, expressed in the equivalence between image and identity, the secret art of invisibleness of which the migrant poet speaks, changes the very terms of our recognition of the person.

This change is precipitated by the peculiar temporality whereby the subject cannot be apprehended without the absence or invisibility that constitutes it – 'as even now you look/but never see me' – so that the subject speaks, and is seen, from where it is *not*; and the migrant woman can subvert the perverse satisfaction of the racist, masculinist gaze that disavowed her presence, by presenting it with an anxious absence, a countergaze that turns the discriminatory look, which denies her cultural and sexual difference, back on itself.

It is this familiar, postmodernist space of the Other (in the process of identification) that develops a graphic historical and cultural specificity in the splitting of the postcolonial or migrant subject. In place of that 'I' – institutionalized in the visionary, authorial ideologies of *Eng. Lit.* or the notion of 'experience' in the empiricist accounts of slave history – there emerges the challenge to see what is invisible, the look that cannot 'see me,' a certain problem of the object of the gaze that constitutes a problematic referent for the language of the Self. The elision of the eye, represented in a narrative of negation and repetition – *no . . . no . . . never* – insists that the phrase of identity cannot be spoken, except by putting the eye/I in the impossible position of enunciation. *To see* a missing person, or *to look* at Invisibleness, is to emphasize the subject's *transitive* demand for a *direct* object of self-reflection, a point of presence that would maintain its privileged enunciatory position *qua subject*. To see a *missing person* is to *transgress* that demand; the 'I' in the position of mastery is, at *that same time*, the place of its absence, its *re*-presentation. What we witness is the alienation of the eye with the sound of the signifier as the desire (to look/to be looked at) emerges and is erased in the *feint of writing*:

> But faintly pencilled
> behind a shirt,
> a trendy jacket or tie
> *if* he catches your eye,
> he'll come screaming at you like a jet –
> savage of no sensational paint,
> fangs cancelled.

Why does the faintly penciled person fail to catch your eye? What is the secret of Invisibleness that enables the woman migrant to look without being seen?

What is transformed in the postmodern perspective is not simply the image of the person, but an interrogation of the discursive and disciplinary place from which questions of identity are strategically and institutionally posed. Through the progress of this poem 'you' are continually positioned in the space between a range of contradictory places that coexist. So that you find yourself at the point at which the Orientalist stereotype is evoked and erased *at the same time*; in the place where Eng. Lit. is *Entstellt* in the ironic mimicry of its Indo-Anglian repetition. And this space of re-inscription must be thought outside of those metaphysical philosophies of self-doubt, where the otherness of identity is the anguished *presence* within the Self of an existentialist agony that emerges when you look perilously through a glass darkly.

What is profoundly unresolved, even erased, in the discourses of poststructuralism is that *perspective of depth* through which the authenticity of identity comes to be reflected in the glassy metaphorics of the mirror and its mimetic or realist narratives. In shifting the frame of identity from the field of vision to the space of writing, postmodernism interrogates that third dimensionality that gives profundity to the representation of Self and Other and creates that depth of perspective that cineastes call the fourth wall; literary theorists describe it as the transparency of realist metanarratives. Barthes brilliantly diagnoses this as *l'effet du reel*, the 'profound, geological dimension'[4] of signification, achieved by arresting the linguistic sign in its *symbolic* function. The bilateral space of the symbolic consciousness, Barthes writes, massively privileges *resemblance*, constructs an *analogical* relation between signifier and signified that ignores the question of form, and creates a vertical dimension within the sign. In this scheme the signifier is always predetermined by the signified – that conceptual or real space that is placed prior to, and outside of, the act of signification.

From our point of view, this verticality is significant for the light it sheds on that *dimension of depth* that provides the language of identity with its sense of reality, a measure of the 'me,' which emerges from an acknowledgment of my inwardness, the depth of my character, the profundity of my person, to mention only a few of those adjectives through which we commonly articulate our self-consciousness. My argument about the importance of *depth* in the representation of a unified image of the self is borne out by the most decisive and influential formulation on personal identity in the English empiricist tradition.

John Locke's famous criteria of the continuity of consciousness ensuring the sameness of a rational being could quite legitimately be read as written in the symbolic sign of resemblance and analogy. For the consciousness of the past, crucial to the argument – 'as far as this consciousness can be extended *backwards* to any past action or thought, so far reaches the identity of that person' – is precisely that unifying third dimension, that agency of *depth*, that brings together in an analogical relation (dismissive of the differences that construct temporality and signification), 'that same consciousness uniting those distant actions into the same person, *whatever substances contributed to their production*' (my emphasis).[5]

Barthes's description of the sign-as-symbol is conveniently analogous to the language we use to designate identity. At the same time, it sheds light on the concrete linguistic concepts with which we can grasp how the language of personhood comes to be invested with a visuality or visibility of depth. This makes the moment of self-consciousness at once refracted and transparent; the question of identity always posed uncertainly, tenebrously, between shadow and substance. The symbolic consciousness gives the sign (of the Self) a sense of autonomy or solitariness 'as if it stands by itself in the world' privileging an individuality and a unitariness whose integrity is expressed in a certain richness of agony and anomie. Barthes calls it a mythic prestige, almost totemic in 'its form [which is] constantly exceeded by the power and movement of its content; . . . much less a codified form of communication than an (affective) instrument of participation.'[6]

This image of human identity and, indeed, human identity as *image* – both familiar frames or mirrors of selfhood that speak from deep within Western culture – are inscribed in the sign of resemblance. The analogical relation unifies the experience of self-consciousness by finding, within the mirror of nature, the symbolic certitude of the sign of culture based 'on an analogy with the compulsion to believe when staring at an object'.[7] This, as Rorty writes, is part of the West's obsession that our primary relation to objects and ourselves is analogous to visual perception. Preeminent among these representations has been the reflection of the self that develops in the symbolic consciousness of the sign, and marks out the discursive space from which *The real Me* emerges initially as an assertion of the authenticity of the person and then lingers on to reverberate – *The real Me???* – as a questioning of identity.

My purpose here is to define the space of the inscription or writing of identity – beyond the visual depths of Barthes's symbolic sign. The postmodernist experience of the disseminating self-image goes beyond representation as the analogical consciousness of resemblance. The problem is not of the nature of dialectical contradiction, the antagonistic consciousness of master and slave, that can be sublated and transcended. The impasse or aporia of consciousness that seems to be the representative postmodernist experience is a peculiar strategy of doubling.

Each time the encounter with identity occurs at the point at which something exceeds the frame of the image, it eludes the eye, evacuates the self as site of identity and autonomy and – most important – leaves a resistant trace, a stain of the subject, a sign of resistance. We are no longer confronted with an ontological problem of being but with the discursive strategy of the moment of interrogation, a moment in which the demand for identification becomes, primarily, a response to other questions of signification and desire, culture and politics.

In place of the symbolic consciousness that gives the sign of identity its integrity and unity, its *depth*, we are faced with a dimension of doubling; a spatialization of the subject, that is occluded in the illusory perspective of, what I have called, the 'third dimension' of the mimetic frame or visual image of identity. The figure of the double – to which I now turn – cannot be contained within the analogical sign of resemblance, which, as Barthes said, developed its totemic, vertical dimension only because 'what interests it in the sign is the signified: the signifier is always a determined element.' For poststructuralist discourse, it is the priority (and play) of the signifier that reveals the space of doubling (not depth) that is the very articulatory principle of discourse. It is through that space of enunciation that problems of meaning and being enter the discourses of poststructuralism, as the problematic of subjection and identification.

What emerges in the preceding poems, as the line drawing of trendy jacket and tie, or the eerie, avengeful disembodied eye, must not be read as revelations of some suppressed truth of the postcolonial psyche/subject. In the world of double inscriptions that we have now entered, in this space of *writing*, there can be no such immediacy of a visualist perspective, no such face-to-face epiphanies in the mirror of nature, that Rorty attributed to the tradition of epistemological knowledge. On one level, what confronts you, the reader, in the incomplete portrait of the postcolonial bourgeois – who looks uncannily like the trendy metropolitan intellectual *you* are yourself – is the ambivalence of your desire for the Other: '*You! hypocrite lecteur! – mon semblable, – mon frere!*'

That disturbance of your voyeuristic look enacts the complexity and contradictions of your desire *to see, to fix* cultural difference in a container-able, *visible* object, or as a fact of nature, when it can only be articulated in the uncertainty or undecidability that circulates through the processes of language and identification. The desire for the Other is doubled by the desire in language, which *splits the difference* between Self and Other so that both positions are partial; neither is sufficient unto itself. As I have just shown in the portrait of the missing person, the very question of identi-fication only emerges *in between* disavowal and designation. It is per-formed in the agonistic struggle between the epistemological, visual demand for a knowledge of the Other, and its representation in the act of articulation and enunciation.

> Look a Negro . . . Mama, see the Negro! I'm frightened . . . I could no longer laugh, because I already know where there were legends, stories, history, and above all *historicity* . . . Then, assailed at various points, the corporeal schema crumbled, its place taken by a racial epidermal schema . . . It was no longer a question of being aware of my body in the third person but in a triple person . . . I was responsible for my body, for my race, for my ancestors.[8]

Fanon's *Black Skin, White Masks* reveals the doubling of identity: the difference between personal identity as an intimation of reality, or an intuition of being, and the psychoanalytic problem of identification that, in a sense, always begs the question of the subject: 'What does a man want?' The emergence of the human subject as socially and psychically authen-ticated depends on the *negation* of an originary narrative of fulfillment or an imaginary coincidence between individual interest or instinct and the General Will. Such binary, two-part, identities function in a kind of nar-cissistic reflection of the One in the Other that is confronted in the language of desire by the psychoanalytic process of identification. For identification, identity is never an *a priori*, nor a finished product; it is only ever the problematic process of access to an image of totality. The discursive conditions of this psychic image of identification will be clarified if we think of the perilous perspective of the concept of the image itself. For the image – as point of identification – marks the site of an ambivalence. Its representation is always spatially split – it makes *present* something that is *absent* – and temporally deferred: it is the representation of a time that is always elsewhere, a repetition. The image is only ever an *appurtenance* to authority and identity; it must never be read mimetically as the appearance or a reality. The access to the image of identity is only ever possible in the *negation* of any sense of originality or plenitude, through the principle of displacement and differentiation (absence/presence, representation/repetition) that always renders it a liminal reality. The image is at once a metaphoric substitution, an illusion of presence and by that same token a metonym, a sign of its absence and loss. It is precisely from this edge of meaning and being, from this shifting boundary of otherness within identity, that Fanon asks: 'What does a *black* man want?'

> When it encounters resistance from the other, self-consciousness undergoes the experience of desire . . . As soon as I desire I ask to be considered. I am not merely here and now, sealed into thingness. I am for somewhere else and for something else. I demand that notice be taken of my negating activity in so far as I pursue something other than life . . . I occupied space. I moved towards the other . . . and the evanescent other, hostile, but not opaque, transparent, not there, disappeared. Nausea.[9]

From that overwhelming emptiness of nausea Fanon makes his answer: the black man wants the objectifying confrontation with otherness; in the colonial psyche there is an unconscious disavowal of the negating, splitting moment of desire. The place of the Other must not be imaged as Fanon sometimes suggests as a fixed phenomenological point, opposed to the self, that represents a culturally alien consciousness. The Other must be seen as the necessary negation of a primordial identity – cultural or psychic – that introduces the system of differentiation that enables the cultural to be signified as a linguistic, symbolic, historic reality. If, as I have suggested, the subject of desire is never simply a Myself, then the Other is never simply an *It-self*, a front of identity, truth, or misrecognition.

As a principle of identification, the Other bestows a degree of objectivity but its representation – be it the social process of the Law or the psychic process of the Oedipus – is always ambivalent, disclosing a lack. For instance, the common, conversational distinction between the letter and spirit of the Law displays the otherness of Law itself; the ambiguous grey area between Justice and judicial procedure is, quite literally, a conflict of judgment. In the language of psychoanalysis, the Law of the Father or the paternal metaphor, again, cannot be taken at its word. It is a process of substitution and exchange that inscribes a normative, normalizing place for the subject; but that metaphoric access to identity is exactly the place of prohibition and repression, precisely a conflict of authority. Identification, as it is spoken in the *desire of the Other*, is always a question of interpretation for it is the elusive assignation of myself with a one-self, the elision of person and place.

If the differentiating force of the Other is the process of the subject's signification in language and society's objectification in Law, then how can the Other disappear? Can desire, the moving spirit of the subject, ever evanesce? [. . .]

Notes

1   Adil Jussawalla, *Missing Person* (Bombay: Clearing House, 1976), pp. 14–29.
2   Meiling Jin, 'Strangers on a hostile landscape', in *Watchers and Seekers*, ed. Cobham and Collins (London: The Women's Press), pp. 126–7.
3   Edward Said, *Orientalism* (London, Routledge and Kegan Paul, 1978), pp. 26–7.
4   Roland Barthes, 'The imagination of the sign', in *Critical Essays* (Evanston, Ill.: Northwestern University Press, 1972), pp. 206–7.
5   John Locke, *An Essay Concerning Human Understanding* (London, Fontana, 1969), pp. 212–13.
6   Barthes, 'Imagination of the sign', p. 207.
7   Richard Rorty, 'Mirroring', in *Philosophy and the Mirror of Nature* (Oxford, Blackwell, 1980), pp. 162–3.
8   Frantz Fanon, *Black Skin, White Masks* (London, Pluto Press, 1991), p. 112
9   Ibid., pp. 112, 218

10

Domain **Michel Foucault**

Sexuality must not be described as a stubborn drive, by nature alien and of necessity disobedient to a power which exhausts itself trying to subdue it and often fails to control it entirely. It appears rather as an especially dense transfer point for relations of power: between men and women, young people and old people, parents and offspring, teachers and students, priests and laity, an administration and a population. Sexuality is not the most intractable element in power relations, but rather one of those endowed with the greatest instrumentality: useful for the greatest number of maneuvers and capable of serving as a point of support, as a linchpin, for the most varied strategies.

There is no single, all-encompassing strategy, valid for all of society and uniformly bearing on all the manifestations of sex. For example, the idea that there have been repeated attempts, by various means, to reduce all of sex to its reproductive function, its heterosexual and adult form, and its matrimonial legitimacy fails to take into account the manifold objectives aimed for, the manifold means employed in the different sexual politics concerned with the two sexes, the different age groups and social classes.

In a first approach to the problem, it seems that we can distinguish four great strategic unities which, beginning in the eighteenth century, formed specific mechanisms of knowledge and power centering on sex. These did not come into being fully developed at that time; but it was then that they took on a consistency and gained an effectiveness in the order of power, as well as a productivity in the order of knowledge, so that it is possible to describe them in their relative autonomy.

This chapter, originally published in 1976, is taken from *The History of Sexuality*, Volume I: An Introduction (Harmondsworth, Penguin, 1984), pp. 103–11.

1   *A hysterization of women's bodies:* a threefold process whereby the feminine body was analyzed – qualified and disqualified – as being

thoroughly saturated with sexuality; whereby it was integrated into the sphere of medical practices, by reason of a pathology intrinsic to it; whereby, finally, it was placed in organic communication with the social body (whose regulated fecundity it was supposed to ensure), the family space (of which it had to be a substantial and functional element), and the life of children (which it produced and had to guarantee, by virtue of a biologico-moral responsibility lasting through the entire period of the children's education): the Mother, with her negative image of 'nervous woman,' constituted the most visible form of this hysterization.

2   *A pedagogization of children's sex*: a double assertion that practically all children indulge or are prone to indulge in sexual activity; and that, being unwarranted, at the same time 'natural' and 'contrary to nature,' this sexual activity posed physical and moral, individual and collective dangers; children were defined as 'preliminary' sexual beings, on this side of sex, yet within it, astride a dangerous dividing line. Parents, families, educators, doctors, and eventually psychologists would have to take charge, in a continuous way, of this precious and perilous, dangerous and endangered sexual potential: this pedagogization was especially evident in the war against onanism, which in the West lasted nearly two centuries.

3   *A socialization of procreative behavior*: an economic socialization via all the incitements and restrictions, the 'social' and fiscal measures brought to bear on the fertility of couples; a political socialization achieved through the 'responsibilization' of couples with regard to the social body as a whole (which had to be limited or on the contrary reinvigorated), and a medical socialization carried out by attributing a pathogenic value – for the individual and the species – to birth-control practices.

4   *A psychiatrization of perverse pleasure*: the sexual instinct was isolated as a separate biological and psychical instinct; a clinical analysis was made of all the forms of anomalies by which it could be afflicted; it was assigned a role of normalization or pathologization with respect to all behavior; and finally, a corrective technology was sought for these anomalies.

Four figures emerged from this preoccupation with sex, which mounted throughout the nineteenth century – four privileged objects of knowledge, which were also targets and anchorage points for the ventures of knowledge: the hysterical woman, the masturbating child, the Malthusian couple, and the perverse adult. Each of them corresponded to one of these strategies which, each in its own way, invested and made use of the sex of women, children, and men.

What was at issue in these strategies? A struggle against sexuality? Or were they part of an effort to gain control of it? An attempt to regulate it more effectively and mask its more indiscreet, conspicuous, and intractable aspects? A way of formulating only that measure of knowledge about it that was acceptable or useful? In actual fact, what was involved, rather, was the very production of sexuality. Sexuality must not be thought of as a kind of natural given which power tries to hold in check, or as an obscure domain which knowledge tries gradually to uncover. It is the name that can be given to a historical construct: not a furtive reality that is difficult to grasp, but a great surface network in which the stimulation of bodies, the intensification of pleasures, the incitement to discourse, the formation of special knowledges, the strengthening of controls and resistances, are linked to one another, in accordance with a few major strategies of knowledge and power.

It will be granted no doubt that relations of sex gave rise, in every society, to a *deployment of alliance*: a system of marriage, of fixation and development of kinship ties, of transmission of names and possessions. This deployment of alliance, with the mechanisms of constraint that ensured its existence and the complex knowledge it often required, lost some of its importance as economic processes and political structures could no longer rely on it as an adequate instrument or sufficient support. Particularly from the eighteenth century onward, Western societies created and deployed a new apparatus which was superimposed on the previous one, and which, without completely supplanting the latter, helped to reduce its importance. I am speaking of the *deployment of sexuality*: like the *deployment of alliance*, it connects up with the circuit of sexual partners, but in a completely different way. The two systems can be contrasted term by term. The deployment of alliance is built around a system of rules defining the permitted and the forbidden, the licit and the illicit, whereas the deployment of sexuality operates according to mobile, polymorphous, and contingent techniques of power. The deployment of alliance has as one of its chief objectives to reproduce the interplay of relations and maintain the law that governs them; the deployment of sexuality, on the other hand, engenders a continual extension of areas and forms of control. For the first, what is pertinent is the link between partners and definite statutes; the second is concerned with the sensations of the body, the quality of pleasures, and the nature of impressions, however tenuous or imperceptible these may be. Lastly, if the deployment of alliance is firmly tied to the economy due to the role it can play in the transmission or circulation of wealth, the deployment of sexuality is linked to the economy through numerous and subtle relays, the main one of which, however, is the body – the body that produces and consumes. In a word, the deployment of alliance is attuned to a homeostasis of the social body, which it has the function of maintaining; whence its privileged link with the law; whence too the fact that the important phase for it is 'reproduction.' The deployment of sexuality has its reason for being, not in reproducing itself, but in proliferating, innovating, annexing, creating, and penetrating bodies in an increasingly detailed way, and in controlling populations in an increasingly comprehensive way. We are compelled, then, to accept three or four hypotheses which run counter to the one on which the theme of a sexuality repressed by the modern forms of society is based: sexuality is tied to recent devices of power; it has been expanding at an increasing rate since the seventeenth century; the arrangement that has sustained it is not governed by reproduction; it has been linked from the outset with an intensification of the body – with its exploitation as an object of knowledge and an element in relations of power.

It is not exact to say that the deployment of sexuality supplanted the deployment of alliance. One can imagine that one day it will have replaced it. But as things stand at present, while it does tend to cover up the deployment of alliance, it has neither obliterated the latter nor rendered it useless. Moreover, historically it was around and on the basis of the deployment of alliance that the deployment of sexuality was constructed. First the practice of penance, then that of the examination of conscience and spiritual direction, was the formative nucleus: [. . .] what was at issue to begin with at the tribunal of penance was sex insofar as it was the basis of relations; the questions posed had to do with the commerce allowed or forbidden (adultery, extramarital relations, relations with a person pro-hibited by blood or statute, the legitimate or illegitimate character of the act of sexual congress); then, coinciding with the new pastoral and its application in seminaries, secondary schools, and convents, there was a gradual progression away from the problematic of relations toward a problematic of the 'flesh,' that is, of the body, sensation, the nature of pleasure, the more secret forms of enjoyment or acquiescence. 'Sexuality' was taking shape, born of a technology of power that was originally focused on alliance. Since then, it has not ceased to operate in conjunction with a system of alliance on which it has depended for support. The family cell, in the form in which it came to be valued in the course of the eighteenth century, made it possible for the main elements of the deploy-ment of sexuality (the feminine body, infantile precocity, the regulation of births, and to a lesser extent no doubt, the specification of the perverted) to develop along its two primary dimensions: the husband–wife axis and the parents–children axis. The family, in its contemporary form, must not be understood as a social, economic, and political structure of alliance that excludes or at least restrains sexuality, that diminishes it as much as possible, preserving only its useful functions. On the contrary, its role is to anchor sexuality and provide it with a permanent support. It ensures the production of a sexuality that is not homogeneous with the privileges of alliance, while making it possible for the systems of alliance to be imbued with a new tactic of power which they would otherwise be impervious to. The family is the interchange of sexuality and alliance: it conveys the law and the juridical dimension in the deployment of sexuality; and it conveys the economy of pleasure and the intensity of sensations in the regime of alliance.

[. . .]

What has taken place since the seventeenth century can be interpreted in the following manner: the deployment of sexuality which first developed on the fringes of familial institutions (in the direction of conscience and pedagogy, for example) gradually became focused on the family: the alien, irreducible, and even perilous effects it held in store for the deployment of alliance (an awareness of this danger was evidenced in the criticism often directed at the indiscretion of the directors, and in the entire controversy, which occurred somewhat later, over the private or public, institutional or familial education of children)[1] were absorbed by the family, a family that was reorganized, restricted no doubt, and in any case intensified in comparison with the functions it formerly exercised in the deployment of alliance. In the family, parents and relatives became the chief agents of a deployment of sexuality which drew its outside support from doctors, educators, and later psychiatrists, and which began by competing with the relations of alliance but soon 'psychologized' or 'psychiatrized' the latter. Then these new personages made their appearance: the nervous woman, the frigid wife, the indifferent mother – or worse, the mother beset by murderous obsessions – the impotent, sadistic, perverse husband, the hysterical or neurasthenic girl, the precocious and already exhausted child, and the young homosexual who rejects marriage or neglects his wife. These were the combined figures of an alliance gone bad and an abnormal sexuality; they were the means by which the disturbing factors of the latter were brought into the former and yet they also provided an opportunity for the alliance system to assert its prerogatives in the order of sexuality. Then a pressing demand emanated from the family: a plea for help in reconciling these unfortunate conflicts between sexuality and alliance; and, caught in the grip of this deployment of sexuality which had invested it from without, contributing to its solidification into its modern form, the family broadcast the long complaint of its sexual suffering to doctors, educators, psychiatrists, priests, and pastors, to all the 'experts' who would listen. It was as if it had suddenly discovered the dreadful secret of what had always been hinted at and inculcated in it: the family, the keystone of alliance, was the germ of all the misfortunes of sex. And lo and behold, from the mid-nineteenth century onward, the family engaged in searching out the slightest traces of sexuality in its midst, wrenching from itself the most difficult confessions, soliciting an audience with everyone who might know something about the matter, and opening itself unreservedly to endless examination. The family was the crystal in the deployment of sexuality: it seemed to be the source of a sexuality which it actually only reflected and diffracted. By virtue of its permeability, and through that process of reflections to the outside, it became one of the most valuable tactical components of the deployment. [. . .]

Note

1   Molière's *Tartuffe* and Jakob Michael Lenz's *Tutor*, separated by more than a century, both depict the interference of the deployment of sexuality in the family organization, apropos of spiritual direction in *Tartuffe* and education in *The Tutor*.

11

Critically queer **Judith Butler**

Performative power

Eve Sedgwick's recent reflections on queer performativity ask us not only to consider how a certain theory of speech acts applies to queer practices, but how it is that 'queering' persists as a defining moment of performativity.[1] The centrality of the marriage ceremony in J.L. Austin's examples of performativity suggests that the heterosexualization of the social bond is the paradigmatic form for those speech acts which bring about what they name. 'I pronounce you . . .' puts into effect the relation that it names. But from where and when does such a performative draw its force, and what happens to the performative when its purpose is precisely to undo the presumptive force of the heterosexual ceremonial?

Performative acts are forms of authoritative speech: most performatives, for instance, are statements that, in the uttering, also perform a certain action and exercise a binding power.[2] Implicated in a network of authorization and punishment, performatives tend to include legal sentences, baptisms, inaugurations, declarations of ownership, statements which not only perform an action, but confer a binding power on the action performed. If the power of discourse to produce that which it names is linked with the question of performativity, then the performative is one domain in which power acts *as* discourse.

Importantly, however, there is no power, construed as a subject, that acts, but only, to repeat an earlier phrase, a reiterated acting that *is* power in its persistence and instability. This is less an 'act,' singular and deliberate, than a nexus of power and discourse that repeats or mimes the discursive gestures of power. Hence, the judge who authorizes and installs the situation he names invariably *cites* the law that he applies, and it is the

This chapter is taken from *Bodies that Matter* (London, Routledge, 1993), pp. 224–42.

power of this citation that gives the performative its binding or conferring power. And though it may appear that the binding power of his words is derived from the force of his will or from a prior authority, the opposite is more true: it is *through* the citation of the law that the figure of the judge's 'will' is produced and that the 'priority' of textual authority is established.[3] Indeed, it is through the invocation of convention that the speech act of the judge derives its binding power; that binding power is to be found neither in the subject of the judge nor in his will, but in the citational legacy by which a contemporary 'act' emerges in the context of a chain of binding conventions.

Where there is an 'I' who utters or speaks and thereby produces an effect in discourse, there is first a discourse which precedes and enables that 'I' and forms in language the constraining trajectory of its will. Thus there is no 'I' who stands *behind* discourse and executes its volition or will *through* discourse. On the contrary, the 'I' only comes into being through being called, named, interpellated, to use the Althusserian term, and this discursive constitution takes place prior to the 'I'; it is the transitive invocation of the 'I.' Indeed, I can only say 'I' to the extent that I have first been addressed, and that address has mobilized my place in speech; paradoxically, the discursive condition of social recognition *precedes and conditions* the formation of the subject: recognition is not conferred on a subject, but forms that subject. Further, the impossibility of a full recognition, that is, of ever fully inhabiting the name by which one's social identity is inaugurated and mobilized, implies the instability and incompleteness of subject-formation. The 'I' is thus a citation of the place of the 'I' in speech, where that place has a certain priority and anonymity with respect to the life it animates: it is the historically revisable possibility of a name that precedes and exceeds me, but without which I cannot speak.

[. . .]

Gender performativity and drag

How, if at all, is the notion of discursive resignification linked to the notion of gender parody or impersonation? First, what is meant by understanding gender as an impersonation? Does this mean that one puts on a mask or persona, that there is a 'one' who precedes that 'putting on,' who is something other than its gender from the start? Or does this miming, this impersonating precede and form the 'one,' operating as its formative precondition rather than its dispensable artifice?

The construal of gender-as-drag according to the first model appears to be the effect of a number of circumstances. One of them I brought on myself by citing drag as an example of performativity, a move that was taken then, by some, to be *exemplary* of performativity. If drag is performative, that does not mean that all performativity is to be understood as drag. The publication of *Gender Trouble* coincided with a number of publications that did assert that 'clothes make the woman,' but I never did think that gender was like clothes, or that clothes make the woman. Added to these, however, are the political needs of an emergent queer movement in which the publicization of theatrical agency has become quite central.[4]

The practice by which gendering occurs, the embodying of norms, is a compulsory practice, a forcible production, but not for that reason fully determining. To the extent that gender is an assignment, it is an assignment which is never quite carried out according to expectation, whose addressee never quite inhabits the ideal s/he is compelled to approximate. Moreover, this embodying is a repeated process. And one might construe repetition as precisely that which *undermines* the conceit of voluntarist mastery designated by the subject in language.

[. . .] [D]rag is not unproblematically subversive. It serves a subversive function to the extent that it reflects the mundane impersonations by which heterosexually ideal genders are performed and naturalized and undermines their power by virtue of effecting that exposure. But there is no guarantee that exposing the naturalized status of heterosexuality will lead to its subversion. Heterosexuality can augment its hegemony *through* its denaturalization, as when we see denaturalizing parodies that reidealize heterosexual norms *without* calling them into question.

On other occasions, though, the transferability of a gender ideal or gender norm calls into question the abjecting power that it sustains. For an occupation or reterritorialization of a term that has been used to abject a population can become the site of resistance, the possibility of an enabling social and political resignification. And this has happened to a certain extent with the notion of 'queer.' The contemporary redeployment enacts a prohibition and a degradation against itself, spawning a different order of values, a political affirmation from and through the very term which in a prior usage had as its final aim the eradication of precisely such an affirmation.

It may seem, however, that there is a difference between the embodying or performing of gender norms and the performative use of discourse. Are these two different senses of 'performativity,' or do they converge as modes of citationality in which the compulsory character of certain social imperatives becomes subject to a more promising deregulation? Gender norms operate by requiring the embodiment of certain ideals of femininity and masculinity, ones that are almost always related to the idealization of the heterosexual bond. In this sense, the initiatory performative, 'It's a girl!' anticipates the eventual arrival of the sanction, 'I pronounce you man and wife.' Hence, also, the peculiar pleasure of the cartoon strip in which the infant is first interpellated into discourse with 'It's a lesbian!' Far from an essentialist joke, the queer appropriation of the performative mimes and exposes both the binding power of the heterosexualizing law *and its expropriability.*

To the extent that the naming of the 'girl' is transitive, that is, initiates the process by which a certain 'girling' is compelled, the term or, rather, its symbolic power, governs the formation of a corporeally enacted femininity that never fully approximates the norm. This is a 'girl,' however, who is compelled to 'cite' the norm in order to qualify and remain a viable subject. Femininity is thus not the product of a choice, but the forcible citation of a norm, one whose complex historicity is indissociable from relations of discipline, regulation, punishment. Indeed, there is no 'one' who takes on a gender norm. On the contrary, this citation of the gender norm is necessary in order to qualify as a 'one,' to become viable as a 'one,' where subject-formation is dependent on the prior operation of legitimating gender norms.

It is in terms of a norm that compels a certain 'citation' in order for a viable subject to be produced that the notion of gender performativity calls to be rethought. And precisely in relation to such a compulsory citationality that the theatricality of gender is also to be explained. Theatricality need not be conflated with self-display or self-creation. Within queer politics, indeed, within the very signification that is 'queer,' we read a resignifying practice in which the desanctioning power of the name 'queer' is reversed to sanction a contestation of the terms of sexual legitimacy. Paradoxically, but also with great promise, the subject who is 'queered' into public discourse through homophobic interpellations of various kinds *takes up* or *cites* that very term as the discursive basis for an opposition. This kind of citation will emerge as *theatrical* to the extent that it *mimes and renders hyperbolic* the discursive convention that it also *reverses*. The hyperbolic gesture is crucial to the exposure of the homophobic 'law' that can no longer control the terms of its own abjecting strategies.

[. . .]

Melancholia and the limits of performance

The critical potential of 'drag' centrally concerns a critique of a prevailing truth-regime of 'sex,' one that I take to be pervasively heterosexist: the distinction between the 'inside' truth of femininity, considered as psychic disposition or ego-core, and the 'outside' truth, considered as appearance or presentation, produces a contradictory formation of gender in which no fixed 'truth' can be established. Gender is neither a purely psychic truth, conceived as 'internal' and 'hidden,' nor is it reducible to a surface appearance; on the contrary, its undecidability is to be traced as the play *between* psyche and appearance (where the latter domain includes what appears *in words*). Further, this will be a 'play' regulated by heterosexist constraints though not, for that reason, fully reducible to them.

In no sense can it be concluded that the part of gender that is performed is therefore the 'truth' of gender; performance as bounded 'act' is distinguished from performativity insofar as the latter consists in a reiteration of norms which precede, constrain, and exceed the performer and in that sense cannot be taken as the fabrication of the performer's 'will' or 'choice'; further, what is 'performed' works to conceal, if not to disavow, what remains opaque, unconscious, unperformable. The reduction of performativity to performance would be a mistake.

The rejection of an expressive model of drag which holds that some interior truth is exteriorized in performance needs, however, to be referred to a psychoanalytic consideration on the relationship between how gender *appears* and what gender *signifies*. Psychoanalysis insists that the opacity of the unconscious sets limits to the exteriorization of the psyche. It also argues, rightly I think, that what is exteriorized or performed can only be understood through reference to what is barred from the signifier and from the domain of corporeal legibility.

How precisely do repudiated identifications, identifications that do not 'show,' circumscribe and materialize the identifications that do? Here it seems useful to rethink the notion of gender-as-drag in terms of the analysis of gender melancholia.[5] Given the iconographic figure of the melancholic drag queen, one might consider whether and how these terms work together. Here, one might ask also after the disavowal that occasions performance and that performance might be said to enact, where performance engages 'acting out' in the psychoanalytic sense.[6] If melancholia in Freud's sense is the effect of an ungrieved loss (a sustaining of the lost object/Other as a psychic figure with the consequence of heightened identification with that Other, self-beratement, and the acting out of unresolved anger and love),[7] it may be that performance, understood as 'acting out,' is significantly related to the problem of unacknowledged loss. Where there is an ungrieved loss in drag performance (and I am sure that such a generalization cannot be universalized), perhaps it is a loss that is refused and incorporated in the performed identification, one that reiterates a gendered idealization and its radical uninhabitability. This is neither a territorialization of the feminine by the masculine nor an 'envy' of the masculine by the feminine, nor a sign of the essential plasticity of gender. What it does suggest is that gender performance allegorizes a loss it cannot grieve, allegorizes the incorporative fantasy of melancholia whereby an object is phantasmatically taken in or on as a way of refusing to let it go.

The analysis above is a risky one because it suggests that for a 'man' performing femininity or for a 'woman' performing masculinity (the latter is always, in effect, to perform a little less, given that femininity is often cast as the spectacular gender) there is an attachment to and a loss and refusal of the figure of femininity by the man, or the figure of masculinity by the woman. Thus, it is important to underscore that drag is an effort to negotiate cross-gendered identification, but that cross-gendered identification is not the exemplary paradigm for thinking about homosexuality, although it may be one. In this sense, drag allegorizes some set of melancholic incorporative fantasies that stabilize *gender*. Not only are a vast number of drag performers straight, but it would be a mistake to think that homosexuality is best explained through the performativity that is drag. What does seem useful in this analysis, however, is that drag exposes or allegorizes the mundane psychic and performative practices by which heterosexualized genders form themselves through the renunciation of the *possibility* of homosexuality, a foreclosure that produces a field of heterosexual objects at the same time that it produces a domain of those whom it would be impossible to love. Drag thus allegorizes *heterosexual melancholy*, the melancholy by which a masculine gender is formed from the refusal to grieve the masculine as a possibility of love; a feminine gender is formed (taken on, assumed) through the incorporative fantasy by which the feminine is excluded as a possible object of love, an exclusion never grieved, but 'preserved' through the heightening of feminine identification itself. In this sense, the 'truest' lesbian melancholic is the strictly straight woman, and the 'truest' gay male melancholic is the strictly straight man.

What drag exposes, however, is the 'normal' constitution of gender presentation in which the gender performed is in many ways constituted by a set of disavowed attachments or identifications that constitute a different domain of the 'unperformable.' Indeed, it may well be that what constitutes the *sexually* unperformable is performed instead as *gender identification*.[8] To the extent that homosexual attachments remain unacknowledged within normative heterosexuality, they are not merely constituted as desires that emerge and subsequently become prohibited. Rather, these are desires that are proscribed from the start. And when they do emerge on the far side of the censor, they may well carry that mark of impossibility with them, performing, as it were, as the impossible within the possible. As such, they will not be attachments that can be openly grieved. This is, then, less *the refusal* to grieve (a formulation that accents the choice involved) than a preemption of grief performed by the absence of cultural conventions for avowing the loss of homosexual love. And it is this absence that produces a culture of heterosexual melancholy, one that can be read in the hyperbolic identifications by which mundane heterosexual masculinity and femininity confirm themselves. The straight man *becomes* (mimes, cites, appropriates, assumes the status of) the man he 'never' loved and 'never' grieved; the straight woman *becomes* the woman she 'never' loved and 'never' grieved. It is in this sense, then, that what is most apparently performed as gender is the sign and symptom of a pervasive disavowal.

[. . .]

Gendered and sexual performativity

How then does one link the trope by which discourse is described as 'performing' and that theatrical sense of performance in which the hyperbolic status of gender norms seems central? What is 'performed' in drag is, of course, *the sign* of gender, a sign that is not the same as the body that it figures, but that cannot be read without it. The sign, understood as a gender imperative – 'girl!' – reads less as an assignment than as a command and, as such, produces its own insubordinations. The hyperbolic conformity to the command can reveal the hyperbolic status of the norm itself, indeed, can become the cultural sign by which that cultural imperative might become legible. Insofar as heterosexual gender norms produce inapproximable ideals, heterosexuality can be said to operate through the regulated production of hyperbolic versions of 'man' and 'woman.' These are for the most part compulsory performances, ones which none of us choose, but which each of us is forced to negotiate. I write 'forced to negotiate' because the compulsory character of these norms does not always make them efficacious. Such norms are continually haunted by their own inefficacy; hence, the anxiously repeated effort to install and augment their jurisdiction.

The resignification of norms is thus a function of their *inefficacy*, and so the question of subversion, of *working the weakness in the norm*, becomes a matter of inhabiting the practices of its rearticulation. The critical promise of drag does not have to do with the proliferation of genders, as if a sheer increase in numbers would do the job, but rather with the exposure or the failure of heterosexual regimes ever fully to legislate or contain their own ideals. Hence, it is not that drag *opposes* heterosexuality, or that the proliferation of drag will bring down heterosexuality; on the contrary, drag tends to be the allegorization of heterosexuality and its constitutive melancholia. As an allegory that works through the hyperbolic, drag brings into relief what is, after all, determined only in relation to the hyperbolic: the understated, taken-for-granted quality of heterosexual performativity. At its best, then, drag can be read for the way in which hyperbolic norms are dissimulated as the heterosexual mundane. At the same time these same norms, taken not as commands to be obeyed, but as imperatives to be 'cited,' twisted, queered, brought into relief as heterosexual imperatives, are not, for that reason, necessarily subverted in the process.

It is important to emphasize that although heterosexuality operates in part through the stabilization of gender norms, gender designates a dense site of significations that contain and exceed the heterosexual matrix. Although forms of sexuality do not unilaterally determine gender, a non-causal and non-reductive connection between sexuality and gender is nevertheless crucial to maintain. Precisely because homophobia often operates through the attribution of a damaged, failed, or otherwise abject gender to homosexuals, that is, calling gay men 'feminine' or calling lesbians 'masculine,' and because the homophobic terror over performing homosexual acts, where it exists, is often also a terror over losing proper gender ('no longer being a real or proper man' or 'no longer being a real or proper woman'), it seems crucial to retain a theoretical apparatus that will account for how sexuality is regulated through the policing and the shaming of gender.

[. . .]

In psychoanalytic terms, the relation between gender and sexuality is in part negotiated through the question of the relationship between identification and desire. And here it becomes clear why refusing to draw lines of causal implication between these two domains is as important as keeping open an investigation of their complex interimplication. For, if to identify as a woman is not necessarily to desire a man, and if to desire a woman does not necessarily signal the constituting presence of a masculine identification, whatever that is, then the heterosexual matrix proves to be an *imaginary* logic that insistently issues forth its own unmanageability. The heterosexual logic that requires that identification and desire be mutually exclusive is one of the most reductive of heterosexism's psychological instruments: if one identifies *as* a given gender, one must desire a different gender. On the one hand, there is no one femininity with which to identify, which is to say that femininity might itself offer an array of identificatory sites, as the proliferation of lesbian femme possibilities attests. On the other hand, it is hardly descriptive of the complex dynamic exchanges of lesbian and gay relationships to presume that homosexual identifications 'mirror' or replicate one another. The vocabulary for describing the difficult play, crossing, and destabilization of masculine and feminine identifications within homosexuality has only begun to emerge within theoretical language: the non-academic language historically embedded in gay communities is here much more instructive. The thought of sexual difference *within* homosexuality has yet to be theorized in its complexity.

For one deciding issue will be whether social strategies of regulation, abjection, and normalization will not continue to relink gender and sexuality such that the oppositional analysis will continue to be under pressure to theorize their interrelations. This will not be the same as reducing gender to prevailing forms of sexual relations such that one 'is' the effect of the sexual position one is said to occupy. Resisting such a reduction, it ought to be possible to assert a set of non-causal and non-reductive relations between gender and sexuality, not only to link feminism and queer theory, as one might link two separate enterprises, but to establish their constitutive interrelationship. Similarly, the inquiry into both homosexuality and gender will need to cede the priority of *both* terms in the service of a more complex mapping of power that interrogates the formation of each in specified racial regimes and geopolitical spatializations. And the task, of course, does not stop here, for no one term can serve as foundational, and the success of any given analysis that centers on any one term may well be the marking of its own limitations as an exclusive point of departure.

The goal of this analysis, then, cannot be pure subversion, as if an undermining were enough to establish and direct political struggle. Rather than denaturalization or proliferation, it seems that the question for thinking discourse and power in terms of the future has several paths to follow: how to think power as resignification together with power as the convergence or interarticulation of relations of regulation, domination, constitution? How to know what might qualify as an affirmative resignification – with all the weight and difficulty of that labor – and how to run the risk of reinstalling the abject at the site of its opposition? But how, also, to rethink the terms that establish and sustain bodies that matter?

[. . .]

Performativity describes this relation of being implicated in that which one opposes, this turning of power against itself to produce alternative modalities of power, to establish a kind of political contestation that is not a 'pure' opposition, a 'transcendence' of contemporary relations of power, but a difficult labor of forging a future from resources inevitably impure.

How will we know the difference between the power we promote and the power we oppose? Is it, one might rejoin, a matter of 'knowing?' For one is, as it were, in power even as one opposes it, formed by it as one reworks it, and it is this simultaneity that is at once the condition of our partiality, the measure of our political unknowingness, and also the condition of action itself. The incalculable effects of action are as much a part of their subversive promise as those that we plan in advance.

The effects of performatives, understood as discursive productions, do not conclude at the terminus of a given statement or utterance, the passing of legislation, the announcement of a birth. The reach of their signifiability cannot be controlled by the one who utters or writes, since such productions are not owned by the one who utters them. They continue to signify in spite of their authors, and sometimes against their authors' most precious intentions.

It is one of the ambivalent implications of the decentering of the subject to have one's writing be the site of a necessary and inevitable expropriation. But this yielding of ownership over what one writes has an important set of political corollaries, for the taking up, reforming, deforming of one's words does open up a difficult future terrain of community, one in which the hope of ever fully recognizing oneself in the terms by which one signifies is sure to be disappointed. This not owning of one's words is there from the start, however, since speaking is always in some ways the speaking of a stranger through and as oneself, the melancholic reiteration of a language that one never chose, that one does not find as an instrument to be used, but that one is, as it were, used by, expropriated in, as the unstable and continuing condition of the 'one' and the 'we,' the ambivalent condition of the power that binds.

Acknowledgements

This [chapter] was originally published in *GLQ*, vol. 1, no. 1 (Fall 1993). I thank David Halperin and Carolyn Dinshaw for their useful editorial suggestions. This chapter is an altered version of that essay.

Notes

1   See Eve Kosofsky Sedgwick's 'Queer performativity' *GLQ*, 1(1) (spring 1993). I am indebted to her provocative work and for prompting me to rethink the relationship between gender and performativity.

2   It is, of course, never quite right to say that language or discourse 'performs', since it is unclear that language is primarily constituted as a set of 'acts'. After all, this description of an 'act' cannot be sustained through the trope that established the act as a singular event, for the act will turn out to refer to prior acts and to a reiteration of 'acts' that is perhaps more suitably described as a citational chain. Paul de Man points out in 'Rhetoric of persuasion' that the distinction between constative and performative utterances is confounded by the fictional status of both: 'the possibility for language to perform is just as fictional as the possibility for language to assert' (p. 129). Further, he writes, 'considered as persuasion, rhetoric is performative, but considered as a system of tropes, it deconstructs its own performance'; *Allegories of Reading* (New Haven, CT, Yale University Press, 1987), pp. 130–1.

3   In what follows, that set of performatives that Austin terms illocutionary will be at issue, those in which the binding power of the act *appears* to be derived from the intention or will of the speaker. In 'Signature, event, context', Derrida argues that the binding power that Austin attributes to the speaker's intention in such illocutionary acts is more properly attributable to a citational force of the speaking, the iterability that establishes the authority of the speech act, but which establishes the non-singular character of that act. In this sense, every 'act' is an echo or citational chain, and it is its citationality that constitutes its performative force (in, Margins of Philosophy, Trans. Alan Bass. Chicago, IL: University of Chicago Press).

4   Theatricality is not for that reason fully intentional, but I might have made that reading possible through my reference to gender as 'intentional and non-referential' in 'Performative acts and gender constitution', an essay published in Sue-Ellen Case (ed.), *Performing Feminisms* (Baltimore, MD, Johns Hopkins University, 1991), pp. 270–82. I use the term 'intentional' in a specifically phenomenological sense. 'Intentionality' within phenomenology does not mean voluntary or deliberate, but is, rather, a way of characterizing consciousness (or language) as *having an object*, more specifically, as directed toward an object which may or may not exist. In this sense, an act of consciousness may intend (posit, constitute, apprehend) an *imaginary* object. Gender, in its ideality, might be construed as an intentional object, an ideal which is constituted but which does not exist. In this sense, gender would be like 'the feminine' as it is discussed as an impossibility by Drucilla Cornell in *Beyond Accommodation* (New York, Routledge, 1992).

5   Judith Butler, *Gender Trouble* (London, Routledge, 1990), pp. 57–65. See also my 'Melancholy genders, refused identifications', in *Psychoanalytic Dialogues* (forthcoming).

6   I thank Laura Mulvey for asking me to consider the relation between performativity and disavowal, and Wendy Brown for encouraging me to think about the relation between melancholia and drag and for asking whether the denaturalization of gender norms is the same as their subversion. I also thank Mandy Merck for numerous enlightening questions that led to these speculations, including the suggestion that if disavowal conditions performativity, then perhaps gender itself might be understood on the model of the fetish.

7   See 'Freud and the melancholia of gender', in Butler, *Gender Trouble*.

8   This is not to suggest that an exclusionary matrix rigorously distinguishes between how one identifies and how one desires; it is quite possible to have overlapping identification and desire in heterosexual or homosexual exchange, or in a bisexual history of sexual practice. Further, 'masculinity' and 'femininity' do not exhaust the terms for either eroticized identification or desire.

PSYCHOANALYSIS AND PSYCHOSOCIAL RELATIONS

Introduction
Jessica Evans

Part II presents alternative psychoanalytic accounts to those dominated by the concept of 'the subject in language' which have become established in cultural studies and cultural theory and were represented in Part I of the Reader. It seeks to establish the grounds on which psychoanalysis provides particular insights of its own, and it does this by disentangling psychoanalysis from its subordination to linguistic theory. Furthermore, the readings represent another tradition of thinking within psychoanalysis: that of the Kleinian and object-relations schools of thought which have characterized the British clinical scene since the Second World War. A number of readings also allow us to confront the spread of a therapeutic ethos as an 'abstract system' throughout contemporary cultural life, as well as the relationship of this phenomenon to the traditional psychoanalytic canon (see Chapters 20 and 21). However, the selections in this part remain confined to those who speak as psychoanalytic practitioners or otherwise as promulgators of psychoanalysis as a method of apprehending unconscious processes.

In contrast to those in Part III, the readings in this part adhere to a perspective which would oppose post-Foucauldian genealogical interpreters of psychoanalysis who seek to historicize the unconscious and in so doing regard it as an 'invented' category which creates a certain kind of subject – one who has the capacity for self-knowledge; one who is instructed to find the truth of him or herself within his or her own past (Foucault, 1981; Rose, 1989). This governmental argument, that psychoanalysis is an instrument for making individuals recognize themselves in certain ways and thus be made amenable for new forms of self-management, is not directly addressed by the readings, for quite clearly they were not written with this task in mind. But it is a debate which should open up as a consequence of juxtaposing these two groups of readings (see *the General introduction*).

The aim of these readings is to pose some questions about the conception of the human material upon which different psychoanalytic models are based. As was stated in the General introduction, clinical psychoanalysis may be regarded as necessarily encompassing a 'thick' rather than a 'thin' conception of this human material (see Cousins and Hussain, 1984). One way of explaining this is to say that, almost by definition, psychoanalysis involves the observation, analysis and treatment of an individual or a group, understood as an entity which has evolved over time and has a structural depth underlying appearances. It could further be argued that there are 'thicker' and 'thinner' conceptions of the human person *within* different psychoanalytic schools, and that the Kleinian and object-relations psychoanalytic schools have an even thicker conception of the human person than the post-structuralist theories represented in Part I. For example, Kleinian psychoanalysis – as represented by our first reading by Melanie Klein (Chapter 12) – presents strong arguments for a conception of an 'inner world' which acknowledges the necessity of conflicting fantasies born out of the anxieties inherent in the intense intimacies of early dependency and love. Around Kleinian and object-relations theory has grown up a view that the inner world has its own complex space such that individuals unconsciously use aspects of the external world to represent aspects of their own internal world. These 'internal objects' (mental concepts or representations of others that are not identical with the qualities of *real* others) are allowed a relative autonomy; they can be destructive, or creative – destructive when splitting and projection overwhelm the capacity to distinguish between the different realities of the internal and external worlds. For some writers (Craib, 1998: 9), it is this psychodynamic view that provides a necessary corrective to the 'normotic' and overly cognitive assumptions of the postmodern or post-structuralist or even just plain sociological theorist for whom inner life is an effect of outer life and does not in itself generate anything new: as if we do not have any experience of our own. Indeed, one central aim of a psychodynamic psychotherapy or psychoanalytic treatment could be said to be to *enlarge* the inner world of the patient and at the same time to help the patient recognize its boundaries (Craib, 1998: 169). A key element in the recognition of a boundary is for the patient to shift from a position in which the nature of inner reality is such that it is little affected by subsequent changes or opportunities in the external world to a situation in which the present can be seen and used creatively for itself – as separate and different from the past world (see Casement, 1985: 125–36). So another fruitful debate that should emerge for readers is provided by the contrast between the readings in this part and the other parts of the book, where there are presented (very different kinds of) arguments for, in effect, 'thinning' down the boundaries between inner and outer worlds.

As Michael Rustin (1995) has indicated, the difference in settings of Lacanian-derived theories and Kleinian and object-relations approaches illuminates a divergence in the wider political ethos of each form of psychoanalysis. In Britain, the reception and defence of Lacanian theory, travelling to the UK as a central component of post-1960s French philosophy, have been found in the mainly non-analytic community of academic publications and university departments. Lacan's theory is famously known for adhering to the anti-naturalistic in its refusal of a model of psychic health, associating positive terms with authoritarian closure, and seeking to destabilize the seeming fixity of the subject's place in the symbolic order. In contrast, the Kleinian and object-relations traditions of psychoanalytic thought have their main base in the clinical work of public mental health services, the voluntary sector and private psychotherapeutic practice. In this sense they have forged, though certainly not always easily, a certain identification with the social democratic institutions of the post-war welfare state (see Riley, 1983; Rustin, 1991, 1995; Rose, 1989). None the less, it would be incorrect to say that the Kleinian perspective is more normative than Lacanian theory, and it certainly pays no less attention to 'negative' feelings. However, it can be said to be grounded by a more explicit conception of the difference between the healthy and the mature and the relatively unwell or pathological in the psychic life of individuals and institutions. Kleinian and post-Kleinian theory is distinctive in allowing, with the provision of containment and attention to transference and counter-transference, a movement in the internal and largely unconscious object relations of the individual so that some integration and maturity can be achieved.

The British psychoanalyst and paediatrician D.W. Winnicott noted that, in psychoanalytic terms, after the war, the English returned to the mother and the French returned to the father (see Skelton, 1994). Certainly Klein, Winnicott and other post-Kleinian psychoanalysts characteristically emphasize the pre-Oedipal life of the infant, and assert that unconscious fantasy and a differentiated self born of part-object relating is there from birth, necessarily preceding and in fact making possible the acquisition of language and symbolization. Klein's significant reform of Freudian theory lay in her concepts of the paranoid-schizoid and depressive positions, through which the differences between the self and the other in very early life are variously constructed. These are at first developmental phases but, more importantly, they are positions between which adults can oscillate in ordinary neurosis. Klein's play technique with young children showed that from very early on in the infant's life fantasies are experienced as localized somatic as well as mental phenomena, relating first to part-objects such as the life-giving mother's breast and proceeding to the parents as whole people. Generally, in its struggle to cope with good and bad experiences, the infant tries to retain good feelings and introject good objects, making them part of itself, whilst expelling bad objects and projecting bad feelings on to some outside object. The process of splitting involves the attempt to prevent the bad feeling or object from contaminating the good feeling or object so that objects are split, or the bad object split off and disowned. In her paper of 1946, 'Notes on some schizoid mechanisms' (Chapter 12), Klein describes the effects of this splitting of the ego and develops for the first time her concept of projective identification as part of schizoid mechanisms. In normal development, where the mother successfully contains the projected parts of the infant self, the child is able to work through the paranoic-schizoid position and achieve less paranoic, less projection-dominated object relating. In this, the depressive position, the infant's fragmented identification with part-objects transforms into a recognition or introjection of the (m)other as a whole and separate person; she is at one and the same time someone whom the baby is utterly dependent upon and one who has an independent existence. The depressive position is the realization that the (m)other is the source both of good and bad, allowing the child to remember and retain love for the good object even while hating it or feeling its absence – for example during weaning (referred to by Winnicott in Chapter 14, p. 158). One cannot underestimate the importance of this for how Kleinians understand psychic health: the anxieties of the depressive position are at the same time signs of nascent *moral* capacities – of ambivalence, mourning, dependency, responsibility for others, and guilt (see Segal, 1973).

Chapter 13, D.W. Winnicott's 'Mirror-role of mother and family in child development', is of interest in part because it allows us to grasp some of the central differences between a Lacanian and a 'British School' perspective. Critics of Lacan (Macey, 1995) have noted that his theory relies upon a curiously 'affectless' psychoanalysis, one in which the intense anxieties and conflicts – in short, sufferings – of the human subject take the back seat while the grand epic of the subject's entry into language and the symbolic is in the driving seat. Jane Flax has argued that it is indeed typical that Lacan's conception of the most important developmental moment of the infant's life should be constituted by a series of encounters between the infant and a reflecting surface, a mirror (Flax, 1990: 89–96; see Lacan, Chapter 4). The 'I' comes into being alone in Lacan's theory, as she puts it (1990: 93). The effects of 'language' upon the subject appear to have no dependence upon, nor do they interact with, the child's relations with actual others; this is in large part the crux of the difference between Lacan and Winnicott. For Winnicott's 'mirror' is not conceptualized as an illusory reflective object, but as the loving gaze of a person (who for Winnicott is normally the mother, but does not have to be) who, if all goes well, does not reflect back her own defences but recognizes and confirms what the baby is presenting to her. One can see how for Winnicott the child's relationship to the mother should, ideally, lead to a strengthening of the ego. However, for Lacanians the formation of the ego is a moment of primary narcissism based on idealization and deceit. Built from successive identifications it is a defence against persecutory feelings of disintegration. The reading also points to one important way in which Winnicott's ideas took a different direction from those of Klein. Whereas, for Klein, psychic states operate at the level of unconscious fantasy ('phantasy') and do not necessarily correspond to the external modes of parental care, for Winnicott it was unfeasible to refer to the psychic world of the young child without taking into account the growth-enabling quality of its immediate environment, i.e. the actual nature of its parenting. Our other selection from Winnicott's writings, 'Transitional objects and transitional phenomena' (Chapter 14), also taken from *Playing and Reality* (1971), shows his highly original investigation of the interstitial and illusory areas of childhood experience, represented by the 'transitional object'. Direct observation of children's play showed him the importance of these first 'not-me' possessions that become a central part of the depressive position: they are integrated into the child's early auto-erotic experiences and become objects for fantasizing, but they also act as a bridgehead for the child's emerging relationship with an environment beginning to be understood as separate from it, rather than merged with it. Here the child enters into the paradox of feeling that he or she has created and discovered the object at one and the same time. Winnicott's thinking in this reading is supported by his 1941 paper on the spatula game (Winnicott, 1975), as well as the 'squiggle' method he developed in the 1950s (Winnicott, 1989, and see Chapter 14, p. 160). He consistently argues that the more healthy relationship to the transitional object is one that is spontaneous, rather than compliant. If a child is hurried or directed, then this object does not acquire meaning invested in it by the infant and it feels as if creativity cannot originate from within him or her. Instead, it remains (or becomes) an alien object belonging to the world of the adults; if this experience is persistent enough, in later life creativity may be associated with fraudulence, or with envy of, or, alternatively, passive compliance with, later mentors or teachers. At the end of the extract, a case study serves to illustrate just how traumatic separations can effect a more pathological relationship to transitional objects. It is upon the basis of his ideas about the transitional object that Winnicott also developed his theories about the necessity for the psychoanalyst to demonstrate a non-intrusive availability (see Chapter 13, pp. 148–9 and Winnicott, 1971)

Isabel Menzies Lyth's 'Social systems as a defense against anxiety' (Chapter 15) is a famous piece of Kleinian organizational consultancy, first published in 1959: a case study of hospital nurses in a large teaching hospital. It offers extensive insight into the psychodynamics of an institution – how feeling-states, bits of experience and emotions are taken in, given out, and *moved around* by individual members of a social organization to the extent that individuals lose parts of themselves in that institution, which then becomes a projective system. The presenting symptom in this case derived from the fact that nurses were being trained at the same time as they were being expected to be *the* nursing staff of the hospital. Menzies Lyth's work uncovered pervasive defensive 'techniques' at work which operated as a collective defence against the inevitable anxieties of nursing work, that is, they encouraged the repression rather than the containment of these anxieties which would have helped nurses to develop a more fulfilling working experience. Although the social defence system in the hospital developed originally from the combination of each individual's need, it rapidly became fixed and rigid – something which each new intake of student nurses introjected. Menzies Lyth presents a particular view of group dynamics, namely that the group can be seen as a small-scale society in which there are better and worse modes of social organization that either contain and manage unconscious dynamics or encourage distress and anxiety.

Michael Rustin's paper of 1991, 'Psychoanalysis, racism and anti-racism' (Chapter 16), also written from a Kleinian perspective, concentrates on the inner world of the racist individual, but it also contains a provocative argument about what he regards as the problematic strategies of anti-racist campaigns and their likely effects. His work shows the advantage of a psychodynamic account: that it seems to explain some of the passion which is invested in racism and the primitive chain of associations it evokes. It is interesting to compare Rustin's reading with the extract forming Chapter 17, Frantz Fanon's 'The negro and psychopathology', taken from his *Black Skins, White Masks* (1956), a text which drives home the painful and destructive effects of racism on the personalities of its victims. Drawing from his own clinical experience as well as observations of cultural life, Fanon explains how the colonial subject comes to feel inadequate as a result of being immersed in a white world (e.g. the Antillean who has arrived in Paris). Although in his or her country of origin the black person has already internalized a value system which pictures Europeans as the pinnacle of civilized achievement (the 'final stage of his personality', p. 220), it is only upon arrival in France that he has to confront his new identity as a *negro*. Fanon identifies the specific mechanisms of projection on to the black man (in contrast to the Jewish person) as deriving from corporeal – mostly genital – fixations. His analysis is couched in Freudian terms: the negro is made to represent the repressed (and often incestuous) sexual desires of the white man, or, as in the case of the final case study, of the white woman.

The last four readings of Part II represent, in their different ways, a critical engagement with the cultural values of psychoanalysis itself as well as its relationship to more popular therapeutic practices. Chapter 18, 'The narcissistic personality of our time', is taken from Christopher Lasch's extensively discussed and criticized *The Culture of Narcissism* (1979). In this book, as in *The Minimal Self* (1984), Lasch put a distinctive but not entirely unprecedented case, especially for those familiar with the work of the Frankfurt School, that a certain narcissistic character disorder is becoming dominant in a contemporary American society steered both by the over-extension of marketization and commodification, and by the intrusion of welfare professionals into the private domain. Lasch's psychoanalytic contribution is, as evidenced in the extract in which he draws upon the work of American analyst Otto Kernberg, to consider at the individual level the costs of a culture which makes impossible lasting relationships, loyalty to institutions, stable employment, and trust in authority. For the narcissist, the external world is experienced as an extension of the self; intimacy, commitment and feelings of dependency cannot be tolerated; and a voracious sense of omnipotence and control along with a perpetual sense of dissatisfaction abound. Lasch's account, as an encyclopaedic survey of contemporary culture, only shows in metaphorical terms how individual pathology actually relates to wider social patterns; the actual and concrete mechanisms remain unexplained (see Rose, Chapter 24). At times, clinical categories and data tend to be used in an instrumental and impressionistic sense. None the less, his attempt to portray the feeling of narcissism as a seemingly unavoidable response to contemporary cultural values remains provocative. A number of more important criticisms of Lasch's work on narcissism have been made, most notably from feminist quarters (Barrett and McIntosh, 1982). The main target of these was Lasch's conservative tendency, following on from the earlier Frankfurt School theses of the 'fatherless family', to lament a golden age when paternal authority underpinned a strong and 'private' family that could provide the basis for a sense of responsibility and continuity in identity. In Chapter 19, an extract from her book *The Bonds of Love* (1988), Jessica Benjamin provides a feminist psychoanalytic challenge to those theorists, such as Lasch, who would posit a dichotomy between the father-orientated post-Oedipal superego of autonomy and self-restraint and the mother-dominated pre-Oedipal narcissist for whom separation and individuation has not been achieved (an argument Lasch later modified, see Lasch, 1984). Benjamin has developed a feminist object-relations theory that draws both upon the Frankfurt School's critiques of rationality as well as on the work of Winnicott and the British 'attachment' theorist John Bowlby. But it has also been strongly inflected by the North American feminists Dorothy Dinnerstein and Carol Gilligan and their studies of the effects of traditional gender-differentiated parenting on girls' and boys' intersubjective capacities for autonomy, dependency and empathy. 'The oedipal riddle' (Chapter 19) shows how existing hierarchical value systems and cultural symptoms – that mothers cannot represent to their children a model of separation and agency and that fathers cannot emotionally nurture their children for they are only possessors of the phallus – actually infuse the central postulate of Freudian psychoanalytic theory itself, the oedipal complex. Her contention is that the oedipal riddle involves a deep faultline between a mother of dependency and a father of liberation from the merging with the mother. The symbolic system as it currently still exists, she argues, 'locks into place the sense of the mother's dangerous but alluring power and the need for paternal defence against it' (p. 244). One of her proposals is that women will only be attributed an independent subjectivity when the internal object of the mother is based on a positive introjection of her, rather than on a defensive repudiation of her as the 'other' of dependency.

The last two readings present particular interpretations of contemporary post-analytic therapeutic developments. It can be argued that these have departed in a number of significant ways from the values and emphases of the classical psychoanalytic tradition.

In 'The trajectory of the self' (Chapter 20), Anthony Giddens takes a rather different view of the newer self-actualization therapies by putting them in the context of a wider argument, developed across a number of books (see Giddens, 1990), about the emergence of contemporary 'post-traditional' culture. External anchors and restraints supplied by others – rooted in ideas of obligation, duty and permanence – are now usurped by the 'reflexive' project of the self, he argues. A high premium is placed upon the self-constructing and protean self, a self that is what it makes of itself (p. 252) and with whom responsibility lies. Hence, in the realm of relationships to others, Giddens cites the emergence of the 'pure relationship', one that is to be based on the satisfactions it delivers in the here and now; one in which each person perpetually makes a cost–benefit assessment of all the gains and losses to the self in entering into or maintaining this or that relationship. Janette Rainwater's transformative therapy manual, *Self-therapy*, is treated not so much as a discursive entity but as a transparent measure of 'the way we are now'. A psychoanalyst might regard her text as narcissism incarnate in its illusion of self-sufficiency and denial of the limits of our power to manipulate the world. Ian Craib's 'What's happening to mourning?' (Chapter 21) presents a strong argument to the effect that altered social conditions of death and dying, particularly the specialization process, have subjected mourning and bereavement so that grief is effectively 'tamed'. Furthermore, the original insights of Freud and Klein into mourning have become effectively railroaded by the standardized methodology of the modern bereavement counsellor. Illness, dying and bereavement were once integrated, and there were ritualistic ways of making them publicly meaningful; in the past 200 years they have become increasingly segregated and made subjects of the health and psychotherapy professions – with their own programmatic practices. Craib questions the treatment aims of bereavement counselling, and asks if they represent a pathologization of grieving as an illness, given their emphasis on abstract guidelines to take patients through a predictable set of symptoms. From Craib's psychodynamic perspective, modern bereavement texts, rather like Rainwater's manual, have very little to do with any of the classical traditions of psychoanalytic thought, in their lack of acknowledgement of the often irrational and neurotic elements which will, it is argued, always be bound up with attachment to – and loss of – an object: guilt, obligation, anger and disappointment.

References

Barrett, M. and McIntosh, M. (1982) *The Anti-social Family*. London: Verso.

Benjamin, Jessica (1988) *The Bonds of Love: Psychoanalysis, Feminism and the Problem of Domination*. London: Virago.

Casement, Patrick (1985) *On Learning From the Patient*. London: Tavistock/Routledge.

Cousins, M. and Hussain, A. (1984) *Michel Foucault*. Basingstoke: Macmillan.

Craib, Ian (1998) *Experiencing Identity*. London: Sage.

Fanon, Frantz (1956) *Black Skins, White Masks*. London: Pluto Press.

Flax, Jane (1990) 'Lacan and Winnicott: splitting and regression in psychoanalytic theory', *Thinking in Fragments: Psychoanalysis, Feminism, and Postmodernism in the Contemporary West*. Berkeley, CA: University of California Press.

Foucault, Michel (1981) *The History of Sexuality*, volume 1. Harmondsworth: Penguin.

Giddens, A. (1990) *The Consequences of Modernity*. Cambridge: Polity Press.

Klein, Melanie (1986) [1935] 'The psychogenesis of manic-depressive states', in J. Mitchell (ed.), *The Selected Melanie Klein*. Harmondsworth: Penguin.

Lasch, Christopher (1979) *The Culture of Narcissism*. New York: W.W. Norton.

Lasch, Christopher (1984) *The Minimal Self: Psychic Survival in Troubled Times*. London: Picador.

Macey, David (1995) 'On the subject of Lacan', in A. Elliot and S. Frosh (eds), *Psychoanalysis in Contexts: Paths between Theory and Modern Culture*. London: Routledge.

Rainwater, Janette (1989) *Self-Therapy: a Guide to Becoming Your Own Therapist*. London: Crucible.

Riley, Denise (1983) *War in the Nursery: Theories of the Child and Mother*. London, Virago.

Rose, Nikolas (1989) *Governing the Soul*. London: Sage.

Rustin, Michael (1991) *The Good Society and the Inner World*. London: Verso.

Rustin, Michael (1995) 'Lacan, Klein and politics', in A. Elliot and S. Frosh (eds), *Psychoanalysis in Contexts: Paths between Theory and Modern Culture*. London: Routledge.

Segal, Hanna (1973) *Introduction to the Work of Melanie Klein*. London: Karnac Books/The Institute of Psychoanalysis.

Skelton, Ross (1994) 'Lacan for the feint-hearted', *The British Journal of Psychotherapy*, 10 (3) (spring). pp. 418–29.

Winnicott, D.W. (1964) *The Child, the Family, and the Outside World*. Harmondsworth: Penguin.

Winnicott, D.W. (1971) *Playing and Reality*. London: Tavistock Press.

Winnicott, D.W. (1975) 'The observation of infants in a set situation', in *Collected Papers: Through Paediatrics to Psycho-analysis*. London: Hogarth Press.

Winnicott, D.W. (1989) *Psycho-analytic Explorations*. London: Karnac Books.

12

Notes on some schizoid mechanisms   **Melanie Klein**

Introduction

The present [chapter][1] is concerned with the importance of early paranoid and schizoid anxieties and mechanisms. I have given much thought to this subject for a number of years, even before clarifying my views on the depressive processes in infancy. In the course of working out my concept of the infantile depressive position, however, the problems of the phase preceding it again forced themselves on my attention. I now wish to formulate some hypotheses at which I have arrived regarding the earlier anxieties and mechanisms.[2]

    [. . .]

At the outset it will be useful to summarize briefly the conclusions regarding the earliest phases of development which I have already put forward.[3]

In early infancy anxieties characteristic of psychosis arise which drive the ego to develop specific defence mechanisms. In this period the fixation points for all psychotic disorders are to be found. This hypothesis led some people to believe that I regarded all infants as psychotic: but I have already dealt sufficiently with this misunderstanding on other occasions. The psychotic anxieties, mechanisms and ego defences of infancy have a profound influence on development in all its aspects, including the development of the ego, superego and object relations.

This chapter, first published in 1946, is taken from *The Selected Melanie Klein*, ed. J. Mitchell (Harmondsworth, Penguin, 1986), pp. 176–200.

I have often expressed my view that object relations exist from the beginning of life, the first object being the mother's breast which to the child becomes split into a good (gratifying) and bad (frustrating) breast; this splitting results in a severance of love and hate. I have further suggested that the relation to the first object implies its introjection and projection, and thus from the beginning object relations are moulded by an interaction between introjection and projection, between internal and external objects and situations. These processes participate in the building up of the ego and superego and prepare the ground for the onset of the Oedipus complex in the second half of the first year.

From the beginning the destructive impulse is turned against the object and is first expressed in phantasied oral-sadistic attacks on the mother's breast, which soon develop into onslaughts on her body by all sadistic means. The persecutory fears arising from the infant's oral-sadistic impulses to rob the mother's body of its good contents, and from the anal-sadistic impulses to put his excrements into her (including the desire to enter her body in order to control her from within) are of great importance for the development of paranoia and schizophrenia.

I enumerated various typical defences of the early ego, such as the mechanisms of splitting the object and the impulses, idealization, denial of inner and outer reality and the stifling of emotions. I also mentioned various anxiety contents, including the fear of being poisoned and devoured. Most of these phenomena – prevalent in the first few months of life – are found in the later symptomatic picture of schizophrenia.

This early period (first described as the 'persecutory phase') I later termed 'paranoid position',[4] and held that it precedes the depressive position. If persecutory fears are very strong, and for this reason (among others) the infant cannot work through the paranoid-schizoid position, the working through of the depressive position is in turn impeded. This failure may lead to a regressive reinforcing of persecutory fears and strengthen the fixation points for severe psychoses (that is to say, the group of schizophrenias). Another outcome of serious difficulties arising during the period of the depressive position may be manic-depressive disorders in later life. I also concluded that in less severe disturbances of development the same factors strongly influence the choice of neurosis.

While I assumed that the outcome of the depressive position depends on the working through of the preceding phase, I nevertheless attributed to the depressive position a central role in the child's early development. For with the introjection of the object as a whole the infant's object relation alters fundamentally. The synthesis between the loved and hated aspects of the complete object gives rise to feelings of mourning and guilt which imply vital advances in the infant's emotional and intellectual life. This is also a crucial juncture for the choice of neurosis or psychosis. To all these conclusions I still adhere.

[. . .] I also differ from Fairbairn's view that 'the great problem of the schizoid individual is how to love without destroying by love, whereas the great problem of the depressive individual is how to love without destroying by hate'.[5] This conclusion is in line not only with his rejecting Freud's concept of primary instincts but also with his underrating the role which aggression and hatred play from the beginning of life. As a result of this approach, he does not give enough weight to the importance of early anxiety and conflict and their dynamic effects on development.

Certain problems of the early ego

[. . .] So far, we know little about the structure of the early ego. [. . .] I would [. . .] say that the early ego largely lacks cohesion, and a tendency towards integration alternates with a tendency towards disintegration, a falling into bits.[6] I believe that these fluctuations are characteristic of the first few months of life.

We are, I think, justified in assuming that some of the functions which we know from the later ego are there at the beginning. Prominent amongst these functions is that of dealing with anxiety. I hold that anxiety arises from the operation of the death instinct within the organism, is felt as fear of annihilation (death) and takes the form of fear of persecution. The fear of the destructive impulse seems to attach itself at once to an object – or rather it is experienced as the fear of an uncontrollable over-powering object. Other important sources of primary anxiety are the trauma of birth (separation anxiety) and frustration of bodily needs; and these experiences too are from the beginning felt as being caused by objects. Even if these objects are felt to be external, they become through introjection internal persecutors and thus reinforce the fear of the destructive impulse within.

The vital need to deal with anxiety forces the early ego to develop fundamental mechanisms and defences. The destructive impulse is partly projected outwards (deflection of the death instinct) and, I think, attaches itself to the first external object, the mother's breast. As Freud has pointed out, the remaining portion of the destructive impulse is to some extent bound by the libido within the organism. However, neither of these processes entirely fulfils its purpose, and therefore the anxiety of being destroyed from within remains active. It seems to me in keeping with the lack of cohesiveness, that under the pressure of this threat the ego tends to fall to pieces.[7] This falling to pieces appears to underlie states of disintegration in schizophrenics.

The question arises whether some active splitting processes within the ego may not occur even at a very early stage. As we assume, the early ego splits the object and the relation to it in an active way, and this may imply some active splitting of the ego itself. In any case, the result of splitting is a dispersal of the destructive impulse which is felt as the source of danger. I suggest that the primary anxiety of being annihilated by a destructive force within, with the ego's specific response of falling to pieces or splitting itself, may be extremely important in all schizophrenic processes.

Splitting processes in relation to the object

The destructive impulse projected outwards is first experienced as oral aggression. I believe that oral-sadistic impulses towards the mother's breast are active from the beginning of life, though with the onset of teething the cannibalistic impulses increase in strength – a factor stressed by Abraham.

In states of frustration and anxiety the oral-sadistic and cannibalistic desires are reinforced, and then the infant feels that he has taken in the nipple and the breast *in bits*. Therefore in addition to the divorce between a good and a bad breast in the young infant's phantasy, the frustrating breast – attacked in oral-sadistic phantasies – is felt to be in fragments; the gratifying breast, taken in under the dominance of the sucking libido, is felt to be complete. This first internal good object acts as a focal point in the ego. It counteracts the processes of splitting and dispersal, makes for cohesiveness and integration, and is instrumental in building up the ego.[8] The infant's feeling of having inside a good and complete breast may, however, be shaken by frustration and anxiety. As a result, the divorce between the good and bad breast may be difficult to maintain, and the infant may feel that the good breast too is in pieces.

I believe that the ego is incapable of splitting the object – internal and external – without a corresponding splitting taking place within the ego. Therefore the phantasies and feelings about the state of the internal object vitally influence the structure of the ego. The more sadism prevails in the process of incorporating the object, and the more the object is felt to be in pieces, the more the ego is in danger of being split in relation to the internalized object fragments.

The processes I have described are, of course, bound up with the infant's phantasy life; and the anxieties which stimulate the mechanism of splitting are also of a phantastic nature. It is in phantasy that the infant splits the object and the self, but the effect of this phantasy is a very real one, because it leads to feelings and relations (and later on, thought processes) being in fact cut off from one another.

Splitting in connection with projection and introjection

So far, I have dealt particularly with the mechanism of splitting as one of the earliest ego mechanisms and defences against anxiety. Introjection and projection are from the beginning of life also used in the service of this primary aim of the ego. Projection, as Freud described, originates from the deflection of the death instinct outwards and in my view it helps the ego to overcome anxiety by ridding it of danger and badness. Introjection of the good object is also used by the ego as a defence against anxiety.

Closely connected with projection and introjection are some other mechanisms. Here I am particularly concerned with the connection between splitting, idealization and denial. As regards splitting of the object, we have to remember that in states of gratification love feelings turn towards the gratifying breast, while in states of frustration hatred and persecutory anxiety attach themselves to the frustrating breast.

Idealization is bound up with the splitting of the object, for the good aspects of the breast are exaggerated as a safeguard against the fear of the persecuting breast. While idealization is thus the corollary of persecutory fear, it also springs from the power of the instinctual desires which aim at unlimited gratification and therefore create the picture of an inexhaustible and always bountiful breast – an ideal breast.

We find an instance of such a cleavage in infantile hallucinatory gratification. The main processes which come into play in idealization are also operative in hallucinatory gratification, namely, splitting of the object and denial both of frustration and of persecution. The frustrating and persecuting object is kept widely apart from the idealized object. However, the bad object is not only kept apart from the good one but its very existence is denied, as is the whole situation of frustration and the bad feelings (pain) to which frustration gives rise. This is bound up with denial of psychic reality. The denial of psychic reality becomes possible only through strong feelings of omnipotence – an essential characteristic of early mentality. Omnipotent denial of the existence of the bad object and of the painful situation is in the unconscious equal to annihilation by the destructive impulse. It is, however, not only a situation and an object that are denied and annihilated – *it is an object relation* which suffers this fate; and therefore a part of the ego, from which the feelings towards the object emanate, is denied and annihilated as well.

In hallucinatory gratification, therefore, two interrelated processes take place: the omnipotent conjuring up of the ideal object and situation, and the equally omnipotent annihilation of the bad persecutory object and the painful situation. These processes are based on splitting both the object and the ego.

In passing I would mention that in this early phase splitting, denial and omnipotence play a role similar to that of repression at a later stage of ego development. [. . .]

So far, in dealing with persecutory fear, I have singled out the oral element. However, while the oral libido still has the lead, libidinal and aggressive impulses and phantasies from other sources come to the fore and lead to a confluence of oral, urethral and anal desires, both libidinal and aggressive. Also the attacks on the mother's breast develop into attacks of a similar nature on her body, which comes to be felt as it were as an extension of the breast, even before the mother is conceived of as a complete person. The phantasied onslaughts on the mother follow two main lines: one is the predominantly oral impulse to suck dry, bite up, scoop out and rob the mother's body of its good contents. (I shall discuss the bearing of these impulses on the development of object relations in connection with introjection.) The other line of attack derives from the anal and urethral impulses and implies expelling dangerous substances (excrements) out of the self and into the mother. Together with these harmful excrements, expelled in hatred, split-off parts of the ego are also projected on to the mother or, as I would rather call it, *into* the mother.[9] These excrements and bad parts of the self are meant not only to injure but also to control and to take possession of the object. In so far as the mother comes to contain the bad parts of the self, she is not felt to be a separate individual but is felt to be *the* bad self.

Much of the hatred against parts of the self is now directed towards the mother. This leads to a particular form of identification which establishes the prototype of an aggressive object relation. I suggest for these processes the term 'projective identification'. When projection is mainly derived from the infant's impulse to harm or to control the mother,[10] he feels her to be a persecutor. In psychotic disorders this identification of an object with the hated parts of the self contributes to the intensity of the hatred directed against other people. As far as the ego is concerned the excessive splitting off and expelling into the outer world of part of itself considerably weaken it. For the aggressive component of feelings and of the personality is intimately bound up in the mind with power, potency, strength, knowledge and many other desired qualities.

It is, however, not only the bad parts of the self which are expelled and projected, but also good parts of the self. Excrements then have the significance of gifts; and parts of the ego which, together with excrements, are expelled and projected into the other person represent the good, i.e. the loving parts of the self. The identification based on this type of projection again vitally influences object relations. The projection of good feelings and good parts of the self into the mother is essential for the infant's ability to develop good object relations and to integrate his ego. However, if this projective process is carried out excessively, good parts of the personality are felt to be lost, and in this way the mother becomes the ego ideal; this process too results in weakening and impoverishing the ego. Very soon such processes extend to other people, and the result may be an over-strong dependence on these external representatives of one's own good parts. Another consequence is a fear that the capacity to love has been lost because the loved object is felt to be loved predominantly as a representative of the self.

The processes of splitting off parts of the self and projecting them into objects are thus of vital importance for normal development as well as for abnormal object relations.

The effect of introjection on object relations is equally important. The introjection of the good object, first of all the mother's breast, is a precondition for normal development. I have already described that it comes to form a focal point in the ego and makes for cohesiveness of the ego. One characteristic feature of the earliest relation to the good object – internal and external – is the tendency to idealize it. In states of frustration or increased anxiety, the infant is driven to take flight to his internal idealized object as a means of escaping from persecutors. From this mechanism various serious disturbances may result: when persecutory fear is too strong, the flight to the idealized object becomes excessive, and this severely hampers ego development and disturbs object relations. As a result the ego may be felt to be entirely subservient to and dependent on the internal object – only a shell for it. With an unassimilated idealized object there goes a feeling that the ego has no life and no value of its own.[11] I would suggest that the condition of flight to the unassimilated idealized object necessitates further splitting processes within the ego. For parts of the ego attempt to unite with the ideal object, while other parts strive to deal with the internal persecutors.

The various ways of splitting the ego and internal objects result in the feeling that the ego is in bits. This feeling amounts to a state of disintegration. In normal development, the states of disintegration which the infant experiences are transitory. Among other factors, gratification by the external good object[12] again and again helps to break through these schizoid states. The infant's capacity to overcome temporary schizoid states is in keeping with the strong elasticity and resilience of the infantile mind. If states of splitting and therefore of disintegration, which the ego is unable to overcome, occur too frequently and go on for too long, then in my view they must be regarded as a sign of schizophrenic illness in the infant, and some indications of such illness may already be seen in the first few months of life. In adult patients, states of depersonalization and of schizophrenic dissociation seem to be a regression to these infantile states of disintegration.

In my experience, excessive persecutory fears and schizoid mechanisms in early infancy may have a detrimental effect on intellectual development in its initial stages. Certain forms of mental deficiency would therefore have to be regarded as belonging to the group of schizophrenias. Accordingly, in considering mental deficiency in children at any age one should keep in mind the possibility of schizophrenic illness in early infancy.

I have so far described some effects of excessive introjection and projection on object relations. I am not attempting to investigate here in any detail the various factors which in some cases make for a predominance of introjective and in other cases for a predominance of projective processes. As regards normal personality, it may be said that the course of ego development and object relations depends on the degree to which an optimal balance between introjection and projection in the early stages of development can be achieved. This in turn has a bearing on the integration of the ego and the assimilation of internal objects. Even if the balance is disturbed and one or the other of these processes is excessive, there is some interaction between introjection and projection. For instance the projection of a predominantly hostile inner world which is ruled by persecutory fears leads to the introjection – in taking back – of a hostile external world; and vice versa, the introjection of a distorted and hostile external world reinforces the projection of a hostile inner world.

Another aspect of projective processes, as we have seen, concerns the forceful entry into the object and control of the object by parts of the self. As a consequence, introjection may then be felt as a forceful entry from the outside into the inside, in retribution for violent projection. This may lead to the fear that not only the body but also the mind is controlled by other people in a hostile way. As a result there may be a severe disturbance in introjecting good objects – a disturbance which would impede all ego functions as well as sexual development and might lead to an excessive withdrawal to the inner world. This withdrawal is, however, caused not only by the fear of introjecting a dangerous external world but also by the fear of internal persecutors and an ensuing flight to the idealized internal object.

I have referred to the weakening and impoverishment of the ego resulting from excessive splitting and projective identification. This weakened ego, however, becomes also incapable of assimilating its internal objects, and this leads to the feeling that it is ruled by them. Again, such a weakened ego feels incapable of taking back into itself the parts which it projected into the external world. These various disturbances in the interplay between projection and introjection, which imply excessive splitting of the ego, have a detrimental effect on the relation to the inner and outer world and seem to be at the root of some forms of schizophrenia.

Projective identification is the basis of many anxiety situations, of which I shall mention a few. The phantasy of forcefully entering the object gives rise to anxieties relating to the dangers threatening the subject from within the object. For instance, the impulses to control an object from within it stir up the fear of being controlled and persecuted inside it. By introjecting and reintrojecting the forcefully entered object, the subject's feelings of inner persecution are strongly reinforced; all the more since the reintrojected object is felt to contain the dangerous aspects of the self. The accumulation of anxieties of this nature, in which the ego is, as it were, caught between a variety of external and internal persecution-situations, is a basic element in paranoia.

I have previously described[13] the infant's phantasies of attacking and sadistically entering the mother's body as giving rise to various anxiety situations (particularly the fear of being imprisoned and persecuted within her) which are at the bottom of paranoia. I also showed that the fear of being imprisoned (and especially of the penis being attacked) inside the mother is an important factor in later disturbances of male potency (impotence) and also underlies claustrophobia.[14]

Schizoid object relations

To summarize now some of the disturbed object relations which are found in schizoid personalities: the violent splitting of the self and excessive projection have the effect that the person towards whom this process is directed is felt as a persecutor. Since the destructive and hated part of the self which is split off and projected is felt as a danger to the loved object and therefore gives rise to guilt, this process of projection in some ways also implies a deflection of guilt from the self on to the other person. Guilt has, however, not been done away with, and the deflected guilt is felt as an unconscious responsibility for the people who have become representatives of the aggressive part of the self.

Another typical feature of schizoid object relations is their narcissistic nature which derives from the infantile introjective and projective processes. For, as I suggested earlier, when the ego ideal is projected into another person, this person becomes predominantly loved and admired because he contains the good parts of the self. Similarly, the relation to another person on the basis of projecting bad parts of the self into him is of a narcissistic nature, because in this case as well the object strongly represents one part of the self. Both these types of a narcissistic relation to an object often show strong obsessional features. The impulse to control other people is, as we know, an essential element in obsessional neurosis. The need to control others can to some extent be explained by a deflected drive to control parts of the self. When these parts have been projected excessively into another person, they can only be controlled by controlling the other person. One root of obsessional mechanisms may thus be found in the particular identification which results from infantile projective processes. This connection may also throw some light on the obsessional element which so often enters into the tendency for reparation. For it is not only an object about whom guilt is experienced but also parts of the self which the subject is driven to repair or restore.

All these factors may lead to a compulsive tie to certain objects or – another outcome – to a shrinking from people in order to prevent both a destructive intrusion into them and the danger of retaliation by them. The fear of such dangers may show itself in various negative attitudes in object relations. For instance, one of my patients told me that he dislikes people who are too much influenced by him, for they seem to become too much like himself and therefore he gets tired of them.

Another characteristic of schizoid object relations is a marked artificiality and lack of spontaneity. Side by side with this goes a severe disturbance of the feeling of the self or, as I would put it, of the relation to the self. This relation, too, appears to be artificial. In other words psychic reality and the relation to external reality are equally disturbed.

The projection of split-off parts of the self into another person essentially influences object relations, emotional life and the personality as a whole. To illustrate this contention I will select as an instance two universal phenomena which are interlinked: the feeling of loneliness and fear of parting. We know that one source of the depressive feelings accompanying parting from people can be found in the fear of the destruction of the object by the aggressive impulses directed against it. But it is more specifically the splitting and projective processes which underlie this fear. If aggressive elements in relation to the object are predominant and strongly aroused by the frustration of parting, the individual feels that the split-off components of his self, projected into the object, control his object in an aggressive and destructive way. At the same time the internal object is felt to be in the same danger of destruction as the external one in whom one part of the self is felt to be left. The result is an excessive weakening of the ego, a feeling that there is nothing to sustain it, and a corresponding feeling of loneliness. While this description applies to neurotic individuals, I think that in some degree it is a general phenomenon.

One need hardly elaborate the fact that some other features of schizoid object relations, which I described earlier, can also be found in minor degrees and in a less striking form in normal people – for instance shyness, lack of spontaneity or, on the other hand, a particularly intense interest in people.

In similar ways normal disturbances in thought-processes link up with the developmental paranoid-schizoid position. For all of us are liable at times to a momentary impairment of logical thinking which amounts to thoughts and associations being cut off from one another and situations being split off from one another; in fact, the ego is temporarily split.

The depressive position in relation to the paranoid-schizoid position

I now wish to consider further steps in the infant's development. So far I have described the anxieties, mechanisms and defences which are characteristic of the first few months of life. With the introjection of the complete object in about the second quarter of the first year marked steps in integration are made. This implies important changes in the relation to objects. The loved and hated aspects of the mother are no longer felt to be so widely separated, and the result is an increased fear of loss, states akin to mourning and a strong feeling of guilt, because the aggressive impulses are felt to be directed against the loved object. The depressive position has come to the fore. The very experience of depressive feelings in turn has the effect of further integrating the ego, because it makes for an increased understanding of psychic reality and better perception of the external world, as well as for a greater synthesis between inner and external situations.

The drive to make reparation, which comes to the fore at this stage, can be regarded as a consequence of greater insight into psychic reality and of growing synthesis, for it shows a more realistic response to the feelings of grief, guilt and fear of loss resulting from the aggression against the loved object. Since the drive to repair or protect the injured object paves the way for more satisfactory object relations and sublimations, it in turn increases synthesis and contributes to the integration of the ego.

During the second half of the first year the infant makes some fundamental steps towards working through the depressive position. However, schizoid mechanisms still remain in force, though in a modified form and to a lesser degree, and early anxiety situations are again and again experienced in the process of modification. The working through of the persecutory and depressive positions extends over the first few years of childhood and plays an essential part in the infantile neurosis. In the course of this process, anxieties lose in strength; objects become both less idealized and less terrifying, and the ego becomes more unified. All this is interconnected with the growing perception of reality and adaptation to it.

If development during the paranoid-schizoid position has not proceeded normally and the infant cannot – for internal or external reasons – cope with the impact of depressive anxieties a vicious circle arises. For if persecutory fear, and correspondingly schizoid mechanisms, are too strong, the ego is not capable of working through the depressive position. This forces the ego to regress to the paranoid-schizoid position and reinforces the earlier persecutory fears and schizoid phenomena. Thus the basis is established for various forms of schizophrenia in later life; for when such a regression occurs, not only are the fixation points in the schizoid position reinforced, but there is a danger of greater states of disintegration setting in. Another outcome may be the strengthening of depressive features.

External experiences are, of course, of great importance in these developments. For instance, in the case of a patient who showed depressive and schizoid features, the analysis brought up with great vividness his early experiences in babyhood, to such an extent that in some sessions physical sensations in the throat or digestive organs occurred. The patient had been weaned suddenly at four months of age because his mother fell ill. In addition, he did not see his mother for four weeks. When she returned, she found the child greatly changed. He had been a lively baby, interested in his surroundings, and he seemed to have lost this interest. He had become apathetic. He had accepted the substitute food fairly easily and in fact never refused food. But he did not thrive on it any more, lost weight and had a good deal of digestive trouble. It was only at the end of the first year, when other food was introduced, that he again made good physical progress.

Much light was thrown in the analysis on the influence these experiences had on his whole development. His outlook and attitudes in adult life were based on the patterns established in this early stage. For instance, we found again and again a tendency to be influenced by other people in an unselective way – in fact to take in greedily whatever was offered – together with great distrust during the process of introjection. This process was constantly disturbed by anxieties from various sources, which also contributed to an increase of greed.

Taking the material of this analysis as a whole, I came to the conclusion that at the time when the sudden loss of the breast and of the mother occurred, the patient had already to some extent established a relation to a complete good object. He had no doubt already entered the depressive position but could not work through it successfully and the paranoid-schizoid position became regressively reinforced. This expressed itself in the 'apathy' which followed a period when the child had already shown a lively interest in his surroundings. The fact that he had reached the depressive position and had introjected a complete object showed in many ways in his personality. He had actually a strong capacity for love and a great longing for a good and complete object. A characteristic feature of his personality was the desire to love people and trust them, unconsciously to regain and build up again the good and complete breast which he had once possessed and lost.

Connection between schizoid and manic-depressive phenomena

Some fluctuations between the paranoid-schizoid and the depressive positions always occur and are part of normal development. No clear division between the two stages of development can therefore be drawn; moreover, modification is a gradual process and the phenomena of the two positions remain for some time to some extent intermingled and interacting. [. . .]

Some schizoid defences

It is generally agreed that schizoid patients are more difficult to analyse than manic-depressive types. Their withdrawn, unemotional attitude, the narcissistic elements in their object relations (to which I referred earlier), a kind of detached hostility which pervades the whole relation to the analyst create a very difficult type of resistance. I believe that it is largely the splitting processes which account for the patient's failure in contact with the analyst and for his lack of response to the analyst's interpretations. The patient himself feels estranged and far away, and this feeling corresponds to the analyst's impression that considerable parts of the patient's personality and of his emotions are not available. Patients with schizoid features may say: 'I hear what you are saying. You may be right, but it has no meaning for me.' Or again they say they feel they are not there. The expression 'no meaning' in such cases does not imply an active rejection of the interpretation but suggests that parts of the personality and of the emotions are split off. These patients can, therefore, not deal with the interpretation; they can neither accept it nor reject it.

[. . .]

The violent splitting off and destroying of one part of the personality under the pressure of anxiety and guilt is in my experience an important schizoid mechanism. To refer briefly to an [. . .] instance: a woman patient had dreamed that she had to deal with a wicked girl child who was determined to murder somebody. The patient tried to influence or control the child and to extort a confession from her which would have been to the child's benefit; but she was unsuccessful. I also entered into the dream and the patient felt that I might help her in dealing with the child. Then the patient strung up the child on a tree in order to frighten her and also prevent her from doing harm. When the patient was about to pull the rope and kill the child, she woke. During this part of the dream the analyst was also present but again remained inactive.

I shall give here only the essence of the conclusions I arrived at from the analysis of this dream. In the dream the patient's personality was split into two parts: the wicked and uncontrollable child on the one hand, and on the other hand the person who tried to influence and control her. The child, of course, stood also for various figures in the past, but in this context she mainly represented one part of the patient's self. Another conclusion was that the analyst was the person whom the child was going to murder; and my role in the dream was partly to prevent this murder from taking place. Killing the child – to which the patient had to resort – represented the annihilation of one part of her personality.

The question arises how the schizoid mechanism of annihilating part of the self connects with repression which, as we know, is directed against dangerous impulses. This, however, is a problem with which I cannot deal here.

[. . .] I have repeatedly found that advances in synthesis are brought about by interpretations of the specific causes for splitting. Such interpretations must deal in detail with the transference situation at that moment, including of course the connection with the past, and must contain a reference to the details of the anxiety situations which drive the ego to regress to schizoid mechanisms. The synthesis resulting from interpretations on these lines goes along with depression and anxieties of various kinds. Gradually such waves of depression – followed by greater integration – lead to a lessening of schizoid phenomena and also to fundamental changes in object relations. [. . .]

Notes

1   This chapter is the revised version of the original paper of 1946 published in the *International Journal of Psycho-Analysis*, vol. 27, pp. 99–110. This revised version was published in 1952, in *Developments in Psycho-Analysis*, eds. M. Klein and J. Riviere (London: Hogarth Press). In it she added the following footnotes and one new paragraph.

2   Before completing this [chapter] I discussed its main aspects with Paula Heimann and am much indebted to her for stimulating suggestions in working out and formulating a number of the concepts presented here.

3   Cf. my *Psycho-analysis of Children*, Collected Works, vol. 11, 1932, and 'A contribution to the psychogenesis of manic-depressive states' (1935), in *The Selected Melanie Klein*, ed. J. Mitchell (Harmondsworth, Penguin, 1986), ch. 6.

4   When this [chapter] was first published in 1946, I was using my term 'paranoid position' synonymously with W.R.D. Fairbairn's 'schizoid position'. On further deliberation I decided to combine Fairbairn's term with mine and throughout the present book [*Developments in Psycho-analysis*, 1952, in which this [chapter] was published] I am using the expression 'paranoid-schizoid position'.

5   Cf. W.R.D. Fairbairn, 'A revised psychopathology of the psychoses and psycho-neuroses', *International Journal of Psycho-Analysis*, 22, 1941. pp. 250–79.

6   The greater or lesser cohesiveness of the ego at the beginning of postnatal life should be considered in connection with the greater or lesser capacity of the ego to tolerate anxiety which, as I have previously contended (*The Psycho-analysis of Children*, partic.

p. 49), is a constitutional factor. Cf. D.W. Winnicott, 'Primitive emotional development (1945). In this paper Winnicott also described the pathological outcome of states of unintegration; for instance, the case of a woman patient who could not distinguish between her twin sister and herself.

7   Ferenczi in 'Notes and fragments', [written in 1930–2], in Sandor Ferenczi (1980), *Final Contributions to the Problems and Methods of Psycho-Analysis*, ed. Michael Balint, (New York: Brunner-Mazel) suggests that most likely every living organism reacts to unpleasant stimuli by fragmentation, which might be an expression of the death instinct. Possibly, complicated mechanisms (living organisms) are only kept as an entity through the impact of external conditions. When these conditions become unfavourable the organism falls to pieces.

8   D.W. Winnicott ('Primitive emotional development', in (1975) *Collected Papers: Through Paediatrics to Psycho-Analysis* (London, Hogarth Press)) referred to the same process from another angle: he described how integration and adaptation to reality depend essentially on the infant's experience of the mother's love and care.

9   The description of such primitive processes suffers from a great handicap, for these phantasies arise at a time when the infant has not yet begun to think in words. In this context, for instance, I am using the expression 'to project *into* another person' because this seems to me the only way of conveying the unconscious process I am trying to describe.

10 M.G. Evans, in a short unpublished communication (read to the British Psycho-Analytical Society, January 1946) gave some instances of patients in whom the following phenomena were marked: lack of sense of reality, a feeling of being divided and parts of the personality having entered the mother's body in order to rob and control her; as a consequence the mother and other people similarly attacked came to represent the patient. M.G. Evans related these processes to a very primitive stage of development.

11 Cf. 'A contribution to the problem of sublimation and its relation to the processes of internalization' (1942), *International Journal of Psycho-Analysis*, 23, 8–17, where Paula Heimann described a condition in which the internal objects act as foreign bodies embedded in the self. Whilst this is more obvious with regard to the bad objects, it is true even for the good ones, if the ego is compulsively subordinated to their preservation. When the ego serves its good internal objects excessively, they are felt as a source of danger to the self and come close to exerting a persecuting influence. Paula Heimann introduced the concept of the assimilation of the internal objects and applied it specifically to sublimation. As regards ego development, she pointed out that such assimilation is essential for the successful exercise of ego functions and for the achievement of independence.

12 Looked at in this light, the mother's love and understanding of the infant can be seen as the infant's greatest standby in overcoming states of disintegration and anxieties of a psychotic nature.

13 *Psycho-Analysis of Children*, ch. 8, esp. p. 131, and ch. 12, esp. p. 242.

14 Joan Riviere, in an unpublished paper 'Paranoid attitudes seen in everyday life and in analysis' (read before the British Psycho-Analytical Society in 1948), reported a great deal of clinical material in which projective identification became apparent. Unconscious phantasies of forcing the whole self into the inside of the object (to obtain control and possession) led, through the fear of retaliation, to a variety of persecutory anxieties such as claustrophobia, or to such common phobias as of burglars, spiders, invasion in wartime. These fears are connected with the unconscious 'catastrophic' phantasies of being dismembered, disembowelled, torn to pieces and of total internal disruption of the body and personality and loss of identity – fears which are an elaboration of the fear of annihilation (death) and have the effect of reinforcing the mechanisms of splitting and the process of ego disintegration as found in psychotics.

13

Mirror-role of mother and family in child development
D.W. Winnicott

In individual emotional development *the precursor of the mirror is the mother's face.* I wish to refer to the normal aspect of this and also to its psychopathology.

Jacques Lacan's paper 'Le stade du miroir'[1] has certainly influenced me. He refers to the use of the mirror in each individual's ego development. However, Lacan does not think of the mirror in terms of the mother's face in the way that I wish to do here.

I refer only to infants who have sight. The wider application of the idea to cover infants with poor sight or no sight must be left over till the main theme is stated. The bare statement is this: in the early stages of the emotional development of the human infant a vital part is played by the environment which is in fact not yet separated off from the infant by the infant. Gradually the separating-off of the not-me from the me takes place, and the pace varies according to the infant and according to the environment. The major changes take place in the separating-out of the mother as an objectively perceived environmental feature. If no one person is there to be mother the infant's developmental task is infinitely complicated.

Let me simplify the environmental function and briefly state that it involves:

This chapter, which was first published in 1967, is taken from *Playing and Reality* (Harmondsworth, Penquin, 1971), pp. 130–8.

1   Holding
2   Handling
3   Object-presenting.

The infant may respond to these environmental provisions, but the result in the baby is maximal personal maturation. By the word maturation at this stage I intend to include the various meanings of the word integration, as well as psychosomatic inter-relating and object-relating.

A baby is held, and handled satisfactorily, and with this taken for granted is presented with an object in such a way that the baby's legitimate experience of omnipotence is not violated. The result can be that the baby is able to use the object, and to feel as if this object is a subjective object, and created by the baby.

All this belongs to the beginning, and out of all this come the immense complexities that comprise the emotional and mental development of the infant and child.[2]

Now, at some point the baby takes a look round. Perhaps a baby at the breast does not look at the breast. Looking at the face is more likely to be a feature.[3] What does the baby see there? To get to the answer we must draw on our experience with psychoanalytic patients who reach back to very early phenomena and yet who can verbalize (when they feel they can do so) without insulting the delicacy of what is preverbal, unverbalized, and unverbalizable except perhaps in poetry.

What does the baby see when he or she looks at the mother's face? I am suggesting that, ordinarily, what the baby sees is himself or herself. In other words the mother is looking at the baby and *what she looks like is related to what she sees there*. All this is too easily taken for granted. I am asking that this which is naturally done well by mothers who are caring for their babies shall not be taken for granted. I can make my point by going straight over to the case of the baby whose mother reflects her own mood or, worse still, the rigidity of her own defences. In such a case what does the baby see?

Of course nothing can be said about the single occasions on which a mother could not respond. Many babies, however, do have to have a long experience of not getting back what they are giving. They look and they do not see themselves. There are consequences. First, their own creative capacity begins to atrophy, and in some way or other they look around for other ways of getting something of themselves back from the environment. They may succeed by some other method, and blind infants need to get themselves reflected through other senses than that of sight. Indeed, a mother whose face is fixed may be able to respond in some other way. Most mothers can respond when the baby is in trouble or is aggressive, and especially when the baby is ill. Second, the baby gets settled in to the idea that when he or she looks, what is seen is the mother's face. The mother's face is not then a mirror. So perception takes the place of apperception, perception takes the place of that which might have been the beginning of a significant exchange with the world, a two-way process in which self-enrichment alternates with the discovery of meaning in the world of seen things.

Naturally, there are half-way stages in this scheme of things. Some babies do not quite give up hope and they study the object and do all that is possible to see in the object some meaning that ought to be there if only it could be felt. Some babies, tantalized by this type of relative maternal failure, study the variable maternal visage in an attempt to predict the mother's mood, just exactly as we all study the weather. The baby quickly learns to make a forecast: 'Just now it is safe to forget the mother's mood and to be spontaneous, but any minute the mother's face will become fixed or her mood will dominate, and my own personal needs must then be withdrawn otherwise my central self may suffer insult.'

Immediately beyond this in the direction of pathology is predictability, which is precarious, and which strains the baby to the limits of his or her capacity to allow for events. This brings a threat of chaos, and the baby will organize withdrawal, or will not look except to perceive, as a defence. A baby so treated will grow up puzzled about mirrors and what the mirror has to offer. If the mother's face is unresponsive, then a mirror is a thing to be looked at but not to be looked into.

To return to the normal progress of events, when the average girl studies her face in the mirror she is reassuring herself that the mother-image is there and that the mother can see her and that the mother is *en rapport* with her. When girls and boys in their secondary narcissism look in order to see beauty and to fall in love, there is already evidence that doubt has crept in about their mother's continued love and care. So the man who falls in love with beauty is quite different from the man who loves a girl and feels she is beautiful and can see what is beautiful about her.

I will not try to press home my idea, but instead I will give some examples so that the idea I am presenting can be worked over by the reader.

Illustration I

I refer first to a woman of my acquaintance who married and brought up three fine male children. She was also a good support to her husband who had a creative and important job. Behind the scenes this woman was always near to depression. She seriously disturbed her marital life by waking every morning in a state of despair. She could do nothing about it. The resolution of the paralysing depression came each day when at last it was time to get up and, at the end of her ablutions and dressing, she could 'put on her face'. Now she felt rehabilitated and could meet the world and take up her family responsibilities. This exceptionally intelligent and responsible person did eventually react to a misfortune by developing a chronic depressive state which in the end became transformed into a chronic and crippling physical disorder.

Here is a recurring pattern, easily matched in the social or clinical experience of everyone. What is illustrated by this case only exaggerates that which is normal. The exaggeration is of the task of getting the mirror to notice and approve. The woman had to be her own mother. If she had had a daughter she would surely have found great relief, but perhaps a daughter would have suffered because of having too much importance in correcting her mother's uncertainty about her own mother's sight of her.

[. . .]

I see that I am linking apperception with perception by postulating a historical process (in the individual) which depends on being seen:

When I look I am seen, so I exist.
I can now afford to look and see.
I now look creatively and what I apperceive I also perceive.
In fact I take care not to see what is not there to be seen (unless I am tired).

[. . .]

Illustration III

I have a research case, a woman who has had a very long analysis. This patient has come through, late in life, to feeling real, and a cynic might say: to what end? But she feels it has been worth while, and I myself have learned a great deal of what I know of early phenomena through her.

This analysis involved a serious and deep regression to infantile dependence. The environmental history was severely disturbing in many respects, but here I am dealing with the effect on her of her mother's depression. This has been worked over repeatedly and as analyst I have had to displace this mother in a big way in order to enable the patient to get started as a person.[4]

Just now, near the end of my work with her, the patient has sent me a portrait of her nurse. I had already had her mother's portrait and I have got to know the rigidity of the mother's defences very intimately. It became obvious that the mother (as the patient said) had chosen a depressed nurse to act for her so that she might avoid losing touch with the children altogether. A lively nurse would automatically have 'stolen' the children from the depressed mother.

This patient has a marked absence of just that which characterizes so many women, an interest in the face. She certainly had no adolescent phase of self-examination in the mirror, and now she looks in the mirror only to remind herself that she 'looks like an old hag' (patient's own words).

This same week this patient found a picture of my face on a book-cover. She wrote to say she needed a bigger version so that she could see the lines and all the features of this 'ancient landscape'. I sent the picture (she lives away and I see her only occasionally now) and at the same time I gave her an interpretation based on what I am trying to say in this chapter.

This patient thought that she was quite simply acquiring the portrait of this man who had done so much for her (and I have). But what she needed to be told was that my lined face had some features that link for her with the rigidity of the faces of her mother and her nurse.

I feel sure that it was important that I knew this about the face, and that I could interpret the patient's search for a face that could reflect herself, and at the same time see that, because of the lines, my face in the picture reproduced some of her mother's rigidity.

Actually this patient has a thoroughly good face, and she is an exceptionally sympathetic person when she feels like it. She can let herself be concerned with other people's affairs and with their troubles for a limited period of time. How often this characteristic has seduced people into thinking of her as someone to be leaned on! The fact is, however, that the moment my patient feels herself being involved, especially in someone's depression, she automatically withdraws and curls up in bed with a hot-water bottle, nursing her soul. Just here she is vulnerable.

Illustration IV

After all this had been written a patient brought material in an analytic hour which might have been based on this that I am writing. This woman is very much concerned with the stage of the establishment of herself as an individual. In the course of this particular hour she brought in a reference to 'Mirror mirror on the wall' etc. and then she said: 'Wouldn't it be awful if the child looked into the mirror and saw nothing!'

The rest of the material concerned the environment provided by her mother when she was a baby, the picture being of a mother talking to someone else unless actively engaged in a positive relating to the baby. The implication here was that the baby would look at the mother and see her talking to someone else. The patient then went on to describe her great interest in the paintings of Francis Bacon and she wondered whether to lend me a book about the artist. She referred to a detail in the book. Francis Bacon 'says that he likes to have glass over his pictures because then when people look at the picture what they see is not just a picture; they might in fact see themselves.'[5]

After this the patient went on to speak of 'Le stade du miroir' because she knows of Lacan's work, but she was not able to make the link that I feel I am able to make between the mirror and the mother's face. It was not my job to give this link to my patient in this session because the patient is essentially at a stage of discovering things for herself, and premature interpretation in such circumstances annihilates the creativity of the patient and is traumatic in the sense of being against the maturational process. This theme continues to be important in this patient's analysis, but it also appears in other guises.

This glimpse of the baby's and child's seeing the self in the mother's face, and afterwards in a mirror, gives a way of looking at analysis and at the psychotherapeutic task. Psychotherapy is not making clever and apt interpretations; by and large it is a long-term giving the patient back what the patient brings. It is a complex derivative of the face that reflects what is there to be seen. I like to think of my work this way, and to think that if I do this well enough the patient will find his or her own self, and will be able to exist and to feel real. Feeling real is more than existing; it is finding a way to exist as oneself, and to relate to objects as oneself, and to have a self into which to retreat for relaxation.

[. . .]

This to which I have referred in terms of the mother's role of giving back to the baby the baby's own self continues to have importance in terms of the child and the family. Naturally, as the child develops and the maturational processes become sophisticated, and identifications multiply, the child becomes less and less dependent on getting back the self from the mother's and the father's face and from the faces of others who are in parental or sibling relationships.[6] Nevertheless, when a family is intact and is a going concern over a period of time each child derives benefit from being able to see himself or herself in the attitude of the individual members or in the attitudes of the family as a whole. We can include in all this the actual mirrors that exist in the house and the opportunities the child gets for seeing the parents and others looking at themselves. It should be understood, however, that the actual mirror has significance mainly in its figurative sense.

This could be one way of stating the contribution that a family can make to the personality growth and enrichment of each one of its individual members.

Notes

1 Jacques Lacan, 'Le stade du miroir comme formateur, de la fonction du je, telle qu'elle nous est révélée dans l'experience psychanalytique', in *Ecrits* (Paris, Editions du Seuil, 1966).

2 For further and detailed discussion of these ideas, the reader can consult my paper, 'The theory of the parent–infant relationship', in *The Maturational Processes and the Facilitating Environment* (London, Hogarth Press and the Institute of Psycho-Analysis, 1965).

3 D. Gough, 'The behaviour of infants in the first year of life', *Proceedings of the Royal Society of Medicine*, 55.

4 An aspect of this case was reported by me in my paper 'Metapsychological and clinical aspects of regression within the psycho-analytical set-up' (1954), in *Collected Papers: Through Paediatrics to Psycho-Analysis* (London, Tavistock Publications, 1958).

5 See *Francis Bacon: Catalogue Raisonné and Documentation* (Alley, 1964).

6 See my paper 'Ego distortion in terms of true and false self', in *The Maturational Processes and the Facilitating Environment*.

14

Transitional objects and transitional phenomena
D.W. Winnicott

In this chapter I give the original hypothesis[1] as formulated in 1951, and I then follow this up with two clinical examples.

Original hypothesis

It is well known that infants as soon as they are born tend to use fist, fingers, thumbs in stimulation of the oral erotogenic zone, in satisfaction of the instincts at that zone, and also in quiet union. It is also well known that after a few months infants of either sex become fond of playing with dolls, and that most mothers allow their infants some special object and expect them to become, as it were, addicted to such objects.

There is a relationship between these two sets of phenomena that are separated by a time interval, and a study of the development from the earlier into the later can be profitable, and can make use of important clinical material that has been somewhat neglected.

The first possession

This chapter, first published in 1951, is taken from *Playing and Reality* (Harmondsworth, Penguin, 1971), pp. 1–21.

Those who happen to be in close touch with mothers' interests and problems will be already aware of the very rich patterns ordinarily displayed by babies in their use of the first 'not-me' possession. These patterns, being displayed, can be subjected to direct observation.

There is a wide variation to be found in a sequence of events that starts with the newborn infant's fist-in-mouth activities, and leads eventually on to an attachment to a teddy, a doll or soft toy, or to a hard toy.

It is clear that something is important here other than oral excitement and satisfaction, although this may be the basis of everything else. Many other important things can be studied, and they include:

1 The nature of the object.
2 The infant's capacity to recognize the object as 'not-me'.
3 The place of the object – outside, inside, at the border.
4 The infant's capacity to create, think up, devise, originate, produce an object.
5 The initiation of an affectionate type of object-relationship.

I have introduced the terms 'transitional objects' and 'transitional phenomena' for designation of the intermediate area of experience, between the thumb and the teddy bear, between the oral erotism and the true object-relationship, between primary creative activity and projection of what has already been introjected, between primary unawareness of indebtedness and the acknowledgement of indebtedness ('Say: "ta"').

By this definition an infant's babbling and the way in which an older child goes over a repertory of songs and tunes while preparing for sleep come within the intermediate area as transitional phenomena, along with the use made of objects that are not part of the infant's body yet are not fully recognized as belonging to external reality.

Inadequacy of usual statement of human nature It is generally acknowledged that a statement of human nature in terms of interpersonal relationships is not good enough even when the imaginative elaboration of function and the whole of fantasy both conscious and unconscious, including the repressed unconscious, are allowed for. There is another way of describing persons that comes out of the researches of the past two decades. Of every individual who has reached to the stage of being a unit with a limiting membrane and an outside and an inside, it can be said that there is an *inner reality* to that individual, an inner world that can be rich or poor and can be at peace or in a state of war. This helps, but is it enough?

My claim is that if there is a need for this double statement, there is also need for a triple one: the third part of the life of a human being, a part that we cannot ignore, is an intermediate area of *experiencing*, to which inner reality and external life both contribute. It is an area that is not challenged, because no claim is made on its behalf except that it shall exist as a resting-place for the individual engaged in the perpetual human task of keeping inner and outer reality separate yet interrelated.

It is usual to refer to 'reality-testing', and to make a clear distinction between apperception and perception. I am here staking a claim for an intermediate state between a baby's inability and his growing ability to recognize and accept reality. I am therefore studying the substance of *illusion*, that which is allowed to the infant, and which in adult life is inherent in art and religion, and yet becomes the hallmark of madness when an adult puts too powerful a claim on the credulity of others, forcing them to acknowledge a sharing of illusion that is not their own. We can share a respect for *illusory experience,* and if we wish we may collect together and form a group on the basis of the similarity of our illusory experiences. This is a natural root of grouping among human beings.

I hope it will be understood that I am not referring exactly to the little child's teddy bear or to the infant's first use of the fist (thumb, fingers). I am not specifically studying the first object of object-relationships. I am concerned with the first possession, and with the intermediate area between the subjective and that which is objectively perceived.

Development of a personal pattern   There is plenty of reference in psychoanalytic literature to the progress from 'hand to mouth' to 'hand to genital', but perhaps less to further progress to the handling of truly 'not-me' objects. Sooner or later in an infant's development there comes a tendency on the part of the infant to weave other-than-me objects into the personal pattern. To some extent these objects stand for the breast, but it is not especially this point that is under discussion.

In the case of some infants the thumb is placed in the mouth while fingers are made to caress the face by pronation and supination movements of the forearm. The mouth is then active in relation to the thumb, but not in relation to the fingers. The fingers caressing the upper lip, or some other part, may be or may become more important than the thumb engaging the mouth. Moreover, this caressing activity may be found alone, without the more direct thumb–mouth union.

In common experience one of the following occurs, complicating an auto-erotic experience such as thumb-sucking:

1   with the other hand the baby takes an external object, say a part of a sheet or blanket, into the mouth along with the fingers; or

2   somehow or other the bit of cloth is held and sucked, or not actually sucked; the objects used naturally include napkins and (later) handkerchiefs, and this depends on what is readily and reliably available; or

3   the baby starts from early months to pluck wool and to collect it and to use it for the caressing part of the activity; less commonly, the wool is swallowed, even causing trouble; or

4   mouthing occurs, accompanied by sounds of 'mum-mum', babbling, anal noises, the first musical notes, and so on.

One may suppose that thinking, or fantasying, gets linked up with these functional experiences.

All these things I am calling *transitional phenomena.* Also, out of all this (if we study one infant) there may emerge something or some phenomenon – perhaps a bundle of wool or the corner of a blanket or eiderdown, or a word or tune, or a mannerism – that becomes vitally important to the infant for use at the time of going to sleep, and is a defence against anxiety, especially anxiety of depressive type. Perhaps some soft object or other type of object has been found and used by the infant, and this then becomes what I am calling a *transitional object*. This object goes on being important. The parents get to know its value and carry it round when travelling. The mother lets it get dirty and even smelly, knowing that by washing it she introduces a break in continuity in the infant's experience, a break that may destroy the meaning and value of the object to the infant.

I suggest that the pattern of transitional phenomena begins to show at about four to six to eight to twelve months. Purposely I leave room for wide variations.

Patterns set in infancy may persist into childhood, so that the original soft object continues to be absolutely necessary at bedtime or at time of loneliness or when a depressed mood threatens. In health, however, there is a gradual extension of range of interest, and eventually the extended range is maintained, even when depressive anxiety is near. A need for a specific object or a behaviour pattern that started at a very early date may reappear at a later age when deprivation threatens.

This first possession is used in conjunction with special techniques derived from very early infancy, which can include or exist apart from the more direct auto-erotic activities. Gradually in the life of an infant teddies and dolls and hard toys are acquired. Boys to some extent tend to go over to use hard objects, whereas girls tend to proceed right ahead to the acquisition of a family. It is important to note, however, that *there is no noticeable difference between boy and girl in their use of the original 'not-me' possession*, which I am calling the transitional object.

As the infant starts to use organized sounds ('mum', 'ta', 'da') there may appear a 'word' for the transitional object. The name given by the infant to these earliest objects is often significant, and it usually has a word used by the adults partly incorporated in it. For instance, 'baa' may be the name, and the 'b' may have come from the adult's use of the word 'baby' or 'bear'.

I should mention that sometimes there is no transitional object except the mother herself. Or an infant may be so disturbed in emotional development that the transition state cannot be enjoyed, or the sequence of objects used is broken. The sequence may nevertheless be maintained in a hidden way.

Summary of special qualities in the relationship

1   The infant assumes rights over the object, and we agree to this assumption. Nevertheless, some abrogation of omnipotence is a feature from the start.

2   The object is affectionately cuddled as well as excitedly loved and mutilated.

3   It must never change, unless changed by the infant.

4   It must survive instinctual loving, and also hating and, if it be a feature, pure aggression.

5   Yet it must seem to the infant to give warmth, or to move, or to have texture, or to do something that seems to show it has vitality or reality of its own.

6   It comes from without from our point of view, but not so from the point of view of the baby. Neither does it come from within; it is not a hallucination.

7   Its fate is to be gradually allowed to be decathected, so that in the course of years it becomes not so much forgotten as relegated to limbo. By this I mean that in health the transitional object does not 'go inside' nor does the feeling about it necessarily undergo repression. It is not forgotten and it is not mourned. It loses meaning, and this is because the transitional phenomena have become diffused, have become spread out over the whole intermediate territory between 'inner psychic reality' and 'the external world as perceived by two persons in common', that is to say, over the whole cultural field.

At this point my subject widens out into that of play, and of artistic creativity and appreciation, and of religious feeling, and of dreaming, and also of fetishism, lying and stealing, the origin and loss of affectionate feeling, drug addiction, the talisman of obsessional rituals, etc.

Relationship of the transitional object to symbolism   It is true that the piece of blanket (or whatever it is) is symbolical of some part-object, such as the breast. Nevertheless, the point of it is not its symbolic value so much as its actuality. Its not being the breast (or the mother), although real, is as important as the fact that it stands for the breast (or mother).

When symbolism is employed the infant is already clearly distinguishing between fantasy and fact, between inner objects and external objects, between primary creativity and perception. But the term 'transitional object', according to my suggestion, gives room for the process of becoming able to accept difference and similarity. I think there is use for a term for the root of symbolism in time, a term that describes the infant's journey from the purely subjective to objectivity; and it seems to me that the transitional object (piece of blanket, etc.) is what we see of this journey of progress towards experiencing.

It would be possible to understand the transitional object while not fully understanding the nature of symbolism. It seems that symbolism can be properly studied only in the process of the growth of an individual and that it has at the very best a variable meaning. For instance, if we consider the water of the Blessed Sacrament, which is symbolic of the body of Christ, I think I am right in saying that for the Roman Catholic community it *is* the body, and for the Protestant community it is a *substitute*, a reminder, and is essentially not, in fact, actually the body itself. Yet in both cases it is a symbol.

[. . .]

Theoretical study

There are certain comments that can be made on the basis of accepted psychoanalytic theory:

1   The transitional object stands for the breast, or the object of the first relationship.

2   The transitional object antedates established reality-testing.

3   In relation to the transitional object the infant passes from (magical) omnipotent control to control by manipulation (involving muscle erotism and coordination pleasure).

4   The transitional object may eventually develop into a fetish object and so persist as a characteristic of the adult sexual life.[2]

5   The transitional object may, because of anal erotic organization, stand for faeces (but it is not for this reason that it may become smelly and remain unwashed).

Relationship to internal object (Klein) It is interesting to compare the transitional object concept with Melanie Klein's concept of the internal object.[3] The transitional object is *not an internal object* (which is a mental concept) – it is a possession. Yet it is not (for the infant) an external object either.

The following complex statement has to be made. The infant can employ a transitional object when the internal object is alive and real and good enough (not too persecutory). But this internal object depends for its qualities on the existence and aliveness and behaviour of the external object. Failure of the latter in some essential function indirectly leads to deadness or to a persecutory quality of the internal object. After a persistence of inadequacy of the external object, the internal object fails to have meaning to the infant, and then, and then only, does the transitional object become meaningless too. The transitional object may therefore stand for the 'external' breast, but *indirectly*, through standing for an 'internal' breast.

The transitional object is never under magical control like the internal object, nor is it outside control as the real mother is.

Illusion–Disillusionment In order to prepare the ground for my own positive contribution to this subject I must put into words some of the things that I think are taken too easily for granted in many psychoanalytic writings on infantile emotional development, although they may be understood in practice.

There is no possibility whatever for an infant to proceed from the pleasure principle to the reality principle or towards and beyond primary identification,[4] unless there is a good-enough mother. The good-enough 'mother' (not necessarily the infant's own mother) is one who makes active adaptation to the infant's needs, an active adaptation that gradually lessens, according to the infant's growing ability to account for failure of adaptation and to tolerate the results of frustration. Naturally, the infant's own mother is more likely to be good enough than some other person, since this active adaptation demands an easy and unresented preoccupation with the one infant; in fact, success in infant care depends on the fact of devotion, not on cleverness or intellectual enlightenment.

The good-enough mother, as I have stated, starts off with an almost complete adaptation to her infant's needs, and as time proceeds she adapts less and less completely, gradually, according to the infant's growing ability to deal with her failure.

The infant's means of dealing with this maternal failure include the following:

1   The infant's experience, often repeated, that there is a time-limit to frustration. At first, naturally, this time-limit must be short.
2   Growing sense of process.
3   The beginnings of mental activity.
4   Employment of auto-erotic satisfactions.
5   Remembering, reliving, fantasying, dreaming; the integrating of past, present, and future.

[. . .]

Illusion and the value of illusion The mother, at the beginning, by an almost 100-per-cent adaptation affords the infant the opportunity for the *illusion* that her breast is part of the infant. It is, as it were, under the baby's magical control. [. . .] The mother's eventual task is gradually to disillusion the infant, but she has no hope of success unless at first she has been able to give sufficient opportunity for illusion.

In another language, the breast is created by the infant over and over again out of the infant's capacity to love or (one can say) out of need. A subjective phenomenon develops in the baby, which we call the mother's breast.[5] The mother places the actual breast just where the infant is ready to create, and at the right moment.

From birth, therefore, the human being is concerned with the problem of the relationship between what is objectively perceived and what is subjectively conceived of, and in the solution of this problem there is no health for the human being who has not been started off well enough by the mother. *The intermediate area to which I am referring is the area that is allowed to the infant between primary creativity and objective perception based on reality-testing.* The transitional phenomena represent the early stages of the use of illusion, without which there is no meaning for the human being in the idea of a relationship with an object that is perceived by others as external to that being.

The idea illustrated in Figure 14.1 is this: that at some theoretical point early in the development of every human individual an infant in a certain setting provided by the mother is capable of conceiving of the idea of something that would meet the growing need that arises out of instinctual tension. The infant cannot be said to know at first what is to be created. At this point in time the mother presents herself. In the ordinary way she gives her breast and her potential feeding urge. The mother's adaptation to the infant's needs, when good enough, gives the infant the *illusion* that there is an external reality that corresponds to the infant's own capacity to create. In other words, there is an overlap between what the mother supplies and what the child might conceive of. To the observer, the child perceives what the mother actually presents, but this is not the whole truth. The infant perceives the breast only in so far as a breast could be created just there and then. There is no interchange between the mother and the infant. Psychologically the infant takes from a breast that is part of the infant, and the mother gives milk to an infant that is part of herself. In psychology, the idea of interchange is based on an illusion in the psychologist.

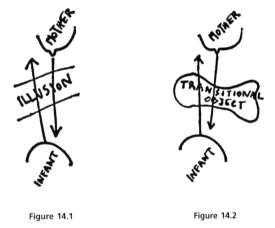

Figure 14.1   Figure 14.2

In Figure 14.2 a shape is given to the area of illusion, to illustrate what I consider to be the main function of the transitional object and of transitional phenomena. The transitional object and the transitional phenomena start each human being off with what will always be important for them, i.e. a neutral area of experience which will not be challenged. *Of the transitional object it can be said that it is a matter of agreement between us and the baby that we will never ask the question: 'Did you conceive of this or was it presented to you from without?' The important point is that no decision on this point is expected. The question is not to be formulated.*

This problem, which undoubtedly concerns the human infant in a hidden way at the beginning, gradually becomes an obvious problem on account of the fact that the mother's main task (next to providing opportunity for illusion) is disillusionment. This is preliminary to the task of weaning, and it also continues as one of the tasks of parents and educators. In other words, this matter of *illusion* is one that belongs inherently to human beings and that no individual finally solves for himself or herself, although a *theoretical* understanding of it may provide a *theoretical* solution. If things go well, in this gradual disillusionment process, the stage is set for the frustrations that we gather together under the word weaning; but it should be remembered that when we talk about the phenomena (which Klein has specifically illuminated in her concept of the depressive position)[6] that cluster round weaning we are assuming the underlying process, the process by which opportunity for illusion and gradual disillusionment is provided. If illusion–disillusionment has gone astray the infant cannot get to so normal a thing as weaning, nor to a reaction to weaning, and it is then absurd to refer to weaning at all. The mere termination of breast-feeding is not a weaning.

We can see the tremendous significance of weaning in the case of the normal child. When we witness the complex reaction that is set going in a certain child by the weaning process, we know that this is able to take place in that child because the illusion–disillusionment process is being carried through so well that we can ignore it while discussing actual weaning.

Development of the theory of illusion–disillusionment   It is assumed here that the task of reality-acceptance is never completed, that no human being is free from the strain of relating inner and outer reality, and that relief from this strain is provided by an intermediate area of experience[7] which is not challenged (arts, religion, etc.). This intermediate area is in direct continuity with the play area of the small child who is 'lost' in play.

In infancy this intermediate area is necessary for the initiation of a relationship between the child and the world, and is made possible by good-enough mothering at the early critical phase. Essential to all this is continuity (in time) of the external emotional environment and of particular elements in the physical environment such as the transitional object or objects.

The transitional phenomena are allowable to the infant because of the parents' intuitive recognition of the strain inherent in objective perception, and we do not challenge the infant in regard to subjectivity or objectivity just here where there is the transitional object.

Should an adult make claims on us for our acceptance of the objectivity of his subjective phenomena we discern or diagnose madness. If, however, the adult can manage to enjoy the personal intermediate area without making claims, then we can acknowledge our own corresponding intermediate areas, and are pleased to find a degree of overlapping, that is to say common experience between members of a group in art or religion or philosophy.

[. . .]

An application of the theory

It is not the object, of course, that is transitional. The object represents the infant's transition from a state of being merged with the mother to a state of being in relation to the mother as something outside and separate. This is often referred to as the point at which the child grows up out of a narcissistic type of object-relating, but I have refrained from using this language because I am not sure that it is what I mean; also, it leaves out the idea of dependence, which is so essential at the earliest stages before the child has become sure that anything can exist that is not part of the child.

Psychopathology manifested in the area of transitional phenomena

I have laid great stress on the normality of transitional phenomena. Nevertheless, there is a psychopathology to be discerned in the course of the clinical examination of cases. As an example of the child's management of separation and loss I draw attention to the way in which separation can affect transitional phenomena.

As is well known, when the mother or some other person on whom the infant depends is absent, there is no immediate change owing to the fact that the infant has a memory or mental image of the mother, or what we call an internal representation of her, which remains alive for a certain length of time. If the mother is away over a period of time which is beyond a certain limit measured in minutes, hours, or days, then the memory or the internal representation fades. As this takes effect, the transitional phenomena become gradually meaningless and the infant is unable to experience them. We may watch the object becoming decathected. Just before loss we can sometimes see the exaggeration of the use of a transitional object as part of *denial* that there is a threat of its becoming meaningless. To illustrate this aspect of denial I shall give a short clinical example of a boy's use of string.

String[8]   A boy aged seven years was brought to the Psychology Department of the Paddington Green Children's Hospital by his mother and father in March 1955. The other two members of the family also came: a girl aged ten, attending an ESN school, and a rather normal small girl aged four. The case was referred by the family doctor because of a series of symptoms indicating a character disorder in the boy. [. . .]

I first saw the parents in a long interview in which they gave a clear picture of the boy's development and of the distortions in his development. They left out one important detail, however, which emerged in an interview with the boy.

It was not difficult to see that the mother was a depressive person, and she reported that she had been hospitalized on account of depression. From the parents' account I was able to note that the mother cared for the boy until the sister was born when he was three years three months. This was the first separation of importance, the next being at three years eleven months, when the mother had an operation. When the boy was four years nine months the mother went into a mental hospital for two months, and during this time he was well cared for by the mother's sister. By this time everyone looking after this boy agreed that he was difficult, although showing very good features. He was liable to change suddenly and to frighten people by saying, for instance, that he would cut his mother's sister into little pieces. He developed many curious symptoms, such as a compulsion to lick things and people; he made compulsive throat noises; often he refused to pass a motion and then made a mess. [. . .]

After this interview with the parents I saw the boy in a personal interview. There were present two psychiatric social workers and two visitors. The boy did not immediately give an abnormal impression and he quickly entered into a squiggle game with me. (In this squiggle game I make some kind of an impulsive line-drawing and invite the child whom I am interviewing to turn it into something, and then he makes a squiggle for me to turn into something in my turn.)

The squiggle game in this particular case led to a curious result. The boy's laziness immediately became evident, and also nearly everything I did was translated by him into something associated with string. Among his ten drawings there appeared the following:

lasso
whip
crop
a yo-yo string
a string in a knot
another crop
another whip

After this interview with the boy I had a second one with the parents, and asked them about the boy's preoccupation with string. They said that they were glad that I had brought up this subject, but they had not mentioned it because they were not sure of its significance. They said that the boy had become obsessed with everything to do with string, and in fact whenever they went into a room they were liable to find that he had joined together chairs and tables; and they might find a cushion, for instance, with a string joining it to the fireplace. They said that the boy's preoccupation with string was gradually developing a new feature, one that had worried them instead of causing them ordinary concern. He had recently tied a string round his sister's neck (the sister whose birth provided the first separation of this boy from his mother).

In this particular kind of interview I knew I had limited opportunity for action: it would not be possible to see these parents or the boy more frequently than once in six months, since the family lived in the country. I therefore took action in the following way. I explained to the mother that this boy was dealing with a fear of separation, attempting to deny separation by his use of string, as one would deny separation from a friend by using the telephone. She was sceptical, but I told her that should she come round to finding some sense in what I was saying I should like her to open up the matter with the boy at some convenient time, letting him know what I had said, and then developing the theme of separation according to the boy's response.

I heard no more from these people until they came to see me about six months later. The mother [. . .] had felt that what I had said was silly, but one evening she had opened the subject with the boy and found him to be eager to talk about his relation to her and his fear of a lack of contact with her. She went over all the separations she could think of with him with his help, and she soon became convinced that what I had said was right, because of his responses. Moreover, from the moment that she had this conversation with him the string play ceased. There was no more joining of objects in the old way. She had had many other conversations with the boy about his feeling of separateness from her, and she made the very significant comment that she felt the most important separation to have been his loss of her when she was seriously depressed; it was not just her going away, she said, but her lack of contact with him because of her complete preoccupation with other matters.

At a later interview the mother told me that a year after she had had her first talk with the boy there was a return to playing with string and to joining together objects in the house. She was in fact due to go into hospital for an operation, and she said to him: 'I can see from your playing with string that you are worried about my going away, but this time I shall only be away a few days, and I am having an operation which is not serious.' After this conversation the new phase of playing with string ceased. [. . .]

Notes

1   Published in the *International Journal of Psycho-Analysis*, 34(2) (1953); and in D.W. Winnicott, *Collected Papers: Through Paediatrics to Psycho-Analysis* (London, Tavistock Publications, 1958).

2   See Wulff's development of the theme in M. Wulff, 'Fetishism and object choice in early childhood', *Psychoanalytical Quarterly*, 15 (1946).

3   Melanie Klein, 'A contribution to the psychogenesis of manic depressive states', in *Contributions to Psycho-Analysis 1921–1945* (London, Hogarth Press and the Institute of Psycho-Analysis, 1948).

4   See Sigmund Freud, *The Ego and the Id* in *The Standard Edition of the Works of Sigmund Freud*, ed. James Strachey (London, Hogarth Press and the Institute of Psychoanalysis, 1953), volume 19.

5   I include the whole technique of mothering. When it is said that the first object is the breast, the word 'breast' is used, I believe, to stand for the technique of mothering as well as for the actual flesh. It is not impossible for a mother to be a good-enough mother (in my way of putting it) with a bottle for the actual feeding.

6   Melanie Klein, 'Mourning and its relation to manic-depressive states', in *Contributions to Psycho-Analysis 1921–1945*.

7   Cf. Joan Riviere, 'On the genesis of psychical conflict in earliest infancy', *International Journal of Psycho-Analysis*, 17 (1936).

8   Published in *Child Psychology and Psychiatry*, vol, 1 (1960); and in Winnicott, *The Maturational Processes and the Facilitating Environment* (London, Hogarth Press and the Institute of Psychoanalysis, 1965).

15

Social systems as a defense against anxiety
Isabel Menzies Lyth

This chapter, first published in 1960, is taken from *The Social Engagement of Social Science, Volume I: The Socio-Psychological Perspective* eds E. Trist and H. Murray (London, Free Association Books, 1990), pp. 439–62.

This study was initiated by the nursing service of a general teaching hospital in London which sought help in planning the training of student nurses of whom there were 500 in the hospital. Trained nursing staff numbered 150. The student nurses spent all but six months of their three years of undergraduate training working full-time in wards and departments as 'staff' while learning and practicing nursing skills. They carried out most of the actual nursing. The task with which the nursing service was struggling was effectively to reconcile two needs: for wards and departments to have adequate numbers of appropriate student nurses as staff; for student nurses, as students, to have the practical experience required for their training. Senior nurses feared the system was at the point of breakdown with serious consequences for student nurse training since patient care naturally tended to take priority whenever there was conflict. [. . .] While doing this 'diagnostic' exploration we became aware of the high level of tension, distress and anxiety in the nursing service. How could nurses tolerate so much anxiety? We found much evidence that they could not. Withdrawal from duty was common. One-third did not complete their training; the majority of these left at their own request. Senior staff changed their jobs appreciably more frequently than workers at similar levels in other professions. Sickness rates were high, especially for minor illnesses requiring only a few days' absence from duty.

The relief of this anxiety seemed to us an important therapeutic task in itself and, moreover, proved to have a close connection with the development of more effective techniques of student-nurse allocation. In this paper I attempt to elucidate the nature and effect of the anxiety level in the hospital.

Nature of the anxiety

The primary task of a hospital is to care for ill people who cannot be cared for in their own homes. The major responsibility for this task lies with the nursing service, which provides continuous care, day and night, all year around. The nursing service bears the full, immediate and concentrated impact of stress arising from patient-care.

The situations likely to evoke stress in nurses are familiar. Nurses are in constant contact with people who are physically ill or injured, often seriously. The recovery of patients is not certain and may not be complete. [. . .] Nurses face the reality of suffering and death as few lay people do. Their work involves carrying out tasks which, by ordinary standards, are distasteful, disgusting and frightening. Intimate physical contact with patients arouses libidinal and erotic wishes that may be difficult to control. The work arouses strong and conflicting feelings: pity, compassion and love; guilt and anxiety; hatred and resentment of the patients who arouse these feelings; envy of the care they receive.

The objective situation confronting the nurse bears a striking resemblance to the phantasy[1] situations that exist in every individual in the deepest and most primitive levels of the mind. The intensity and complexity of the nurse's anxieties are to be attributed primarily to the peculiar capacity of the objective features of the work to stimulate afresh these early situations and their accompanying emotions.

The elements of these phantasies may be traced back to earliest infancy.[2] The infant experiences two opposing sets of feelings and impulses, libidinal and aggressive. These stem from instinctual sources and are described by the constructs of the life-instinct and the death-instinct. Feeling omnipotent and attributing dynamic reality to these feelings and impulses, the infant believes that the libidinal impulses are literally life-giving and the aggressive impulses death-dealing; similar feelings, impulses and powers are attributed to other people and to important parts of people. The objects and the instruments of the libidinal and aggressive impulses are phantasized as the infant's own and other people's bodies and bodily products. Physical and psychic experiences are intimately interwoven. The infant's psychic experience of objective reality is greatly influenced by its own feelings and phantasies, moods and wishes.

[. . .]

Patients and relatives had complicated feelings towards the hospital, which were expressed particularly and most directly to nurses, and often puzzled and distressed them. Patients and relatives showed appreciation, gratitude, affection, respect; a touching relief that the hospital coped; helpfulness and concern for the nurses. But patients often resented their dependence; accepted grudgingly the discipline imposed by treatment and hospital routine; envied nurses their health and skills; were demanding, possessive and jealous. Patients, like nurses, found strong libidinal and

SOCIAL SYSTEMS AS DEFENSE AGAINST ANXIETY

erotic feelings stimulated by nursing care, and sometimes behaved in ways that increased the nurses' difficulties, for example by unnecessary physical exposure. [. . .]

In a more subtle way, both patients and relatives made psychological demands on nurses that increased their experience of stress. The hospital was expected to do more than accept the ill patients, care for their physical needs, and help realistically with their psychological stress. Implicitly it was expected to accept and, by so doing, free patients and relatives from, certain aspects of the emotional problems aroused by the patient and the illness. The hospital, particularly the nurses, had projected into them feelings such as depression and anxiety, fear of the patient and the illness, disgust at the illness and necessary nursing tasks. Patients and relatives treated the staff in such a way as to ensure that the nurses experienced these feelings instead of, or partly instead of, themselves, for example by refusing or trying to refuse to participate in important decisions about the patient and so forcing responsibility and anxiety back on the hospital. Thus, to the nurses' own deep and intense anxieties were psychically added those of other people. [. . .]

The nurses projected infantile phantasy-situations into current work-situations and experienced the objective situations as a mixture of objective reality and phantasy. They then re-experienced painfully and vividly in relation to current objective reality many of the feelings appropriate to the phantasies. In thus projecting phantasy-situations into objective reality, the nurses were using an important and universal technique for mastering anxiety and modifying the phantasy-situations. The objective situations symbolize the phantasy-situations and successful mastery of the objective situations gives reassurance about the mastery of the phantasy-situations. To be effective, such symbolization requires that the symbol *represents* the phantasy object, but *is not equated* with it. The symbol's own distinctive, objective characteristics must also be recognized and used. If, for any reason, the symbol and the phantasy object become almost or completely equated, the anxieties aroused by the phantasy object are aroused in full intensity by the symbolic object. The symbol then ceases to perform its function in containing and modifying anxiety (Segal, 1957). The close resemblance of the phantasy and objective situations in nursing constitutes a threat that symbolic representation will degenerate into symbolic equation and that nurses will consequently experience the full force of their primitive infantile anxieties in consciousness. Modified instances of this phenomenon were not uncommon in this hospital. For example, a nurse whose mother had had several gynecological operations broke down and had to give up nursing shortly after beginning her tour of duty on the gynecological ward.

To understand the sources of the anxiety was one thing: to understand why overt anxiety remained chronically at so high a level was another. Therefore our attention was directed to the adaptive and defensive techniques within the nursing service.

Defensive techniques in the nursing service

In developing a structure, culture and mode of functioning, a social organization is influenced by a number of interacting factors, crucial among which is its primary task, i.e. the task it was created to perform (Rice, 1958) and the technology that this requires. The influences of the primary task and technology can easily be exaggerated. Indeed, I would prefer to regard them as limiting factors. [. . .] Within these limits, the culture, structure and mode of functioning are determined by the psychological needs of the members (Trist and Bamforth, 1951).

The need of the members of the organization to use it in the struggle against anxiety leads to the development of socially structured defense mechanisms, which appear as elements in the structure, culture and mode of functioning of the organization (Jaques, 1955). [. . .] A social defense system develops over time through collusive interaction and agreement, often unconscious, between members of the organization as to what form it shall take. The socially structured defense mechanisms then tend to become an aspect of external reality with which old and new members of the institution must come to terms.

[. . .]

Splitting up the nurse/patient relationship

The focus of anxiety for the nurse lay in the relation with the patient. The closer and more concentrated this relationship, the more the nurse was likely to experience the impact of anxiety. The nursing service attempted to protect the individual nurse from anxiety by splitting up contact with patients. It is hardly too much to say that the nurse did not nurse patients. The total work-load of a ward or department was broken down into lists of tasks, each of which was allocated to a particular student nurse, who performed patient-centered tasks for a large number of patients, perhaps as many as all the patients in a ward. As a corollary, the student performed only a few tasks for, and had restricted contact with, any one patient, and was thus prevented from contact with the totality of any one patient and his or her illness.

Depersonalization, categorization and denial of the significance of the individual

The protection afforded by the task-list system was reinforced by a number of other devices that inhibited the development of a full person-to-person relationship between nurse and patient. The implicit aim of such devices, which operated both structurally and culturally, may be described as depersonalization or elimination of individual distinctiveness in both nurse and patient. For example, nurses often talked about patients not by name but by bed number or by disease or diseased organ: 'the liver in bed 10' or 'the pneumonia in bed 15.' Nurses themselves deprecated this practice, but it persisted. There was an almost explicit 'ethic' that any patient must be the same as any other patient. It must not matter to the nurses whom they nursed or what illness. Nurses found it difficult to express preferences even for types of patients or for men or women patients. Conversely, it should not matter to the patient which nurse attended or, indeed, how many different nurses did. By implication it was the duty, as well as the need and privilege, of the patient to be nursed and of the nurse to nurse, regardless of the fact that a patient might need to 'nurse' a distressed nurse and nurses might sometimes need to be 'nursed.' Outside the specific requirements of physical illness and treatment, the way patients were nursed was determined largely by their membership in the category patient and minimally by idiosyncratic wants and needs. For example, there was only one way of bed-making except when the physical illness required another, only one time to wash all patients – in the morning.

The nurses' uniforms were a symbol of an expected inner and behavioral uniformity; a nurse became a kind of agglomeration of nursing skills, without individuality; each was thus interchangeable with another of the same seniority. Socially permitted differences between nurses tended to be restricted to a few major categories, outwardly differentiated by minor differences in insignia on the same basic uniform. This attempted to create an operational identity between all nurses in the same category. To an extent indicating clearly the need for 'blanket' decisions, duties and privileges were allotted to categories of people and not to individuals according to their personal capacities and needs. [. . .]

Detachment and denial of feelings

The entrant into any profession that works with people needs to develop adequate professional detachment. He or she must learn to control feelings, refrain from excessive involvement, avoid disturbing identifications and maintain professional independence against manipulation and demands for unprofessional behavior. The reduction of individual distinctiveness aided detachment by minimizing the mutual interaction of personalities, which might lead to 'attachment.' It was reinforced by an implicit operational policy of 'detachment.' 'A good nurse doesn't mind moving.' A good nurse is willing and able without disturbance to move from ward to ward or hospital to hospital at a moment's notice. The implicit rationale appeared to be that a student nurse would learn to be detached psychologically if given sufficient experience of being detached literally and physically. This approach comes dangerously close to concrete thinking. Most senior nurses did not subscribe personally to this implicit rationale. They were aware of the personal distress as well as the operational disturbance caused by over-frequent moves. However, in their formal roles they continued to initiate frequent moves and made little other training provision for developing genuine professional detachment. The pain and distress of breaking relationships and the importance of stable and continuing relationships were implicitly denied by the system, although they were often stressed personally by people in the system.

This denial was reinforced by denial of the disturbing feelings that arose within relationships. Interpersonal repressive techniques were culturally required and typically used to deal with emotional stress. Both student nurses and staff showed panic about emotional outbursts. Brisk, reassuring behavior and advice of the 'stiff upper lip,' 'pull yourself together' variety were characteristic. Student nurses suffered severely from emotional strain and habitually complained that the senior staff did not understand and made no effort to help them. Indeed, when the emotional stress arose from nurses having made a mistake, they were usually reprimanded instead of being helped. A student nurse told me that she had made a mistake that hastened the death of a dying patient. She was reprimanded separately by four senior nurses, and not comforted. However, student nurses were wrong when they said that senior nurses did not understand or feel for their distress. In personal conversation with us, seniors showed considerable understanding and sympathy and often remembered surprisingly vividly some of the agonies of their own training. But they lacked confidence in their ability to handle emotional stress in any way other than by repressive techniques, and often said, 'In any case, the students won't come and talk to us.'

The attempt to eliminate decisions by ritual task-performance

Making a decision implies making a choice between different possible courses of action and committing oneself to one of them, the choice being made in the absence of full factual information about the effects of the choice. All decisions are thus attended by uncertainty about their outcome and consequently by some conflict and anxiety. The anxiety consequent on decision-making is likely to be acute if a decision affects the treatment and welfare of patients. To spare staff this anxiety, the nursing service attempted to minimize the number and variety of decisions. For example, the student nurse was instructed to perform the task-list in a way reminiscent of performing a ritual. Precise instructions were given about the way each task must be performed, the order of the tasks and the time for their performance, although such precise instructions were not objectively necessary, or even wholly desirable.

Much time and effort were expended in standardizing nursing procedures in cases where there were a number of effective alternatives. Both teachers and practical-work supervisors impressed on the student nurse the importance of carrying out the ritual, reinforcing this by fostering an attitude to work that regarded every task as almost a matter of life and death, to be treated with appropriate seriousness. This attitude applied even to those tasks that could be effectively performed by an unskilled lay person. As a corollary, student nurses were actively discouraged from using their own discretion and initiative to plan their work realistically in relation to the objective situation, for example, at times of crisis to discriminate between tasks on the grounds of urgency or relative importance and act accordingly. [. . .]

Reducing the weight of responsibility in decision-making by checks and counter-checks

The psychological burden of anxiety arising from a final, committing decision by a single person was dissipated in a number of ways, so that its impact was reduced. The final act of commitment was postponed by checking and re-checking decisions for validity and postponing action as long as possible. Executive action following decisions was also checked and re-checked at intervening stages. Individuals spent much time in private rumination over decisions and actions. Whenever possible, they involved other nurses in decision-making and in reviewing actions. [. . .] Nurses consulted not only their immediate seniors but also their juniors and nurses or other staff with whom they had no functional relationship but who happened to be available.

Collusive social redistribution of responsibility and irresponsibility

Each nurse had to face and, in some way, resolve a painful conflict over accepting the responsibility of the role. Nursing tends to evoke a strong sense of responsibility, and nurses often discharged their duties at considerable personal cost. On the other hand, the heavy burden of responsibility was difficult to bear consistently, and nurses were tempted to abandon it. Each nurse had wishes and impulses that would lead to irresponsible action, to skipping boring, repetitive tasks or to becoming libidinally or emotionally attached to patients. The balance of opposing forces in the conflict varied between individuals; some are naturally 'more responsible' than others, but the conflict was always present. To experience this conflict fully and intrapsychically would be extremely stressful. The intrapsychic conflict was alleviated by a technique that partly converted it into an interpersonal conflict. People in certain roles tended to be described by themselves and others as responsible, while people in other roles were described as irresponsible. Nurses habitually complained that other nurses were irresponsible, behaved carelessly and impulsively, and in consequence needed to be ceaselessly supervised and disciplined. The complaints commonly referred not to individuals or to specific incidents but to whole categories of nurses, usually a category junior to the speaker. The implication was that the juniors were not only less responsible now than the speaker, but also less responsible than she was when she was in the same junior position. Few nurses recognized or admitted such tendencies in themselves. Many people complained that their seniors, as a category, imposed unnecessarily strict and repressive discipline, and treated them as though they had no sense of responsibility. Few senior staff seemed able to recognize such features in their own behavior to subordinates. These juniors and seniors were, with few exceptions, the same people viewed from above or below, as the case might be.

We came to realize that the complaints stemmed from a collusive system of denial, splitting and projection that was culturally acceptable to, indeed culturally required of, nurses. Each nurse tended to split off aspects of herself from her conscious personality and to project them into other nurses. Her irresponsible impulses, which she feared she could not control, were attributed to her juniors. Her painfully severe attitude to these impulses and burdensome sense of responsibility were attributed to her seniors. Consequently, she identified juniors with her irresponsible self and treated them with the severity that self was felt to deserve. Similarly, she identified seniors with her own harsh disciplinary attitude to her irresponsible self and expected harsh discipline. There was psychic truth in the assertion that juniors were irresponsible and seniors harsh disciplinarians. These were the roles assigned to them. There was also objective truth, since people acted objectively on the psychic roles assigned to them. Discipline was often harsh and sometimes unfair, since the multiple projection also led the senior to identify all juniors with her irresponsible self and so with each other. Thus, she failed to discriminate between them sufficiently. Nurses complained about being reprimanded for other people's mistakes while no serious effort was made to find the real culprit. A staff nurse[3] said, 'If a mistake has been made, you must reprimand someone, even if you don't know who really did it.' Irresponsible behavior was also quite common, mainly in tasks remote from direct patient care. The inter-personal conflict was painful but was less so than experiencing the conflict fully intrapsychically, and it could more easily be evaded. The disciplining eye of seniors could not follow juniors all the time, nor did the junior confront her senior with irresponsibility all the time.

Purposeful obscurity in the formal distribution of responsibility

Additional protection from the impact of responsibility for specific tasks was given by the fact that the formal structure and role system failed to define fully enough who was responsible for what and to whom. This matched and objectified the obscurity about the location of psychic responsibility that inevitably arose from the massive system of projection described above. The content and boundaries of roles were obscure, especially at senior levels. The responsibilities were more onerous at this level so that protection was felt as very necessary. Also the more complex roles and role-relationships made it easier to evade definition. The content of the role of the student nurse was rigidly prescribed by her task-list. However, in practice, she was unlikely to have the same task-list for any length of time. She might, and frequently did, have two completely different task-lists in a single day. There was therefore a lack of stable person/role constellations, and it became very difficult to assign responsibility finally to a person, a role or a person/role constellation.

Responsibility and authority on wards were generalized in a way that made them non-specific and prevented them from falling firmly on one person, even the sister. Each nurse was held to be responsible for the work of every nurse junior to her. Junior, in this context, implied no hierarchical relationship, and was determined only by the length of time a student nurse had been in training, and all students were 'junior' to trained staff. Every nurse was expected to initiate disciplinary action in relation to any failure by any junior nurse. Such diffused responsibility meant, of course, that responsibility was not generally experienced specifically or seriously. This was a policy for inactivity.

The reduction of the impact of responsibility by delegation to superiors

Delegation in the hospital seemed to move in a direction opposite to the usual one. Tasks were frequently forced upwards in the hierarchy so that all responsibility for their performance could be disclaimed. Insofar as this happened, the heavy burden of responsibility on the individual was reduced.

The results of years of this practice were visible in the nursing service at the time of the study. We were struck by the low level of tasks carried out by nursing staff and students in relation to their personal ability, skill and position in the hierarchy. Formally and informally, tasks were assigned to staff at a level well above that at which one found comparable tasks in other institutions. The task of allocating student nurses to practical duties was a case in point. This work was carried out by the first and second assistant matrons[4] and took up a considerable proportion of their working-time. The task was such that, if policy were clearly defined and the task appropriately organized, it could be efficiently performed by a competent clerk part-time under the supervision of a senior nurse. We saw this delegation upward in operation a number of times as new tasks developed for nurses out of changes resulting from our study. The senior staff decided to change the practical training for post-graduate students so that they might have better training in administration and supervision. The students were now to spend six months continuously in one operational unit during which time they would act as understudy-cum-shadow to the sister or staff nurse. Personal compatibility was felt to be important, and it was suggested that, with training, the sisters should take part in the selection of the fourth-year students for their own wards, a task within their competence. At first there was enthusiasm for the proposal, but as definite plans were made and the ward sisters began to feel that they had no developed skill for selection, they requested that, after all, senior staff should continue to select for them as they had always done. The senior staff, although already overburdened, accepted the task.

The repeated occurrence of such incidents by mutual collusive agreement between superiors and subordinates is hardly surprising considering the mutual projection system described above. Nurses as subordinates tended to feel very dependent on their superiors in whom they had psychically vested, by projection, some of the best and most competent parts of themselves. They felt that their projections gave them the right to expect their superiors to undertake their tasks and make decisions for them. On the other hand, nurses as superiors did not feel they could fully trust their subordinates in whom they had psychically vested the irresponsible and incompetent parts of themselves. Their acceptance of their subordinates' projections also conveyed a sense of duty to accept their subordinates' responsibilities.

[. . .]

Avoidance of change

Change is an excursion into the unknown. It implies a commitment to future events that are not entirely predictable and to their consequences, and inevitably provokes doubt and anxiety. Any significant change within a social system implies changes in existing social relationships and in social structure, which implies in turn a change in the operation of the social system as a defense system. While this change is proceeding, anxiety is likely to be more open and intense. This is a familiar experience while the individual's defenses are being restructured in the course of psychoanalytic therapy. Jaques (1955) has stressed that resistance to social change can be better understood if it is seen as the resistance of groups of people unconsciously clinging to existing institutions because changes threaten existing social defenses against deep and intense anxieties.

It is understandable that the nursing service, whose tasks stimulated such primitive and intense anxieties, should anticipate change with unusually severe anxiety. In order to avoid this anxiety, the service tried to avoid change wherever possible and to cling to the familiar, even when the familiar had obviously ceased to be appropriate or relevant. Changes tended to be initiated only at the point of crisis. The presenting problem was a good example of the difficulty in initiating and carrying through change. Staff and student nurses had long felt that the methods in operation were unsatisfactory and had wanted to change them. They had, however, been unable to do so. The problem was approaching the point of breakdown and the limits of the capacities of the people concerned when we were called in. Other examples of this clinging to the inappropriate familiar could be observed. Changes in medical practice and the initiation of the National Health Service had led to more rapid patient turnover, an increase in the proportion of acutely ill patients, a wider range of illness to be nursed in each ward and greater variation in the work-load of a ward from day to day. These changes pointed to the need for increasing flexibility in the work organization in wards. In fact, no such increase had taken place. Indeed, the difficulty inherent in trying to deal with a fluctuating work-load by the rather rigid system described above tended to be handled by increased prescription and rigidity and by reiteration of the familiar. The greater the anxiety the greater the need for reassurance in rather compulsive repetition.

Commentary on the social defense system

The characteristic feature of the social defense system was its orientation to helping the individual to avoid the conscious experience of anxiety, guilt, doubt and uncertainty. This was done by eliminating situations, events, tasks, activities and relationships that caused anxiety or, more correctly, evoked anxieties connected with primitive psychological remnants in the personality. Little attempt was made positively to help the individual confront the anxiety-evoking experiences and, by so doing, to develop her capacity to tolerate and deal more effectively with them. Basically, the potential anxieties in the nursing situation were felt to be too deep and dangerous for full confrontation. They threatened personal disruption and social chaos. In fact, of course, the attempt to avoid such confrontation could never be completely successful. A compromise was inevitable between the implicit aims of the social defense system and the demands of reality as expressed in the need to pursue the primary task.

It followed that the psychic defense mechanisms that had, over time, been built into the socially structured defense system of the nursing service were, in the main, those which by evasion give protection from the full experience of anxiety. These were derived from the most primitive psychic defense mechanisms typical of the young infant's attempts to deal, mainly by evasion, with the severe anxieties aroused by the interplay of instincts. Individuals vary in the extent to which they are able, as they grow older, to modify or abandon their early defense mechanisms and develop other methods of dealing with their anxieties. Notably, these other methods include the ability to confront the anxiety situations in their original or symbolic forms and to work them over; to approach and tolerate psychic and objective reality; to differentiate between them and to perform con- structive and objectively successful activities in relation to them. Every individual is at risk that objective or psychic events stimulating acute anxiety will lead to partial or complete abandonment of the more mature methods of dealing with anxiety and to regression to more primitive methods of defense. The intense anxiety evoked by the nursing task had precipitated just such individual regression to primitive types of defense. These had been projected and given objective existence in the social structure and culture of the nursing service, with the result that anxiety was to some extent contained, but that true mastery of anxiety by deep working-through and modification was seriously inhibited. Thus, it was to be expected that nurses would persistently experience a higher degree of anxiety than was justified by the objective situation.

Consideration in more detail of how the socially structured defense system failed to support the individual in the struggle towards more effective mastery of anxiety may be approached from two different but related points of view. First, I will consider how far the current functioning of the nursing service gave rise to experiences that reassured nurses or aroused anxiety. As a direct consequence of the social organization, many situations and incidents arose that aroused anxiety. On the other hand, the social system frequently deprived nurses of necessary reassurance and satisfaction. In other words, the social defense system itself aroused a good deal of secondary anxiety as well as failing to alleviate primary anxiety.

Threat of crisis and operational breakdown

From the operational point of view, the nursing service was cumbersome and inflexible. It could not easily adapt to short- or long-term changes in conditions. The task-list system and minutely prescribed task-performance made it difficult to adjust work-loads when necessary by postponing or omitting less urgent or important tasks. [. . .] Recurrent shortages of second-year or third-year nurses occurred while they spent six weeks in school; sickness or leave frequently reduced numbers. The work/staff ratio, therefore, varied considerably and often suddenly. Since work could not easily be reduced, this generated considerable pressure, tension and uncertainty among staff and students. [. . .] Nurses were haunted by fear of failing to carry out their duties adequately as pressure of work increased. Conversely, they rarely experienced the satisfaction and lessening of anxiety that came from knowing they had the ability to carry out their work realistically and efficiently.

The nursing service was organized in a way that made it difficult for one person, or even a close group of people, to make a rapid and effective decision. Diffusion of responsibility prevented adequate and specific concentration of authority for making and implementing decisions. The organization of working groups made it difficult to achieve adequate con-centration of knowledge. In a ward, only the sister and the staff nurse were in a position to collect and coordinate knowledge. However, they had to do this for a unit of such size and complexity that it was impossible to do it effectively. They were, inevitably, badly briefed. We came across many cases where the sister did not remember how many nurses were on duty or what each was supposed to do, and had to have recourse to a written list. Such instances cannot be attributed primarily to individual inadequacy. Decisions tended to be made, therefore, by people who felt that they lacked adequate knowledge of relevant and ascertainable facts. This led to both anxiety and anger. [. . .]

Excessive movement of student nurses

The fact that a rise in work/staff ratios could be met only within very narrow limits by a reduction in the work-load meant that it was often necessary to have staff reinforcements, usually to move student nurses. The defense of rigid work organization thus appeared as a factor contributory to the presenting problem of student allocation, and the consequent distress and anxiety. Denial of the importance of relationships and feelings did not adequately protect the nurses, especially since the moves most directly affected student nurses, who had not yet fully developed these defenses. Nurses grieved and mourned over broken relationships with patients and other nurses; they felt they were failing their patients. They felt strange in new surroundings. They had to learn new duties and make relationships with new patients and staff, and probably had to nurse types of illness they had never nursed before. Until they got to know more about the new situation they suffered anxiety, uncertainties and doubts. Senior staff estimated that it took a student two weeks to settle down in a new ward. We regarded this as an underestimate. The suddenness of many moves increased the difficulty. [. . .] Patients could not be handed over properly to other nurses. [. . .] Nurses tended to feel acutely deprived by [the] lack of preparation. As one young woman said, 'If only I had known a bit sooner that I was going to the diabetic ward, I would have read up about diabetics and that would have helped a lot.' [. . .]

This situation did indeed help to produce a defensive psychological detachment. Students protected themselves against the pain and anxiety of transfers, or the threat of transfers, by limiting their psychological involvement in any situation, with patients or other staff. This reduced their interest and sense of responsibility and fostered a 'don't care' attitude of which nurses and patients complained bitterly. Nurses felt anxious and guilty when they detected such feelings in themselves, and angry, hurt and disappointed when they found them in others. The resulting detachment also reduced the possibility of satisfaction from work well done in a job one deeply cared about.

Under-employment of student nurses

Understandably, since work-loads were so variable and it was difficult to adjust tasks, the nursing service tried to plan its establishment to meet peak rather than average loads. As a result, student nurses quite often had too little work. They hardly ever complained of overwork but rather a number complained of not having enough work, although they still complained of stress. We observed obvious under-employment in spite of the fact that student nurses were apt to make themselves look busy doing something and talked of having to look busy to avoid censure from the sister. [. . .]

Student nurses were also under-employed in terms of level of work. A number of elements in the defense system contributed to this. Consider, for example, the assignment of duties to whole categories of student nurses. Since nurses found it so difficult to tolerate inefficiency and mistakes, the level of duties for each category was pitched low, near to the expected level of the least competent nurse in the category. In addition, the policy that made student nurses the effective nursing staff of the hospital condemned them to the repetitive performance of simple tasks to an extent far beyond that necessary for their training. The performance of simple tasks need not of itself imply that the student nurse's role was at a low level. The level depends also on how much opportunity was given for the use of discretion and judgment in the organization of the tasks – which, when and how. In fact, the social defense system specifically minimized the exercise of discretion and judgment in the student nurse's organization of tasks, for example, through the task-list system. [. . .]

Under-employment of this kind stimulates anxiety and guilt, which are particularly acute when under-employment implies failing to use one's capacities fully in the service of other people in need. Nurses found the limitations on their performance very frustrating. They often experienced a painful sense of failure when they had faithfully performed their prescribed tasks, and expressed guilt and concern about incidents in which they had carried out instructions to the letter, but, in so doing, had practiced what they considered to be bad nursing. For example, a nurse had been told to give a patient who had been sleeping badly a sleeping draught at a certain time. In the interval he had fallen into a deep natural sleep. Obeying her orders, she woke him up to give him the medicine. Her common sense and judgment told her to leave him asleep and she felt very guilty that she had disturbed him. The nurses felt they were being forced to abandon common-sense principles of good nursing, and they resented it.

Jaques (1956) discussed the use of discretion and came to the conclusion that the level of responsibility experienced in a job was related solely to the exercise of discretion and not to carrying out the prescribed elements. We may say that the level of responsibility in the nurse's job is minimized by the attempt to eliminate the use of discretion. Nurses felt insulted, indeed almost assaulted, by being deprived of the opportunity to be more responsible. They felt, and were, devalued by the social system. They were intuitively aware that the further development of their capacity for responsibility was being inhibited by the work and training situation and they greatly resented this. The bitterness of the experience was intensified because they were constantly being exhorted to behave responsibly, which, in the ordinary usage of the word in a work-situation, they were prevented from doing. We came to the conclusion that senior staff tended to use the word 'responsible' differently from ordinary usage. For them, a responsible nurse was one who carried out prescriptions to the letter. There was an essential conflict between staff and students that greatly added to stress and bitterness on both sides. Jaques (1956) stated that workers in industry cannot rest content until they have reached a level of work that deploys to the full their capacity for discretionary responsibility. Student nurses, who were, in effect, workers in the hospital for most of their time, were certainly not content.

Deprivation of personal satisfactions

The nursing service seemed to provide unusually little in the way of direct satisfaction for staff and students. Although the dictum 'nursing should be a vocation' implied that nurses should not expect ordinary job satisfaction, its absence added to stress. Mention has already been made of a number of ways in which nurses were deprived of positive satisfactions potentially existent in the profession. Satisfaction was also reduced by the attempt to evade anxiety by splitting up the nurse–patient relationship and converting patients who need nursing into tasks that must be performed. Although the nursing *service* had considerable success in nursing patients, the individual nurse had little direct experience of success. Success and satisfaction were dissipated in much the same way as anxiety. Nurses missed the reassurance of seeing patients get better in a way they could easily connect with their own efforts. The nurses' longing for this kind of experience was shown in the excitement and pleasure felt by a nurse who was chosen to 'special' a patient, that is give special, individual care to a very ill patient in a crisis. The gratitude of patients, an important reward for nurses, was also dissipated. Patients' were grateful to the hospital or to the nurses for their treatment and recovery, but they could not easily express gratitude in any direct way to individual nurses. There were too many and they were too mobile. [. . .]

The nursing service inhibited in a number of ways the realization of satisfactions in relationships with colleagues. The traditional relationship between staff and students was such that students were singled out by staff almost solely for reprimand or criticism. Good work was taken for granted and little praise given. Students complained that no one noticed when they worked well, when they stayed late on duty, or when they did some extra task for a patient's comfort. Work-teams were notably impermanent. Even three-monthly moves of student nurses made it difficult to weld together a strong, cohesive work-team. The more frequent moves, and the threat of moves, made it almost impossible. In such circumstances, it was difficult to build a team that functioned effectively on the basis of real knowledge of the strengths and weaknesses of each member, her needs as well as her contribution, and adapted to the way of working and type of relationship each person preferred. Nurses felt hurt and resentful about the lack of importance attached to their personal contribution to the work, and the work itself was less satisfying when it had to be done not only in accord- ance with the task-list system, but also within an informal, but rigid, organization. [. . .]

[. . .]

I go on now to consider the second general approach to the failure of the social defense to alleviate anxiety. This arose from the direct impact of the social defense system on the individual, regardless of specific experiences, that is, from the more directly psychological interaction between the social defense system and the individual nurse.

Although I have used the term 'socially structured defense system' as a construct to describe certain features of the nursing service as a continuing social institution, I wish to make it clear that I do not imply that the nursing service *as an institution* operates the defenses. Defenses are, and can be, operated only by individuals. Their behavior is the link between their psychic defenses and the institution. Membership necessitates an adequate degree of matching between individual and social defense systems. I will not attempt to define the degree of matching, but state simply that if the discrepancy between social and individual defense systems is too great, some breakdown in the individual's relation with the institution is inevitable. The form of breakdown varies, but it commonly takes the form of a temporary or permanent break in the individual's membership. For example continuing to use one's own defenses and to follow one's own idiosyncratic behavior patterns may make an individual intolerable to other members of the institution who are more adapted to the social defense system. They may then respond with rejection. Trying to behave in a way consistent with the social defense system rather than individual defenses will increase anxieties and make it impossible for the individual to continue membership. Theoretically, matching between social and individual defenses can be achieved by a re-structuring of the social defense system to match the individual, by a re-structuring of the individual defense system to match the social, or by a combination of the two. The processes by which an adequate degree of matching is achieved are too complicated to describe here in detail. It must suffice to say that they depend heavily on repeated projection of the psychic defense system into the social defense system and repeated introjection of the social defense system into the psychic defense system. This allows continuous testing of match and fit as the individual experiences his or her own and other people's reactions (Heimann, 1952).

The social defense system of the nursing service has been described as an historical development through collusive interaction between individuals to project and reify relevant elements of their psychic defense systems. However, from the point of view of new entrants to the nursing service, the social defense system at the time of entry is a datum, an aspect of external reality to which they must react and adapt. Fenichel (1946) makes a similar point. He states that social institutions arise through the efforts of human beings to satisfy their needs, but that social institutions then become external realities comparatively independent of individuals which affect the structure of the individual. The student nurses were faced with a particularly difficult task in adapting to the nursing service and developing an adequate match between the social defense system and their psychic defense systems. It will be clear that the nursing service was very resistant to change, especially change in the functioning of its defense system. For the student nurses, this meant that the social defense system was to an unusual extent immutable. In the process of matching between the psychic and social defense systems, the emphasis was heavily on the modification of the individual's psychic defenses. This meant in practice that the social defense system had to be incorporated and used more or less as it was found, and psychic defenses re-structured as necessary to match it.

An earlier section of this paper described how the social defense system of the hospital was built on primitive psychic defenses, those characteristic of the earliest phases of infancy. The fact that the student nurses had to incorporate and use this defense system has certain intrapsychic consequences. These defenses are oriented to the violent, terrifying situations of infancy, and rely heavily on violent splitting which dissipates the anxiety. They avoid the experience of anxiety and effectively prevent the individual from confronting it. Thus, the individual cannot bring the content of the phantasy anxiety situations into effective contact with reality. Unrealistic or pathological anxiety cannot be differentiated from realistic anxiety arising from real dangers. Therefore, anxiety tends to remain permanently at a level determined more by the phantasies than by the reality. The forced introjection of the hospital defense system, therefore, perpetuates in the individual a considerable degree of pathological anxiety.

The enforced use of this defense system inhibited maturation in many ways and even led to regression. It interfered with the capacity for symbol formation; it inhibited the capacity for abstract thought and conceptualization; it prevented full development of the individual's knowledge, understanding and skills. The social defense system inhibited the psychic integration on which the development of such capacities depends. Individuals were prevented from realizing to the full their capacity for concern, compassion and sympathy, and for action based on these feelings which would strengthen their belief in their own good aspects and capacity to use them. The defense system struck directly, therefore, at the roots of sublimatory activities in which infantile anxieties could be re-worked in symbolic form and modified.

In general, one may say that forced introjection of the defense system prevented the personal defensive maturation that alone would allow for the modification of the remnants of infantile anxiety and diminish the extent to which early anxieties may be re-evoked and projected into current real situations. Indeed, in many cases, it forced the individual to regress to a maturational level below that achieved before entering the hospital. In this, the nursing service failed its individual members desperately. [. . .]

Conclusion

Attention has been concentrated mainly on the way in which the social defense system in the nursing service was ineffective in containing anxiety in its members. It did not help them work it through. Incidentally, however, mention was made from time to time of the effect of the social defense system on diminishing the efficiency of task-performance. The inefficiencies were not so great as to prevent task-performance from continuing, although at a less than optimum level and accompanied by fears that it might be in jeopardy.

Inefficiencies noted include high staff/patient ratios, bad nursing practice, excessive staff turnover, failure to train students effectively for their future roles. Further, the high level of anxiety in nurses added to the stress of illness and hospitalization for patients and had adverse effects on such factors as recovery rates. A later investigation (Revans, 1959) connected recovery rates of patients quite directly with the morale of the nursing staff. Thus the social structure of the nursing service is defective not only as a means of handling anxiety, but also as a method of organizing its tasks. These two aspects of the situation cannot be regarded as separate. The inefficiency is an inevitable consequence of the chosen defense system.

The success and viability of a social institution are intimately connected with the techniques it uses to contain anxiety. Analogous hypotheses about the individual have long been widely accepted. Freud (1948) put forward such ideas as his work developed. The work of Melanie Klein and her colleagues has given a central position to anxiety and the defenses in personality development and ego-functioning (Klein, 1948). Similarly, an understanding of this aspect of the functioning of a social institution is an important diagnostic and therapeutic tool in facilitating social change. Bion (1955) and Jaques (1955) stress the importance of understanding these phenomena and relate difficulties in achieving social change to difficulty in tolerating the anxieties that are released as social defenses are re-structured. The many failures experienced by social scientists and others in attempts to change social institutions would seem to be connected with their not taking sufficient account of the need to analyze anxieties and defenses.

The nursing service illustrated the problem of achieving social change to a marked degree. Efforts to initiate serious change were often met with acute anxiety and hostility. The people concerned felt very threatened, the threat being of nothing less than social chaos and individual breakdown. To give up known ways of behavior and embark on the unknown were felt to be intolerable. In general, it may be postulated that resistance to social change is likely to be greatest in institutions whose social defense systems are dominated by primitive psychic defense mechanisms, those which have been collectively described by Melanie Klein as the paranoid-schizoid defenses (Klein, 1952a, 1959). One may compare this socio-therapeutic experience with the common experience in psychoanalytical therapy, that the most difficult work is with patients whose defenses are mainly of this kind, or in phases of the analysis when such defenses predominate.

Some therapeutic results were achieved in the hospital, notably in relation to the presenting symptom. For example, a planned set of courses was prepared for student nurses, which jointly ensured that the student nurse had adequate training and that the hospital was adequately staffed, and took more realistic account of the real discrepancies between training and staffing needs. To prevent emergencies from interfering with the implementation of the planned courses, a reserve pool of mobile nurses was created. The common feature of the changes, however, was that they involved minimal disturbance of the existing defense system. Indeed, it might be more correct to say that they involved reinforcing and strengthening the existing type of defense. Proposals were made for more far-reaching change, involving a re-structuring of the social defense system. For example, one suggestion was that a limited experiment be done in ward organization, eliminating the task-list system and substituting some form of patient assignment. However, although the senior staff discussed such proposals with courage and seriousness, they did not feel able to proceed with the plans. This happened in spite of our clearly expressed view that, unless there were some fairly radical changes in the system, the problems of the nursing service might well become extremely serious. The decision seemed to us quite comprehensible, however, in view of the anxiety and the defense system. These would have made the therapeutic task of accomplishing change very difficult for both the nursing service and the therapist.

Notes

1 Throughout this paper I follow the convention of using 'fantasy' to mean conscious fantasy and 'phantasy' to mean unconscious phantasy.
2 In my description of infantile psychic life I follow the work of Freud, particularly as developed and elaborated by Melanie Klein (1952b, 1959).
3 In the nursing service, a 'sister' is the head nurse in a ward and a 'staff nurse' is a fully qualified nurse who is her deputy.
4 The nurses third and fourth in seniority in administration.

References

Bion, W.R. (1955) 'Group dynamics: a review', in M. Klein, P. Heimann and R.E. Money-Kyrle (eds), *New Directions in Psycho-Analysis*. London: Tavistock Publications.
Fenichel, O. (1946) *The Psycho-Analytic Theory of the Neuroses*. New York: Norton.
Freud, S. (1948) *Inhibitions, Symptoms and Anxiety*. London: Hogarth Press and Institute of Psychoanalysis.
Heimann, P. (1952) 'Certain functions of introjection and projection in earliest infancy', in J. Riviere (ed.), *Developments in Psycho-Analysis*. London: Hogarth Press and Institute of Psychoanalysis.
Jaques, E. (1955) 'Social systems as a defence against persecutory and depressive anxiety', in M. Klein, P. Heimann and R.E. Money-Kyrle (eds), *New Directions in Psycho-Analysis*. London: Tavistock Publications.
Jaques E. (1956) *Measurement of Responsibility: a Study of Work, Payment, and Individual Capacity*. London: Tavistock Publications.

Klein, M. (1948) 'The importance of symbol formation in the development of the ego', in *Contributions to Psycho-Analysis 1921–1945*. London: Hogarth Press and Institute of Psychoanalysis.

Klein M. (1952a) 'Notes on some schizoid mechanisms', in J. Riviere (ed.), *Developments in Psycho-Analysis*. London: Hogarth Press and Institute of Psychoanalysis [see Chapter 12, this volume].

Klein, M. (1952b) 'Some theoretical conclusions regarding the emotional life of the infant', in J. Riviere (ed.), *Developments in Psycho-Analysis*. London: Hogarth Press and Institute of Psychoanalysis.

Klein, M. (1959) 'Our adult world and its roots in infancy', *Human Relations*, 12: 291–303.

Revans, R.W. (1959) 'The hospital as an organism: a study in communications and morale', *Proceedings of the Sixth Annual International Meeting of the Institute of Management Sciences*. London and New York: Pergamon Press.

Rice, A.K. (1958) *Productivity and Social Organization: the Ahmedabad Experiment*. London: Tavistock Publications (reissued 1987, New York: Garland).

Segal, H. (1957) 'Notes on symbol formation', *International Journal of Psycho-Analysis*, 38: 391–7.

Trist, E.L. and Bamforth K.W. (1951) 'Some social and psychological consequences of the Longwall method of coal getting', *Human Relations*, 4: 3–38.

16

Psychoanalysis, racism and anti-racism
Michael Rustin

Race in social science

'Race' is both an empty category and one of the most destructive and powerful forms of social categorization. How is this paradox to be explained, and how are its negative consequences for human lives to be resisted? These are the central issues to be explored in this chapter.

Amongst the attributes that can be chosen as grounds for categorizing people, those of race are widely recognized to have the least power to explain any significant differences between them.[1] The distinctions of national culture, religion and class mark out some significant properties and differences between members of groups defined in these terms.[2] To share the assumptions of the dominant culture of France, in regard to such matters as the meaning of 'culture', the proper role of the state, or the significance of food, is to think differently from English middle-class society about these aspects of life. To be brought up as a member of a Nonconformist Protestant community is to share beliefs, habits of thought, a particular cast of moral feelings, distinct from those of a Roman Catholic, a Jew, or a humanistic atheist. Equally, to share the values of a class or status group is to hold some set of implicit attitudes, derived ultimately from the common economic situation of those similarly positioned.

Such differences are likely to be expressed by the choice of distinct principles and habits of classification, expressing not so much a clear opposition to other groups as different principles of cognitive and moral selection. Of course, where groups are antagonistically placed in relation to one another (Protestants and Catholics; rival nationalities; opposed social classes) there will also be disagreements of an explicit kind – members of

This chapter is taken from *The Good Society and the Inner World* (London, Verso, 1991), pp. 57–84.

one group will be forced to take note, in a negating way, of the dominant definitions of the other's existence. But even in such cases of open antagonism, there will probably be positive as well as negative grounds of identity. A Protestant is not merely a bundle of non-Catholic characteristics; even more obviously this is true of national identities; class identities, even if formed in relation to antagonistic classes, usually develop some positive values and categorizations of their own, which do not need the threat of the other class to keep them in being.

[. . .]

By contrast with this series of attributes, differences of biological race are largely lacking in substance. Racial differences go no further, in their essence, than superficial variations in bodily appearance and shape – modal tallness of different groups, colour of skin, facial shape, hair, etc. Given the variations that occur within so-called racial groups, and give rise to no general categorizations or clusterings (the physically stronger, more symmetrically featured, larger, leaner, etc.), it is hard to find any significance in these difference except those which are quite arbitrarily assigned to them. [. . .] Racial differences depend on the definition given to them by the other – that is to say, on the definition of the other – and the most powerful definitions of these kinds are those which are negative – definitions that we can call racist. Because the differences marked out by race are inherently so trivial (in terms of the human capacities they describe) they are to be explained largely as a myth, or counter-myth, in a sense that does not in the main apply to the other dimensions of difference discussed above, though these can be – and often are – also turned into myths.

Of course, these 'empty' categories of race are nevertheless immensely powerful as markers and boundaries in many human societies. Identification with one 'racial group' and against another, oppression of one racial group by another, and resistance to such racial oppression by groups who define themselves in racial terms for this purpose, are among the most important forms of social cleavage, domination and resistance. Sociologists, being concerned to understand and explain the world as it is, note this line of cleavage as a social fact, and have been able to demonstrate its prevalence, its origins, its relation to other lines of division (especially those of class, nation, and empire) and its dire human effects. But in so doing they tend to lose sight of an important issue: how is it that a categorization that is so empty and arbitrary can nevertheless give rise to such powerful, oppressive, and even catastrophic social effects? What is the mechanism or principle that can explain how a nothing, an objectively insignificant no-thing, can become and remain so disastrously and dismally important in its effects on human lives?

It is significant that supposedly 'natural' differences of race appear to be insignificant or unnoticed in the discriminations of others made by small children, whether of adults or others of their own age. Very young children, shaped in this presumably by their genetic inheritance, relate to adults in terms of their familiarity or friendliness, not in terms of their superficial bodily characteristics. It is mainly at the age of latency – both when cultural definitions are gaining greater influence in children's minds, and when there are powerful positive and negative feelings making themselves felt outside the holding setting of the immediate family – that racial patterns emerge in thinking and social behaviour. The more negative feeling and anxiety that is having to be processed by children and adolescents in their social milieu (such as school), the more likely this is to be projected in persecutory ways into negatively defined 'out-groups'. Racial feeling among children seems to be a product of group life and culture, not instinctual nature.

From a sociological point of view, this may not seem a very interesting question. A social fact is a social fact. Among the most causally important of social facts are shared beliefs about the world, whatever their justification or otherwise from the viewpoint of the scientific observer. Sociologists often seem to be committed to a kind of epistemological neutrality about the beliefs they study.[3] Their interest in beliefs is in their facticity and causal potency; it seems to them to be some other discipline's job to explain where this potency comes from. Other disciplines have not, in the particular case of beliefs in the significance of race – what we can thus accurately describe as race-ism – come forward with very powerful explanations.

Clarifying the differences between beliefs which have rational grounds, and those which do not, and explaining how each comes to be held, nevertheless seems to me to be a crucial task for the social sciences. It is hard to imagine a distinction between good societies and bad ones, or tolerable ones and intolerable ones, which doesn't turn on the pervasiveness or otherwise of rational, well-informed and intelligent ways of thinking, and their opposites – irrational, ignorant and stupid ways. [. . .] Societies which are relatively rational in their ways of adjudicating human claims and of responding to human needs may be ill-informed in their understanding of nature. Conversely, societies which are highly rational in their technical understanding and practices may be completely deluded in their social beliefs. The Azande (as they were described by Evans-Pritchard in 1976) might thus be regarded as mostly sensible and well ordered in their social practices, but limited in their scientific understanding. The Nazis, on the other hand, were rational in their organizational and technical methods, but maniacs in their thinking about and dealings with human beings. These distinctions do not follow merely from arbitrary cultural and ethical preferences. Consistency and inconsistency in thought, respect and disrespect for contextually known facts, are empirically observable attributes of practices and beliefs about the social world, as well as about the natural. Simple societies may be rationally well ordered, in their everyday social actions, or not. On the other hand, whilst technological progress may be, empirically, a precondition of many morally desirable states of affairs (less suffering, longer life spans, etc.),[4] it does not necessarily bring these into existence, and can indeed enlarge rather than reduce the scale of human suffering.

It is important to retain the criterion of rationality as discriminating between different kinds of individual and social behaviour, if there is to be any ground for making moral judgements, whether of acts, individuals, or societies. If one recognizes that the categories of 'rational' and 'irrational' are separately applicable to many different spheres of life, it is possible to avoid the privileging of 'Eurocentric' and 'Western' world-views which has followed from post-Enlightenment faith in reason, and has made Western rationality sometimes seem like one ideological face of imperialism. [. . .]

Similarly, Freud's stance of scepticism towards the claims to unquestionable rationality of those he analysed – and indeed, of society in general – led him not to indifference to the value of human reason but to a life's work designed to strengthen its sway in all human lives.

Since beliefs in racial difference are among the most irrational that men and women hold, it seems that the science of the irrational, psychoanalysis (that is to say, the science which seeks to understand the sources of the irrational in the human mind), is one science to which we ought to look for their explanation. [. . .]

Psychoanalysis and racism

A valuable starting point for thinking about a psychoanalytic approach to race and racism is Sartre's brilliant essay *Anti-Semite and Jew*.[5] Though he makes no reference to psychoanalytic ideas in this piece of writing, the core of Sartre's argument immediately grasps what in psychoanalytic terms is the key phenomenon to be understood. 'Anti-Semitism', he says, 'is a passion.' What he means by this is that the attitudes of the anti-Semite are made up of opposite and inconsistent attributions, involve sensations of physical repulsion and disgust, and explicitly deny any reason or need to be ordinarily logical:

> I noted earlier that anti-Semitism is a passion. Everybody understands that emotions of hate or anger are involved. But ordinarily, hate and anger have a provocation: I hate someone who has made me suffer, someone who contemns or insults me. We have just seen that anti-Semitic passion could not have such a character. It precedes the facts that are supposed to call it forth; it seeks them out to nourish itself upon them; it must even interpret them in a special way so that they may become truly offensive. Indeed, if you so much as mention a Jew to an anti-Semite, he will show signs of a lively irritation. If we recall that we must always consent to anger before it can manifest itself and that, as is indicated so accurately by the French idiom, we 'put ourselves' into anger, we shall have to agree that the anti-Semite has chosen to live on the plane of passion.

The anti-Semite has chosen hate because hate is a faith; at the outset he has chosen to devalue words and reasons. How entirely at ease he feels as a result. How futile and frivolous discussions about the rights of the Jew appear to him. He has placed himself on other ground from the beginning. If out of courtesy he consents for a moment to defend his point of view, he lends himself but does not give himself. He tries simply to project his intuitive certainty on to the plane of discourse.[6]

What Sartre calls 'a passion' (the opposite, in his view of the world, of reason, linked indissolubly with compulsion; as, conversely, reason is the means and expression of freedom) we might in psychoanalytic terms describe as a psychotic state. The essence of the argument that follows is that beliefs about race, when they are suffused with intense feeling, are akin to psychotic states of mind. This is not, of course, to say that they are beliefs only or mainly held by a particular category of psychotics – how much that would simplify the matter if it were so! The psychoanalytic argument is a different one. It is that psychotic attributes of mind are universal, original and latent components of human mentality; never wholly banished from the self; liable to become more salient in conditions of fear and anxiety than in more benign settings; and of course more central and pathogenic in some individuals than in others, sometimes for explicable reasons in an individual's psychic history.[7]

The mechanisms of psychotic thought find in racial categorizations an ideal container. These mechanisms include the paranoid splitting of objects into the loved and hated, the suffusion of thinking processes by intense, unrecognized emotion, confusion between self and object due to the splitting of the self and massive projective identification, and hatred of reality and truth. The arbitrariness and baselessness of racial categories, their embodiment of a pure spirit of otherness, are an advantage if one 'wants to think' (as Sartre would see it, from his perspective of unlimited individual responsibility for acts of self), or is compelled to think (as psychoanalysts would be more likely to see it), in a psychotic way. There is nothing, in reality, to think about, no real external object (at least, none that wouldn't cut across these organizing categories if its real properties were recognized) to impede the free flow of projected feelings, or the projective identifications of different and unwanted parts of the self. The emptiness of racial categories renders them particularly good vehicles for pseudo-thinking, and for what Bion calls lies – that is, pseudo-thinking intended to defend against the apprehension of reality.[8] Concepts that are useless for the purposes of understanding anything are effective enough for the transfer of Sartre's 'passions' – that is, unwanted states of feeling.

Of course, many other systems of categories will do for the same purpose. Religion, class, nationality can all provide blank screens, or crude outlines, on which the phantasies of the unconscious can be written. Mental constructions of animal species will do as well, and racial categorizations have often been represented through the metaphors of the bestiary, as Leo Kuper has pointed out.[9] (Who isn't irrationally afraid, in some part of themselves, of some animal or other, whether spider, snake, or rat?) But in these other cases of social discrimination there is more real difference to intrude, more complications to consider, in making any descriptive use of these categories. In the racial case, virtually no differences are caught by 'black' or 'white', except those which are the effects of something else – culture, nationality, the experience of discrimination or of oppression; the results of hostility to the racial category as such. These differences are in the main the product, perhaps over a long period of history, of the irrational regard (and actions) of the other. This is paradoxically the source of racism's power. It is the fact that this category means nothing in itself that makes it able to bear so much meaning – mostly psychologically primitive in character – with so little innate resistance from the conscious mind.

One unconscious source of these projections, underestimated in Sartre's unduly rationalist view of the mind, may, however, be the significance of bodily sensation in early infancy. In physical contact between parents and infants, sensations of touch, smell, the feel of hair, the perception of family resemblance, become suffused with intense feeling. In so far as early attachment is textured in these ways, physical characteristics remain potential objects of powerful emotions, both positive and negative. (Such physical characteristics are subsequently given typical or idealized form in cultural representations, tapping and reinforcing the early identifications of dominant groups and alienating or severing contact with those of subordinate or marginalized ones, which is why argument over the diffused range and plurality of representations is an important one.) This is not to say that human beings naturally remain fixated for life on these dimensions of similarity and difference. If this were the case, attachment would be exclusively within family groups, and incest would be the norm. It does, however, suggest that the 'passions' Sartre so brilliantly denounces are more firmly rooted in human identities than he might wish. Rationality and the capacity to enjoy differences depend on a continuing developmental struggle within each individual and social group, and cannot be accomplished by a simple act of rational will. This is consistent with Freud's more general view of the possibility and precariousness of reason and the reality principle in human life.

The relevance of the Kleinian tradition in psychoanalysis

The psychoanalytic ideas from which these characterizations of racial categorizations are drawn are those of Melanie Klein and analysts influenced by her.[10] [. . .]

[. . .]

The 'schizoid mechanisms' described by Klein include splitting, idealization and denigration, and she refers to these processes as liable to be wholly unrestrained by considerations of logic and rationality. These psychotic mechanisms do not usually take the form of artfully disguised rationalizations, of thought processes merely distorted or biased by the pressure of unconscious impulse in the matter of neurotic symptoms. In this more primitive field of mental operations, reason does not merely become rationalization; it may cease to operate at all, or be in evidence only in episodic moments.

Bion's work has further developed these ideas, through his closer attention to the mechanisms and preconditions of thought and disorders of thought.[11] He identified the desire for knowledge and understanding as an innate human need, parallel in its functional importance to the desires of love and the aversions of hate. This developed Klein's idea of an 'epistemophilic instinct', or innate appetite for knowledge, with which she explained the infant's interest in and phantasies about parental intercourse in writings on the early stages of the Oedipus complex. Where Klein's model of the mind was mainly constructed around the antonyms of love and hate, Bion adds a third dimension of knowledge.[12] Attacks on the understanding (sometimes called 'attacks on linking' in his writing)[13] form a specific dimension of malfunction and perversion, taking the form sometimes of lies (minus K) or of total refusal to enter the treacherous field of communication through language. Perversions of thought thus become in Bion's view – and in that of Donald Meltzer, who has further developed some of these ideas[14] – a specific kind of individual and social pathology.

The relevance of these conceptions to the phenomena of racism derives from the importance of irrational projections and states of projective identification in racial attributions. Dichotomous versions of racial difference are paranoid in their structure, since they function mainly not as cognitive mapping devices intended to identify facts, but as ways of channelling and condensing basic feelings of positive and negative identification. They are modes of mental splitting, idealization, and denigration (Leo Kuper points out the significant etymology of this last term)[15] *par excellence*.

Explicit vilification seems to be a more prominent element in the racism of dominant groups than self-idealization, even though idealization and its opposite are usually linked. The effect of getting rid of bad feelings into the other is to allow the self to perceive itself as wholly good. The idea that the subject- or subordinate- or pariah-race (whether blacks or Jews in different contexts) is inferior or repellent nevertheless seems to carry more intuitive conviction than triumphalist assertions of the perfection of the dominant group, though these occur too. The most active process at work in such racisms is the projection of negative, repressed, or inaccessible aspects of the individual and social self. Cultures of racial domination, since they are founded on greed, cruelty and the exploitation of weakness, will have many such hateful states of mind to get rid of somewhere. This process can have a self-reinforcing dynamic, in which the evidence of damage inflicted on projected internal objects generates still more violent persecution, which is again projected on to powerless victims.

One location in which the other side of this psychic coin, idealization, is to be found at the present time is in the form of practices and ideologies intended to attach positive value to attributes deemed to be inherent in the subordinate group. Here the emphasis, so far as racial definition is concerned, is on positive, not negative, feelings in the propagation of ideologies and sentiments of racial pride. One hardly wishes to call in question practices whose purpose is to improve the self-esteem of members of oppressed or stigmatized groups, and to defend them against hostile attributions. But there are possible costs here, too, in subordination of the vital and virtuous habits of mind of truth-seeking, and in the unnoticed negative side of all idealizing modes of thought. Ideological attributions of goodness to a group defined as falling on one side of a dividing line tend to involve implicit attributions of badness to those on the other.

Other evidence of the psychotic roots of racism are to be found in the primitive mental associations and accompaniments of racist thinking. Enoch Powell gave expression to one symptom of this when he referred in his infamous Birmingham speech[16] to excrement being pushed through an old lady's letter-box. Deep psychic confusion is revealed when faeces become such important carriers of meaning as they have been in the mythology of race relations in Britain. It is clear that disgusting and degraded aspects of the self are here being dealt with by being either ascribed to, or literally dumped on, the unwanted group. Anxieties about fecundity and sexual potency of other racial groups are an indication of another source of primitive disturbance. Oral phantasies of cannibalism lie deep in the colonialist memory – Caliban is a near-anagram of cannibal,[17] and Robinson Crusoe rescues the slave/servant he names Friday from being eaten by pursuers of a different tribe. While the idea of cannibalism as such has often been treated in modern times as a joke (giving rise to a standard cartoon format of persons about to be cooked in large cauldrons with some witty caption) the lasting preoccupation with the idea of cannibalism (out of all proportion to its historical or anthropological significance) seems to indicate deeper unconscious roots. (The idea comes nearer to the surface in the classic fairy tales and in some more recent children's fiction.)[18] The connection between primitive oral phantasy and contemporary racism can be seen in the way emotions and anxieties about food suffuse racial prejudice today. *The Observer* of 22 November 1987 reported (among many other incidents) severe harassment and attacks on an Asian family in Thamesmead initiated when 'the next-door neighbour banged on the door and said: "Your curry is making the whole street stink."' The passions and disgusts thus evoked by food habits reveal deep preoccupations with, and probable confusions about, bodily functions and their inner meanings. (There are mythologies about what other races and peoples eat.) All the three levels of bodily fixation described by Freud – oral, anal and genital – seem to be conspicuously in evidence in the everyday mythologies of racism.

The schizoid mechanisms described by Klein in the context of infantile life, and in their manifestation in the experience of individual psychoanalysis, have also been described as processes in the mental life of groups, by Bion and others.[19] This idea can be extended to a societal level, to explain the processes by which powerful transitive communications take place between members of imaginary collectivities; what is thus communicated are emotions or aspects of identity of high negative valency. What is expelled by the group expressing prejudice or hatred, and what has to be borne (or resisted, or got rid of, if that is possible) by their recipients, are powerful doses of bad psychic stuff. Such transactions are more potent, psychologically primitive, and damaging than the mere mental definitions or images that are usually written about in this context. It is just because these communications do not operate merely at a cognitive level, as statements of opinion, that they are so hard for their recipients to deal with. Expressions of prejudice, rejection, or distaste fulfil active, albeit unconscious, emotional needs for those who make them – they get rid of something unwanted or uncomfortable out of the self, where they cause mental conflict and pain, into some external container, whose pain is either disregarded as of no account or, worse still, has a perverse value for those who project it in its visible existence outside the self. One can easily see how social groups made to receive the projections of collectivities superior to them will be filled with the desire to push them on to some group still more vulnerable than they, and thus how maltreatment is passed down the social status ladder from group to group. Racism can thus be seen to involve states of projective identification, in which hated self-attributes of members of the group gripped by prejudice are phantasied to exist in members of the stigmatized race. An example of this mechanism is to be found in Jeremy Seabrook's account of racist attitudes in Blackburn in the 1960s, in his *City Close-up*.[20] The paradox of the hostility expressed by members of the white working class to Asians was that the Asians then, in Seabrook's view, had come to embody in reality many of the virtues of solid working-class family life, while it was the prejudiced white community that was experiencing a shaming loss of these qualities in the context of its economic and social disintegration. What the white community described by Seabrook did was to project on to the Asians the demoralized and disintegrated state which was being acutely experienced as a degradation by the depleted white working class.

Theories which don't take note of these psychic roots of racist practices can't adequately account either for the deep pain and damage they cause to their victims, or for their persistence as a social pathology. The tendency to see racism as a system of ideological or false beliefs, to be banished by anti-racist teaching and propaganda, fails to see that its main power lies at an unconscious level. Racist ways of thinking may be so resistant to argument precisely because they don't derive from or really engage with these levels of mental functioning. They derive from preconceptions, not observed facts, and pay little regard to rules of consistency or rational inference in the formation of judgements and strong opinions. The racist, as Sartre said of the anti-Semite, 'takes his stand from the start on the ground of irrationalism'.[21] Rather than attending, as much recent writing about racism does, to the prejudiced content of thoughts about race and their historical and social origins, perhaps we should pay more attention to their psychic form, to the process rather than the product of thoughts and feelings about race.

These psychoanalytic insights suggest how processes of thoughts are driven and overdetermined by unconscious emotional forces. Splitting between positive and negative feelings, and corresponding processes of idealization and denigration, are inherent in racist attributions. Klein and her early colleagues gave most attention to the power of the emotions of love and hate unconsciously to shape states of mind and relationships to internal and external objects. The later Kleinian interest in the nature of thought processes also has relevance to racist beliefs, however. What Bion, Rosenfeld, Meltzer, and others came to understand was that sadistic attacks on absent or lost external objects could lead to a perverse idealization of the 'bad self' – that is, the self as the author of denigratory and sadistic attacks. Such destructive narcissism could extend to the self's own pathological and destructive ways of thinking. The 'lie' in this system of personality organization becomes positively valued, as carrying for the self an important aspect of its defences against weakness, loss, or negative judgement. The idea that negative attitudes to the truth, as well as more familiarly towards persons and objects, can become part of pathological organizations of the personality may explain something about the extraordinary tenacity of racist beliefs in certain conditions. This qualifies only to a degree the view earlier expressed that the primary hold of racism comes from the domain of sentiment rather than reason. This is because whilst this view acknowledges that kinds of 'reasoning' may be clung to as important defences of identity and motives to action, the 'reasoning' in question is itself a representative of hatred of the truth, and the reciprocal exchanges and relationships on which truthful apprehension of reality must be based. The gangster's stylized mockery of 'conventional' values and morality, and of 'straight' ways of thinking, and the Nazi's frenzied denunciations of 'alien' kinds of thinking, indicate a deep hatred of rational processes as such. This is what explains the almost arrogant indifference to reason or evidence described by Sartre in his discussion of anti-Semitism.

There is a parallel between the arguments made here about the relevance of psychoanalysis to the understanding of racism and those of some feminists on the implications of psychoanalysis for women's oppression. In each case, the psychoanalytic argument draws attention to the unconscious roots of mechanisms of domination and subordination, and suggests that reasoning about the issues – that is, discourse on a level of superficial rationality – is unlikely to shift the balance of social relations very much. Feminists like Mitchell, Dinnerstein and Chodorow[22] argued that gender identities were established by unconscious processes of repression and identification during infancy. Only by radically altering the family (Mitchell) or in a more reformist vein by altering the balance of male and female parental responsibility within it (Dinnerstein and Chodorow) could more equal gender identities be forged – more equal but nevertheless different in general pattern, I would say.

There is, however, an important difference between the psychoanalytic view advanced here in regard to race, and the above argument as it has addressed feminist issues. Feminist writers on this topic have tended to think of women-feminists even – as their principal readership, drawing attention to obstacles to emancipation lodged inside themselves, and trying to describe and account for some deep-rooted conservative attachments among women to traditional identities (for example those of mother and wife) even where these conflict with feminist ideals. The psychoanalytic view of racism is not, however, intended to be principally addressed to racism's victims – as a way of reflecting on how hard it is to overcome negative self-definitions, for example. It is worth drawing attention to the emotional damage caused by projections of the kind referred to above, but more important to think about their causes and possible removal. Racism is primarily to be located as a problem of those who perpetrate its practices, not of its victims.

Obviously racism is not wholly explicable by reference to the operation of social sentiments, or by psychoanalysis's analysis of these in terms of unconscious mental processes. It would be crassly reductionist not to recognize the interaction of racial oppression with the oppression of class, or to fail to acknowledge the enormous role of imperialist domination in creating conditions for, and legitimizing, racial domination. It can even be argued that rational-choice theories have some leverage on this (and other) forms of social cleavage. That is to say, for members of a social category, however constituted, the use of membership of that category as a criterion of inclusion or exclusion, advantage or disadvantage, clearly potentially serves to advance the interests of individuals favourably classified. For white South Africans competing for scarce resources, power and status, it is clearly advantageous, by many common-sense definitions, to be able *a priori* to exclude blacks from virtually all competition. Similarly, exclusions by gender, or status group, benefit some by restricting competition from others, and indeed by the idea of superiority embodied in the principles of exclusion.

The point that is being made here is not that these forms of exclusion or domination do not exist, or do not count. Patently they do, and the social forces that contribute to them obviously need to be understood as well as possible, and vigorously challenged. What is being argued is that societies or groups that commit themselves to enforcing discriminations and disadvantages on a racial basis *ipso facto* commit themselves to irrational ways of conducting their affairs. Gains in material or other interest by particular groups are achieved at the expense of a denial of truth and reason – in effect, by adopting the strategy of the 'useful' lie.

Imperialist doctrines of 'natural' inferiority, or more opportunistic exclusionary practices based on more blatant kinds of self-interest, are founded on misrepresentations, and inevitably invade the capacity of those who hold them to cling on to rational mental functions and the respect these demand for the apprehension of reality and for the reciprocal conversations by which this is sustained. Projections, splittings of good and bad, and delusional phantasies are inevitably engendered by such commitments to lies, even where they do not provide their primary source.

It is not, of course, being argued that these social and political levels of oppression have no reality. The point is rather that a crucial means by which such structures are upheld is through irrational mental process, and that this dimension needs to be recognized and confronted as such. Above all, it is vital for those opposed to racist definitions not to fall victim to similar delusional and wilfully untruthful systems of thought as those which dominate the worlds of their oppressors.

Anti-racism as a strategy for overcoming racism

Nevertheless, it does seem vital to assess correctly what racism is, before deciding upon anti-racist strategies. Theories which characterize racism primarily as an ideology, as a system of false beliefs derived from imperialist history and as representing in a displaced form the interests of conflicting social classes,[23] may in part misrepresent the nature of the phenomenon, and therefore generate mistaken strategies for dealing with it.

This now-influential view has emerged in part from recent approaches to popular culture, which have extended the understanding of ideologies and their functioning. Where an earlier 'sociology of knowledge' and its Marxist cognate, the theory of ideology, viewed 'knowledge' as formalized, systematic bodies of ideas, more recent approaches – for example, those developed at the Centre for Contemporary Cultural Studies in Birmingham – have instead devoted attention to popular, everyday beliefs.[24] [. . .] While systematic social theories remain important to neo-Marxist analyses of culture, it is argued that popularly held beliefs do more work, so to speak.

Popular racist mentalities, however, have proved more tenacious and hard to uproot than scientific or quasi-scientific theories of racial difference had earlier been. Whilst theories of racial superiority and inferiority, influenced by Social Darwinist ideas, enjoyed great influence in the West in the latter part of the nineteenth and the early twentieth century[25] [. . .] they have in recent years been eclipsed by theories critical of biological explanations of human behaviour. [. . .] It has been hard to find sound evidence of biologically given differences between racially defined groups, in contrast to the relatively large and obvious differences traceable to cultural and social causes. It is hard to know what significance could be attached to such differences as have been asserted (even if they could be proved to exist), given the much greater range of attributes found within every so-called racial group.

Unfortunately, however, the intellectual strength or weakness of racist scientific theories seems to bear little relationship to the corresponding pervasiveness and vigour of popular racism. Intense forms of nationalism have also seemed able to thrive without benefit of rational support, as one would expect from the view of the unconscious sources of prejudice being presented here. It has turned out to be much more difficult to change popular definitions of the situation than it was to modify ideas in their more systematized form. The popular press is one reason for this, since it often serves as a transmitter and relay for currents of unconscious anxiety and hatred. Strong feelings are aroused by the press's attention to violent, distressing, or perverse events in its news coverage, and by the powerful images which dominate it, but seldom is anything written in the *Sun* or its equivalents which helps readers to respond to such events in reflective ways. [. . .] Philip Cohen has described, in the specific context of anti-racist teaching, how tenaciously 'common-sense' world-views are defended by working-class pupils against the more 'rational' anti-racist approaches of their liberal-minded teachers.[26] Conflict between 'racist' and 'anti-racist' definitions are, he shows, subordinated to a more deeply structured contest in working-class comprehensive schools between the 'middle-class' ideas of those in authority, and the 'culture of resistance' of working-class pupils among whom the educational transmission system of the school often fails.

Racist ideas may unwittingly be given an intellectual weight and plausibility they do not in reality justify, if racism is defined by anti-racists mainly as an ideological formation. Once racism is defined as a set of beliefs, it seems obligatory to explore their origins and affinities, and by implication to assign them intellectual significance. Thus biological theories of racial difference, eugenicist programmes of selective breeding, racial theories in cognitive psychology, are dredged up for scrupulous study, even though their current intellectual importance in the relevant social sciences may be trivial. Given the hypothesis that racism is a system of false beliefs, if these theories did not exist it would almost be necessary to invent them in order to demonstrate their falsehood. If, however, the major roots of racism in society have little to do with rationally held beliefs, a strategy which identifies their critique and refutation as a primary aim may be somewhat beside the point. To explain how and why false beliefs arise and are sustained may be a more vital matter than the repeated slaying by logic of ideas that may, to all intents and purposes, be already dead.

Whilst there may be good reason for vigilance to prevent the unchallenged re-emergence of racist theories (which might be more likely to occur without it), there is also a danger that concerns over legitimation or proscription may take the place of objective concerns for the truth. The politicized habits of thought thus induced, though they may seem harmless and even beneficial in the specific sphere of hostility to the pariah-field of racist theory, are hard to combine with the retention of a spirit of truth-seeking and open-mindedness in general. Such a rational and non-repressive climate is broadly the one in which racist thinking is least likely to thrive, and in which, conversely, positive perspectives of social improvement are most likely to develop.

There may be related problems with regard to certain other methods currently adopted to combat racist beliefs, if the argument that racial prejudices are psychologically primitive in origin has validity. In this case, what may be most significant for individuals, including those who hold them, to understand about them is their quality as states of mind rather than their phenomenal content. It seems likely that everyone, without exception, operates in a 'paranoid-schizoid' mode some of the time, though of course with varying objects into or on to which fear, hatred, frustration etc. are projected. Such bad feelings are likely to be dealt with uncon-sciously – as Bion pointed out, merely knowing about such feelings is very different from knowing them in an emotionally real way.[27] Classroom teaching aimed at changing attitudes may therefore do no more than ruffle the surface, for psychological reasons as well as because of the conflicts between the class cultures of teachers and children discussed so insightfully by Cohen. Worse than this, it can have the effect of increasing defensive kinds of psychological organization.

This psychological dimension to racist attitudes also raises questions about what is likely to be appropriate or helpful in teaching 'racism awareness' in educational settings. It seems important to distinguish between states of irrational hatred and projection *per se*, which are virtually universal in their incidence (though varying greatly in degree and intensity both for biographical and social reasons) and need to be understood and contained as such, and their particular manifestation in racial attitudes. Persecutory and guilt-inducing procedures may not be helpful as a technique for dealing with states of mind that are at root paranoid and persecutory in nature. Evoking feelings of guilt and shame in white students may not necessarily throw much light on where irrational antagonisms between groups come from, or in reality help individuals to deal with them.

From a psychoanalytic point of view, persecution seems ill-advised as a technique for dealing with states of mind that are at root paranoid and persecutory. (Persecutory here means deriving from the feeling of being persecuted.) This procedure would seem closely analogous to trying to deal with neurotic or psychotic symptoms (or, say, troubling personality dis-orders such as sexual sadism) by repression. Some apparent success might be achieved by such means, in that individuals susceptible to groups pressure will be led to hide their inclinations or find relief in persecuting them (through projective identification) in someone else. But such change will be superficial, brought about wholly through a strengthened superego and group-mindedness (part of the constituting problem of racism in the first place). Lasting change requires an experience of thinking about states of mind and their origins and meanings, in relatively free and non-accusatory settings. This is why psychoanalysis developed the technique of free association, and works in the mode of understanding rather than moral judgement. Psychoanalysis also makes the assumption that human beings in principle share the same latent dispositions and habits of mind, and that pathologies are not the monopoly of the other. It would seem to follow that in order for learning to take place at any depth, some mental tolerance has to be extended to what is contemplated, in order that it can become an object of conscious reflection and choice. The psychoanalytic assumption that primitive and 'bad' states of mind are universal dispositions seems a necessity for transformative learning.

On this view, racist states of mind are only one of many possible forms of irrational and negative projections of group feeling, whatever one might say about their specific historical and current social power. These states of feeling, in their general form, are not the monopoly of particular national or ethnic groups. Black racism or counter-racism, as well as white, is clearly both conceivable and actual. It seems to me that such states of mind, and their harmful consequences for the relations of individuals and groups, should be the larger subject of 'awareness' teaching, and should be thought about in whatever form they are manifested. It is hard to see how people of different 'races' can learn together about themselves if the fundamental assumption is that members of one group are guilty and members of the other are innocent.

Some related considerations may apply to more politicized versions of anti-racist teaching, in which racism is viewed straightforwardly as an ideological formation to be rooted out wherever it is found. On the surface, such anti-racist movements identify a wholly bad and non-racial object to attack. Since it is hard to find any rational basis for defending this object, the campaigns seem unchallengeably to have both morality and reason on their side. Even here, however, the form of mobilization of group sentiment in this movement, and the apparently overwhelming and self-evident correctness of the argument it makes, should raise some critical questions.

On the surface, anti-racism does not represent a simple reversal of racist feeling. Since its negative object is racism itself, not a racial group, anti-racism seems to invite an inclusive and clearly non-racist form of support. In reality, however, the position is a little more complicated. The 'racism' attacked by the anti-racist movement is not racism in all its forms, but mainly the racism of white society. Its pervasiveness is usually explained in this context by reference to the history of imperialism, and to the class dynamics of capitalism. This is importantly qualified in more sophisticated accounts by the insistence that racial inequalities and conflicts are not reducible to those of class, and have a separate causal weight within a more complex but still unified theoretical model.[28] The 'universalist' frame of reference which implicitly holds all this together is a socialist or neo-Marxist theory, and this framework enables an alliance to be constructed (fragile as it may be) between black radicals concerned mainly with questions of racial disadvantage, and white anti-racists concerned, among other things, with threats from the radical right. Whites identified with racism, or blacks deemed insufficiently hostile towards it, are the primary objects of criticism, not those subscribing to racist definitions of any kind. There is evidently a current of 'counter-racism' among blacks (insisting, for example, in social work on the enforcement of racial uniformity in fostering and adoption policies)[29] which is not subjected to critical reflection within this broadly anti-racist movement. 'Anti-racism' thus seems to allow both for the conduct of a universalist critique of racial discrimination, prejudice, domination etc., and for claims by black spokespersons to obtain control on a racial basis of what is deemed to be 'their own' social space. The ambiguity and slippage in this context between anti-racist and counter-racist arguments perhaps follows from the necessity to win multiracial support in Britain if any action on behalf of racial minorities is to succeed.

The existence in Britain of powerful forms of racism, resistance to attempts at remedy, and the need for a deliberate redress of ethnic disadvantage is not in doubt in this argument. What does need to be reflected on is what forms of investigation, advocacy and political response are most beneficial. On the whole, mere inversions of persecutory ways of thinking by dominant groups, in those few settings where minorities have some local control, may not be the most effective in the long run. Even the apparently righteous inversion inherent in the concept of 'anti-racism' may have its serious drawbacks, in being both manifestly the direct antithesis of racism, yet also bound by it as the central object of thought and feeling. What this concept does not encourage is the dissolution of the empty object of signifier 'race' into more real and individuated kinds of difference. A good society would be one which was not anti-racist but non-racial in its identities.

The danger lies in the powerful feelings of 'unity-in-conflict' evoked by negativistic campaigns, however justified their apparent object. While these states of mind may not be at all racist, they are persecutory in direction and conformity-inducing in their internal structure. The underlying state of mind they induce is massifying and deindividualizing. They are therefore liable to produce unconscious states of mind and hostility psychologically analogous to those of racism, even though they may well have a quite different content.

One might hypothesize further that a function of such antagonistic movements (one which defines itself as 'anti-' cannot be anything else) is to deal with the hostility suffered by victim groups by pushing it outwards, back in the direction of its perpetrators (Fanon's idea of cathartic liberation through acts of revolutionary violence[30] was a more extreme version of the same idea). One can see that this has helped to mobilize black people – and in other circumstances other victims of racial, class, national, or indeed gender domination – to fight to improve their situation, and why this is necessary. The psychic pain brought about by racial discrimination cannot simply be endlessly absorbed without deep damage to individuals' positive feelings and hopefulness about themselves and the world.

On the other hand, there are potential costs in the self-assertion of racial (or national) identities against other groups around them. If the assertion takes (implicitly or explicitly) a racial or communal form, it defines other groups antagonistically and exclusively. The terms of the relationship between insurgent and dominant group are cast in what Bion called, in his work on the psychodynamics of groups,[31] the 'basic assumption' (that is, dominant unconscious definition) of 'fight–flight', the behaviour appropriate in the face of enemies. While concessions may, and ideally will, be made by dominant groups in the face of such conflicts, increased contact and racial integration may be less likely, in part because of the strength of group hostility aroused by the conflict itself.

[. . .]

It may even be that definitions and exposures of racism as part of the dominant ideology may exaggerate its general extent and scope in Britain, seeming to prove its intractability and pervasiveness not least to members of minority groups themselves. The hypothesis that racism is a general state of mind for which all whites should feel themselves responsible, regardless of their individual attitudes, experience and actions, makes a non-racist society seem a utopian idea, and makes it seem rational to avoid the risks of any close inter-racial contact. Anti-racism can become a counter-racism, whose natural outcome is a situation where members of different racial groups choose an uncomfortable racial separation. In the same way, attributions of incorrigible anti-Semitism have been used as arguments within the Jewish community for the maintenance of an exclusive Jewish collective identity, leading to a repudiation of close relations with non-Jews, morally enforced with at least the intensity of the converse rejections from the non-Jewish side.

[. . .]

Individuals should certainly be made aware of the pain and damage caused by racial attributions. But it should also be acknowledged that much prejudice is unwitting, a conductor for inner states of hostility whose origin and mental function need as much attention as their substantive object. Such superficial attitudes may be modified by experience and reflection. [. . .]

[. . .] The widest support for anti-racist positions needs to be sought and maintained. Neither the language of racial separatism, nor an alliance cast in revolutionary terms between the white and black opponents of imperialist capitalism, is likely to be able to deliver a broad constituency or consensus for anti-racist action. The idea of rights of citizenship for all, unqualified by race, would probably provide the strongest support for the aims of a non-discriminatory society, in which life chances are not determined by ethnic attributes. Addressing that sane part of most individuals which is not racist may be a better basis for advance towards a non-racial society than a generalized attribution of racism.

Racial, cultural and national definitions of identity

[. . .] There is of course need for conflict and challenge to racist attitudes, and out of this learning and change do take place. But it is probably best that such conflicts of attitude are contained by structures that are not themselves excessively threatening, and that individuals are brought into touch with realities of other persons, including their capacity for pain and sympathy, rather than driven back on phantasy as their primary means for making sense of the world.

Racism, as a system of distortions and lies, can be successfully fought only through a commitment to the truth, concerning both inner and outer realities. Only societies (and smaller institutions within them) in which habits of reason and individuation are cultivated will be able to resist the sway of states of mind such as racial and communal hatred, which are rooted in paranoia and collective phantasy.

Notes

1   See P.L. Van den Berghe, *Race and Racism: a Comparative Perspective* (London, Wiley, 2nd edn, 1978), ch. 1.

2   See Benedict Anderson, *Imagined Communities: Reflections on the Origin and Spread of Nationalism* (London, Verso, 1983).

3   See the essays in Martin Hollis and Steven Lukes (eds), *Rationality and Relativism* (Oxford, Oxford University Press, 1982); and Ernest Gellner, *Cause and Meaning in the Social Sciences* (London, Routledge, 1973).

4   This argument is central to both Marxist and liberal conceptions of progress. For the former, see G.A. Cohen, *Karl Marx's Theory of History* (Oxford, Oxford University Press, 1980); and for a version of the latter, see Ernest Gellner, *Thought and Change* (London, Weidenfeld and Nicolson, 1964). A more complex view of the cognitive aspects of modernization and their consequences is presented in Gellner's later *Plough, Sword and Book: the Structure of Human History* (Collins Harvill, 1988).

5   Jean-Paul Sartre, *Anti-Semite and Jew* (Schocken, 1948; originally published Paris, 1946).

6   Ibid., pp. 17, 19.

7   The relation of these modes of thought to prejudice is touched on in Hanna Segal, 'Schizoid mechanisms underlying phobia formation', in *The Work of Hanna Segal* (London, Free Association Books/Maresfield Library, 1986).

8   W.R. Bion, *Attention and Interpretation* (1970; republished London, Maresfield Reprints, 1984), ch. 11.

9   Leo Kuper, 'Ideologies of cultural difference in race relations', in *Race, Class and Power* (London, Duckworth, 1974).

10   See J. Mitchell (ed.), *The Selected Melanie Klein* (Harmondsworth, Penguin, 1986); H. Segal, *An Introduction to the Work of Melanie Klein* (London, Heinemann, 1975).

11   W.R. Bion, *Second Thoughts* (London, Heinemann, 1978).

12   Bion writes on the processes by which meaning is constructed from the raw material of

sensation and emotion in *Learning from Experience* (1962; Maresfield Reprint, 1984). This issue, and its relevance to the psychoanalytic process, is also central to his subsequent works, *Elements of Psychoanalysis* (1963), *Transformations* (1965), and *Attention and Interpretation* (1970) (all republished as Maresfield Reprints, 1984). Melanie Klein's idea of the epistemophilic instinct is developed in various papers to be found in M. Klein, *The Psycho-Analysis of Children* (1932; republished Hogarth Press, 1975). Her 1928 paper 'The early stages of the Oedipus complex' is reprinted in Mitchell (ed.), *The Selected Melanie Klein*.

13 Bion, *Learning from Experience*.

14 D. Meltzer. *The Kleinian Development*, Part 3 (Perthshire: Clunie Press, 1978), and *Studies in Extended Metapsychology: Clinical Applications of Bion's Ideas* (Clunie Press, 1986).

15 Kuper, 'Ideologies of cultural difference', p. 96, n. 16.

16 Powell's speech was delivered in Birmingham on 29 April 1968. For a discussion of Powell, see Tom Nairn. *The Break-up of Britain* (London, Verso, 1981), ch. 6.

17 See Octave Mannoni. *Prospero and Caliban* (London, Methuen, 1956).

18 See Bruno Bettelheim. *The Uses of Enchantment* (Harmondsworth, Penguin, 1978); and, on more modern writing for children, M.J. Rustin and M.E. Rustin, *Narratives of Love and Loss* (London, Verso. 1987), esp, ch. 7.

19 See W.R. Bion, *Experiences in Groups* (London, Tavistock, 1981); and for a later Kleinian view, R. Hinshelwood, *What Happens in Groups* (London, Free Association Books, 1987).

20 Jeremy Seabrook, *City Close-up* (Harmondsworth, Penguin, 1973).

21 Sartre, *Anti-Semite and Jew*, p. 25.

22 J. Mitchell, *Psychoanalysis and Feminism* (Harmondsworth, Penguin, 1975); D. Dinnerstein, *The Mermaid and the Minotaur: the Rocking of the Cradle and the Ruling of the World* (New York, Harper and Row, 1976); Nancy Chodorow, *The Reproduction of Mothering* (Berkeley CA, University of California Press, 1978).

23 Centre for Contemporary Cultural Studies, *The Empire Strikes Back* (London, Hutchinson, 1982); for a more complex view, see Paul Gilory, *There Ain't No Black in the Union Jack* (London, Hutchinson, 1987), esp. ch. 1.

24 See, for example, S. Hall and T. Jefferson (eds), *Resistance through Rituals* (London, Hutchinson, 1976); and S. Hall et al., *Policing the Crisis* (London, Macmillan, 1978). For work which relates this approach more specifically to racism, see Philip Cohen, *Racism and Popular Culture: a Cultural Studies Approach* (London, London University Institute of Education, 1987).

25 See Van den Berghe, *Race and Racism*, ch. 1.

26 Philip Cohen, *The Perversions of Inheritance: Studies in the Making of Multi-racial Britain* (forthcoming).

27 Bion develops the distinction between 'knowing' and 'knowing about' in *Learning from Experience*.

28 For example, in Centre for Contemporary Cultural Studies, *The Empire Strikes Back*.

29 A review of research on transracial adoption which does not support making race an over-riding condition in deciding placements is reported in Barbara Tizard and Ann Phoenix (1989) 'Black identity and trans-racial adoption', *New Community*, 15, April.

30 Frantz Fanon, *The Wretched of the Earth* (New York, Grove Press, 1963).

31 Bion, *Experiences in Groups*.

17

The negro and psychopathology   **Frantz Fanon**

Psychoanalytic schools have studied the neurotic reactions that arise among certain groups, in certain areas of civilization. In response to the requirements of dialectic, one should investigate the extent to which the conclusions of Freud or of Adler can be applied to the effort to understand the man of color's view of the world.

It can never be sufficiently emphasized that psychoanalysis sets as its task the understanding of given behavior patterns – within the specific group represented by the family. When the problem is a neurosis experienced by an adult, the analyst's task is to uncover in the new psychic structure an analogy with certain infantile elements, a repetition, a duplication of conflicts that owe their origin to the essence of the family constellation. In every case the analyst clings to the concept of the family as a 'psychic circumstance and object.'[1]

Here, however, the evidence is going to be particularly complicated. In Europe the family represents in effect a certain fashion in which the world presents itself to the child. There are close connections between the structure of the family and the structure of the nation. Militarization and the centralization of authority in a country automatically entail a resurgence of the authority of the father. In Europe and in every country characterized as civilized or civilizing, the family is a miniature of the nation. As the child emerges from the shadow of his parents, he finds himself once more among the same laws, the same principles, the same values. A normal child that has grown up in a normal family will be a normal man. There is no disproportion between the life of the family and the life of the nation. [. . .]

[. . .]

But – and this is a most important point – we observe the opposite in the man of color. A normal Negro child, having grown up within a normal

This chapter, first published in 1956, is taken from *Black Skins, White Masks* (London, Pluto Press, 1991), pp. 141–209.

family, will become abnormal on the slightest contact with the white world. This statement may not be immediately understandable. Therefore let us proceed by going backward. Paying tribute to Dr Breuer, Freud wrote:

> In almost every case, we could see that the symptoms were, so to speak, like residues of emotional experiences, to which for this reason we later gave the name of psychic traumas. Their individual characters were linked to the traumatic scenes that had provoked them. According to the classic terminology, the symptoms were determined by 'scenes' of which they were the mnemic residues, and it was no longer necessary to regard them as arbitrary and enigmatic effects of the neurosis. In contrast, however, to what was expected, it was not always a single event that was the cause of the symptom; most often, on the contrary, it arose out of multiple traumas, frequently analogous and repeated. [. . .]

It could not be stated more positively; every neurosis has its origins in specific *Erlebnisse*. Later Freud added:

> This trauma, it is true, has been quite expelled from the consciousness and the memory of the patient and as a result he has apparently been saved from a great mass of suffering, but the repressed desire continues to exist in the unconscious; it is on watch constantly for an opportunity to make itself known and it soon comes back into consciousness, but in a disguise that makes it impossible to recognize; in other words, the repressed thought is replaced in consciousness by another that acts as its surrogate, its *Ersatz*, and that soon surrounds itself with all those feelings of morbidity that had been supposedly averted by the repression.

These *Erlebnisse* are repressed in the unconscious.

What do we see in the case of the black man? [. . .] A drama is enacted every day in colonized countries. How is one to explain, for example, that a Negro who has passed his baccalaureate and has gone to the Sorbonne to study to become a teacher of philosophy is already on guard before any conflictual elements have coalesced round him? René Ménil accounted for this reaction in Hegelian terms. In his view it was 'the consequence of the replacement of the repressed [African] spirit in the consciousness of the slave by an authority symbol representing the Master, a symbol implanted in the subsoil of the collective group and charged with maintaining order in it as a garrison controls a conquered city.[2]

[. . .] René Ménil has made no misjudgment. Meanwhile we have the right to put a question to ourselves: how is the persistence of this reaction in the twentieth century to be explained when in other ways there is complete identification with the white man? Very often the Negro who becomes abnormal has never had any relations with whites. Has some remote experience been repressed in his unconscious? Did the little black child see his father beaten or lynched by a white man? Has there been a real traumatism? To all of this we have to answer *no*. Well, then?

If we want to answer correctly, we have to fall back on the idea of *collective catharsis*. In every society, in every collectivity, exists – must exist – a channel, an outlet through which the forces accumulated in the form of aggression can be released. This is the purpose of games in children's institutions, of psychodramas in group therapy, and, in a more general way, of illustrated magazines for children – each type of society, of course, requiring its own specific kind of catharsis. The Tarzan stories, the sagas of twelve-year-old explorers, the adventures of Mickey Mouse, and all those 'comic books' serve actually as a release for collective aggression. The magazines are put together by white men for little white men. This is the heart of the problem. In the Antilles – and there is every reason to think that the situation is the same in the other colonies – these same magazines are devoured by the local children. In the magazines the Wolf, the Devil, the Evil Spirit, the Bad Man, the Savage are always symbolized by Negroes or Indians; since there is always identification with the victor, the little Negro, quite as easily as the little white boy, becomes an explorer, an adventurer, a missionary 'who faces the danger of being eaten by the wicked Negroes.' [. . .]

The black schoolboy in the Antilles, who in his lessons is forever talking about 'our ancestors, the Gauls,' identifies himself with the explorer, the bringer of civilization, the white man who carries truth to savages – an all-white truth. There is identification – that is, the young Negro subjectively adopts a white man's attitude. He invests the hero, who is white, with all his own aggression – at that age closely linked to sacrificial dedication, a sacrificial dedication permeated with sadism. An eight-year-old child who offers a gift, even to an adult, cannot endure a refusal. Little by little, one can observe in the young Antillean the formation and crystallization of an attitude and a way of thinking and seeing that are essentially white. When in school he has to read stories of savages told by white men, he always thinks of the Senegalese. As a schoolboy, I had many occasions to spend whole hours talking about the supposed customs of the savage Senegalese. In what was said there was a lack of awareness that was at the very least paradoxical. Because the Antillean does not think of himself as a black man; he thinks of himself as an Antillean. The Negro lives in Africa. Subjectively, intellectually, the Antillean conducts himself like a white man. But he is a Negro. That he will learn once he goes to Europe; and when he hears Negroes mentioned he will recognize that the word includes himself as well as the Senegalese. What are we to conclude on this matter?

[. . .]

The white family is the agent of a certain system. The society is indeed the sum of all the families in it. The family is an institution that prefigures a broader institution: the social or the national group. Both turn on the same axes. The white family is the workshop in which one is shaped and trained for life in society. 'The family structure is internalized in the superego,' Marcus says, 'and projected into political [though I would say social] behavior.'[3]

As long as he remains among his own people, the little black follows very nearly the same course as the little white. But if he goes to Europe, he will have to reappraise his lot. For the Negro in France, which is his country, will feel different from other people. One can hear the glib remark: the Negro makes himself inferior. But the truth is that he is made inferior. The young Antillean is a Frenchman called upon constantly to live with white compatriots. Now, the Antillean family has for all practical purposes no connection with the national – that is, the French, or European – structure. The Antillean has therefore to choose between his family and European society; in other words, the individual who *climbs up* into society – white and civilized – tends to reject his family – black and savage – on the plane of imagination [. . .]. In this case the schema [. . .] becomes

Family ⟵ Individual ⟶ Society

and the family structure is cast back into the *id*.

The Negro recognizes the unreality of many of the beliefs that he has adopted with reference to the subjective attitude of the white man. When he does, his real apprenticeship begins. And reality proves to be extremely resistant. But, it will be objected, you are merely describing a universal phenomenon, the criterion of maturity being in fact adaptation to society. My answer is that such a criticism goes off in the wrong direction, for I have just shown that for the Negro there is a myth to be faced. A solidly established myth. The Negro is unaware of it as long as his existence is limited to his own environment; but the first encounter with a white man oppresses him with the whole weight of his blackness.

Then there is the unconscious. Since the racial drama is played out in the open, the black man has no time to 'make it unconscious.' The white man, on the other hand, succeeds in doing so to a certain extent, because a new element appears: guilt. The Negro's inferiority or superiority complex or his feeling of equality is *conscious*. These feelings forever chill him. They make his drama. In him there is none of the affective amnesia characteristic of the typical neurotic.

[. . .]

With the exception of a few misfits within the closed environment, we can say that every neurosis, every abnormal manifestation, every affective erethism in an Antillean is the product of his cultural situation. In other words, there is a constellation of postulates, a series of propositions that slowly and subtly – with the help of books, newspapers, schools and their texts, advertisements, films, radio – work their way into one's mind and shape one's view of the world of the group to which one belongs.[4] In the Antilles that view of the world is white because no black voice exists. The folklore of Martinique is meager, and few children in Fort-de-France know the stories of 'Compè Lapin,' twin brother of the Br'er Rabbit of Louisiana's Uncle Remus. A European familiar with the current trends of Negro poetry, for example, would be amazed to learn that as late as 1940 no Antillean found it possible to think of himself as a Negro. It was only with the appearance of Aimé Césaire that the acceptance of negritude and the statement of its claims began to be perceptible. The most concrete proof of this, furthermore, is that feeling which pervades each new generation of students arriving in Paris: it takes them several weeks to recognize that contact with Europe compels them to face a certain number of problems that until their arrival had never touched them. And yet these problems were by no means invisible.[5]

[. . .]

What am I getting at? Quite simply this: when the Negro makes contact with the white world, a certain sensitizing action takes place. If his psychic structure is weak, one observes a collapse of the ego. The black man stops behaving as an *actional* person. The goal of his behavior will be The Other (in the guise of the white man), for The Other alone can give him worth. That is on the ethical level: self-esteem. But there is something else.

[. . .] [T]he Negro is phobogenic. What is phobia? I prefer to answer that question by relying on the latest work of Hesnard: 'Phobia is a neurosis characterized by the anxious fear of an object (in the broadest sense of anything outside the individual) or, by extension, of a situation.'[6] Naturally that object must have certain aspects. It must arouse, Hesnard says, both fear and revulsion. But here we encounter a difficulty. Applying the genetic method to the understanding of phobia, Charles Odier wrote that all anxiety derives from a certain subjective insecurity linked to the absence of the mother.[7] This occurs, according to Odier, sometime in the second year of life.

Investigating the psychic structure of the phobic, he comes to this conclusion: 'Before attacking the adult beliefs, all the elements of the infantile structure which produced them must be analyzed.'[8] The choice of the phobic object is therefore *overdetermined*. This object does not come at random out of the void of nothingness; in some situation it has previously evoked an affect in the patient. His phobia is the latent presence of this affect at the root of his world; there is an organization that has been given a form. For the object, naturally, need not be there, it is enough that somewhere it *exist*: it is a possibility. This object is endowed with evil intentions and with all the attributes of a malefic power.[9] In the phobic, affect has a priority that defies all rational thinking. As we can see, the phobic is a person who is governed by the laws of rational prelogic and affective prelogic: methods of thinking and feeling that go back to the age at which he experienced the event that impaired his security. The difficulty indicated here is this: [. . .] In the majority of Negrophobic men has there been an attempt at rape? An attempt at *fellatio?* Proceeding with complete orthodoxy, we should be led by the application of analytic conclusions to this: if an extremely frightening object, such as a more or less imaginary attacker, arouses terror, this is also – for most often such cases are those of women – and especially a terror mixed with sexual revulsion. 'I'm afraid of men' really means, at the bottom of the motivation of the fear, because they might do all kinds of things to me, but not commonplace cruelties: sexual abuses – in other words, immoral and shameful things.[10]

'*Contact* alone is enough to evoke anxiety. For contact is at the same time the basic schematic type of initiating sexual action (touching, caresses – sexuality).[11] Since we have learned to know all the tricks the ego uses in order to defend itself, we know too that its denials must in no case be taken literally. Are we not now observing a complete inversion? Basically, does this *fear* of rape not itself cry out for rape? Just as there are faces that ask to be slapped, can one not speak of women who ask to be raped? In *If He Hollers Let Him Go*, Chester Himes describes this type very well. The big blonde trembles whenever the Negro goes near her. Yet she has nothing to fear, since the factory is full of white men. In the end, she and the Negro go to bed together.

When I was in military service I had the opportunity to observe the behavior of white women from three or four European countries when they were among Negroes at dances. Most of the time the women made involuntary gestures of flight, of withdrawing, their faces filled with a fear that was not feigned. And yet the Negroes who asked them to dance would have been utterly unable to commit any act at all against them, even if they had wished to do so. The behavior of these women is clearly under-standable from the standpoint of imagination. That is because the Negro-phobic woman is in fact nothing but a putative sexual partner – just as the Negrophobic man is a repressed homosexual.

In relation to the Negro, everything takes place on the genital level. A few years ago, I remarked to some friends during a discussion that in a general sense the white man behaves toward the Negro as an elder brother reacts to the birth of a younger. [. . .]

On the phenomenological level there would be a double reality to be observed. The Jew is feared because of his potential for acquisitiveness. 'They' are everywhere. The banks, the stock exchanges, the government are infested with 'them.' 'They' control everything. Soon the whole country will belong to 'them.' 'They' do better in examinations than the 'real' Frenchmen. Soon 'they' will be making the laws for us. Not long ago, an acquaintance studying for the civil service said to me, 'Say what you want, "they" take good care of one another. When Moch was in power, for instance, the number of kikes in government jobs was appalling.' In the medical profession the situation is no different. Every Jewish student who wins a prize in a competition does it through 'pull.' As for the Negroes, they have tremendous sexual powers. What do you expect, with all the freedom they have in their jungles! They copulate at all times and in all places. They are really genital. They have so many children that they cannot even count them. Be careful, or they will flood us with little mulattoes.

[. . .]

For the sexual potency of the Negro is hallucinating. That is indeed the word: this potency *must be* hallucinating. Psychoanalysts who study the problem soon enough find the mechanisms of every neurosis. Sexual anxiety is predominant here. All the Negrophobic women I have known had abnormal sex lives. Their husbands had left them; or they were widows and they were afraid to find a substitute for the dead husband; or they were divorced and they had doubts at the thought of a new object investment. All of them endowed the Negro with powers that other men (husbands, transient lovers) did not have. And besides there was also an element of perversion, the persistence of infantile formations: God knows how they make love! It must be terrifying.

There is one expression that through time has become singularly eroticized: the black athlete. There is something in the mere idea, one young woman confided to me, that makes the heart skip a beat. A prostitute told me that in her early days the mere thought of going to bed with a Negro brought on an orgasm. She went in search of Negroes and never asked them for money. But, she added, 'going to bed with them was no more remarkable than going to bed with white men. It was before I did it that I had the orgasm. I used to think about (imagine) all the things they might do to me: and that was what was so terrific.'

Still on the genital level, when a white man hates black men, is he not yielding to a feeling of impotence or of sexual inferiority? Since his ideal is an infinite virility, is there not a phenomenon of diminution in relation to the Negro, who is viewed as a penis symbol? Is the lynching of the Negro not a sexual revenge? We know how much of sexuality there is in all cruelties, tortures, beatings. One has only to reread a few pages of the Marquis de Sade to be easily convinced of the fact. Is the Negro's superiority real? Everyone *knows* that it is not. But that is not what matters. The prelogical thought of the phobic has decided that such is the case. [. . .] I knew a Negro medical student who would not dare to make a vaginal examination of any patient in the gynecological clinic. He told me that one day he had heard one of them say, 'There's a nigger in there. If he touches me, I'll slap his face. You never know with them. He must have great big hands; and besides he's sure to be rough.'

If one wants to understand the racial situation psychoanalytically, not from a universal viewpoint but as it is experienced by individual consciousnesses, considerable importance must be given to sexual phenomena. In the case of the Jew, one thinks of money and its cognates. In that of the Negro, one thinks of sex. Anti-Semitism can be rationalized on a basic level. It is because he takes over the country that the Jew is a danger. An acquaintance told me recently that although he was not an anti-Semite he had been constrained to admit that the majority of Jews whom he had known during the war had behaved very badly. I tried in vain to get him to concede that such a statement was the fruit of a determined desire to find the essence of the Jew wherever it might exist.

THE NEGRO AND PSYCHOPATHOLOGY

[. . .]

Jean-Paul Sartre has made a masterful study of the problem of anti-Semitism; let us try to determine what are the constituents of Negrophobia. This phobia is to be found on an instinctual, biological level. At the extreme, I should say that the Negro, because of his body, impedes the closing of the postural schema of the white man – at the point, naturally, at which the black man makes his entry into the phenomenal world of the white man. This is not the place in which to state the conclusions I drew from studying the influence exerted on the body by the appearance of another body. (Let us assume, for example, that four fifteen-year-old boys, all more or less athletic, are doing the high jump. One of them wins by jumping four feet ten inches. Then a fifth boy arrives and tops the mark by a half-inch. The four other bodies experience a destructuration.) What is important to us here is to show that with the Negro the cycle of the *biological* begins.[12]

No anti-Semite, for example, would ever conceive of the idea of castrating the Jew. He is killed or sterilized. But the Negro is castrated. The penis, the symbol of manhood, is annihilated, which is to say that it is denied. The difference between the two attitudes is apparent. The Jew is attacked in his religious identity, in his history, in his race, in his relations with his ancestors and with his posterity; when one sterilizes a Jew, one cuts off the source; every time that a Jew is persecuted, it is the whole race that is persecuted in his person. But it is in his corporeality that the Negro is attacked. It is as a concrete personality that he is lynched. It is as an actual being that he is a threat. The Jewish menace is replaced by the fear of the sexual potency of the Negro. O. Mannoni said:

> An argument widely used by racialists against those who do not share their convictions is worthy of mention for its revealing character. 'What,' they say, 'if you had a daughter, do you mean to say that you would marry her to a negro?' I have seen people who appeared to have no racialist bias lose all critical sense when confronted with this kind of question. The reason is that such an argument disturbs certain uneasy feelings in them (more exactly, *incestuous* feelings) and they turn to racialism as a defence reaction.[13]

Before we go further, it seems important to make this point: granted that unconscious tendencies toward incest exist, why should these tendencies emerge more particularly with respect to the Negro? In what way, taken as an absolute, does a black son-in-law differ from a white son-in-law? Is there not a reaction of unconscious tendencies in both cases? Why not, for instance, conclude that the father revolts because in his opinion the Negro will introduce his daughter into a sexual universe for which the father does not have the key, the weapons, or the attributes?

Every intellectual gain requires a loss in sexual potential. The civilized white man retains an irrational longing for unusual eras of sexual license, of orgiastic scenes, of unpunished rapes, of unrepressed incest. In one way these fantasies respond to Freud's life instinct. Projecting his own desires onto the Negro, the white man behaves 'as if' the Negro really had them. When it is a question of the Jew, the problem is clear: he is suspect because he wants to own the wealth or take over the positions of power. But the Negro is fixated at the genital; or at any rate he has been fixated there. Two realms: the intellectual and the sexual. An erection on Rodin's *Thinker* is a shocking thought. One cannot decently 'have a hard on' everywhere. The Negro symbolizes the biological danger; the Jew, the intellectual danger.

To suffer from a phobia of Negroes is to be afraid of the biological. For the Negro is only biological. The Negroes are animals. They go about naked. And God alone knows. . . . Mannoni said further: 'In his urge to identify the anthropoid apes, Caliban, the Negroes, even the Jews with the mythological figures of the satyrs, man reveals that there are sensitive spots in the human soul at a level[14] where thought becomes confused and where sexual excitement is strangely linked with violence and aggressiveness.'[15] [. . .]

[. . .]

The Negro symbolizes the biological. First of all, he enters puberty at the age of nine and is a father at the age of ten; he is hot-blooded, and his blood is strong; he is tough. As a white man remarked to me not long ago, with a certain bitterness: 'You all have strong constitutions.' What a beautiful race – look at the Senegalese . . . Weren't they called *our Black Devils* during the war? . . . But they must be brutal . . . I just can't see them putting those big hands of theirs on my shoulders. I shudder at the mere thought of it . . . Well aware that in certain cases one must interpret by opposites, I understand this extra-fragile woman: at bottom what she wants most is to have the powerful Negro bruise her frail shoulders. [. . .] I have always been struck by the speed with which 'handsome young Negro' turns into 'young colt' or 'stallion.' [. . .]

[. . .] 'What is important in phenomenology is less the study of a large number of instances than the intuitive and deep understanding of a few individual cases.[16] The question that arises is this: can the white man behave healthily toward the black man and can the black man behave healthily toward the white man?

A pseudo-question, some will say. But when we assert that European culture has an *imago* of the Negro which is responsible for all the conflicts that may arise, we do not go beyond reality. In the chapter on language [in *Black Skin, White Masks*] we saw that on the screen the Negro faithfully reproduces that *imago*. Even serious writers have made themselves its spokesmen. So it was that Michel Cournot could write:

> The black man's sword is a sword. When he has thrust it into your wife, she has really felt something. It is a revelation. In the chasm that it has left, your little toy is lost. Pump away until the room is awash with your sweat, you might as well just be singing. This is *good-bye* . . . Four Negroes with their

penises exposed would fill a cathedral. They would be unable to leave the building until their erections had subsided; and in such close quarters that would not be a simple matter.

To be comfortable without problems, they always have the open air. But then they are faced with a constant insult: the palm tree, the breadfruit tree, and so many other proud growths that would not slacken for an empire, erect as they are for all eternity, and piercing heights that are not easily reached at any price.[17]

When one reads this passage a dozen times and lets oneself go – that is, when one abandons oneself to the movement of its images – one is no longer aware of the Negro but only of a penis; the Negro is eclipsed. He is turned into a penis. He is a penis. It is easy to imagine what such descriptions can stimulate in a young girl in Lyon. Horror? Lust? Not indifference, in any case. Now, what is the truth? The average length of the penis among the black men of Africa, Dr Palès says, rarely exceeds 120 millimeters (4.6244 inches). Testut, in his *Traité d'anatomie humaine*, offers the same figure for the European. But these are facts that persuade no one. The white man is convinced that the Negro is a beast; if it is not the length of the penis, then it is the sexual potency that impresses him. Face to face with this man who is 'different from himself,' he needs to defend himself. In other words, to personify The Other. The Other will become the mainstay of his preoccupations and his desires. [. . .]

One thing must be mentioned in this connection: a white woman who has had a Negro lover finds it difficult to return to white men. Or so at least it is believed, particularly by white men: 'Who knows what "they" can give a woman?' Who indeed does know? Certainly 'they' do not. On this subject I cannot overlook this comment by Etiemble:

> Racial jealousy produces the crimes of racism: To many white men, the black is simply that marvelous sword which, once it has transfixed their wives, leaves them forever transfigured. My statistical sources have been able to provide me with no documentation on this point. I have, however, known some Negroes; some white women who have had Negroes; and finally, some Negro women who have had white lovers. I have heard enough confidences from all of them to be able to deplore the fact that M. Cournot applies his talents to the rejuvenation of a fable in which the white man will always be able to find a specious argument: shameful, dubious, and thus doubly effective.[18]

An endless task, the cataloguing of reality. We accumulate facts, we discuss them, but with every line that is written, with every statement that is made, one has the feeling of incompleteness. [. . .]

[. . .]

We can now stake out a marker. For the majority of white men the Negro represents the sexual instinct (in its raw state). The Negro is the incarnation of a genital potency beyond all moralities and prohibitions. The women among the whites, by a genuine process of induction, invariably view the Negro as the keeper of the impalpable gate that opens into the realm of orgies, of bacchanals, of delirious sexual sensations . . . We have shown that reality destroys all these beliefs. But they all rest on the level of the imagined, in any case on that of a paralogism. The white man who ascribes a malefic influence to the black is regressing on the intellectual level, since, as we have shown, his perception is based on a mental age of eight years (the comic books). Is there not a concurrent regression to and fixation at pregenital levels of sexual development? Self-castration? (The Negro is taken as a terrifying penis.) Passivity justifying itself by the recognition of the superiority of the black man in terms of sexual capacity? It is obvious what a variety of questions it would be interesting to raise. There are, for instance, men who go to 'houses' in order to be beaten by Negroes; passive homosexuals who insist on black partners.

[. . .]

The Negro is the genital. Is this the whole story? Unfortunately not. The Negro is something else. Here again we find the Jew. He and I may be separated by the sexual question, but we have one point in common. Both of us stand for Evil. The black man more so, for the good reason that he is black. Is not whiteness in symbols always ascribed in French to Justice, Truth, Virginity? I knew an Antillean who said of another Antillean 'His body is black, his language is black, his soul must be black too.' This logic is put into daily practice by the white man. The black man is the symbol of Evil and Ugliness.

[. . .]

Confronted by such a tide of aggression, this Jew will have to take a stand. Here is all the ambiguity that Sartre describes. Certain pages of *Anti-Semite and Jew* are the finest that I have ever read. The finest, because the problem discussed in them grips us in our guts.[19]

The Jew, authentic or inauthentic, is struck down by the fist of the 'salaud.' His situation is such that everything he does is bound to turn against him. For naturally the Jew prefers himself, and it happens that he forgets his Jewishness, or hides it, hides himself from it. That is because he has then admitted the validity of the Aryan system. There are Good and Evil. Evil is Jewish. Everything Jewish is ugly. Let us no longer be Jews. I am no longer a Jew. Down with the Jews. In such circumstances, these are the most aggressive. Like that patient of Baruk who had a persecution complex and who, seeing the doctor one day wearing his yellow star, grabbed him by the lapel and shouted: 'I, sir, am a Frenchman.' Or this woman: 'Making rounds in the ward of my colleague, Dr Daday, I encountered a Jewish patient who had been the target of taunts and insults from her fellow-patients. A non-Jewish patient had gone to her defense. The Jewish patient thereupon turned on the woman who had defended the Jews, hurling every possible anti-Semitic calumny at her and demanding that that Jewess be got rid of.'[20]

This is a fine example of reactional phenomenon. In order to react against anti-Semitism, the Jew turns himself into an anti-Semite. [. . .]

Fault, Guilt, refusal of guilt, paranoia – one is back in homosexual territory. In sum, what others have described in the case of the Jew applies perfectly in that of the Negro.

Good–Evil, Beauty–Ugliness, White–Black: such are the characteristic pairings of the phenomenon that, making use of an expression of Dide and Guiraud, we shall call 'manicheism delirium.'[21]

[. . .]

Continuing to take stock of reality, endeavoring to ascertain the instant of symbolic crystallization, I very naturally found myself on the threshold of Jungian psychology. European civilization is characterized by the presence, at the heart of what Jung calls the collective unconscious, of an archetype: an expression of the bad instincts, of the darkness inherent in every ego, of the uncivilized savage, the Negro who slumbers in every white man. And Jung claims to have found in uncivilized peoples the same psychic structure that his diagram portrays. Personally, I think that Jung has deceived himself. Moreover, all the peoples that he has known – whether the Pueblo Indians of Arizona or the Negroes of Kenya in British East Africa – have had more or less traumatic contacts with the white man. I said earlier that in his Salavinizations[22] the young Antillean is never black; and I have tried to show what this phenomenon corresponds to. Jung locates the collective unconscious in the inherited cerebral matter. But the collective unconscious, without our having to fall back on the genes, is purely and simply the sum of prejudices, myths, collective attitudes of a given group. It is taken for granted, to illustrate, that the Jews who have settled in Israel will produce in less than a hundred years a collective unconscious different from the ones that they had before 1945 in the countries which they were forced to leave.

On the level of philosophic discussion, this would be the place to bring up the old problem of instinct and habit: instinct, which is inborn (we know how we must view this 'innateness'), invariable, specific; habit, which is acquired. On this level one would have only to demonstrate that Jung has confused instinct and habit. In his view, in fact, the collective unconscious is bound up with the cerebral structure, the myths and archetypes are permanent engrams of the race. I hope I have shown that nothing of the sort is the case and that in fact the collective unconscious is cultural, which means acquired. [. . .] *In Europe, the black man is the symbol of Evil.* One must move softly, I know, but it is not easy. The torturer is the black man, Satan is black, one talks of shadows, when one is dirty one is black – whether one is thinking of physical dirtiness or of moral dirtiness. It would be astonishing, if the trouble were taken to bring them all together, to see the vast number of expressions that make the black man the equivalent of sin. In Europe, whether concretely or symbolically, the black man stands for the bad side of the character. As long as one cannot understand this fact, one is doomed to talk in circles about the 'black problem.' Blackness, darkness, shadow, shades, night, the labyrinths of the earth, abysmal depths, blacken someone's reputation; and, on the other side, the bright look of innocence, the white dove of peace, magical, heavenly light. A magnificent blond child – how much peace there is in that phrase, how much joy, and above all how much hope! There is no comparison with a magnificent black child: literally, such a thing is unwonted. Just the same, I shall not go back into the stories of black angels. In Europe, that is to say, in every civilized and civilizing country, the Negro is the symbol of sin. The archetype of the lowest values is represented by the Negro. [. . .] How else is one to explain, for example, that the unconscious representing the base and inferior traits is colored black? [. . .] When I descend I see caverns, grottoes where savages dance. Let there be no mistake, above all. For example, in one of the waking-dream sessions that Desoille describes for us, we find Gauls in a cave. But, it must be pointed out, the Gaul is a simple fellow. A Gaul in a cave, it is almost like a family picture – a result, perhaps, of 'our ancestors, the Gauls.' I believe it is necessary to become a child again in order to grasp certain psychic realities. This is where Jung was an innovator: he wanted to go back to the childhood of the world, but he made a remarkable mistake: he went back only to the childhood of Europe.

In the remotest depth of the European unconscious an inordinately black hollow has been made in which the most immoral impulses, the most shameful desires lie dormant. And as every man climbs up toward whiteness and light, the European has tried to repudiate this uncivilized self, which has attempted to defend itself. When European civilization came into contact with the black world, with those savage peoples, everyone agreed: those Negroes were the principle of evil.

Jung consistently identifies the foreign with the obscure, with the tendency to evil: he is perfectly right. This mechanism of projection – or, if one prefers, transference – has been described by classic psychoanalysis. In the degree to which I find in myself something unheard-of, something reprehensible, only one solution remains for me: to get rid of it, to ascribe its origin to someone else. In this way I eliminate a short circuit that threatens to destroy my equilibrium. One must be careful with waking dreams in the early sessions, because it is not good if the obscenity emerges too soon. The patient must come to understand the workings of sub-limation before he makes any contact with the unconscious. If a Negro comes up in the first session, he must be removed at once; to that end, suggest a stairway or a rope to the patient, or propose that he let himself be carried off in a helicopter. Infallibly, the Negro will stay in his hole. In Europe the Negro has one function: that of symbolizing the lower emo-tions, the baser inclinations, the dark side of the soul. In the collective unconscious of *homo occidentalis*, the Negro – or, if one prefers, the color black – symbolizes evil, sin, wretchedness, death, war, famine. All birds of prey are black. In Martinique, whose collective unconscious makes it a European country, when a 'blue' Negro – a coal-black one – comes to visit, one reacts at once: 'What bad luck is he bringing?'

The collective unconscious is not dependent on cerebral heredity; it is the result of what I shall call the unreflected imposition of a culture. Hence there is no reason to be surprised when an Antillean exposed to waking-dream therapy relives the same fantasies as a European. It is because the Antillean partakes of the same collective unconscious as the European.

If what has been said thus far is grasped, this conclusion may be stated: it is normal for the Antillean to be anti-Negro. Through the collective unconscious the Antillean has taken over all the archetypes belonging to the European. The *anima* of the Antillean Negro is almost always a white woman. In the same way, the *animus* of the Antilleans is always a white man. That is because in the works of Anatole France, Balzac, Bazin, or any of the rest of 'our' novelists, there is never a word about an ethereal yet ever present black woman or about a dark Apollo with sparkling eyes . . . But I too am guilty, here I am talking of Apollo! There is no help for it: I am a white man. For unconsciously I distrust what is black in me, that is, the whole of my being.

I am a Negro – but of course I do not know it, simply because I am one. When I am at home my mother sings me French love songs in which there is never a word about Negroes. When I disobey, when I make too much noise, I am told to 'stop acting like a nigger.'

Somewhat later I read white books and little by little I take into myself the prejudices, the myths, the folklore that have come to me from Europe. But I will not accept them all, since certain prejudices do not apply in the Antilles. Anti-Semitism, for instance, does not exist there, for there are no Jews, or virtually none. Without turning to the idea of collective catharsis, it would be easy for me to show that, without thinking, the Negro selects himself as an object capable of carrying the burden of original sin. The white man chooses the black man for this function, and the black man who is white also chooses the black man. The black Antillean is the slave of this cultural imposition. After having been the slave of the white man, he enslaves himself. The Negro is in every sense of the word a victim of white civilization. It is not surprising that the artistic creations of Antillean poets bear no special watermark: these men are white. To come back to psychopathology, let us say that the Negro lives an ambiguity that is extraordinarily neurotic. At the age of twenty – at the time, that is, when the collective unconscious has been more or less lost, or is resistant at least to being raised to the conscious level – the Antillean recognizes that he is living an error. Why is that? Quite simply because – and this is very important – the Antillean has recognized himself as a Negro, but, by virtue of an ethical transit, he also feels (collective unconscious) that one is a Negro to the degree to which one is wicked, sloppy, malicious, instinctual. Everything that is the opposite of these Negro modes of behavior is white. This must be recognized as the source of Negrophobia in the Antillean. In the collective unconscious, black = ugliness, sin, darkness, immorality. In other words, he is Negro who is immoral. If I order my life like that of a moral man, I simply am not a Negro. Whence the Martinican custom of saying of a worthless white man that he has 'a nigger soul.' Color is nothing, I do not even notice it, I know only one thing, which is the purity of my conscience and the whiteness of my soul. 'Me white like snow,' the other said.

Cultural imposition is easily accomplished in Martinique. The ethical transit encounters no obstacle. But the real white man is waiting for me. As soon as possible he will tell me that it is not enough to try to be white, but that a white totality must be achieved. It is only then that I shall recognize the betrayal. Let us conclude. An Antillean is made white by the collective unconscious, by a large part of his individual unconscious, and by the virtual totality of his mechanism of individuation. The color of his skin, of which there is no mention in Jung, is black. All the inabilities to under-stand are born of this blunder.

[. . .]

Moral consciousness implies a kind of scission, a fracture of con-sciousness into a bright part and an opposing black part. In order to achieve morality, it is essential that the black, the dark, the Negro vanish from consciousness. Hence a Negro is forever in combat with his own image.

If in like manner one allows M. Hesnard his scientific conception of the moral life, and if the world of moral sickness is to be understood by starting from Fault and Guilt, a normal person will be one who has freed himself of this guilt, or who in any case has managed not to submit to it. More directly, each individual has to charge the blame for his baser drives, his impulses, to the account of an evil genius, which is that of the culture to which he belongs (we have seen that this is the Negro). This collective guilt is borne by what is conventionally called the scapegoat. Now the scapegoat for white society – which is based on myths of progress, civilization, liberalism, education, enlightenment, refinement – will be precisely the force that opposes the expansion and the triumph of these myths. This brutal opposing force is supplied by the Negro.

In the society of the Antilles, where the myths are identical with those of the society of Dijon or Nice, the young Negro, identifying himself with the civilizing power, will make the nigger the scapegoat of his moral life.

[. . .]

One can understand why Sartre views the adoption of a Marxist position by black poets as the logical conclusion of Negrohood. In effect, what happens is this: as I begin to recognize that the Negro is the symbol of sin, I catch myself hating the Negro. But then I recognize that I am a Negro. There are two ways out of this conflict. Either I ask others to pay no attention to my skin, or else I want them to be aware of it. I try then to find value for what is bad – since I have unthinkingly conceded that the black man is the color of evil. In order to terminate this neurotic situation, in which I am compelled to choose an unhealthy, conflictual solution, fed on fantasies, hostile, inhuman in short, I have only one solution: to rise above this absurd drama that others have staged round me, to reject the two terms that are equally unacceptable, and, through one human being, to reach out for the universal. [. . .]

[. . .]

Recently, in a children's paper, I read a caption to a picture in which a young black Boy Scout was showing a Negro village to three or four white scouts: 'This is the kettle where my ancestors cooked yours.' One will gladly concede that there are no more Negro cannibals, but we should not allow ourselves to forget . . . Quite seriously, however, I think that the writer of that caption has done a genuine service to Negroes without knowing it. For the white child who reads it will not form a mental picture of the Negro in the act of eating the white man, but rather as having eaten him. Unquestionably, this is progress.

Before concluding this chapter, I should like to abstract a case study, for access to which I must thank the medical director of the women's division of the psychiatric hospital of Saint-Ylie. The case clarifies the point of view that I am defending here. It proves that, at its extreme, the myth of the Negro, the idea of the Negro, can become the decisive factor of an authentic alienation.

Mlle B. was nineteen years old when she entered the hospital in March. Her admission sheet reads:

> The undersigned, Dr P., formerly on the staff of the Hospitals of Paris, certifies that he has examined Mlle B., who is afflicted with a nervous disease consisting of periods of agitation, motor instability, tics, and spasms which are conscious but which she cannot control. These symptoms have been increasing and prevent her from leading a normal social life. Her commitment for observation is required under the provisions laid down by the law of 1838 regarding voluntary commitments.

[. . .]

Her immediate family had no history of pathological manifestations. Puberty occurred at the age of sixteen. [. . .]

An interview made it possible to isolate these details: 'It's especially when I'm working that the tics come.' (The patient was working at a job that entailed her living away from home.) The tics affected the eyes and the forehead; she panted and yelped. She slept quite well, without nightmares, and ate well. She was not out of sorts during menstruation. When she went to bed, the facial tics were constant until she fell asleep.

[. . .]

She uttered sounds. It was never possible to understand what she was saying. This manifestation ended in quite loud, inarticulate cries. As soon as she was spoken to, these stopped.

The psychiatrist in charge decided to employ waking-dream therapy. A preliminary interview had brought out the existence of hallucinations in the form of terrifying circles, and the patient had been asked to describe them. Here is an excerpt from the notes on the first session:

Deep and concentric, the circles expanded and contracted to the rhythm of a Negro tom-tom. This tom-tom made the patient think of the danger of losing her parents, especially her mother.

I then asked her to make the sign of the cross over these circles, but they did not disappear. I told her to take a cloth and rub them out, and they vanished.

She turned in the direction of the tom-tom. She was surrounded by half-naked men and women dancing in a frightening way. I told her not to be afraid to join the dance. She did so. Immediately the appearance of the dancers changed. It was a splendid party. The men and women were well dressed and they were dancing a waltz, *The Snow Star*.

I told her to go closer to the circles; she could no longer see them. I told her to think of them; they appeared, but they were broken. I told her to go in through the opening. 'I'm not completely surrounded any more,' she said spontaneously, 'I can get out again.' The circle broke into two pieces and then into several. Soon there were only two pieces, and then they disappeared. There were frequent throat and eye tics while she was talking.

A succession of such sessions will bring about the sedation of the motor disturbance.

Here are notes on another session:

I told her to bring back the circles. She could not see them at first; then they came. They were broken. She entered them. They broke, rose again, then gently, one after another, fell away into the void. I told her to listen to the tom-tom. She did not hear it. She called to it. She heard it on the left.

I suggested to her that an angel would go with her to the tom-tom: She wanted to go all alone. But someone was coming down from the sky. It was an angel. He was smiling; he took her close to the tom-tom. There were only black men there, and they were dancing round a large fire and looked evil. The angel asked her what they were going to do; she said they were going to burn a white man. She looked for him everywhere. She could not see him.

'Ah, I see him! He's a white man about fifty years old. He's half undressed.'

The angel began to negotiate with the black chief (for she was afraid). The black chief said that this white man was not from their country and so they were going to burn him. But he had done nothing wrong.

They set him free and went back to their dancing, joyfully. She refused to take part in the dance.

I sent her to talk to the chief. He was dancing alone. The white man had disappeared. She wanted to go away and seemed to have no desire to know the Negroes. She wanted to go away with her angel, somewhere where she would really be at home, with her mother, her brothers, and her sisters.

When the tics had ceased, the treatment was dropped. A few days later the patient was seen again because she had had a relapse. These are the notes of that session:

The circles kept coming closer. She hit them with a stick. They broke into fragments. The stick was a magic wand. It changed these bits of iron into something shining and beautiful.

She turned toward a fire. It was the fire round which the Negroes were dancing. She wanted to know the chief, and she approached him.

One Negro who had stopped dancing started again, but in a new rhythm. She danced round the fire and let the Negroes take her hands. [. . .]

I take this passage from the notes of another session:

She began to think about the circles again. Each was broken into a single piece, on the right of which something was missing. The smaller circles remained intact. She wanted to break them. She took them in her hands and bent them, and then they broke. One, however, was still left. She went through it. On the other side she found she was in darkness. But she was not afraid. She called someone and her guardian angel came down, friendly and smiling. He led her to the right, back into the daylight.

In this case, the waking-dream therapy produced appreciable results. But as soon as the patient was once more *alone* the tics returned.

I do not want to elaborate on the infrastructure of this psycho-neurosis. The questions put by the chief psychiatrist had brought out a fear of imaginary Negroes – a fear first experienced at the age of twelve.

I had a great many talks with this patient. When she was ten or twelve years old, her father, 'an old-timer in the Colonial Service,' liked to listen to programs of Negro music. The tom-tom echoed through their house every evening, long after she had gone to bed. Besides, as we have pointed out, it is at this age that the savage–cannibal–Negro makes his appearance. The connection was easily discernible.

In addition, her brothers and sisters, who had discovered her weak point, amused themselves by scaring her. Lying in bed and hearing the tom-toms, she virtually *saw* Negroes. She fled under the covers, trembling. Then smaller and smaller circles appeared, blurring the Negroes. These circles are easily recognizable as a kind of defense mechanism against her hallucinosis. Later, the circles appeared without the Negroes – the defense mechanism had taken over without reference to what had brought it on.

I talked with the girl's mother, who corroborated what the patient had said. The girl was very emotional, and at the age of twelve she had often been observed to tremble in her bed. My presence on her ward made no perceptible difference in her mental state. By now it was the circles *alone* that produced the motor reactions: outcries, facial tics, random gesticulation.

Even when one concedes a constitutional factor here, it is clear that her alienation is the result of a fear of the Negro, a fear aggravated by determining circumstances. Although the patient had made considerable progress, it was doubtful whether she would soon be able to resume a normal life in society.

Notes

1   Jacques Lacan, 'Le complèxe, facteur concret de la psychologie familiale', *Encyclopédie française*, 8–40, 5.

2   A quotation borrowed from Michel Leiris, 'Martinique, Guadeloupe, Hait', *Les Temps Modernes* (February, 1950), p. 1346.

3   Joachim Marcus, 'Structure familiale et comportements politiques: l'autorite dans la famille et dans l'Etat', *Revue Française de Psychoanalyse*, (April–June, 1949).

4   I recommend the following experiment to those who are unconvinced. Attend showings of a Tarzan film in the Antilles and in Europe. In the Antilles, the young Negro identifies himself *de facto* with Tarzan against the Negroes. This is much more difficult for him in a European theater, for the rest of the audience, which is white, automatically identifies him with the savages on the screen. It is a conclusive experience. The Negro learns that one is not black without problems. A documentary film on Africa produces similar reactions when it is shown in a French city and in Fort-de-France. I will go farther and say that Bushmen and Zulus arouse even more laughter among the young Antilleans. It would be interesting to show how in this instance the reactional exaggeration betrays a hint of recognition. In France a Negro who sees this documentary is virtually petrified. There he has no more hope of flight: he is at once Antillean, Bushman, and Zulu.

5   More especially, they become aware that the line of self-esteem that they had chosen should be inverted. We have seen in fact that the Antillean who goes to France pictures this journey as the final stage of his personality. Quite literally I can say without any risk of error that the Antillean who goes to France in order to convince himself that he is white will find his real face there.

6   A. Hesnard, *L'univers morbide de la faute* (Paris, Presses Universitaires de France, 1949) p. 37.

7   Charles Odier, *Anxiety and Magic Thinking* (New York, International Universities Press, 1956), p. 46. Originally, *L'angoisse et la pensée magique* (Neuchâtel, Delachaux, 1947).

8   Ibid., p. 76.

9   Ibid., pp. 58, 68.

10   Hesnard, *L'univers morbide de la faute*, p. 38.

11   Ibid., p. 40.

12   It would indeed be interesting, on the basis of Lacan's theory of the *mirror period*, to investigate the extent to which the *imago* of his fellow built up in the young white at the usual age would undergo an imaginary aggression with the appearance of the Negro. When one has grasped the mechanism described by Lacan, one can have no further doubt that the real Other for the white man is and will continue to be the black man. And conversely. Only for the white man The Other is perceived on the level of the body image, absolutely as the not-self – that is, the unidentifiable, the unassimilable. For the black man, as we have shown, historical and economic realities come into the picture. 'The subject's recognition of his image in the mirror', Lacan says, 'is a phenomenon that is doubly significant for the analysis of this stage: the phenomenon appears after six months, and the study of it at that time shows in convincing fashion the tendencies that currently constitute reality for the subject; the mirror image, precisely because of these affinities, affords, a good symbol of that reality: of its affective value, illusory like the image, and of its structure, as it reflects the human form' (*Encyclopédie française*, 8–40, 9 and 10). [. . .]

      In addition, I suggest that those who are interested in such questions read some of the compositions written in French by Antillean children between the ages of ten and fourteen. Given as a theme 'My feelings before I went on vacation', they reacted like real little Parisians and produced such things as, 'I like vacation because then I can run through the fields, breathe fresh air, and come home with *rosy* cheeks.' It is apparent that one would hardly be mistaken in saying that the Antillean does not altogether apprehend the fact of his being a Negro. [. . .]

It may perhaps be objected that if the white man is subject to the elaboration of the *imago* of his peer, an analogous phenomenon should occur in the Antillean, visual perception being the sketch for such an elaboration. But to say this is to forget that in the Antilles perception always occurs on the level of the imaginary. It is in white terms that one perceives one's fellows. People will say of someone, for instance, that he is 'very black'; there is nothing surprising, within a family, in hearing a mother remark that 'X is the blackest of my children' – it means that X is the least white. I can only repeat the observation of a European acquaintance to whom I had explained this: in terms of people, it is nothing but a mystification. Let me point out once more that every Antillean expects all the others to perceive him in terms of the essence of the white man. In the Antilles, just as in France, one comes up against the same myth; a Parisian says, 'He is black but he is very intelligent'; a Martinican expresses himself no differently. [. . .]

13   [Dominique] O. Mannoni, *Prospero and Caliban: the Psychology of Colonization* (New York, Praeger, 1964), p. 111, n. 1.

14   When we consider the responses given in waking-dream therapy we shall see that these mythological figures, or 'archetypes,' do reside very deep in the human mind. Whenever the individual plunges down, one finds the Negro, whether concretely or symbolically.

15   Mannoni, *Prospero and Caliban*, p. 111.

16   Karl Jaspers, *Psychopathologie générale*, French translation by Kastler and Mendousse, p. 49.

17   Michel Cournot, *Martinique* (Paris, Collection Metamorphoses, Gallimard, 1948), pp. 13–14.

18   Etiemble, 'Sur le *Martinique* de M. Michel Cournot', *Les Temps Modernes* (February, 1950), p. 1505.

19   I am thinking particularly of this passage:

> Such then is this haunted man, condemned to make his choice of himself on the basis of false problems and in a false situation, deprived of the metaphysical sense by the hostility of the society that surrounds him, driven to a rationalism of despair. His life is nothing but a long flight from others and from himself. He has been alienated even from his own body; his emotional life has been cut in two; he has been reduced to pursuing the impossible dream of universal brotherhood in a world that rejects him.
>
> Whose is the fault? It is our eyes that reflect to him the unacceptable image that he wishes to dissimulate. It is our words and our gestures – *all* our words and *all* our gestures – our anti-Semitism, but equally our condescending liberalism – that have poisoned him. It is we who constrain him to choose to be a Jew *whether through flight from himself or through self-assertion*; it is we who force him into the dilemma of Jewish authenticity or inauthenticity . . . This species that bears witness for essential humanity better than any other because it was born of secondary reactions within the body of humanity – this quintessence of man, disgraced, uprooted, destined from the start to either inauthenticity or martyrdom. In this situation there is not one of us who is not totally guilty and even criminal; the Jewish blood that the Nazis shed falls on all our heads (Sartre, *Anti-Semite and Jew*, pp. 135–6).

20   Henri Baruk, *Précis de psychiatrie* (Paris, Masson, 1950), pp. 372–3.

21   Dide and Guiraud, *Psychiatrie du médecin praticien* (Paris, Masson, 1922), p. 164.

22   *Translator's note*: Salavin is a character created by Georges Duhamel, and who is the prototype of the ineffectual man: a mediocrity, a creature of fleeting impulse, and always the victim of his own chimeras.

The narcissistic personality of our time
Christopher Lasch

[. . .] Psychoanalysis best clarifies the connection between society and the individual, culture and personality, precisely when it confines itself to careful examination of individuals. It tells us most about society when it is least determined to do so. Freud's extrapolation of psychoanalytic principles into anthropology, history, and biography can be safely ignored by the student of society, but his clinical investigations constitute a storehouse of indispensable ideas, once it is understood that the unconscious mind represents the modification of nature by culture, the imposition of civilization on instinct.

> Freud should not be reproached [wrote T.W. Adorno] for having neglected the concrete social dimension, but for being all too untroubled by the social origin of . . . the rigidity of the unconscious, which he registers with the undeviating objectivity of the natural scientist . . . In making the leap from psychological images to historical reality, he forgets what he himself discovered – that all reality undergoes modification upon entering the unconscious – and is thus misled into positing such factual events as the murder of the father by the primal horde.[1]

Those who wish to understand contemporary narcissism as a social and cultural phenomenon must turn first to the growing body of clinical writing on the subject, which makes no claim to social or cultural significance and deliberately repudiates the proposition that 'changes in contemporary culture', as Otto Kernberg writes, 'have effects on patterns of object relations.'[2] In the clinical literature, narcissism serves as more than a metaphoric term for self-absorption. As a psychic formation in which 'love rejected turns back to the self as hatred,' narcissism has come to be

This chapter is taken from *The Culture of Narcissism* (New York, W.W. Norton, 1979), pp. 34–44.

recognized as an important element in the so-called character disorders that have absorbed much of the clinical attention once given to hysteria and obsessional neuroses. A new theory of narcissism has developed, grounded in Freud's well-known essay on the subject (which treats narcissism – libidinal investment of the self – as a necessary precondition of object love) but devoted not to primary narcissism but to secondary or pathological narcissism: the incorporation of grandiose object images as a defense against anxiety and guilt. Both types of narcissism blur the boundaries between the self and the world of objects, but there is an important difference between them. The newborn infant – the primary narcissist – does not yet perceive his mother as having an existence separate from his own, and he therefore mistakes dependence on the mother, who satisfies his needs as soon as they arise, with his own omnipotence. 'It takes several weeks of postnatal development . . . before the infant perceives that the source of his need . . . is within and the source of gratification is outside the self.'

Secondary narcissism, on the other hand, 'attempts to annul the pain of disappointed [object] love' and to nullify the child's rage against those who do not respond immediately to his needs; against those who are now seen to respond to others beside the child and who therefore appear to have abandoned him. Pathological narcissism, 'which cannot be considered simply a fixation at the level of normal primitive narcissism,' arises only when the ego has developed to the point of distinguishing itself from surrounding objects. If the child for some reason experiences this separation trauma with special intensity, he may attempt to reestablish earlier relationships by creating in his fantasies an omnipotent mother or father who merges with images of his own self. 'Through internalization the patient seeks to recreate a wished-for love relationship which may once have existed and simultaneously to annul the anxiety and guilt aroused by aggressive drives directed against the frustrating and disappointing object.'

Narcissism in recent clinical literature

The shifting emphasis in clinical studies from primary to secondary narcissism reflects both the shift in psychoanalytic theory from study of the id to study of the ego and a change in the type of patients seeking psychiatric treatment. Indeed the shift from a psychology of instincts to ego psychology itself grew partly out of a recognition that the patients who began to present themselves for treatment in the 1940s and 1950s 'very seldom resembled the classical neuroses Freud described so thoroughly.' In the last twenty-five years, the borderline patient, who confronts the psychiatrist not with well-defined symptoms but with diffuse dissatisfactions, has become increasingly common. He does not suffer from debilitating fixations or phobias or from the conversion of repressed sexual energy into nervous ailments; instead he complains 'of vague, diffuse dissatisfactions with life' and feels his 'amorphous existence to be futile and purposeless.' He describes 'subtly experienced yet pervasive feelings of emptiness and depression,' 'violent oscillations of self-esteem,' and 'a general inability to get along.' He gains 'a sense of heightened self-esteem only by attaching himself to strong, admired figures whose acceptance he craves and by whom he needs to feel supported.' Although he carries out his daily responsibilities and even achieves distinction, happiness eludes him, and life frequently strikes him as not worth living.[3]

Psychoanalysis, a therapy that grew out of experience with severely repressed and morally rigid individuals who needed to come to terms with a rigorous inner 'censor', today finds itself confronted more and more often with a 'chaotic and impulse-ridden character.' It must deal with patients who 'act out' their conflicts instead of repressing or sublimating them. These patients, though often ingratiating, tend to cultivate a protective shallowness in emotional relations. They lack the capacity to mourn, because the intensity of their rage against lost love objects, in particular against their parents, prevents their reliving happy experiences or treasuring them in memory. Sexually promiscuous rather than repressed, they nevertheless find it difficult to 'elaborate the sexual impulse' or to approach sex in the spirit of play. They avoid close involvements, which might release intense feelings of rage. Their personalities consist largely of defenses against this rage and against feelings of oral deprivation that originate in the pre-Oedipal stage of psychic development.

Often these patients suffer from hypochondria and complain of a sense of inner emptiness. At the same time they entertain fantasies of omnipotence and a strong belief in their right to exploit others and be gratified. Archaic, punitive, and sadistic elements predominate in the superegos of these patients, and they conform to social rules more out of fear of punishment than from a sense of guilt. They experience their own needs and appetites, suffused with rage, as deeply dangerous, and they throw up defenses that are as primitive as the desires they seek to stifle.

On the principle that pathology represents a heightened version of normality, the 'pathological narcissism' found in character disorders of this type should tell us something about narcissism as a social phenomenon. Studies of personality disorders that occupy the borderline between neurosis and psychosis, though written for clinicians and making no claims to shed light on social or cultural issues, depict a type of personality that ought to be immediately recognizable, in a more subdued form, to observers of the contemporary cultural scene: facile at managing the impressions he gives to others, ravenous for admiration but contemptuous of those he manipulates into providing it; unappeasably hungry for emotional experiences with which to fill an inner void; terrified of aging and death.[4]

The most convincing explanations of the psychic origins of this borderline syndrome draw on the theoretical tradition established by Melanie Klein. In her psychoanalytic investigations of children, Klein discovered that early feelings of overpowering rage, directed especially against the mother and secondarily against the internalized image of the mother as a ravenous monster, make it impossible for the child to synthesize 'good' and 'bad' parental images. In his fear of aggression from the bad parents – projections of his own rage – he idealizes the good parents who will come to the rescue.

Internalized images of others, buried in the unconscious mind at an early age, become self-images as well. If later experience fails to qualify or to introduce elements of reality into the child's archaic fantasies about his parents, he finds it difficult to distinguish between images of the self and of the objects outside the self. These images fuse to form a defense against the bad representations of the self and of objects, similarly fused in the form of a harsh, punishing superego. Melanie Klein analyzed a ten-year-old boy who unconsciously thought of his mother as a 'vampire' or 'horrid bird' and internalized this fear as hypochondria. He was afraid that the bad presences inside him would devour the good ones. The rigid separation of good and bad images of the self and of objects, on the one hand, and the fusion of self- and object images on the other, arose from the boy's inability to tolerate ambivalence or anxiety. Because his anger was so intense, he could not admit that he harbored aggressive feelings towards those he loved. 'Fear and guilt relating to his destructive phantasies moulded his whole emotional life.'

A child who feels so gravely threatened by his own aggressive feelings (projected onto others and then internalized again as inner 'monsters') attempts to compensate himself for his experiences of rage and envy with fantasies of wealth, beauty, and omnipotence. These fantasies, together with the internalized images of the good parents with which he attempts to defend himself, become the core of a 'grandiose conception of the self.' A kind of 'blind optimism,' according to Otto Kernberg, protects the narcissistic child from the dangers around and within him – particularly from dependence on others, who are perceived as without exception undependable. 'Constant projection of "all bad" self and object images perpetuates a world of dangerous, threatening objects, against which the "all good" self images are used defensively, and megalomanic ideal self images are built up.' The splitting of images determined by aggressive feelings from images that derive from libidinal impulses makes it impossible for the child to acknowledge his own aggression, to experience guilt or concern for objects invested simultaneously with aggression and libido, or to mourn for lost objects. Depression in narcissistic patients takes the form not of mourning with its admixture of guilt, described by Freud in 'Mourning and melancholia,' but of impotent rage and 'feelings of defeat by external forces.'

Because the intrapsychic world of these patients is so thinly populated – consisting only of the 'grandiose self,' in Kernberg's words, 'the devalued, shadowy images of self and others, and potential persecutors – they experience intense feelings of emptiness and inauthenticity. Although the narcissist can function in the everyday world and often charms other people (not least with his 'pseudo-insight into his personality'), his devaluation of others, together with his lack of curiosity about them, impoverishes his personal life and reinforces the 'subjective experience of emptiness.' Lacking any real intellectual engagement with the world – notwithstanding a frequently inflated estimate of his own intellectual abilities – he has little capacity for sublimation. He therefore depends on others for constant infusions of approval and admiration. He 'must attach [himself] to someone, living an almost parasitic' existence. At the same time, his fear of emotional dependence, together with his manipulative, exploitive approach to personal relations, makes these relations bland, superficial, and deeply unsatisfying. 'The ideal relationship to me would be a two month relationship,' said a borderline patient. 'That way there'd be no commitment. At the end of the two months I'd just break it off.'

Chronically bored, restlessly in search of instantaneous intimacy – of emotional titillation without involvement and dependence – the narcissist is promiscuous and often pansexual as well, since the fusion of pregenital and Oedipal impulses in the service of aggression encourages polymorphous perversity. The bad images he has internalized also make him chronically uneasy about his health, and hypochondria in turn gives him a special affinity for therapy and for therapeutic groups and movements.

As a psychiatric patient, the narcissist is a prime candidate for interminable analysis. He seeks in analysis a religion or way of life and hopes to find in the therapeutic relationship external support for his fantasies of omnipotence and eternal youth. The strength of his defenses, however, makes him resistant to successful analysis. The shallowness of his emotional life often prevents him from developing a close connection to the analyst, even though he 'often uses his intellectual insight to agree verbally with the analyst and recapitulates in his own words what has been analysed in previous sessions.' He uses intellect in the service of evasion rather than self-discovery, resorting to some of the same strategies of obfuscation that appear in the confessional writing of recent decades. 'The patient uses the analytic interpretations but deprives them quickly of life and meaning, so that only meaningless words are left. The words are then felt to be the patient's own possession, which he idealizes and which give him a sense of superiority.' Although psychiatrists no longer consider narcissistic disorders inherently unanalyzable, few of them take an optimistic view of the prospects for success.

According to Kernberg, the great argument for making the attempt at all, in the face of the many difficulties presented by narcissistic patients, is the devastating effect of narcissism on the second half of their lives – the certainty of the terrible suffering that lies in store. In a society that dreads old age and death, aging holds a special terror for those who fear dependence and whose self-esteem requires the admiration usually reserved for youth, beauty, celebrity, or charm. The usual defenses against the ravages of age – identification with ethical or artistic values beyond one's immediate interests, intellectual curiosity, the consoling emotional warmth derived from happy relationships in the past – can do nothing for the narcissist. Unable to derive whatever comfort comes from identification with historical continuity, he finds it impossible, on the contrary, 'to accept the fact that a younger generation now possesses many of the previously cherished gratifications of beauty, wealth, power and, particularly, creativity. To be able to enjoy life in a process involving a growing identification with other people's happiness and achievements is tragically beyond the capacity of narcissistic personalities.'[5]

Social influences on narcissism

Every age develops its own peculiar forms of pathology, which express in exaggerated form its underlying character structure. In Freud's time, hysteria and obsessional neurosis carried to extremes the personality traits associated with the capitalist order at an earlier stage in its development – acquisitiveness, fanatical devotion to work, and a fierce repression of sexuality. In our time, the preschizophrenic, borderline, or personality disorders have attracted increasing attention, along with schizophrenia itself. This 'change in the form of neuroses has been observed and described since World War II by an ever-increasing number of psychiatrists.' According to Peter L. Giovacchini, 'Clinicians are constantly faced with the seemingly increasing number of patients who do not fit current diagnostic categories' and who suffer not from 'definitive symptoms' but from 'vague, ill-defined complaints.' 'When I refer to "this type of patient,"' he writes, 'practically everyone knows to whom I am referring.' The growing prominence of 'character disorder' seems to signify an underlying change in the organization of personality, from what has been called inner-direction to narcissism.[6]

Allen Wheelis argued in 1958 that the change in 'the patterns of neuroses' fell 'within the personal experience of older psychoanalysts,' while younger ones 'become aware of it from the discrepancy between the older descriptions of neuroses and the problems presented by the patients who come daily to their offices. The change is from symptom neuroses to character disorders.'[7] Heinz Lichtenstein, who questioned the additional assertion that it reflected a change in personality structure, nevertheless wrote in 1963 that the 'change in neurotic patterns' already constituted a 'well-known fact.'[8] In the seventies, such reports have become increasingly common. 'It is no accident,' Herbert Hendin notes, 'that at the present time the dominant events in psychoanalysis are the rediscovery of narcissism and the new emphasis on the psychological significance of death.'[9] 'What hysteria and the obsessive neuroses were to Freud and his early colleagues . . . at the beginning of this century,' writes Michael Beldoch:

> the narcissistic disorders are to the workaday analyst in these last few decades before the next millennium. Today's patients by and large do not

suffer from hysterical paralyses of the legs or hand-washing compulsions; instead it is their very psychic selves that have gone numb or that they must scrub and rescrub in an exhausting and unending effort to come clean.[10]

These patients suffer from 'pervasive feelings of emptiness and a deep disturbance of self-esteem.' Burness E. Moore notes that narcissistic disorders have become more and more common.[11] According to Sheldon Bach, 'You used to see people coming in with hand-washing compulsions, phobias, and familiar neuroses. Now you see mostly narcissists.'[12] Gilbert J. Rose maintains that the psychoanalytic outlook, 'inappropriately transplanted from analytic practice' to everyday life, has contributed to 'global permissiveness' and the 'over-domestication of instinct,' which in turn contributes to the proliferation of 'narcissistic identity disorders.'[13] According to Joel Kovel the stimulation of infantile cravings by advertising, the usurpation of parental authority by the media and the school, and the rationalization of inner life accompanied by the false promise of personal fulfillment, have created a new type of 'social individual.'

> The result is not the classical neuroses where an infantile impulse is suppressed by patriarchal authority, but a modern version in which impulse is stimulated, perverted and given neither an adequate object upon which to satisfy itself nor coherent forms of control . . . The entire complex, played out in a setting of alienation rather than direct control, loses the classical form of symptom – and the classical therapeutic opportunity of simply restoring an impulse to consciousness.[14]

The reported increase in the number of narcissistic patients does not necessarily indicate that narcissistic disorders are more common than they used to be, in the population as a whole, or that they have become more common than the classical conversion neuroses. Perhaps they simply come more quickly to psychiatric attention. Ilza Veith contends that:

> with the increasing awareness of conversion reactions and the popularization of psychiatric literature, the 'old-fashioned' somatic expressions of hysteria have become suspect among the more sophisticated classes, and hence most physicians observe that obvious conversion symptoms are now rarely encountered and, if at all, only among the uneducated.[15]

The attention given to character disorders in recent clinical literature probably makes psychiatrists more alert to their presence. But this possibility by no means diminishes the importance of psychiatric testimony about the prevalence of narcissism, especially when this testimony appears at the same time that journalists begin to speculate about the new narcissism and the unhealthy trend toward self-absorption. The narcissist comes to the attention of psychiatrists for some of the same reasons that he rises to positions of prominence not only in awareness movements and other cults but in business corporations, political organizations, and government bureaucracies. For all his inner suffering, the narcissist has many traits that make for success in bureaucratic institutions, which put a premium on the manipulation of interpersonal relations, discourage the formation of deep personal attachments, and at the same time provide the narcissist with the approval he needs in order to validate his self-esteem. Although he may resort to therapies that promise to give meaning to life and to overcome his sense of emptiness, in his professional career the narcissist often enjoys considerable success. The management of personal impressions comes naturally to him, and his mastery of its intricacies serves him well in political and business organizations where performance now counts for less than 'visibility,' 'momentum,' and a winning record. As the 'organization man' gives way to the bureaucratic 'gamesman' – the 'loyalty era' of American business to the age of the 'executive success game' – the narcissist comes into his own. [. . .]

Notes

1   T.W. Adorno, 'Sociology and psychology', *New Left Review*, 47 (1968), pp. 80, 96.

2   Otto F. Kernberg, *Borderline Conditions and Pathological Narcissism* (New York, Jason Aronson, 1975), p. 223.

3   For recent theories of narcissism, see Warren R. Brodey, 'Image, object, and narcissistic relationships', *American Journal of Orthopsychiatry*, 31 (1961), p. 505 ('love rejected'); Therese Benedek, Parenthood as a developmental phase', *Journal of the American Psychoanalytic Association*, 7 (1959), pp. 389–90 ('several weeks of post-natal development'); Thomas Freeman, 'The concept of narcissism in schizophrenic states', *International Journal of Psychoanalysis* 44 (1963), p. 295 ('annul the pain'; 'recreate a wished-for love relationship'); Kernberg, *Borderline Conditions*, p. 283 ('cannot be considered'). On the distinction between primary and secondary narcissism and the characteristics of the latter, see also H.G. Van der Waals, 'problems of narcissism', *Bulletin of the Menninger Clinic*, 29 (1965), pp. 293–310; Warren M. Brodey, 'On the dynamics of narcissism', *Psychoanalytic Study of the Child*, 20 (1965), pp. 165–93; James F. Bing and Rudolph O. Marburg, 'Narcissism', *Journal of the American Psychoanalytic Association*, 10 (1962), pp. 593–605; Lester Schwartz, 'Techniques and prognosis in treatment of the narcissistic personality', *Journal of the American Psychoanalytic Association*, 21 (1973), pp. 617–32; Edith Jacobson, *The Self and the Object World* (New York, International Universities Press, 1964), ch. 1, esp. pp. 17–19; James F. Bing, Francis McLaughlin and Rudolph Marburg, 'The meta-psychology of narcissism', *Psychoanalytic Study of the Child*, 14 (1959), pp. 9–28. Freud's 'On narcissism: an introduction' (1914) appears in *The Standard Edition of the Works of Sigmund Freud*, ed. James Strachey (London, Hogarth Press and the Institute of Psychoanalysis, 1953), volume 3, pp. 30–59.

4   For the characteristics of character disorders, see Peter L. Giovacchini, *Psychoanalysis of Character Disorders* (New York, Jason Aronson, 1975), pp. xv ('very seldom resembled the classical neuroses'), p. 1 ('vague, diffuse dissatisfactions'), p. 31 ('general inability to get along'); Heinz Kohut, *The Analysis of the Self* (New York, International Universities Press, 1971), p. 16 ('feelings of emptiness and depression'), p. 62 ('sense of heightened self-esteem'), p. 172 ('elaborate the sexual impulse'); Annie Reich, 'Pathologic forms of self-esteem regulation', *Psychoanalytic Study of the Child*, 15 (1960), p. 224 ('violent oscillations'). See also for an early description of borderline

conditions, Robert P. Knight, 'Borderline states' (1953), in Robert P. Knight and Cyrus R. Freidman (eds), *Psychoanalytic Psychiatry and Psychology: Clinical and Theoretical Papers* (New York, International Universities Press, 1954), pp. 97–109; and for the importance of magical thinking in these conditions, Thomas Freeman, 'The concept of narcissism in schizophrenic states', *International Journal of Psychoanalysis*, 44 (1963), pp. 293–303; Géza Róheim, *Magic and Schizophrenia* (New York, International Universities Press, 1955).

5   For the psychodynamics of pathological narcissism, see Melanie Klein, 'The Oedipus complex in the light of early anxieties' (1945), in her *Contributions to Psychoanalysis* (New York, McGraw-Hill, 1964), pp. 339–67; Melanie Klein, 'Notes on some schizoid mechanisms' (1946) and Paula Heimann, 'Certain functions of introjection and projection in early infancy', in Melanie Klein et al., *Developments in Psychoanalysis* (London: Hogarth Press, 1952), pp. 122–68, 292–320; Paula Heimann, 'A contribution to the reevaluation of the Oedipus complex: the early stages', in Melanie Klein et al., *New Directions in Psychoanalysis* (New York, Basic Books, 1957), pp. 23–38; Kernberg, *Borderline Conditions*, esp. p. 36 (constant projection), p. 38 ('blind optimism'), p. 161 ('pseudo-insight'), p. 213 ('emptiness'), p. 282 ('grandiose self'), pp. 310–11 (aging and death); Roy R. Grinker et al., *The Borderline Syndrome* (New York, Basic Books, 1968), p. 102 ('parasitic' attachments), p. 105 ('two month relationship'); Otto Kernberg, 'A contribution to the ego-psychological critique of the Kleinian School', *International Journal of Psychoanalysis*, 50 (1969), pp. 317–33 (quoting Herbert A. Rosenfeld on the narcissistic patient's use of words to defeat interpretation).

       On the psychogenesis of secondary narcissim, see also Kohut, *Analysis of the Self*; Giovacchini, *Psychoanalysis of Character Disorders*; Brodey, 'Dynamics of narcissism'; Thomas Freeman, 'Narcissim and defensive processes in schizophrenic states', *International Journal of Psychoanalysis*, 43 (1962), pp. 415–25; Nathaniel Ross, 'The "as if" concept', *Journal of the American Psychoanalytic Association*, 15 (1967), pp. 59–83.

       On mourning, see Freud's 'Mourning and Melancholia' (1917), *The Standard Edition*, volume 8, pp. 152–70; Martha Wolfenstein. 'How is mourning possible?', *Psychoanalytic Study of the Child*, 21 (1966), pp. 93–126; and on psychoanalysis as a way of life, Gilbert J. Rose, 'Some misuses of analysis as a way of life: analysis interminable and interminable "analysts"', *International Review of Psychoanalysis*, 1 (1974), pp. 509–15.

6   Giovacchini, *Psychoanalysis of Character Disorders*, pp. 316–17.

7   Allen Wheelis, *The Quest for Identity* (New York, Norton, 1958), pp. 40–1.

8   Heinz Lichtenstein, 'The dilemma of human identity', *Journal of the American Psychoanalytic Association*, 11 (1963), pp. 186–7.

9   Herbert Hendin, *The Age of Sensation* (New York, Norton, 1975), p. 13.

10   Michael Beldoch, 'The therapeutic as narcissist,' *Salmagundi*, 20 (1972), pp. 136, 138.

11   Burness E. Moore, 'Toward a clarification of the concept of narcissism', *Psychoanalytic Study of the Child*, 30 (1975), p. 265.

12   Sheldon Bach, quoted in *Time*, 20 September 1976, p. 63.

13   Rose, 'Some misuses of analysis', p. 513.

14   Joel Kovel, *A Complete Guide to Therapy* (New York, Pantheon, 1976), p. 252.

15   Ilza Veith, *Hysteria: the History of a Disease* (Chicago, University of Chicago Press, 1965), p. 273.

19

The oedipal riddle   **Jessica Benjamin**

The route to individuality that leads through identificatory love of the father is a difficult one for women to follow. The difficulty lies in the fact that the power of the liberator-father is used to defend against the engulfing mother. Thus however helpful a specific change in the father's relationship to the daughter may be in the short run, it cannot solve the deeper problem: the split between a father of liberation and a mother of dependency. For children of both sexes, this split means that identification and closeness with the mother must be traded for independence; it means that being a subject of desire requires repudiation of the maternal role, of feminine identity itself.

Curiously enough, psychoanalysis has not found this split, with its devaluation of the maternal, to be a problem. As long as the father provided the boy with a way into the world and broke up the mother–son bond, no problem seemed to exist. After years of resistance, however, psychoanalysis seems finally ready to accept the idea that girls, too, need a pathway to the wider world, and that a girl's need to assert her subjectivity is not merely an envy-inspired rejection of her proper attitude. Nevertheless, man's occupation of this world remains a given; and few imagine that the mother may be capable of leading the way into it. By and large, the mainstream of psychoanalytic thought has been remarkably indifferent to feminist criticism of the split between a mother of attachment and a father of separation.

In questioning the terms of the sexual polarity, then, we cannot, as in the case of woman's desire, adapt a problem (penis envy) already identified by Freud. Rather, we have to illuminate a problem which psychoanalysis scarcely acknowledges. To do so, we will have to challenge the most fundamental postulates of psychoanalytic thinking as they appear in the

This chapter is taken from *The Bonds of Love: Psychoanalysis, Feminism and the Problem of Domination* (London, Virago, 1988), pp. 133–81.

centerpiece of Freud's theory, the Oedipus complex. For Freud, the Oedipus complex is the nodal point of development, the point at which the child comes to terms with both generational difference and sexual difference. It is the point when the child (the boy, more precisely)[1] accepts his ordained position in the fixed constellation of mother, father, and child.

This construction of difference, as we will see, harbors the crucial assumptions of domination. Analyzing the oedipal model in Freud's original formulations and in the work of later psychoanalysts, we find this common thread: the idea of the father as the protector, or even savior, from a mother who would pull us back to what Freud called the 'limitless narcissism' of infancy. This privileging of the father's role (whether or not it is considered the inevitable result of his having the phallus) can be found in almost every version of the oedipal model. It also underlies the current popular diagnosis of our social malaise: a rampant narcissism that stems from the loss of authority or the absence of the father.

Paradoxically, the image of the liberating father undermines the acceptance of difference that the Oedipus complex is meant to embody. For the idea of the father as the protection against 'limitless narcissism' at once authorizes his idealization and the mother's denigration. The father's ascendancy in the Oedipus complex spells the denial of the mother's subjectivity, and thus the breakdown of mutual recognition. At the heart of psychoanalytic theory lies an unacknowledged paradox: the creation of difference *distorts*, rather than fosters, the recognition of the other. Difference turns out to be governed by the code of domination.

The reader may well wonder that I have given so much credit [in previous chapters] to the father in preoedipal life only to diminish his importance in oedipal life. Having argued that little girls should have use of this very father, I now question his role as liberator. But this is not as contradictory as it seems. In the identification with the *rapprochement* father we saw both a defensive and a positive aspect. What I will argue is that in the Oedipus complex, this defensive aspect becomes much more pronounced. The boy does not merely disidentify with the mother, he repudiates her and all feminine attributes. The incipient split between mother as source of goodness and father as principle of individuation is hardened into a polarity in which her goodness is redefined as a seductive threat to autonomy. Thus a paternal ideal of separation is formed which, under the current gender arrangement, comes to embody the repudiation of femininity. It enforces the split between male subject and female object, and with it, the dual unity of domination and submission.

But we must not forget that every idealization defends against something: the idealization of the father masks the child's fear of his power. The myth of a good paternal authority that is rational and prevents regression purges the father of all terror and, as we will see, displaces it onto the mother, so that she bears the badness for both of them. The myth of the good father (and the dangerous mother) is not easily dispelled. That is why the critique of the oedipal model is so crucial. Perhaps the best way to understand domination is to analyze how it is legitimated in what is the most influential modern construction of psychic life.

Under father's protection

[. . .] According to recent cultural criticism, Narcissus has replaced Oedipus as the myth of our time. Narcissism is now seen to be at the root of everything from the ill-fated romance with violent revolution to the enthralled mass consumption of state-of-the-art products and the 'lifestyles of the rich and famous.' The longing for self-aggrandizement and gratification, in this view, is no longer bound by authority and superego to the moral values of work and responsibility that once characterized the autonomous individual. Instead, people seek immediate experiences of power, glamor, and excitement, or, at least, identification with those who appear to possess them.

This social critique, best articulated by Christopher Lasch in *The Culture of Narcissism*, argues that the unleashing of narcissism reflects the decline of Oedipal Man.[2] The Oedipus complex, this critique continues, was the fundament for the autonomous, rational indivudal, and today's unstable families with their less authoritarian fathers no longer foster the Oedipus complex as Freud described it. The individual who could internalize the father's authority into his own conscience and power is an endangered species. Whereas Oedipus represented responsibility and guilt, Narcissus represents self-involvement and denial of reality. [. . .]

[. . .]

The cultural critique of narcissism is based on this idea of too little guilt. It interprets the Oedipus complex primarily as the source of the superego, favoring a rather old-fashioned reading of Freud's theory. In Freud's conception, the Oedipus complex crystallizes the male child's triangular relationship with the parents. The boy loves his mother and wishes to possess her, hates his father and wishes to replace or murder him. Given the father's superior power (the threat of castration), the boy renounces the incestuous wish toward the mother and internalizes the prohibition and the paternal authority itself. [. . .]

Now the boy's superego will perform the paternal function within his own psyche: internal guilt has replaced fear of the father. Structurally, this means a differentiation within the psyche, a new arrangement of the agencies of superego, ego, and id.[3] The resolution of the complex includes the transition from fear of external authority to self-regulation, the replacement of authority and the desire for approval by conscience and self-control. The cultural critique emphasizes the importance of this process of internalization for the creation of the autonomous individual; and it interprets the current social malaise as the direct result of the weakening of authority and superego, the eclipse of the father. But in its lament for the lost prestige and normative power of Oedipal Man, it oversimplifies the psychoanalytic position. Thus Lasch presents a simple scheme in which the preoedipal fantasy of authority is archaic, primitive, 'charged with sadistic rage,' while the oedipal one is realistic and 'formed by later experience with love and respected models of social conduct.'[4] Implicit in this scheme is the assumption that the narcissistic or infantile components of the psyche are the more destructive ones, that psychological development is a progress away from badness. The comparison between Oedipal Man and the New Narcissist is permeated with nostalgia for old forms of authority and morality. The old authority may have engendered Guilty Man's conflicts but it spared him Tragic Man's disorganization of the self.

Lasch's analysis is a variation on the older theme of the fatherless society, a theory which explained many phenomena, including the popularity of fascism in Germany, as responses to the absence of paternal authority.[5] In Lasch's version, the 'emotional absence of the father' who can provide a 'model of self-restraint' is so devastating because it results in a superego that remains fixated at an early phase, 'harsh and punitive' but without moral values. Other contemporary critics have echoed his analysis, claiming that changes in psychological complaints are the result of shifts in family politics.[6] [. . .]

Sociologically speaking, this viewpoint is one-sided. It simply dismisses all the opposing tendencies that enrich and intensify, as well as complicate, contemporary family life: fewer children per family, shorter working hours for parents, less labor in the home, a culture of family leisure, increased paternal involvement in the early phases of childrearing, and the trend toward understanding rather than merely disciplining children.[7]

As a reading of psychoanalytic discourse, this viewpoint is equally limited. We should start by noting that psychoanalysts do not commonly express the sort of crass nostalgia for authority that we find in the critique of the New Narcissist, even if they are in sympathy with it. It is true that psychoanalysts generally assume that a patient with an oedipal conflict has reached a higher level of development than a patient with a narcissistic or preoedipal one; but what they find positive about Oedipus and the superego, about the father and masculinity, is not primarily framed in terms of the internalization of authority.

Rather, psychoanalysis currently sees the oedipal conflict as the culmination of the preoedipal struggle to separate from the parents. Separation includes giving up the narcissistic fantasy of omnipotence – either as perfect oneness or self-sufficiency. Contemporary psychoanalytic discussions emphasize how the Oedipus complex organizes the great task of coming to terms with difference: when the oedipal child grasps the *sexual* meaning of the difference between himself and his parents, and between mothers and fathers, he has accepted an external reality that is truly outside his control. It is a given, which no fantasy can change. The sexual difference – between genders and between generations – comes to absorb all the childhood experiences of powerlessness and exclusion as well as independence. This interpretation, which understands oedipal development as a step forward into reality and independence, by no means devalues the positive aspect of the child's narcissism in the early relationship with the mother.[8]

This emphasis on separation in the oedipal model becomes problematic, however, because it is linked to the paternal ideal. The idea that the father *intervenes* in the mother – child dyad to bring about a boy's masculine identity and separation is, as I have suggested, hardly innocuous. This idea is actually the manifest form of the deeper (and less scientific) assumption that the father is the only possible liberator and way into the world.[9] Repeatedly, this defense of the father's role as the principle of individuation creeps into the theory even when the element of authority is de-emphasized. Whether the Oedipus complex is interpreted as a theory of separation or of the superego, it still contains the equation of paternity with individuation and civilization.

[. . .]

There are several problems with this point of view. For one thing, the association of the father with oedipal maturity masks his earlier role in *rapprochement* as an ideal imbued with the fantasy of omnipotence. When paternal authority is presented as an alternative to narcissism, its role in preserving that fantasy is ignored. Furthermore, the sanitized view of oedipal authority denies the fear and submission that paternal power has historically inspired.

[. . .]

The repudiation of femininity

[. . .] In the psychoanalytic picture of development, gender polarity and the privileging of the father become far more intense in the oedipal phase. In the preoedipal period, as we saw in the discussion of *rapprochement*, gender difference is still somewhat vague. The boy's ego ideal may still include identification with the mother; he still dresses up in her clothes and, like Freud's famous patient 'Little Hans,' still 'believes' he might have a baby even though he knows he can't. But the oedipal resolution banishes this ambiguity in favour of an exclusively masculine ideal of being the powerful father capable of leaving mother as well as of desiring and uniting with her. In oedipal reality sexual difference becomes a line that can no longer be breached.

After Oedipus, both routes back to mother – identification and object love – are blocked. The boy must renounce not only incestuous love, but also identificatory love of the mother. In this respect the contrary commands of the oedipal father – 'You must be like me' and 'You may not be like me' – unite in a common cause, to repudiate identity with the mother.[10] The oedipal injunctions say, in effect: 'You may not *be like* the mother, and you must *wait* to love her as I do.' Both agencies, paternal ego ideal and superego, push the boy away from dependence, vulnerability, and intimacy with mother. And the mother, the original source of goodness, is now located outside the self, externalized as love object. She may still have ideal properties, but she is not part of the boy's own ego ideal. The good mother is no longer inside; she is something lost – Eden, innocence, gratification, the bounteous breast – that must be regained through love on the outside.

What really changes, then, in the oedipal phase is the nature of the boy's tie to the mother. I have already made the point that the oedipal identification with the father is actually an extension of a powerful erotic connection, identificatory love. In this sense, the term narcissism does not mean self-love or a lack of erotic connection to the other, but a love of someone *like* oneself, a homoerotic love.[11] In the oedipal phase a new kind of love emerges, which Freud, perhaps unfortunately, called object love. But it is not an entirely unhappy phrase, for it does connote that the other is perceived as existing objectively, outside, rather than as part of the self. In the Oedipus complex the important change is the transformation of the original preoedipal object of identification into an oedipal object of 'outside love.' This outside love, according to the theory, would threaten to dissolve back into 'inside love' if the incest barrier did not prohibit it. A major function of the incest barrier thus seems to be making sure the love object and the 'like' object are not the same. It is not just a literal forbidding of sexual union, but also a prohibition on identification with the mother.[12]

In my view – and, in a way, in Freud's view too – the boy's repudiation of femininity is the central thread of the Oedipus complex, no less important than the renunciation of the mother as love object. To be feminine like her would be a throwback to the preoedipal dyad, a dangerous regression. The whole experience of the mother–infant dyad is retrospectively identified with femininity, and vice versa. Having learned that he cannot have babies like mother, nor play her part, the boy can only return as an infant, with the dependency and vulnerability of an infant. Now her nurturance threatens to re-engulf him with its reminder of help-lessness and dependency; it must be countered by his assertion of difference and superiority. To the extent that identification is blocked, the boy has no choice but to overcome his infancy by repudiation of dependency. This is why the oedipal ideal of individuality excludes all dependency from the definition of autonomy.

Generally the road back to the mother is closed off through devalu-ation and denigration; as observed before, the oedipal phase is marked by the boy's contempt for women. Indeed, the boy's scorn, like penis envy, is a readily observable phenomenon, and it often becomes more pronounced once the oedipal stance is consolidated. Consider the great distance between boys and girls during the period of latency: the pejorative charge of 'sissy'; the oedipal boy's insistence that all babies are 'she.'

With the exception of dissidents like Karen Horney, most psycho-analytic writers have denied the extent to which envy and feelings of loss

THE OEDIPAL RIDDLE

underlie the denigration or idealization of women.[13] Male envy of women's fecundity and ability to produce food is certainly not unknown, but little is made of it. Similarly, the anxiety about the penis being cut off is rarely recognized as a metaphor for the annihilation that comes from being 'cut off' from the source of goodness. As Dinnerstein has noted, once the mother is no longer identified with, once she is projected outside the self, then, to a large extent, the boy loses the sense of having this vital source of goodness inside.[14] He feels excluded from the feminine world of nurturance. At times he feels the exclusion more, as when he idealizes the lost paradise of infancy; at other times he feels contempt for that world, because it evokes helplessness and dependency. But even when mother is envied, idealized, sentimentalized, and longed for, she is forever outside the masculine self. The repudiation of the mother, to whom the boy is denied access by the father – and by the outside world, the larger culture that demands that he behave like a little man – engenders a fear of loss, whether the mother is idealized or held in contempt.

[. . .] [T]he identification with the holding mother supplies something vital to the self: in the case of the boy, losing the continuity between himself and mother will subvert his confidence in his 'inside.' The loss of that in-between space cuts him off from the space within. The boy thinks: 'Mother has the good things inside, and now that she is forever separate from me and I may not incorporate her, I can only engage in heroic acts to regain and conquer her in her incarnations in the outside world.' The boy who has lost access to inner space becomes enthralled with conquering outer space.

But in losing the intersubjective space and turning to conquest of the external object, the boy will pay a price in his sense of sexual subjectivity. His adult encounter with woman as an acutely desirable object may rob him of his own desire – he is thrown back into feeling that desire is the property of the object. [. . .] In the oedipal experience of losing the inner continuity with women and encountering instead the idealized, acutely desirable object outside, the image of woman as the dangerous, regressive siren is born. The counterpart of this image is the wholly idealized, masterful subject who can withstand or conquer her.

The upshot of the repudiation of femininity, then, is a stance toward women – of fear, of mastery, of distance – which by no means recognizes her as a different but like subject. Once the unbridgeable sexual difference is established, its dissolution is threatening to male identity, to the precious identification with the father. Holding on to the internalized father, especially by holding on to the ideal phallus, is now the means of protection against being overwhelmed by the mother. But this exclusive identification with the father, achieved at the expense of disavowing all femininity, works against the differentiation that is supposed to be the main oedipal achievement.

We can see this in the fact that the oedipal model equates sexual renunciation of mother with recognition of her independent subjectivity. In giving up the hope of possessing her, in realizing that she belongs to the father, the child presumably comes to terms with the limits of his relationship with her. But true recognition of another person means more than simply not possessing her. In the parents' heterosexual love, the mother belongs to and acknowledges the father, but the father does not necessarily acknowledge her in return. The psychoanalytic literature consistently complains of the mother who denies the child the necessary confrontation with the father's role by pretending that he is unimportant to her, that she loves only the child. Yet seldom do psychoanalysts raise a comparable complaint about the father who denigrates the mother. Realizing that mother belongs to father, or responds to his desire, is not the same as recognizing her as a subject of desire, as a person with a will of her own.

This is the major internal contradiction in the oedipal model. The oedipal resolution is supposed to consolidate the differentiation between self and other – but without recognizing the mother. What the Oedipus complex brings to the boy's erotic life is the quality of outside love for the mother, with all the intensity that separation produces. This erotic potential is further heightened by the incest prohibition, the barrier to transgression, stimulated by the awareness of difference, boundaries, and separation. Yet all of this does not add up to recognition of her as an independently existing subject, outside one's control. It could mean, after all, that she is in the control of someone else whom one takes as one's ideal. The point of the oedipal triangle should be the acknowledgment that 'I must share mother, she is outside my control, she is involved in another relationship besides the one with me.' Yet – and here we come to the unhappy side of the phrase 'object love' – at the same time that the boy acknowledges this outside relationship, he may devalue her and bond with father in feeling superior to her. She is at best a desired object one may not possess.

The problem with the oedipal model should come as no surprise when we consider that men have generally not recognized women as equal independent subjects, but rather perceived them as sexual objects (or maternal helpmates). If the disavowal of identity with the mother is linked to the denial of her equal subjectivity, how can the mother survive as a viable other with whom mutual recognition is possible? Psychoanalysis has been careful to evade this contradiction by defining differentiation not as a tension or balance, not in terms of mutual recognition, but solely as the achievement of separation: as long as the boy gets away from the mother, he has successfully become an individual.

Perhaps the starkest denial by psychoanalysis of the mother's subjectivity is Freud's insistence that children do not know about the existence of the female sexual organs. According to Chasseguet-Smirgel, the real flaw in Freud's thinking was this idea of 'sexual phallic monism,' the assertion that there is only one genital organ of significance to both boys and girls, the penis.[15] No matter what competing evidence he stumbled over, Freud insisted that children do not know about the existence of the vagina until puberty, and that, until then, they perceive woman as castrated men.[16]

The theory of the castrated woman is itself an example of this denial. What is denied, Chasseguet-Smirgel says, is the image of woman and mother as she is known to the unconscious: the frightening and powerful figure created out of the child's helpless dependency. 'The theory of sexual phallic monism (and its derivatives) seems to me to eradicate the narcissistic wound which is common to all humanity, and springs from the child's helplessness, a helplessness which makes him completely dependent upon his mother.'[17] When the oedipal child denies the existence of a vagina in favor of the phallic mother it is because 'the idea of being penetrated by a penis is less invasive than that of a deep and greedy womb.'[18]

The idea of phallic monism is clearly at odds with the acceptance of difference that the Oedipus complex is supposed to embody. It denies the difference between the sexes, or rather it reduces difference to absence, to lack. Difference then means plus-or-minus the penis. There is no range of qualitative divergence; only presence or absence, rich or poor, the haves and the have-nots. There is no such thing as woman: woman is merely that which is not man.[19] Like the oedipal symbolization of the mother as either a lost paradise or a dangerous siren, the denial of her sexual organs makes her always either more or less than human.

[. . .]

Thus the Oedipus complex does not finally resolve the problem of difference, of recognizing an other. The mother is devalued, her power and desire are transferred to the idealized father, and her nurturance is inaccessible. The same phallus that stands for difference and reality also stands for power over and repudiation of women. By assuming the power to represent her sexuality as well as his, it denies women's independent sexuality. Thus, masculinity is defined in opposition to woman, and gender is organized as polarity with one side idealized, the other devalued.

Although the oedipal construction of difference seems to be dominant in our cultural representation of gender, it is not the only possible one. The oedipal phase is, after all, only one point at which gender difference is integrated in the psyche. Once we recognize the consequences of the repudiation of femininity, we may speculate that the boy's stance toward femininity has something in common with the girl's toward masculinity, that it, too, is a reaction to blocked identification. As we have seen in the case of the girl, a successful identificatory love of the father may 'solve' the problem of penis envy. Perhaps repudiation is not all that different from envy, in which it is partially rooted.

Irene Fast's distinction between repudiation and renunciation of femininity suggests another route to the integration of difference. Repudiation, Fast suggests, is an unsuccessful mode of differentiation; 'ideally' boys ought to renounce, not repudiate, femininity, after a period of identification with it.[20] She points out that girls, too, must overcome the primary identification with the mother and replace it with more generalized gender identifications that do not equate all femininity with the mother. If the girl tries to differentiate exclusively by repudiating the mother in favor of the father rather than by also developing generalized gender identifications, she never really separates from the mother: 'Repudiation leaves the primitive identifications and the fusion with the mother intact.'[21] We could then speculate that for boys, repudiation also forecloses the development of a more mature maternal identification; it perpetuates the power of the merging, omnipotent mother in the unconscious. Without this mature identification, the boy does not develop a differentiated mother image. Thus a longer period of 'bisexuality,' of allowing both feminine and masculine identifications to coexist, would aid boys in becoming *more* differentiated from mother and obviate the need for such defenses as repudiation, distance, and control.

Perhaps, then, the way out of the oedipal repudiation of femininity must be sought in the period that comes before it. Between the boy's early disidentification with the mother and his oedipal separation from her is a neglected phase of playful, secondary identification with femininity. Insofar as the culture forecloses this possibility by demanding a premature entry into the oedipal world, gender identity is formed by repudiation rather than by recognition of the other. But the changing social relations of gender have given us a glimpse of another world, of a space in which each sex can play the other and so accept difference by making it familiar. As we give greater value to the preoedipal world, to a more flexible acceptance of difference, we can see that difference is only truly established when it exists in tension with likeness, when we are able to recognize the other in ourselves.

The polarity principle

In the oedipal model, the distinction between the two parents – the holding, nurturing mother and the liberating, exciting father – is expressed as an irreconcilable difference. Even though the *rapprochement* conflict already opposed the father to the mother, it did not wholly abrogate the maternal identification. But in the oedipal construction of difference, this coexistence is no longer possible. Separation takes precedence over connection, and constructing boundaries becomes more important than insuring attachment. The two central elements of recognition – being like and being distinct – are split apart. Instead of recognizing the other who is different, the boy either identifies or disidentifies. Recognition is thus reduced to a one-dimensional identification with likeness; and as distinct from early childhood, where any likeness will do, this likeness is sexually defined.

The denial of identification with the mother also tends to cut the boy off from the intersubjective communication that was part of the primary bond between mother and infant. Emotional attunement, sharing states of mind, empathically assuming the other's position, and imaginatively perceiving the other's needs and feelings – these are now associated with cast-off femininity. Emotional attunement is now experienced as dangerously close to losing oneself in the other; affective imitation is now used negatively to tease and provoke. Thus the intersubjective dimension is increasingly reduced, and the need for mutual recognition must be satisfied with mere identification of likeness (which the industry of mass culture is only too happy to promote in the gender stereotyping of children's playthings). Recognition works more through ideal identifications and less through concrete interaction. What comes to fruition in this psychic phase, then, is a one-sided form of differentiation in which each sex can play only one part. Concrete identifications with the other parent are not lost, but they are excluded from the symbolically organized gender identity.[22]

Although I have dealt with the Oedipal model exclusively in its masculine form, it is easy to see how the model constructs femininity as a simple mirror image of masculinity. The ideal type of femininity (which, as we observed earlier, is constituted as whatever is opposite to masculinity) absorbs all that is cast off by the boy as he flees from mother. The main difference is simply that for girls, masculine traits are not a threat to identity, as feminine traits are for boys, but an unattainable ideal. But for both sexes the important oedipal limit is the same: identify only with the same-sex parent. Even if the mirror relationship does not fit seamlessly in real life, the oedipal model defines gender as just such a complementarity. Each gender is able to represent only one aspect of the polarized self–other relationship.

To the extent that this scheme actually does prevail, no one can truly appreciate difference, for identification with the other parent is blocked. Identification no longer functions as a bridge to the experience of an other; now it can only confirm likeness. Real recognition of the other entails being able to perceive commonality through difference; and true differentiation sustains the balance between separateness and connection in a dynamic tension. But once identification with the other is denied, love becomes only the love of an object, of The Other. Since the mother is deprived of subjectivity, identification with her involves a loss of self. When the oedipal standpoint takes over completely, men no longer confront women as other subjects who can recognize them. Only in other men can they meet their match. Women can gain this power of recognition only by remaining desirable yet unattainable, untouched and unconquered, and ultimately dangerous. Loss of mutual recognition is the most common consequence of gender polarity.

The other important consequence of this polarity is the one-sided ideal of autonomous individuality, the masculine ideal. The identification with the father functions as a denial of dependency. The father's phallus stands for the wholeness and separateness that the child's real helplessness and dependency belie. Denying dependency on the mother by identifying with the phallic ideal amounts to sustaining the *rapprochement* fantasy of omnipotence, only modified by projecting it into the future ('You must *wait* to be like me'). The devaluation of the need for the other becomes a touchstone of adult masculinity.

Thus, I believe, the deep source of discontent in our culture is not repression or, in the new fashion, narcissism, but gender polarity. Many of the persistent symptoms of this discontent – contempt for the needy and dependent, emphasis on individual self-reliance, rejection of social forms of providing nurturance – are not visibly connected to gender. Yet in spite of the fact that these attitudes are almost as common among women as they are among men, they are nevertheless the result of gender polarity. They underlie the mentality of opposition which pits freedom against nurturance: either we differentiate or remain dependent; either we stand alone or are weak; either we relinquish autonomy or renounce the need for love. [. . .]

In spite of the many arguments that individuality is waning, the ideal of a self-sufficient individual continues to dominate our discourse. The power of this ideal is the chief manifestation of male hegemony, far more pervasive than overtly authoritarian forms of male domination. Indeed, this one-sided ideal of individuality has not been diminished by the undermining of paternal authority and superego. It may even have been strengthened: the lack of manifest authority intensifies the pressure to perform independently, to live up to the ideal without leaning on a con-crete person who embodies it. The idealization of masculine values and the disparagement of feminine values persist unabated even though individual men and women are freer to cross over than before. The very idea that this form of individuality is not universal and neutral, but masculine, is highly controversial, as we saw in Lasch's outraged denial of the relevance of gender to narcissism. It challenges the repudiation of femininity, and the equation of masculinity with humanity – and so it challenges men's right to make the world in their own image.

Despite the appearance of gender neutrality and the freedom to be whatever we like, gender polarity persists. And it creates a painful division within the self and between self and other; it constantly frustrates our efforts to recognize ourselves in the world and in each other. My analysis of the oedipal model points beyond the obvious way that sexual difference has been linked to domination – the old authority of the father over children and wife – to its updated, subtler form. It points to a version of male dominion that works through the cultural ideal, the ideal of individuality and rationality that survives even the waning of paternal authority and the rise of more equitable family structures.

What sustains this ideal is the confusion between total loss of self and dependency. As we have seen, in recent versions of the oedipal model the revolt against maternal power is actually portrayed as a reaction against the experience of helplessness. According to the theory, we begin in an original state of primal oneness in which helplessness is not yet realized. The journey of differentiation takes us away from this perfect oneness with

THE OEDIPAL RIDDLE

the beloved source of goodness, into revulsion and fear of fusion with her. But what if the idea of such a state is a symbolic condensation, a retroactive fantasy that 'oversimplifies' a rather complicated intersubjective relationship? As I have shown, that relationship was neither oneness nor perfect – it was always marked by alterations between helplessness and comfort, by the contrast between attunement and disjunction, by an emerging awareness of separation and individual differences.

The vision of perfect oneness, whether of union or of self-sufficiency, is an *ideal* – a symbolic expression of our longing – that we project onto the past. This ideal becomes enlarged in reaction to the experience of helplessness – in the face of circumstance, powerlessness, death – but also by the distance from mother's help that repudiation of her enforces. What makes helplessness more difficult to bear is the feeling that one does not have the source of goodness inside, that one can neither soothe oneself nor find a way to communicate one's needs to someone who can help. It seems to me that the confidence that this other will help, like the confidence created by early attunement, is what mitigates feelings of helplessness. Such confidence is enhanced by a cultural life in which nurturance, responsiveness, and physical closeness are valued and generalized, so that the child can find them everywhere and adopt them himself. It is vitiated when those values are associated exclusively with infancy and must be given up in exchange for autonomy.

When individuals lose access to internal and external forms of maternal identification, independence backfires: it stimulates a new kind of helplessness, one which has to be countered by a still greater idealization of control and self-sufficiency. A usable maternal identification promises the possibility of regaining the satisfactions of dependency, the faith that we can rely on our environment to fulfill us; it is also associated with the confirmation that we contain within ourselves the source of satisfaction. But so long as this identification threatens male identity, men only have access to the mother outside. They react against this dependency by doing without her or by dominating her.

[. . .]

Here we may recall our discussion of the difference between renunciation and repudiation. The persistence of the maternal threat can be explained, at least in part, by the prohibition on maternal identification which deprives the boy of the opportunity to develop a more differentiated image of the mother. The repudiation of the mother gives her the aura of lost perfection, but it also makes her the object of destructive envy: 'Mother does not need me, so I don't need her; she is the source of perfect oneness, but this oneness can turn against me; Mother can retaliate for my envy by "smothering" me with love.' The blocking of identification reduces the mother to the complementary other who easily turns into the enemy, the opposite in the retaliatory power struggle between the sexes. This view of the mother meshes with the defensive stance assumed in reaction to the paradox of recognition, when the power of the one we have depended on may begin to appear threatening to the vulnerable self. When this defensive stance is institutionalized in a coherent symbolic system of gender – as in the Oedipus complex – it cancels access to direct experience of the other. The symbolic system locks into place the sense of the mother's dangerous but alluring power and the need for paternal defense against it. The more violent the repudiation of the source of nurturance, the more dangerous and tempting it begins to appear. The demonic view of maternal love is analogous to the revulsion that repression confers upon a forbidden wish.

[. . .] The effort to destroy or reduce the other is an inevitable part of the childhood struggle for recognition, as well as a way of protecting independence. But it is another matter when – as in the domination of women by men – the other's independent subjectivity really is destroyed, and with it the possibility of mutual recognition. It may be impossible to say where this cycle of real domination and the fantasy of maternal omnipotence begins, but this does not mean that we can never break that cycle and restore the balance of destruction and recognition. The answer awaits the social abolition of gender domination. And this means not just equality for women, but also a dissolution of gender polarity, a reconstruction of the vital tension between recognition and assertion, dependency and freedom.

The new Oedipus

Freud's opposition between rational paternal authority and the maternal underworld still resonates today. And I believe that the father's authority will persist as long as we accept the ideal of rationality as the antithesis of 'limitless narcissism.' The persistence of this dualism alerts us to an unchanging image of the father in the deep strata of the psyche where sexual difference takes hold. This dualism operates just as powerfully, it should be noted, for social critics like Brown and Marcuse, who defend the desire for union with the bounteous mother against the rational reality principle of the father. Their positions accept the characterization of the maternal world as found in the discourse of gender domination: they affirm the 'limitless narcissism' of the babe at the breast who does not recognize the mother's, or anyone else's, equal subjectivity.[23] A deeper critique is necessary, one which rejects the terms of sexual polarity, of subject and object, and so rejects any revolt that merely reverses these terms. The point is to get out of the antithesis between mother and father, this revolving door between the regressive maternal warmth and the icy paternal outside.

One step in the dissolution of this dualism is to reinterpret the Oedipus complex in such a way that it is no longer the summation of development. Rather than emphasizing the overcoming of preoedipal identifications, a new perspective on the Oedipus complex might see it as only a step in mental life, one that leaves room for earlier and later levels of integration. Significantly, Hans Loewald, a prominent exponent of the object relations tendency in American psychoanalysis, proposed in 'The waning of the Oedipus complex' that psychoanalysis should question the exclusion of 'the whole realm of identification and empathy from normality.' The focus on preoedipal life has created 'a growing awareness of the force and validity of another striving, that for unity, symbiosis, fusion, merging, identification.'[24]

The validation of this striving helps to redress the repudiation of the maternal that informed the earlier rationalism of psychoanalysis. It opens a place in the reality principle for bodily continuity with an other; it includes the intersubjective experience of recognition and all the emotional elements that go into appreciating, caring for, touching, and responding to an other, many of which are developed in infancy. I suspect that this change in psychoanalysis is an indirect result of women's increased status and freedom, which have proven that the maternal bond is not founded on a denial of reality. It may also reflect an incipient critique of pure autonomy, based on the observation that the denial of the need for nurturance takes a tremendous toll on those who live by it, as well as on those who cannot or will not live up to it.

[. . .]

The breakdown of paternal authority and the resulting search for a different route to individuation are the context for the controversy over Oedipus and Narcissus with which we began this chapter. But this does not mean that the decline of authority has 'caused' the demise of a once successful form of individuality; rather, it has revealed the contradiction once hidden within that individuality: the inability to confront the independent reality of the other. Men's loss of absolute control over women and children has exposed the vulnerable core of male individuality, the failure of recognition which previously wore the cloak of power, responsibility, and family honor. It is this inability to recognize the other which the psychoanalytic focus on narcissism has finally brought to the surface.

The oedipal model rationalized and concealed this failure by assuming that differentiation cannot occur within the mother–child dyad, that the father must intervene to impose independence. The three pillars of oedipal theory – the primacy of the wish for oneness, the mother's embodiment of this regressive force, and the necessity of paternal intervention – all combine to create the paradox that the only liberation is paternal domination. Oedipal theory thus denies the necessity of mutual recognition between man and woman. Construing the struggle for recognition in terms of the father–son rivalry, the theory reduces woman to a contested point on the triangle, never an other whose different and equal subjectivity need be confronted. By going beyond Oedipus we can envisage a direct struggle for recognition between man and woman, free of the shadow of the father that falls between them. By rejecting the false premise of paternal authority as the only road to freedom, we may recover the promise on which oedipal theory has defaulted: coming to terms with difference.

Notes

1   Much of my argument pertains to the model of the boy's development and requires the pronoun 'he.' At times, however, the oedipal model applies to both sexes, and I will then refer to 'the child.'

2   See Chapter 18 of this volume. Much of the groundwork for Lasch's position had already evolved in his earlier book, *Haven in a Heartless World: the Family Besieged* (New York, Basic Books, 1977). [. . .]

3   Freud elaborates this in *The Ego and the Id* (1923), in *The Standard Edition of the Works of Sigmund Freud*, ed. James Strachey (London, Hogarth Press and the Institute of Psychoanalysis, 1953), volume 19, no 3, pp. 1–66.

4   C. Lasch, *The Culture of Narcissism* (New York, Norton, 1979), p. 41.

5   In formulating his position, Lasch drew heavily on the more sophisticated arguments of the Frankfurt School which had been presented anew in the seventies by Russell Jacoby (see *Social Amnesia*, Boston, Beacon Press, 1975). The main outlines of the thesis relating declining parental authority to loss of oedipal autonomy had been formulated by M. Horkheimer in 'Authority and the family today' (1949), in *Critical Theory* (New York, Seabury Press, 1972) and amplified by H. Marcuse in 'The obsolescence of the Freudian concept of man', in *Five Lectures* (Boston, Beacon Press, 1970).

6   Lasch, *The Culture of Narcissism*, pp. 300–5. [. . .]

7   Joel Kovel suggests how the same intellectual tradition can lead to a different analysis of the family. He recognizes that capitalist development, particularly expanding commodity consumption, has not vitiated but stimulated the growth of personal life, so that the individual is frustrated in the home and confronts a depersonalized public world, which 'is nowhere enriched . . . to the level of demand created by the development of the personal sphere'; Joel Kovel, *The Age of Desire* (New York, Pantheon Press, 1982), p. 117. See also M. Barret and M. McIntosh, *The Anti-Social Family* (London, Verso, 1982).

8   The oedipal model is an internalization theory, in the sense that I discussed earlier, stressing identification with parental functions and ideals. Some psychoanalysis, like Otto Kernberg, in *Borderline Conditions and Pathological Narcissism* (New York, Jason Aronson, 1975), do give the superego an important role. But the formation of the superego is not the only aspect of internalization, and the force that controls insatiable desire and infantile wishes is a less popular concept than the ego that oversees differentiation between self and other. Lasch himself later criticized, in *The Minimal Self* (New York, Norton, 1984), the overemphasis on the superego (while not specifically disavowing his position in *The Culture of Narcissism*) as he came to see that the issue takes a back seat to that of separation.

9   Juliet Mitchell, in *Psychoanalysis and Feminism* (New York, Vintage Books, 1975), states that the father is the necessary intermediary 'if any relationship is to move out of a vicious circle,' and his phallus 'breaks up . . . the dyadic trap' (p. 397). [. . .]

10   Freud, *The Ego and the Id*, p. 34.

11   See Freud's (1914) discussion of homosexual libido, the ego ideal, and love of someone like the self, in 'On narcissism', in *The Standard Edition*, volume 14, pp. 67–102.

12   Hans Loewald, in 'The waning of the Oedipus complex', in *Papers on Psychoanalysis*, (New Haven, CT, Yale University Press, 1979), has also argued that the point of the oedipal prohibitions is to establish a 'barrier between identification and object cathexis.' [. . .]

13   Karen Horney, 'The flight from womanhood', in *Feminine Psychology* (New York, Norton, 1967). See also Dorothy Dinnerstein's discussion of this point in *The Mermaid and the Minotaur* (New York, Harper Row, 1976).

14   Dinnerstein, in *The Mermaid and the Minotaur*, p. 43, speaks of 'the mother-raised boy's sense that the original, most primitive source of life will always lie outside himself.'

15 Janine Chasseguet-Smirgel, 'Freud and female sexuality', *International Journal of Psychoanalysis*, 57 (1976), pp. 275–87.

16 Sigmund Freud, 'Female sexuality' (1931), in *The Standard Edition*, volume 21, pp. 223–43; and 'Feminity', in *New Introductory Lectures on Psychanalysis*, *The Standard Edition*, volume 22, pp. 3–182. See Karen Horney's disagreement, 'The denial of the vagina', in *Feminine Psychology*.

17 Chasseguet-Smirgel, 'Freud and Female sexuality', p. 281.

18 M. Honey and J. Broughton, 'Feminine sexuality: an interview with Janine Chasseguet-Smirgel', *Psychoanalytic Review*, 72 (1985), p. 542.

19 In her remarks on Luce Irigaray's critique of Freud, 'The blind spot in an old dream of symmetry', Jane Gallop emphasizes this point. The blind spot, the denial of women's genitals, prohibits 'any different sexuality.' The other, woman, is circumscribed 'as man's complementary other, his appropriate opposite sex.' Instead of real difference there is only a mirror image: J. Gallop, *The Daughter's Seduction* (Ithaca, NY, Cornell University Press, 1982), p. 58. This is a reading of Irigaray's essay from *Speculum of the Other Woman* (Ithaca, NY, Cornell University Press, 1974). The blind spot is the vagina, obscured by the phallus; it is the blindness of Oedipus, who remains embedded in the phallic phase.

20 Irene Fast, *Gender Identity: a Differentiation Model* (Hillsdale, NJ, The Analytic Press, 1984), pp. 97–8.

21 Ibid., p. 106.

22 The loss of capacities associated with these identifications is more severe in those whose identity is more rigidly defined by gender. See Ricki Levenson, 'Boundaries, autonomy and aggression'.

23 N.O. Brown, *Life Against Death* (Middletown, CT, Wesleyan University Press, 1959), p. 51. The upshot of this position is that all striving is Faustian restlessness and all sociability is repressive. In essence, this position represents a refusal to accept ambivalence, as accepting disillusionment along with hope. Brown, like Marcuse in *Eros and Civilization* (New York, Vintage Books, 1962), juxtaposes a repressive reality principle to the connection to the world achieved through primary narcissism. And so man's ultimate desire is, like the final salvation of Faust by 'Das ewig weibliche,' (the eternal feminine), the image of the virgin mother.

24 Loewald, 'The waning of the Oedipus complex', pp. 772–3.

20

The trajectory of the self   **Anthony Giddens**

[. . .] *Self-therapy*, a work by Janette Rainwater, is a book directly oriented to practice. Like the study by Wallerstein and Blakeslee, it is only one among an indefinite variety of books on its subject, and it figures in this analysis for symptomatic reasons rather than on its own account. Subtitled *a Guide to Becoming your own Therapist*, it is intended as a programme of self-realisation that anyone can use:

> Possibly you're feeling restless. Or you may feel overwhelmed by the demands of wife, husband, children, or job. You may feel unappreciated by those people closest to you. Perhaps you feel angry that life is passing you by and you haven't accomplished all those great things you had hoped to do. Something feels missing from your life. You were attracted by the title of this book and wish that you really were in charge. What to do?[1]

What to do? How to act? Who to be? These are focal questions for everyone living in circumstances of late modernity – and ones which, on some level or another, all of us answer, either discursively or through day-to-day social behaviour. They are existential questions, although, as we shall see later, their relation to the existential issues discussed in the preceding chapter of *Modernity and Self-identity* is problematic.

This chapter is taken from *Modernity and Self-identity* (Cambridge, Polity Press, 1994), pp. 70–98.
A key idea of Rainwater's perspective is set out very early in her book. Therapy with another person – psychiatrist or counsellor – she accepts, is an important, indeed frequently a crucial, part of a process of self-realisation. But, says Rainwater, therapy can only be successful when it involves the individual's own reflexivity: 'when the clients also start learning to do self-therapy.'[2] For therapy is not something which is 'done' to a person, or 'happens' to them; it is an experience which involves the

individual in systematic reflection about the course of her or his life's development. The therapist is at most a catalyst who can accelerate what has to be a process of self-therapy. This proposition applies also, Rainwater notes, to her book, which can inform someone about possible modes and directions of self-change, but which must be interpretatively organised by the person concerned in relation to his or her life's problems.

Self-therapy is grounded first and foremost in continuous self-observation. Each moment of life, Rainwater emphasises, is a 'new moment', at which the individual can ask, 'what do I want for myself?' Living every moment reflectively is a matter of heightened awareness of thoughts, feelings and bodily sensations. Awareness creates potential change, and may actually induce change in and through itself. For instance, the question, 'Are you aware of your breathing right now?', at least when it is first posed, usually produces an instantaneous change. The raising of such an issue may make the person 'aware that she is inhibiting a normal full breathing cycle and allows her body to say "Whew!" in relief, take a deep breath, and then exhale it.' 'And', Rainwater adds parenthetically to the reader, 'how is your breathing right now, after having read this paragraph?'³ – a question that I could echo to whosoever might be reading this particular text . . .

Present-awareness, or what Rainwater calls the 'routine art of self-observation', does not lead to a chronic immersion in current experience. On the contrary, it is the very condition of effectively planning ahead. Self-therapy means seeking to live each moment to the full, but it emphatically does not mean succumbing to the allure of the present. The question 'What do I want for myself right now?' is not the same as taking one day at a time. The 'art of being in the now' generates the self-understanding necessary to plan ahead and to construct a life trajectory which accords with the individual's inner wishes. Therapy is a process of growth, and one which has to encompass the major transitions through which a person's life is likely to pass. Keeping a journal, and developing a notional or actual autobiography, are recommended as means of thinking ahead. The journal, Rainwater suggests, should be written completely for oneself, never with the thought of showing it to anyone else. It is a place where the individual can be completely honest and where, by learning from previously noted experiences and mistakes, she can chart a continuing process of growth. Whether or not the journal itself has the explicit form of an autobiography, 'autobiographical thinking' is a central element of self-therapy. For developing a coherent sense of one's life history is a prime means of escaping the thrall of the past and opening oneself out to the future. The author of the autobiography is enjoined both to go back as far as possible into early childhood and to set up lines of potential development to encompass the future.

The autobiography is a corrective intervention into the past, not merely a chronicle of elapsed events. One of its aspects, for example, is 'nourishing the child-that-you-were'. Thinking back to a difficult or traumatic phase of childhood, the individual talks to the child-that-was, comforting and supporting it and offering advice. In this way, Rainwater argues, feelings of 'if only' can be got over and done with. 'The basic purpose of writing autobiographical material is to help you be done with the past . . .'[4] Another aspect is the 'corrective emotional experience exercise'. The person writes down an event from the past in the form of a short story written in the present, recalling what happened and the feelings involved as accurately as he or she can. Then the story is rewritten in the way the individual would have liked it to happen, with new dialogue, feelings and resolution of the episode.

Reconstruction of the past goes along with anticipation of the likely life trajectory of the future. Self-therapy presumes what Rainwater calls a 'dialogue with time' – a process of self-questioning about how the individual handles the time of her lifespan. Thinking about time in a positive way – as allowing for life to be lived, rather than consisting of a finite quantity that is running out – allows one to avoid a 'helpless–hopeless' attitude. Time which 'carries us along' implies a conception of fate like that found in many traditional cultures, where people are the prisoners of events and preconstructed settings rather than able to subject their lives to the sway of their own self-understanding. Holding a dialogue with time means identifying stressful events (actual events in the past and possible ones to be faced in the future) and coming to terms with their implications. Rainwater offers a 'rating scale' of stressful happenings, based on research literature in the area (pointing out also that such happenings can be causally linked to the onset of physical disease). Examples include death of a spouse, divorce or marital separation, losing one's job, being in financial difficulties, plus many other events or situations.

'Taking charge of one's life' involves risk, because it means confronting a diversity of open possibilities. The individual must be prepared to make a more or less complete break with the past, if necessary, and to contemplate novel courses of action that cannot simply be guided by established habits. Security attained through sticking with established patterns is brittle, and at some point will crack. It betokens a fear of the future rather than providing the means of mastering it:

> People who fear the future attempt to 'secure' themselves – with money, property, health insurance, personal relationships, marriage contracts. Parents attempt to bind their children to them. Some fearful children are reluctant to leave the home nest. Husbands and wives try to guarantee the continuance of the other's life and services. The harsh psychological truth is that there is no permanence in human relationships, any more than there is in the stock market, the weather, 'national security', and so on . . . this clutching at security can be very discouraging to interpersonal relationships, and will impede your own self-growth. The more each of us can learn to be truly in the present with our others, making no rules and erecting no fences

for the future, the stronger we will be in ourselves and the closer and happier in our relationships.

Finally . . . death: 'and the possibility that you're in charge here, too!'[5] Asking people to think about death, Rainwater says, typically provokes one of two attitudes. Either death is associated with fear, as in the case where individuals spend much of their present time worrying about their own death or that of loved ones; or death is regarded as unknowable, and therefore a subject to be avoided as far as possible. Both attitudes – fear of death and denial of death – can be countered by a programme of self-help that draws on the same techniques described elsewhere in Rainwater's book. Thinking back to the past, to the first experience of the death of another person, allows one to begin to ferret out hidden feelings about death. Looking ahead in this case involves contemplating the years of life which the person believes remain, and imagining the setting of one's own future death. An imaginary confrontation with death allows the question to be posed all over again: 'What to do?'

> Imagine that you have been told that you have just three years left to live. You will be in good health for these years . . . What was your immediate response? . . . To start planning how you would spend your time? Or to be angry at how short the time is? Rather than 'raging against the dying of the light' or getting bogged down in the mechanics of how you die in this fantasy, decide how you want to spend your time, *how you want to live these last three years.*
>
> > Where do you want to live?
> > With whom do you want to live?
> > Do you want to work?
> > To study?
> > Are there any ingredients from your fantasy life that you would like to incorporate into your current life?[6]

Self-identity, history, modernity

How distinctive in historical terms are the concerns and orientations expressed in Rainwater's 'self-help manual'? We might, of course, simply say that the search for self-identity is a modern problem, perhaps having its origins in Western individualism. Baumeister claims that in pre-modern times our current emphasis on individuality was absent.[7] The idea that each person has a unique character and special potentialities that may or may not be fulfilled is alien to pre-modern culture. In medieval Europe, lineage, gender, social status and other attributes relevant to identity were all relatively fixed. Transitions had to be made through the various stages of life, but these were governed by institutionalised processes and the individual's role in them was relatively passive. [. . .]

No doubt there is something in these views. But I do not think it is the existence of the 'individual' that is at stake, as a distinctive feature of modernity, and even less so the self. 'Individuality' has surely been valued – within varying limits – in all cultures and so, in one sense or another, has been the cultivation of individual potentialities. Rather than talking in general terms of 'individual', 'self' or even 'self-identity' as distinctive of modernity, we should try to break things down into finer detail. We can begin to do so by charting some of the specific points in, or implications of, Rainwater's portrayal of what therapy is and what it does. The following elements can be drawn out of her text:

(1) The self is seen as a reflexive project, for which the individual is responsible [. . .]. We are, not what we are, but what we make of ourselves. It would not be true to say that the self is regarded as entirely empty of content, for there are psychological processes of self-formation, and psychological needs, which provide the parameters for the reorganisation of the self. Otherwise, however, what the individual becomes is dependent on the reconstructive endeavours in which she or he engages. These are far more than just 'getting to know oneself' better: self-understanding is subordinated to the more inclusive and fundamental aim of building/ rebuilding a coherent and rewarding sense of identity. The involvement of such reflexivity with social and psychological research is striking, and a pervasive feature of the therapeutic outlook advocated.

(2) The self forms a trajectory of development from the past to the anticipated future. The individual appropriates his past by sifting through it in the light of what is anticipated for an (organised) future. The trajectory of the self has a coherence that derives from a cognitive awareness of the various phases of the lifespan. The lifespan, rather than events in the outside world, becomes the dominant 'foreground figure' in the *Gestalt* sense. It is not quite the case that all outside events or institutions are a 'blur', against which only the lifespan has form and is picked out in clear relief; yet such events only intrude in so far as they provide supports for self-development, throw up barriers to be overcome or are a source of uncertainties to be faced.

(3) The reflexivity of the self is continuous, as well as all-pervasive. At each moment, or at least at regular intervals, the individual is asked to conduct a self-interrogation in terms of what is happening. Beginning as a series of consciously asked questions, the individual becomes accustomed to asking, 'how can I use this moment to change?' [. . .] As Rainwater stresses, it is a practised art of self-observation:

What is happening right now?
What am I thinking?
What am I doing?
What am I feeling?
How am I breathing?[8]

(4) It is made clear that self-identity, as a coherent phenomenon, presumes a narrative: the narrative of the self is made explicit. Keeping a journal, and working through an autobiography, are central recommendations for sustaining an integrated sense of self. It is generally accepted among historians that the writing of autobiographies (as well as biographies) only developed during the modern period.[9] Most published autobiographies, of course, are celebrations of the lives or achievements of distinguished individuals: they are a way of singling out the special experiences of such persons from those of the mass of the population. Seen in this way, autobiography seems a rather peripheral feature of individual distinctiveness as a whole. Yet autobiography – particularly in the broad sense of an interpretative self-history produced by the individual concerned, whether written down or not – is actually at the core of self-identity in modern social life. Like any other formalised narrative, it is something that has to be worked at, and calls for creative input as a matter of course.

(5) Self-actualisation implies the control of time – essentially, the establishing of zones of personal time which have only remote connections with external temporal orders (the routinised world of time–space governed by the clock and by universalised standards of measurement). The insistence on the primacy of personal time (the *durée* of day-to-day social life) is everywhere in Rainwater's book – although, as we have seen, it is not offered as a philosophy of the 'absolute present', but as a mode of controlling the available time of the lifespan. 'Holding a dialogue with time' is the very basis of self-realisation, because it is the essential condition of achieving satisfaction at any given moment – of living life to the full. [. . .]

(6) The reflexivity of the self *extends to the body*, where the body (as suggested in the previous chapter of *Modernity and Self-identity*) is part of an action system rather than merely a passive object. Observation of bodily processes – 'How am I breathing?' – is intrinsic to the continuous reflexive attention which the agent is called on to pay to her behaviour. Awareness of the body is basic to 'grasping the fullness of the moment', and entails the conscious monitoring of sensory input from the environment, as well as the major bodily organs and body dispositions as a whole. Body awareness also includes awareness of requirements of exercise and diet. Rainwater points out that people speak of 'going on a diet' – but we are all on a diet! Our diet is what we eat; at many junctures of the day we take decisions about whether or not to eat and drink, and exactly what to eat and drink.

'If you don't like the diet you are on, there is a new minute and a new choice-point coming up, and you can change your diet. You're in charge!'[10]

[. . .]

(7) Self-actualisation is understood in terms of a *balance between opportunity and risk*. Letting go of the past, through the various techniques of becoming free from oppressive emotional habits, generates a multiplicity of opportunities for self-development. The world becomes full of potential ways of being and acting, in terms of experimental involvements which the individual is now able to initiate. It would not be true to say that the psychologically liberated person faces risks while the more traditional self does not; rather, what is at stake is the *secular consciousness of risk*, as inherent in calculative strategies to be adopted in relation to the future.

The individual has to confront novel hazards as a necessary part of breaking away from established patterns of behaviour – including the risk that things could possibly get worse than they were before. Another book on self-therapy describes things in the following way:

> If your life is ever going to change for the better, you'll have to take chances. You'll have to get out of your rut, meet new people, explore new ideas and move along unfamiliar pathways. In a way the risks of self-growth involve going into the unknown, into an unfamiliar land where the language is different and customs are different and you have to learn your way around . . . the paradox is that until we give up all that feels secure, we can never really trust the friend, mate, or job that offers us something. True personal security does not come from without, it comes from within. When we are really secure, we must place our total trust in ourself.
>
> If we reject deliberate risk-taking for self-growth, we will inevitably remain trapped in our situation. Or we end up taking a risk unprepared. Either way, we have placed limits on our personal growth, have cut ourselves off from action in the service of high self-worth.[11]

(8) The moral thread of self-actualisation is one of *authenticity* (although not in Heidegger's sense), based on 'being true to oneself'. Personal growth depends on conquering emotional blocks and tensions that prevent us from understanding ourselves as we really are. To be able to act authentically is more than just acting in terms of a self-knowledge that is as valid and full as possible: it means also disentangling – in Laing's terms – the true from the false self. As individuals we are not able to 'make history' but if we ignore our inner experience, we are condemned to repeat it [. . .].

The morality of authenticity skirts any universal moral criteria, and includes references to other people only within the sphere of intimate relationships – although this sphere is accepted as highly important to the self. To be true to oneself means finding oneself, but since this is an active process of self-construction it has to be informed by overall goals – those of becoming free from dependencies and achieving fulfilment. Fulfilment is in some part a moral phenomenon, because it means fostering a sense that one is 'good', a 'worthy person': 'I know that as I raise my own self-worth, I will feel more integrity, honesty, compassion, energy and love.'[12]

(9) The life course is seen as a series of 'passages'. The individual is likely, or has to go through them, but they are not institutionalised, or accompanied by formalised rites. All such transitions involve loss (as well as, usually, potential gain) and such losses – as in the case of marital separation – have to be mourned if self-actualisation is to proceed on course. Life passages give particular cogency to the interaction of risk and opportunity spoken of earlier – especially, although by no means exclusively, when they are in substantial degree initiated by the individual whom they affect. Negotiating a significant transition in life, leaving home, getting a new job, facing up to unemployment, forming a new relationship, moving between different areas or routines, confronting illness, beginning therapy – all mean running consciously entertained risks in order to grasp the new opportunities which personal crises open up. It is not only in terms of the absence of rites that life passages differ from comparable processes in traditional contexts. More important is that such transitions are drawn into, and surmounted by means of, the reflexively mobilised trajectory of self-actualisation.

(10) The line of development of the self is *internally referential*: the only significant connecting thread is the life trajectory as such. Personal integrity, as the achievement of an authentic self, comes from integrating life experiences within the narrative of self-development: the creation of a personal belief system by means of which the individual acknowledges that 'his first loyalty is to himself.' [. . .]

Of all this, of course, there are questions one could ask. How valid are these conceptions? Are they in some sense ideological? Are they more to do with therapy than with any changes which might have affected the self in modern social conditions? For the moment I want to bracket these issues. It seems to me justified to assert that, partial, inadequate and idiosyncratic as the ideas just outlined may be, they signal something real about self and self-identity in the contemporary world – the world of late modernity. How that may be we can begin to see by connecting them up to the institutional transformations characteristic of that world.

Lifestyles and life plans

The backdrop here is the existential terrain of late modern life. In a post-traditional social universe, reflexively organised, permeated by abstract systems, and in which the reordering of time and space realigns the local with the global, the self undergoes massive change. Therapy, including self-therapy, both expresses that change and provides programmes of realising it in the form of self-actualisation. On the level of the self, a fundamental component of day-to-day activity is simply that of *choice*. Obviously, no culture eliminates choice altogether in day-to-day affairs, and all traditions are effectively choices among an indefinite range of possible behaviour patterns. Yet, by definition, tradition or established habit orders life within relatively set channels. Modernity confronts the individual with a complex diversity of choices and, because it is non-foundational, at the same time offers little help as to which options should be selected. Various consequences tend to follow.

One concerns the primacy of *lifestyle* – and its inevitability for the individual agent. The notion of lifestyle sounds somewhat trivial because it is so often thought of solely in terms of a superficial consumerism [. . .]. But there is something much more fundamental going on than such a conception suggests: in conditions of high modernity, we all not only follow lifestyles, but in an important sense are forced to do so – we have no choice but to choose. A lifestyle can be defined as a more or less integrated set of practices which an individual embraces, not only because such practices fulfil utilitarian needs, but because they give material form to a particular narrative of self-identity.

Lifestyle is not a term which has much applicability to traditional cultures, because it implies choice within a plurality of possible options, and is 'adopted' rather than 'handed down'. Lifestyles are routinised practices, the routines incorporated into habits of dress, eating, modes of acting and favoured milieux for encountering others; but the routines followed are reflexively open to change in the light of the mobile nature of self-identity. Each of the small decisions a person makes every day – what to wear, what to eat, how to conduct himself at work, whom to meet with later in the evening – contributes to such routines. All such choices (as well as larger and more consequential ones) are decisions not only about how to act but who to be. The more post-traditional the settings in which an individual moves, the more lifestyle concerns the very core of self-identity, its making and remaking.

[. . .]

The plurality of choices which confronts individuals in situations of high modernity derives from several influences. First, there is the fact of living in a post-traditional order. To act in, to engage with, a world of plural choices is to opt for alternatives, given that the signposts established by tradition now are blank. Thus someone might decide, for example, to ignore the research findings which appear to show that a diet high in fruit and fibre, and low in sugar, fat and alcohol, is physically beneficial and reduces the risk of contracting some types of illnesses. She might resolutely stick to the same diet of dense, fatty and sugary foods that people in the previous generation consumed. Yet, given the available options in matters of diet and the fact that the individual has at least some awareness of them, such conduct still forms part of a distinctive lifestyle.

Second, there is what Berger calls the 'pluralisation of life-worlds'.[13] As he points out, throughout most of human history, people lived in social settings that were fairly closely connected with each other. Whether in situations of work, leisure or the family, an individual usually lived within a set of milieux of a comparable type – a phenomenon strongly reinforced by the dominance of the local community in most pre-modern cultures. The settings of modern social life are much more diverse and segmented. Segmentation includes particularly the differentiation between the public and private domains – but each of these is also subject internally to pluralisation. Lifestyles are characteristically attached to, and expressive of, specific milieux of action. [. . .]

A third factor conditioning plurality of choice is the existential impact of the contextual nature of warranted beliefs under conditions of modernity. [. . .] [T]he Enlightenment project of replacing arbitrary tradition and speculative claims to knowledge with the certainty of reason proved to be essentially flawed. The reflexivity of modernity operates, not in a situation of greater and greater certainty, but in one of methodological doubt. Even the most reliable authorities can be trusted only 'until further notice'; and the abstract systems that penetrate so much of day-to-day life normally offer multiple possibilities rather than fixed guidelines or recipes for action. Experts can always be turned to, but experts themselves frequently disagree over both theories and practical diagnoses. Consider therapy itself. Someone contemplating therapy faces a bewildering variety of schools of thought and types of programme, and must also reckon with the fact that some psychologists discount the effectiveness of most forms of therapy entirely. [. . .]

Fourth, the prevalence of mediated experience undoubtedly also influences pluralism of choice, in obvious and also in more subtle ways. With the increasing globalisation of media, a multifarious number of milieux are, in principle, rendered visible to anyone who cares to glean the relevant information. The collage effect of television and newspapers gives specific form to the juxtaposition of settings and potential lifestyle choices. [. . .] The media offer access to settings with which the individual may never personally come into contact; but at the same time some boundaries between settings that were previously separate are overcome. [. . .]

In a world of alternative lifestyle options, strategic *life-planning* becomes of special importance. Like lifestyle patterns, life plans of one kind or another are something of an inevitable concomitant of post-traditional social forms.[14] Life plans are the substantial content of the reflexively organised trajectory of the self. Life-planning is a means of preparing a course of future actions mobilised in terms of the self's biography. We may also speak here of the existence of personal calendars or *life-plan calendars* [. . .] timing devices for significant events within the life of the individual, inserting such events within a personalised chronology. Like life plans, personal calendars are typically revised and reconstructed in terms of alterations in an individual's circumstances or frame of mind. 'When I got married,' as a basic date within a life-plan calendar, as the discussion in *Second Chances* indicates, may be largely ousted by 'when the marriage broke up' as a more significant psychological marker. Personal calendars very often incorporate elements of mediated experience – as when, for instance, a couple will remember that they got married 'two weeks after President Kennedy was assassinated'.[15]

[. . .]

Finally, plurality of choice can also be connected directly to relations with others – to the transformation of intimacy.[16] [. . .]

It is characteristic of modern systems of sexual intimacy and friendship that partners are voluntarily chosen from a diversity of possibilities. Of course, proximity is ordinarily necessary for intimate relations to develop, and the extent of real choice varies according to many social and psychological differences. But the lonely hearts column, computer dating and other forms of introduction service demonstrate well enough that plural choice is easy to achieve if one is prepared to shed the last vestiges of traditional ways of doing things. Only when ties are more or less freely chosen can we speak at all of 'relationships' in the sense that term has recently acquired in lay discourse. Reasonably durable sexual ties, marriages and friendship relations all tend to approximate today to the *pure relationship*. In conditions of high modernity, again for reasons to be explored later, the pure relationship (which has nothing to do with sexual purity) comes to be of elementary importance for the reflexive project of the self. This much is evident from Rainwater's book, as it is of virtually all works of therapy, whether self-programmed or not.

The theory and practice of the pure relationship

The following passage appears under a heading 'Emotional Uncertainty in Relationships', in Shere Hite's study *Women and Love*. Hite's research is based on extensive comments obtained from American women about their experiences and feelings in relation to men. One woman responds as follows:

> I have a constant feeling of never being satisfied for some reason. Either he's not calling, or when he's calling, it's not romantic, and so on . . . When I try to talk to him, really talk to him, I feel like I just can't get through . . . It seems to revolve around a constant question of should I be asking myself 'Is everything all right in terms of him (does he still love me)?' or 'Is everything all right in terms of *me*? How am *I*?' If I am unhappy a lot, and he won't talk to me about the problems or resolve the issues, should I say, 'Well, everything is really OK because he's OK and he's still there and still loves me?' Or should I say, 'This relationship is terrible and I will leave it because he is not making me happy?' Loving him makes it difficult to leave him.

Should I want to help him open up more, or should I worry about myself and break up with him? . . . The problem is that first he says he's vulnerable and in love – then later he denies it or doesn't act like it, acts cold. I ask myself, 'Is the goal this man at any cost?' It's almost as if someone is egging me on to go into the deep end of the pool – and then when I get there (with my emotions) and really fall in love, trust him, he says 'What? Why me?' I've been so scared all the way, thinking to myself, no matter what happened, giving him the benefit of the doubt, 'Let me trust, let me trust', not letting myself believe the negative signals, thinking he was just insecure or reacting to something I had done in my *own* effort to seem invulnerable. I've always been so afraid, wondering, 'Will somebody stay?'[17]

These reflections are those of a woman who is not living with the man concerned, and describe a relationship in its fairly early stages; yet, because of their 'exploratory' character, they give some insight into how relationships are constructed. Love is at the centre, and one might suppose that an exploration of intimacy, at least where a sexual component is involved, should concentrate on the nature of romantic attachment. The report recounts the experience of a woman, and although the point of view of the man involved is not given, we might conclude that gender relations should be the prime concern here. Without denying the significance of these features, I want to focus on other things. For there are core elements involved, as I shall try to show, which are also characteristic of other intimate and emotionally demanding relationships – between, for example, same-sex lovers or between very close friends. These are the elements of the pure relationship. They can be spelled out (in ideal-typical form) as follows.

(1) In contrast to close personal ties in traditional contexts, the pure relationship is not anchored in external conditions of social or economic life – it is, as it were, free-floating. Consider, as an illustration, marriage as it once was. Marriage was a contract, often initiated by parents or relatives rather than by the marital partners themselves. The contract was usually strongly influenced by economic considerations, and formed part of wider economic networks and transactions. Even well into modern times, when the old frameworks of marriage had substantially disintegrated, the marital tie was anchored through an internal division of labour, the husband as breadwinner and wife preoccupied with children, hearth and home (although we should not forget that the labour force has always contained a considerable proportion of women). Some of these traditional characteristics of marriage persist, more pronounced among certain socioeconomic groups than others. In general, however, the tendency is towards the eradication of these pre-existing external involvements – a phenomenon originally accompanied by the rise of romantic love as a basic motive for marriage. Marriage becomes more and more a relationship initiated for, and kept going for as long as, it delivers emotional satisfaction to be

derived from close contact with another. Other traits – even such seemingly fundamental ones as having children – tend to become sources of 'inertial drag' on possible separation, rather than anchoring features of the relationship.

Modern friendship exposes this characteristic even more clearly. A friend is defined specifically as someone with whom one has a relationship unprompted by anything other than the rewards that that relationship provides. [. . .]

(2) The pure relationship is sought only for what the relationship can bring to the partners involved. This point is the natural concomitant of (1), and it is precisely in this sense that the relationship is 'pure'. No doubt all personal relations of any duration are testing and tensionful as well as rewarding. But in relationships which only exist for their own sake, anything that goes wrong between the partners intrinsically threatens the relationship itself. Consequently, it is very difficult to 'coast along' in the way in which one can in a social relation dominated by external criteria. If one partner attempts to do so, the other is likely to be disaffected. The peculiar tensions this sets up are well evinced in other material contained in Hite's book, particularly that concerned with marriage:

> Women are deserting marriage in droves, either through divorce, or emotionally, leaving with a large part of their hearts . . . Most, after an initial period of trying, have gone on to find other places to invest their emotional lives. Woman after woman, after the initial years of 'trying to get through' gives up and begins to disengage quietly, gradually, perhaps even unnoticeably.[18]

Yet . . . the vast majority of women do not abandon the quest for love, or for a viable relationship:

> As one woman says, love keeps returning to us, resurfacing perhaps as some kind of key: 'In some way which I cannot find the words for yet, romantic love contains the key to my identity – to discovering myself, my inner being.' Many women feel this way. Why? Perhaps women are right to come back, to try again to make love work or understand why it does not . . . most want not just 'love', but the kind of real love they are talking about. And so it is no surprise that women who are in relationships so often still talk about a 'deeper love' to come, have a hidden part of themselves that believes that there is more, more to life somehow . . . And indeed, shouldn't there be?[19]

Again, one might think that it is love, or the demand for love, which is at issue here, rather than anything specifically to do with relationships as such. However love – ambiguous and difficult notion that it is – is really a codifying force organising the character of the sexual relationship, not in this context an independent value. Moreover, there is plenty of evidence that men are as concerned to find close emotive relationships as women are, and as attached to them.[20] [. . .] The feelings of 'never being satisfied' within the relationship, described by the respondent first quoted, reflect the difficulties inherent in creating or sustaining a relation in which there is balance and reciprocity, satisfactory to both partners, between what each brings and each derives from the tie.

(3) The pure relationship is reflexively organised, in an open fashion, and on a continuous basis. This, too, is apparent enough in the quotation on p. 258, in which the question, 'Is everything all right?' figures as a leading motif. The more a relationship depends only upon itself, the more such a reflexive questioning comes to be its core – and contributes to the tensions noted in (2). The self-examination inherent in the pure relationship clearly connects very closely to the reflexive project of the self. 'How am *I*?' is an interrogation directly bound to the rewards the relationship delivers as well as to the pain it can inflict. [. . .]

(4) 'Commitment' has a central role to play in pure relationships. Commitment would appear generic to many forms of human social activity, and one might readily suppose that it is found in all cultural contexts. For instance, the true believer in a religious order might be said to have a thoroughgoing commitment to the values and practices in question. Yet conviction is not the same as commitment, and when we speak of the second of these in respect of close relationships today we are probably concerned with something that is historically new. Commitment, within the pure relationship, is essentially what replaces the external anchors that close personal connections used to have in pre-modern situations. Love, in the sense of contemporary romantic love, is a form of commitment, but commitment is the wider category of the two. What is the 'committed person' in the context of a close relationship? She or he is someone who, recognising the tensions intrinsic to a relationship of the modern form, is nevertheless willing to take a chance on it, at least in the medium term – and who accepts that the only rewards will be those inherent in the relationship itself. A friend is *ipso facto* a committed person. Someone in a marriage is likely to be so to the degree that the relationship is not kept going only by external involvements or by inertial drag of one kind or another. Commitment is recognised by participants to buy time: to provide emotional support which is guaranteed to persist through at least some of the perturbations which the relationship might undergo (although returns will almost certainly be demanded for this).

Commitment can to some extent be regularised by the force of love, but sentiments of love do not in and of themselves generate commitment, nor do they in any sense authorise it. A person only becomes committed to another when, for whatever reason, she or he decides to be so. The woman in the passage quoted from Hite's study feels she loves her partner, but her love does not supply the commitment she desires. Nor could it, because commitment must almost always be part of an effort-bargain; the pure relationship cannot exist without substantial elements of reciprocity. Rainwater's self-therapy programme recognises this, as do most forms of therapeutic endeavour. One of the reasons why the reflexivity of the self should produce more accurate and insightful self-knowledge is that it helps reduce dependency in close relationships. The well-functioning relationship, she says, is one in which each person is autonomous and sure of his or her self-worth. Where this is not the case, what I have called inertial drag sets in – as is found, for instance, in co-dependent relationships. [. . .]

Commitment is hard to build precisely because it presumes a mutual alignment within the pure relationship. It stands in uneasy connection with the reflexivity that is equally central to how the relationship is ordered. The committed person is prepared to accept the risks which the sacrificing of other potential options entails. In the initial phases of a relationship, each person is likely to be inspecting the activities of the other minutely, since too rapid an advance towards commitment on the part of one person may actively spark the withdrawal of the other from the nascent enterprise altogether. Hite's respondent demonstrates an astute sensitivity to just this aspect of her situation.

(5) The pure relationship is focused on intimacy, which is a major condition of any long-term stability the partners might achieve. Intimacy has to be distinguished from the more negative phenomenon of lack of privacy, characteristic of most circumstances of life in pre-modern Europe and in many non-modern cultures generally. Physical proximity – and, in modern terms, the absence of privacy – were almost inevitable consequences of the architecture of day-to-day life in the small community, but were characteristic of the life of more affluent groups too.[21] Within households, but also in most other contexts of daily life, people were almost always in close range of one another. The development of 'personal' life during the early period of modernity has been well documented by historians, even if the nature of the causal connections involved is a matter of considerable dispute. Intimacy is the other face of privacy, or at least only becomes possible (or desired) given substantial privacy.[22]

[. . .]

The expectation of intimacy provides perhaps the closest links between the reflexive project of the self and the pure relationship. Intimacy, or the quest for it, is at the heart of modern forms of friendship and established sexual relationships. Most manuals of therapy, including that of Rainwater, make it clear that intimacy is usually obtained only through psychological 'work', and that it is only possible between individuals who are secure in their own self-identities. A therapeutic study referred to earlier sums the whole thing up well: an intimate friendship or partnership, the author says, is 'a *choice* between any two people who make a *commitment* to each other to share a meaningful *lifestyle*'.[23] She describes several types of relationship which are distinct from one within which a developed intimacy has been attained. Some relationships are full of conflict, and persistent rows or bickering become normalised: emotional pain becomes a familiar part of the relationship, and without it the relationship in fact might be broken up. Conflict-ridden relationships contrast with 'de-energised' ones. Here there is little direct antagonism between partners, but little in the way of a strong bond either: inertia sustains the relationship. The partners get along with one another in a reasonable enough way in day-to-day matters, but are often bored with and resentful of one another. A 'convenience' relationship is one in which the individuals concerned have overtly or tacitly agreed that they will 'settle for' what they have got in the light of external rewards, or because of the difficulties they might experience if the relationship were dissolved, or for the comfort of not being alone.

All of these 'get by' relationships contrast with intimate ties, which require a commitment to 'the quality of the relationship'; where the relationship threatens to lapse into one of the other types, 'a decision to recommit to each other and make whatever changes and choices necessary to grow close' has to be made. A commitment to 'one's own personal recovery' is also needed if one of the partners is unable to develop the integrity demanded for the pursuit of intimacy.[24] Intimacy, the author stresses, requires a defined measure of privacy on the part of each partner, because a balance between autonomy and the sharing of feelings and experiences has to be obtained if personal closeness is not to be replaced by dependence. [. . .]

(6) The pure relationship depends on mutual trust between partners, which in turn is closely related to the achievement of intimacy. In the pure relationship, trust is not and cannot be taken as 'given': like other aspects of the relationship, it has to be worked at – the trust of the other has to be won. In most pre-modern situations, in which personal relations were stabilised by external criteria, in the sense noted above, trust tended to be geared to established positions. Kinspeople could by no means always be trusted in such settings, as the plots and counterplots between relatives scheming to obtain power in royal households demonstrate. Yet kinship obligations probably were accepted most of the time, and provided reasonably stable environments of trust within which day-to-day life was ordered. Stripped of such qualities, personal ties in the pure relationship require novel forms of trust – precisely that trust which is built through intimacy with the other. Such trust presumes the opening out of the individual to the other, because knowledge that the other is committed, and harbours no basic antagonisms towards oneself, is the only framework for trust when external supports are largely absent.[25]

[. . .] What matters in the building of trust in the pure relationship is that each person should know the other's personality, and be able to rely on regularly eliciting certain sorts of desired responses from the other. This is one reason (not the only one) why authenticity has such an important place in self-actualisation. What matters is that one can rely on what the other says and does. [. . .]

How is trust created in relationships? Again we can turn to the therapeutic manuals to provide a guide. Wegscheider-Cruse offers a range of practical proposals for building trust which derive from systematic research on relationships. One should 'take time to listen to each other daily,' since communication is so central to intimacy. Such talking and listening should not always be limited to trivial events of the day. Where there are substantive issues to be faced, they should be seriously discussed. Partners should 'stick with one issue until resolved, and then be done with it', for 'rehashing the same issues lessens trust and creates new problems.' Old disputes that fester unresolved are often more likely to destroy trust than new difficulties, which may be easier to face. One should 'get to the feelings behind issues,' because surface appearances may hide the true dynamics of a situation, and communication which is not 'in depth' cannot get at these. Other recommendations include nurturing an atmosphere of caring, aiming for a variety of recreational pleasures mutually engaged in, and learning to express anger in a constructive way.[26]

(7) In a pure relationship, the individual does not simply 'recognise the other' and in the responses of that other find his self-identity affirmed. Rather, as follows from the preceding points, self-identity is negotiated through linked processes of self-exploration and the development of intimacy with the other. Such processes help create 'shared histories' of a kind potentially more tightly bound than those characteristic of individuals who share experiences by virtue of a common social position. Such shared histories may be quite divergent from the orderings of time and space that prevail in the wider social world. Yet it is important to emphasise [. . .] that they are characteristically interpolated within that wider world rather than cut off from it. Shared histories are created and sustained, in fact, substantially in terms of how far they integrate participants' life-plan calendars.

[. . .]

Pure relationships come into existence primarily in the domains of sexuality, marriage and friendship. The degree to which intimate spheres are transformed in this way plainly varies according to context and differential socioeconomic position, in common with most of the traits of modernity discussed in this book. Relations between parents and children, and more extended kin relations, stay partly distinct from the purview of the pure relationship. Both remain substantially tied to external criteria: biological connections which form key conditions for the sustaining of the relation. But each also becomes permeated by some of the influences generating the pure relationship. In so far as kinship relations are stripped of their traditional duties and obligations, their continuance tends increasingly to depend on the qualities enumerated above. Either such relations become attenuated and nominal in character or they are reformed through the reflexive achievement of intimacy.

Parent–child relations are something of a special case, because of the radical imbalance of power involved, and because of their centrality for socialisation processes. The close bonds established between parents and children are formed in a context of infantile dependency, but they are also the psychological nexus within which the young child develops capacities to initiate intimate ties in later life. Yet in conditions of modernity, the more a child moves towards adulthood and autonomy, the more elements of the pure relationship tend to come into play. A person who has left home may keep in constant touch with his parents, as a matter of obligation; but reflexively ordered trust must be developed, involving mutually accepted commitment, if the relationship is to be deepened. Where a person becomes a step-parent of an older child, the connections established from the beginning take on the characteristics of the pure relationship. [. . .]

Notes

1   Janette Rainwater, *Self-therapy: a Guide to Becoming your own Therapist* (London, Crucible, 1989), p. 9.

2   Ibid.

3   Ibid., p. 11.

4   Ibid., p. 56.

5   Ibid., p. 194.

6   Ibid., p. 209.

7   Roy F. Baumeister, *Identity, Cultural Change and the Struggle for Self* (New York, Oxford University Press, 1986).

8   Rainwater, *Self-therapy*, p. 15.

9   John O. Lyons, *The Invention of the Self* (Carbondale, Southern Illinois University Press, 1978).

10   Rainwater, *Self-therapy*, p. 172.

11   Sharon Wegscheider-Cruse, *Learning to Love Yourself* (Deerfield Beach, FL, Health Communications, 1987).

12   Ibid., p. 79.

13   Peter Berger et al., *The Homeless Mind* (Harmondsworth, Penguin, 1974).

14   Cf. Berger et al., *Homeless Mind*, pp. 69ff.

15   See Harvey Sacks. 'On members' measurement systems', *Research on Language and Social Interaction*, 22 (1988–9).

16   Anthony Giddens, *The Consequences of Modernity* (Cambridge, Polity Press, 1990).

17   Shere Hite, *Women and Love* (London, Viking, 1988).

18   Ibid., p. 526.

19   Ibid., p. 655.

20   See, for example, Kenneth Solomon and Norman B. Levy, *Men in Transition* (London, Plenum, 1983).

21   See the celebrated analysis by Norbert Elias, *The Civilising Process*, vol. 1 (Oxford, Blackwell, 1978).

22   Goffman has a great deal of interest to say about how privacy is sustained in day-to-day life, and why individuals regard it as so important; on the other hand, he implies that privacy is a universal need, and rarely places his account of it in a historical context.

23 Wegscheider-Cruse, *Learning to Love Yourself*, p. 96 (emphasis added).
24 Ibid., p. 100.
25 Giddens, *Consequences of Modernity*, pp. 114ff.
26 Wegscheider-Cruse, *Learning to Love Yourself*, pp. 101–3.

21

What's happening to mourning?   **Ian Craib**

What I want to do in this chapter is to look at the way in which the meaning of psychoanalytic ideas changes when they are considered outside the consulting room. Something that appears in day-to-day therapeutic work in the consulting room to be a benign and helpful activity can appear in the context of the wider culture in a rather different way. [. . .] This should be no problem for those familiar with the unconscious, but what I am suggesting is that there is also a dimension of the unknown contained in the wider network of social relationships, the sort of society in which we work and out of which we develop. [. . .]

I want to try to make my point through looking at what has happened to the way in which we have thought about and dealt with death and mourning over the last century or so. My suggestion is that there has been a change in what I would call the social organization of mourning, an attempt to organize the process of mourning, and perhaps even of dying itself, in such a way that the real pain and loss is denied, that they can even be seen as 'good things'. At its extreme this becomes a mapping in advance of the mourning process as something through which people should be taken; notions of originality, of each of grief and mourning as being unique, individual and unpleasant seem to disappear.

A number of social processes are at work in this change. At an everyday level, I can see its effects among my undergraduate students and in experiential groups that I lead. Much of the literature on death talks about a twentieth-century taboo, even the 'last great taboo', the subject about which nobody talks. Socially approved mourning rituals have all but disappeared; the bereaved are ignored, or expected to be back in a normal life as soon as possible. I am sure that this is true for some people, but I have noticed that it is certainly not true for others. When I lecture on death

This chapter is taken from *Experiencing Identity* (London, Sage, 1998), pp. 157–67.

and mourning to social science undergraduates, there is a rush to write essays on the subject; it is one of the most popular topics, more popular than sexuality. In the experiential groups, members often enthusiastically embrace death as a metaphor for the ending of the group, sometimes, I think, too enthusiastically, as if they have never felt the fear of death. When I check the library catalogue, the number of books about death, grief or mourning seems to increase monthly. We can add to this the growth of bereavement counselling, of Cruse and of the hospice movement, none of which points to a reluctance to talk about death. So perhaps something else is going on.

One method of thinking about it is in the way that Foucault (1984) discusses sexuality. We tend to see the Victorian period as one in which nobody talked about sex, but Foucault points out that it was a period in which talk about sex exploded. More was written than ever before, by doctors, psychiatrists, psychologists, biologists, etc. It was a period when sexuality was catalogued, classified and brought under the control of professionals, and Freud was part of this. It was also the time when sexuality became what the sociologist Anthony Giddens calls 'sequestered' – split off from the rest of social life and given its own specialized space governed by experts. Perhaps the same thing is happening to death and mourning. I will be looking shortly at the way in which the psychiatric profession and then the therapy and counselling professions have attempted to establish control over mourning. My argument is that this has been at the cost of an understanding of the real complexity of grief and mourning at a theoretical level, if not in everybody's practice. [. . .]

Classic theories of mourning

[. . .] [I]n psychoanalytic theories of mourning I think it is possible to identity a reduction in knowledge content in favour of the 'positive' view of mourning that we can find so often today – a view which under-emphasizes the straightforward strength of the pain that is involved and glosses over the depth of guilt and our inherent ambivalence. This is summed up in a quotation from the review by *Social Work Today* of Colin Murray Parkes' *Bereavement* (1987), cited on the back cover of the book: 'He has helped us all to accept our share in the creative use of suffering.' It seems we should always look on the bright side! Others have noted the same process in relation to dying itself. Anna Witham (1985) talks about the idealization of dying in health professional training and the difficulties that students have when they come up against the real thing; Robert Kastenbaum (1982) has made much the same point.

The earlier psychoanalytic theories of mourning – of Freud, Abraham and Klein – all contain a distinction between normal and pathological mourning and in this sense can be seen in Foucault's terms as illustrating a process of a profession carving out an area of power for itself. But part of my case is that their distinction is qualitatively different from that in the work of more recent writers. Mourning for Freud (1984) involves a withdrawal from the outside world and a concentration of energy on the one who has been lost. This is accompanied by painful feelings of dejection and an inability to find a new love object. We work through mourning, with great expense of energy, by repeated reality testing and finding that the loved one really has gone. We withdraw – de-cathect – our feelings from the lost one until we are ready to find a new love object. The basic model is an energy-flow system. Energy is invested in the loved one, who dies or vanishes. The energy is then withdrawn into the mourner where it stays for a shorter or longer time until the loss is accepted, when it is reinvested in a new love object.

Freud argues that we are familiar with this experience, we know that it will pass and therefore we take it as normal. He went on to identify an abnormal or pathological mourning – melancholia – in which the mourner identifies with the lost loved one and directs the criticism and anger which belongs to the lost one to the mourner. Melancholia, then, is a state in which we have taken the lost loved one inside and kept him or her there, attacking ourselves rather than the person who is lost.

In later developments of the theory, we can see the tenuousness of this distinction in such a way as to suggest that the attempt to maintain it is a result less of understanding what is happening than of establishing the mourning process as an area of professional expertise and control. Abraham (1927), for example, makes the point that the process of internalization of the loved one is a normal part of mourning and in fact the 'successful' mourner is able to internalize the lost one as a good object. The melancholic is unable to achieve this because hostility to the loved one was so great. This moves us closer to the internal world and its complexities and the normal/ pathological now hangs on the degree of hostility in the relationship – or perhaps more accurately in the mourner.

These ideas are developed and rendered more sophisticated in Klein's work (1986) and the idea of pathological mourning changes again. To begin with I will take her example of bereavement (a Mrs A after the sudden death of her son) and examine in particular her first reactions.

Mrs A begins by sorting out letters, keeping her son's and throwing away the others – disposing of the indifferent and hostile, the bad feelings. This is seen as an attempt at restoring her son, to keep him safe inside her, an obsessional mechanism used as a defence against the depressive position; the obsessive action wards off the bad feelings. For the first week there was an (incomplete) withdrawal, a numbness and an absence of dreaming – Mrs A usually dreamt every night. Her first dream brought associations with an occasion when she had recognized that her brother was not as wonderful as she had thought, an event that was experienced as an 'irreparable misfortune'. The event was also associated with guilt, as if it were the result of her own harmful wishes against her brother. Behind these harmful wishes and 'very deeply repressed' was a desire to punish her mother through causing her to lose her son; she was jealous of her mother for possessing such a son. This led her to a death wish against her brother: one of the deeper dream wishes was 'my mother's son has died and not my own'. This was followed by sympathy for her mother and sorrow for herself. Her brother had, in fact, died and besides her earlier sorrow at this event she had, unconsciously, experienced a sense of triumph. Klein argues that some degree of Mrs A's ambivalence to her brother, 'though modified by her strong motherly feelings', had been transferred on to her son and entered into the present grief.

The first defences, then, were the manic defences against grief: denial and triumph. In Mrs A's internal world the grief was transferred to her mother, with the denial that they were one and the same person. Klein goes on to describe the process of movement into sorrow and reconnection with the world, and then the retreat into manic triumphalism and denial. The whole to-and-fro movement is seen as involving the re-establishment of the good internal objects with which the mourner can identify.

I have set out this example at some length because of its focus on the complexity of the psychological processes of mourning, involving feelings with which it is not normally associated: jealousy, triumphalism and a desire to punish. Again it also blurs the line between normal and patho-logical mourning, rooting the latter in a deeper pathology, which in turn is rooted in the earliest stages of life and cannot be 'known in advance'. It seems to me that Klein moves away from thinking about pathological mourning to the pathological personality. In fact Klein is the theorist who least fits into my argument and the interesting thing is that the most recent developments have steadily stripped away the emphasis on the complexity of the internal world, the less acceptable feelings, at the same time as they have established mourning as a subject for professional intervention and control.

The development of contemporary theory

The most recent and dramatic changes in the theory have taken place over the past three decades, beginning with two papers by Bowlby in the early 1960s (1960, 1961) and followed by Parkes (1972). This decade saw the appearance of a number of other books on death and mourning (see, for example, Gorer, 1965; Hinton, 1967) and the beginning of the contem-porary discourse on the subject. The work of both Bowlby and Parkes emphasizes the aetiology of mourning and focuses on 'environmental failure', rather than the dynamics of the internal world. Parkes' book marks the claim of psychiatry over this realm, arguing now that all mourning is pathological and should be regarded as a mental illness. Rather than put forward arguments in favour of such a position, he deals with arguments against it.

The first is the 'labelling' argument: if we call mourning a mental illness, we stigmatize those to whom the label is attached. Parkes' argument is that if we do not call the bereaved mentally ill for this reason, we are reinforcing the stigmatizing connotations of the term. This is fair enough if we accept that mourning is a mental illness. Much more depends on his second argument. He says that people object on the grounds of the normality of mourning, but measles is normal and nobody would suggest that it is not an illness. Grief, he argues, like physical illness, brings discomfort and disturbance of function:

> On the whole, grief resembles a physical injury more closely than any other type of illness. The loss may be spoken of as a 'blow'. As in the case of physical injury, the 'wound' gradually heals; at least it usually does. But occasionally complications set in, healing is delayed or a further injury reopens a healing wound. In such cases, abnormal forms arise, which may even be complicated by the onset of other types of illness. Sometimes it seems that the outcome may be fatal . . . I know of only one functional psychiatric disorder whose cause is known, whose features are distinctive, and whose course is usually predictable, and that is grief, the reaction to loss. Yet this condition has been so neglected by psychiatrists that until recently it was not even mentioned in the indexes of most of the best known general textbooks of psychiatry. (Parkes, 1972: 25–6)

In trying to define grief in terms of presenting symptoms, Parkes settles for the pining or yearning that he immediately relates to separation anxiety and Bowlby's theory of attachment needs. Parkes identifies three stages of grief (the presenting symptoms changing with each one): first a numbness; then pining, then disorganization and despair; recovery only beginning after this last experience.

In the world of the health professional, progress can easily become a matter of having more illnesses added to the list. On the face of it, Parkes' argument is plausible and humane – in fact it is plausible and humane. It also attempts to extend the power of the psychiatric profession in a way instantly recognizable to readers of Foucault and it changes the way we think about mourning in a fairly radical way. One question that emerges is where do we draw the line – should we regard the divorced, the redundant, or anybody suffering from an upheaval in their lives as mentally ill? I would suggest that this problem has been solved by the growth of psychotherapy, which brings almost any human state within the range of treatment without having to medicalize it.

Now what happens in Parkes' account of mourning is that it is seen as less of an internal psychological process of conflicts and reorganization in the internal world and the emphasis is more on the emotions, the external presenting symptoms. By placing it in Bowlby's framework we are moved closer to a quasi-behaviourism. I do not think that what Parkes says is wrong – it is less complete than either the Freudian or Kleinian accounts of mourning, seeing it in terms of cause and effect rather than as an internal processing of experience.

In more recent psychoanalytic accounts of mourning two tendencies sit side by side. On the one hand there is an implicit or even an explicit recognition of the implacability of death, the normality of grief and the never-endingness of mourning. On the other there is the desire to iron all this out, turn it into a positive experience and avoid any depth investigation of the internal world.

A set of three papers in a recent issue of *Group Analysis* is a good illustration, containing accounts of the work of a group of therapists from a hospital in Edmonton, Canada, who have developed a programme of short-term psychotherapy for loss (Lakoff and Azim, 1991; McCallum et al., 1991; Piper and McCallum, 1991). In the first paper, Lakoff and Azim (1991) talk about the contemporary denial of death and the absence of a recognized place for mourning. They also point to the difficulties in understanding what successful or unsuccessful, normal or pathological mourning might be. Quoting a study by Osterweis et al. (1987: 16), they maintain that length of time is no indicator of pathological mourning, but rather the quality and quantity of reactions over time. They also suggest that a change that seems to indicate a 'healthy' recovery in one person could mean the opposite for another. For one person, throwing him or herself into work may be avoidance; for another it may indicate a new flow of creativity.

In the second paper, Piper and McCallum (1991) survey the studies of group interventions in mourning. They begin by lamenting the lack of involvement of health professionals in providing group services for the bereaved. They suggest a classificatory schema involving two dimensions, initial and transitional, and two types, normal and pathological. Help is usually sought in the transitional stage and if the mourning is normal it is mainly a matter of support and practical intervention. Pathological mourning may occur at either stage and may take the form of too much or too little grief – in terms of intensity or duration. However, although they recognize that duration can mean from two months to never and individual differences influence progress through mourning, they then argue that such complication 'may be partially resolved by considering the debilitating impact of the loss in terms of symptomatology and impaired functioning when determining the type of mourning process occurring' (Piper and McCallum, 1991: 365).

The third paper is an account of a study of the effectiveness of twelve-week groups for those caught in pathological mourning according to a standard diagnosis which, presumably, is not derived from the previous discussion: 'Most patients received a DSM-111 Axis 1 diagnosis (usually affective adjustment or anxiety disorder) and about one quarter received an Axis 11 diagnosis (usually dependent personality) (McCallum et al., 1991: 377). The groups were tightly controlled:

> Two experienced therapists each led four of the eight groups. They followed a technical manual and attended a weekly seminar where conceptual and

technical issues were discussed and audiotapes of sessions were played. The theoretical orientation of the twelve-week, time-limited groups was psycho-analytic, and this was checked by conducting a process analysis of seven sessions from each group using the Psychodynamic Work and Object Rating System (Piper and McCallum 1991) which confirmed that the therapists were active, interpretive and group-focused, as intended. (McCallum et al. 1991: 377).

In these papers, we seem to have reached the point where it is simply assumed that professionals should be concerned with the mourning process and their absence is to be remarked upon. Despite all the reservations, a standard diagnostic tool is used to distinguish pathological grief and there are manuals by which to guide a closely regulated therapeutic process. It is clear from the account that while the therapist is listening closely to the group, he or she knows in advance what sort of interpretation he or she will make. It is mapped out according to a view of the appropriate emotions and their expression, rather than on an intimate understanding of the different inner worlds of the group members.

We find here a continued degradation of our understanding of mourning: pathology is defined by a standard measure and 'correct' feelings are laid out in the discussion of the groups. Anger seems OK but not hatred; guilt might be appropriate, but triumph is not mentioned. There is, if you like, a taming of grief and we know what the patient should be doing. There is, further, a move beyond the identification of emotion as a sign of pathology to 'functional impairment' which hands over the definition of 'pathology' to a society which, as many have pointed out, allows no recognized space for mourning. It is a not very large step to the attempt at control and limitation of mourning set out in a recent handbook for healthcare professionals as the aims of a therapeutic assessment of bereavement:

1   To facilitate and consolidate a satisfactorily resolving of bereavement.
2   To provide a framework for specific preventive intervention with bereaved who are at high risk of malresolution.
3   To provide a framework for specific intervention with pathological bereavements so that these may possibly be diverted to a more adaptive course. (Raphael, 1984: 347)

The job becomes getting the machine back on the road.

Psychotherapy as social control

My argument concerns the way in which our conception of mourning has changed, especially over the last thirty years. We have lost the depth that can be found in the work of Freud and Klein, whose papers on mourning have been seminal sources for psychoanalytic thought. The development has been away from the dynamics of the inner world towards classifications based on surface criteria and the development of schemata, programmes for mourning, stages that people have to be moved through. These changes have gone along with the growth of bereavement counselling and division of death and mourning into a separate area of life – its 'sequestration'. I want now to think about the reasons why this has happened. Put as simply as possible, my argument is that as psychoanalytic ideas enter the wider culture they get taken up and transformed – some aspects get lost and others emphasized. Thus the creative dimensions of mourning are emphasized and we are led to think in terms of resolution. It seems to me that this is not a normal human resistance to the horror of death – other societies and our society at other historical periods have thought differently – it has more to do with the sorts of changes we are living through. As these ideas get reinterpreted in this way, so they come to fill a social function which is different from the apparently straightforward activity of helping people with which, at first sight, they are associated. My argument here is that the ideas and the practices they generate become a form of social control, the therapy becoming a play of false selves of which the practitioners are unconscious.

We can see the forms of thinking in the wider culture at work, for example, in the attempt to produce programmed treatments for pathological mourning. One way of looking at it is the development of a therapeutic programming of people to deal with new and different situations. Giddens (1991) argues that the modern forms of self-therapy and popular self-help books are precisely providing formulae for dealing with life in what he calls 'late modernity'. It is possible to push this a bit further. Over the last decade or so the computer has provided new metaphors for talking about human beings. Whereas in the 1960s psychology departments might have been full of rats and pigeons and mazes, they are now full of computers and their object of study is thought of as a computer. The move from behaviourism to cognitive psychology has not been a movement towards intellectual depth. In this context, if some of the insights from psychotherapy can be simplified and standardized, they can be seen as programmes for the human computer. The growth, in the USA, of twelve-step programmes for practically everything is an extreme example. [. . .]

[. . .] In Kohut's (1971) work on narcissism, he comments on the change in family structures since Freud was working – from a situation where there was too much contact between parents and children to one where there is too little. This has been accompanied through this century by the steady loosening of community ties, increased geographical and social mobility (the latter both up and down) and the decline of what we might call 'holding organizations'. I have already mentioned the family and the local community but we can add to those, in this latest rush of fragmentation, business and service organizations (such as British Rail and the

NHS), trade unions and professional associations as self-governing bodies – all the collective entities which could stand between the individual and some much wider, anonymous entity we call society. [. . .]

What happens in such a situation, it seems to me, is first the process of mourning becomes not just a model for major life changes, as it was with the classical theorists, but also a model for everyday life. The modern therapies that Giddens discusses discourage people from trying to make lasting attachments and urge a living for the moment only. Psychoanalysis does not go as far as this, and I doubt that it ever could, but its contribution to the contemporary denial of pain and complexity lies in its approach to grief and mourning. We can turn loss into 'growth' or 'creativity', and perhaps we do not need to think about the loss. In a society which is increasingly frightening, we can think of change as always positive, when in fact it is arguable that it is increasingly destructive – of relationships and lives.

It is arguable that psychotherapy in contemporary society runs the danger of becoming an abstract system, an institution providing formulae for living as psychotherapists try to proselytize in newspaper columns and popular books. [. . .] Returning to grief and mourning, it seems to me that we need comparatively little experience to realize its individuality and the sometimes astonishing way in which a person finds his or her way through it, to a different life or to their own death – or the equally surprising way in which they might decide not to move on from mourning. I suspect that an 'authentic' therapy should respect decisions which, according to an abstract framework, are pathological and perhaps drop the distinction altogether.

This means taking risks, recognizing that we do not possess formulae for living – or for dying – and that we are as isolated and threatened as everybody else. The alternative is that psychotherapy becomes an encounter not between therapist and patient in a joint search for meaning but between two false selves, the therapist hiding behind his or her formulae or programmes which emphasize only one side of our lives, the patient adopting that false self in an attempt to please and reassure the therapist. If mourning is the discovery of the meaning of what has been lost, in all its ambiguity, ambivalence and complexity, then this discovery is prejudged and fenced in if we set out already knowing what should be happening. The more anxious we are, the more we will need to cling on to such formulae; the more our patients will become like the anxious infant trying to protect a more anxious parent by being what the parent wants. In such a situation, our work can seem very successful. On the other hand, we can help the patient to suffer. If we see success as therapists only in enabling creativity and happiness or in being effective in some tangible and possibly measurable way, if, in short, we see ourselves as selling goods on a market to attract customers or to please management, we are developing a false world which will collapse only too easily in the face of our critics.

References

Abraham, K. (1927) *Selected Papers on Psychoanalysis*. London: Hogarth Press.

Bowlby, John (1960) 'Grief and mourning in infancy and childhood', *The Psychoanalytic Study of the Child*, 15: 9–52.

Bowlby, John (1961) 'Processes of Mourning', *International Journal of Psycho-Analysis*, 42: 317–40.

Foucault, Michel (1984) *A History of Sexuality, Volume 1*. Harmondsworth: Penguin.

Freud, Sigmund (1984) 'Mourning and melancholia', in *Collected Works*, volume 11. Harmondsworth: Penguin. pp. 245–68.

Giddens, Anthony (1991) *Modernity and Self-identity: Self and Society in the Late Modern Age*. Cambridge: Polity Press.

Gorer, G. (1965) *Death, Grief and Mourning in Contemporary Britain*. London: Cresset.

Hinton, J. (1967) *Dying*. Harmondsworth: Penguin.

Kastenbaum, R. (1982) 'Dying is healthy and death a bureaucrat: our fantasy machine is alive and well', in M. Dimatteo and H. Friedman (eds), *Interpersonal Issues in Health Care*. London: Academic Press.

Klein (1986) 'Mourning and its relation to manic-depressive states', in J. Mitchell (ed.), *The Selected Melanie Klein*. Harmondsworth: Penguin.

Kohut, H. (1971) *The Analysis of the Self*. New York: International Universities Press.

Lakoff, R.S. and Azim, H.F.A. (1991) 'Society's changing views on mourning', *Group Analysis*, 24: 355–62.

McCallum, M., Piper, E., Hassan, W.E., Azim, A. and Lakoff, R.S. (1991) 'The Edmonton model of short-term group therapy for loss: an integration of theory, practice and research', *Group Analysis*, 24: 375–88.

Osterweis, M., Solomon, F. and Green, M. (1987) 'Bereavement reactions, consequences and care' in Zisook, S. (ed.), *Biophysical Aspects of Bereavement*. Washington, DC: American Psychiatric Press.

Parkes, Colin Murray (1987) *Bereavement: Studies of Grief in Adult Life*. Harmondsworth: Penguin.

Piper, E. and McCallum, M. (1991) 'Group intervention for persons who have experienced loss: description and evaluative research', *Group Analysis*, 24: 363–74.

Raphael, B. (1984) *The Anatomy of Bereavement: a Handbook for the Caring Professions*. London: Unwin Hyman.

Witham, Anna (1985) 'The idealization of dying', *Free Associations*, 3: 80–91.

IDENTITY, SOCIOLOGY, HISTORY

How are we to undertake a sociology of
'persons'? What might the relationship be
between such an endeavour and contemporary
social and cultural theoretical preoccupations
with 'identity' and 'subjectivity'?

The readings in Part III are concerned less
with advancing a simple historical narrative of
changing ideas about the 'person' than in
focusing upon the social relations, techniques,
and forms of training and practice through
which individuals have acquired definite
capacities and attributes for social existence as
particular sorts of 'person'. This shift of focus
involves a movement away from general social
theoretical and psychoanalytical accounts
concerning the formation of 'subjectivity' or
'identity' and towards an understanding of the
limited and specific forms of 'personhood' that
individuals acquire in their passage through

social institutions. With this particularizing and contextualizing emphasis comes recognition of the historical contingency and plurality of 'personae' and the necessity of not separating the properties of particular forms of personhood from the specific cultural milieux or institutional settings in which they are formed.

This section seeks a certain balance of empirical concreteness and theoretical sophistication. One of its key aims is to introduce a certain set of theoretical arguments but also to treat these theories as practical instruments for doing a certain 'sociology' of the person by describing and analyzing the institutional settings in which personal capacities are formed and the practices and techniques through which those capacities are transmitted. These theoretical instruments are associated with a small group of authors whose writing provides this section with its methodological guidelines.

The first reading in Part III (Chapter 22) by the historical sociologist **Norbert Elias** explores the reasons why a particular idea of the 'individual' standing outside 'society' has so frequently been taken as a general starting point for sociologies of 'the person'. Elias indicates how this image of the person (in the singular) as a **'homo clausus'** needs to be strenuously undone if a sociologically satisfactory account of the historical and cultural formation of persons (in the plural) is to be achieved. This challenge is taken up by **Pierre Bourdieu** in his brief but telling essay **'The Biographical Illusion'** (Chapter 23). Focusing on the 'life history' approach Bourdieu highlights some of the theoretical and methodological dangers inherent in presuming the continuity of human beings as subjects of history, essentially equipped with the capacity for bestowing meaning on experience. In particular, Bourdieu explores the ways in which humans' capacities, including the capacity for self-consciousness and self-reflection, depend upon definite forms of discourse and definite sets of activities and techniques in which they are trained and implicated as agents. Categories of persons, we discover, are only intelligible with reference to a definite substratum of discourses and practices which together give agents their – complex and differentiated – forms. As both Bourdieu and Elias make clear, legal, governmental and aesthetic forms of personhood, for example, stand in no general relationship to one another. No claim can be made that one of them is, in fact, *the* person. Each is a definite but limited form of personhood. And these separate and distinct personae are not capable of being summed up into a fully recognized 'whole person' as the classic reading by **T.H. Marshall, 'A Note of Status'** (Chapter 24), makes clear. Here, we learn that forms of personhood depend upon definite arrays of instituted statuses and attributes, rights and duties that organize the practical deportment of individuals and groups. However, these statuses and attributes cannot be unproblematically aligned with an individual's sense of 'self' or 'subjectivity', indeed in some cases they are not attached to individual human beings at all. The task Marshall sets himself and other sociologists is one of describing these instituted statuses and attributes, rights and duties, and thus the different forms of person they constitute, in their own specific terms.

The rest of the readings in this section provide exemplary instances of how to go about conducting just such an exercise. The reading by **Nikolas Rose, 'Identity,**

Genealogy, History' (Chapter 25), functions as something of an orienting device in that it seeks to establish a theoretical and methodological framework for conducting what Rose terms, following Michel Foucault, a 'genealogy of subjectification'. As Rose argues, if we use the term 'subjectification' to refer to the multifarious processes and practices through which human beings come to relate to themselves as persons of a certain sort, then this 'subjectification' can be seen to have its own history, one that it is more practical, technical and less unified than many philosophical and social theoretical accounts usually allow for or appreciate. The variable relations of person, individual and self that Rose articulates are then explored in some detail through an engagement with **Marcel Mauss's** classic published lecture **'A category of the human mind: the notion of "person", the notion of "self"'** (Chapter 26). As Ian Hunter and David Saunders (1995: 72) have argued, Mauss draws important distinctions between person, individual and subject, ones quite different from those that we instinctively deploy today. Whereas individuals' are seen by him as 'relatively unstructured biological and psychological beings ('raw human material'), "persons" represent the definite complexes of instituted statuses and attributes that have provided the means of actually conducting oneself and one's relations with others' (1995: 72). Mauss' distinction, as Hunter and Saunders (1995: 72) point out, rests upon evidence drawn from societies in which not all individuals are or have persons. Moreover, those individuals who are or who have persons do not necessarily bear this personhood in what we moderns would regard as an individual manner – that is within themselves. The forms of being, having, or being a person have varied considerably across time and space; sometimes they have been invested in trans-individual institutions such as name systems or mask-wearing rituals. Finally, 'subjects' differ from persons and individuals in that they represent a 'historically contingent and specific manner in which individuals come to possess the attributes of personhood allocated to them. This manner is one in which the public attributes of the person are internalized and identified with an inner entity (conscience, consciousness) rather than with a public institution such as the totem or religious ritual' (Hunter & Saunders, 1995: 72).

According to Mauss this 'internalization' of personhood does not represent the 'true' or essential form of human subjectivity; rather it is simply one amongst many potential and actual ways of being a 'person'. As he famously argued, 'it was formed only for us, among us'.

This sort of socio-historical approach to studying the formation of persons in distinct instituted cultural settings suggested by Mauss is also the 'central theme' of Max Weber's work, or so Wilhelm Hennis (1988) argues in his classic 'reconstruction' of Weber. Of Weber's historical sociologies of 'personae' perhaps the most famous is that of the Puritan described in some detail in *The Protestant Ethic and the Spirit of Capitalism*. This was 'the persona housed in the distinctive order of living associated with the Protestant sects where life was methodically conducted by daily Bible reading, constant keeping of spiritual account-books, intense monitoring of one's spiritual progress through each day and throughout life' (Saunders, 1997: 106). However, Weber explored many other personae and the contexts in which they are formed: the bureaucrat in the administrative office and the academic in the University, for example. The historical particularity of personae fitted to existence in particular contexts also figured large in **Weber's** famous address on **'The Profession and Vocation of Politics'**. Here Weber drew this lesson for his audience. 'We are placed in different orders of life, each of which is governed by different laws'.

In the light of Mauss's concern with techniques and practices of the person and Weber's concern with the relationship between specific 'conducts of life' and 'departments of existence', the time is now right to introduce Michel Foucault's analysis of the 'self' as a historically and culturally specific comportment of the individual, one dependent on special techniques or procedures of 'subjectification'. In other words, and following Mauss and Weber's lead, Foucault can be seen to be interested in 'the subject' not as some transhistorical object of techniques for being human but as a specific way in which individuals have been enjoined to understand and relate to themselves as 'persons' of a certain sort. 'There is a subject', as Christian Jambet (1992: 238–9) puts it, 'because a certain type of "relationship with the self" comes into being in a culture'. In his final work on 'techniques of the self' in late-antiquity, Foucault analyses the distinction between the code of a morality and the ethic, or way of life, of those attempting to live by the code. Taking as an example the injunction towards conjugal fidelity as a core element of the Christian moral code, Foucault comments that knowledge of this code tells us nothing of the means through which Christians have learned to relate to themselves and conduct themselves as faithful persons. As Ian Hunter (1994: 52) has indicated the 'means of conjugal living are as diverse as the code is seemingly monolithic'. These means can be called *ethical techniques* and they belong to the domain of *spiritual discipline*. **Foucault's** overview of his work on spiritual practices is contained in the **'Introduction to "The Use of Pleasure"'** (Chapter 28). Rather than attempting a general history of the self-reflective subject or conducting a historical dialectic that promises to synthesize this subject, Foucault's work can be viewed as an investigation into the specific spiritual practices through which individuals come to concern themselves with themselves and seek to compose themselves as 'subjects' of their own conduct. The extent to which Foucault succeeds in this endeavour and the manner in which he remains wedded to a certain (romantic) philosophical rather than historical genealogical mode of enquiry is discussed in the reading by **Pierre Hadot**, **'Reflections on the Idea of the "Cultivation of the Self"'** (Chapter 29).

In concluding this section of the reader, attention will be focused on the lessons we can draw from the work under discussion: try not to prise apart personae from their institutional settings; attempt to contextualise and to historicise; try to pay attention to the particularity of the circumstances before reaching a critical judgment. The importance of this lesson is highlighted by the final reading in the section by **Amélie Rorty**. In **'Persons and Personae'** (Chapter 30), Rorty attempts to indicate how, in the vexed debates about identity, apparently conflicting intuitions on the primacy of competing concepts of persons might be reconciled by regionalizing their respective dominance.

Notes

Selection of the readings and for this section, and their interpretative framing, were greatly facilitated by conversations with David Saunders and Ian Hunter.

References

Hennis, W. (1988) *Max Weber: essays in reconstruction*. London: Allen & Unwin.
Hunter, I. (1994) *Re-Thinking the School Sydney*. Allen & Unwin.
Hunter, I & Saunders, D. (1995) 'Walks of Life: Mauss on the human gymnasium', *Body & Society*, 1(2): 65–81.
Jambet, C. (1992) 'The constitution of the subject and spiritual practice: observations on *L'Histoire de la Sexualité*', in T.J. Armstrong (ed. and trans.) *Michel Foucault, Philosopher*. Brighton: Harvester Wheatsheaf pp. 233–47.
Saunders, D. (1997) *The Anti-Lawyers*. London: Routledge
Weber, M. (1930) *The Protestant Ethic and the Spirit of Capitalism*. London: HarperCollins.

In this regard Foucault's notion of 'techniques of the self' can sometimes appear a little misleading, as Rose pointed out in Reading 25. As we have just seen, the 'self' or 'subjecthood' does not form the 'universal' or 'essential' object of techniques of conduct but rather is but one, specialized way in which individuals have been encouraged to relate to themselves as persons. This point is brought home with some precision by Pierre Hadot in the final reading of this section.

Reading

You should now turn to 'Reflections on the Idea of the Cultivation of the Self' by Pierre Hadot which is Chapter 29 of the Reader. As you read this piece try answering the following questions.

1) How useful does Hadot think it is to use the terms 'self' and 'subject' in the context of Antiquity?

2) Why does Hadot accuse Foucault of advancing an interpretation of antique philosophy that is 'too purely aesthetic'? What do his criticisms of Foucault tell us about the importance of historical contextualization for analyzing the formation of persons?

Pierre Hadot is a historian of Antiquity and, in particular, of Ancient philosophy. He has argued for some time that philosophy was not originally conceived as a theoretical discourse but rather as a practical ethical endeavour, a working on the will through the exercise of thought. Only from the seventeenth century did philosophy begin to be conceived of as an authoritative theoretical discourse, developing the idea that truth was the result of 'a process of elaboration, carried out by a reason grounded in itself' (Hadot, 1995: 76). Hadot also insists that the exercises that animated the vocation of philosophy for the Ancients was 'spiritual' in that it involved the transformation of the individual on to a new course of life, yet was also essentially calmative in effect, acting in this sense as a sort of 'therapeutic of the passions' (1995: 83). Taking Stoic philosophy as an example, Hadot (1995: 275) indicates that the task of this philosophy was to develop exercises that would enable individuals to become reconciled to the natural limits of their freedom, and to connect themselves with the 'cosmological' dimensions of existence. Foucault (1987: 8) admits quite openly that the second and third volumes of his History of Sexuality – The Use of Pleasure and The Care of the Self, respectively – owe a considerable debt to the original work of Hadot and as the latter makes clear in the Reading, he and Foucault had been engaged in on-going dialogue until Foucault's untimely demise.

In the reading, Hadot takes issue with some of the key terms Foucault deploys in the latter volumes of the History of Sexuality and he does so on the grounds of their fit with the historical context and with the dynamics they seek to account for. In particular, Hadot questions the explanatory power of 'techniques of the self' and the idea of 'the cultivation of the self' which Foucault deploys to describe Ancient spiritual exercises. For Hadot, the main point of contention is that Foucault's analyses of Ancient 'techniques of the self' are 'too much centred on the "self", or at least on a certain conception of the self'. For Hadot, the 'self' that Foucault is discussing is very much a contemporary Western version of 'the subject'. In part, he argues, this is an outcome of Foucault's attempt not simply to provide an historical account of ancient spiritual practices but to offer them implicitly as a model of life for those living in the here and now – what Foucault (1987: 10) calls an "aesthetics of existence". Foucault (1987: 11) defines the latter as 'those intentional and voluntary actions by which men not only set themselves rules of conduct, but also seek to transform themselves, to change themselves in their singular being, and to make their life into an *oeuvre* that carries certain aesthetic values and meets certain stylistic criteria'. The problem with this formulation, Hadot argues, is that it has no historical fit with either the actual goals or 'psychic content' of Ancient spiritual exercises. As he puts it, 'it seems difficult from a historical point of view to concede that the philosophical practices of the Stoics and the Platonists was related only to the self, to the cultivation of the self and to the pleasure taken in the self'. Rather, these spiritual exercises were aimed not at constructing a subjective identity but rather at freeing 'oneself from one's individuality'. As such, 'one identifies oneself with an "other" which is Nature, universal Reason, which is present in each individual. In this there is a radical transformation of perspective, a universalist and cosmic dimension which Foucault, it seems to me, did not sufficiently stress: interiorisation is going beyond the self in a way which leads to universalisation' (Hadot, 1992: 229).

For Hadot, then, Foucault's error lies in not being historically specific enough, in not embedding the spiritual exercises he describes in their proper historical context. By failing to do this, Foucault is in danger of interpreting the personae of the Stoics, the Epicureans and other Ancients through the prism of a thoroughly modern conception of the person as a self or subject, something which Hadot (1992: 232) argues is problematic precisely because 'it is very difficult to use the terms self and subject in the context of Antiquity'. He sums up his objections to Foucault's terminology in the context of Antiquity in the following manner:

> What I fear is that, by concentrating his interpretation of the cultivation of the self, on concern for the self and on conversion towards the self and, in a general way, by defining his ethical model as an ethic of existence, Foucault might have been advancing a cultivation of the self which was too purely aesthetic – that is to say, I fear, a new form of dandyism, a late twentieth century version (Hadot, 1992: 230).

Hadot is keen not to dismiss Foucault's project in its entirety. In a sense, he wants to hold Foucault accountable to his own stated methodological principles. If, as Foucault argued, 'genealogy is grey, meticulous and patiently documentary' then, Hadot suggests, Foucault needed to be rather more this way inclined himself when studying Ancient spiritual exercises and the persons they constituted. For without such a disposition, Hadot argues, Foucault's analysis was in danger of becoming more theoretical proposition than historical description

***

This is also a point that Pierre Hadot's work sought to emphasize. In undertaking a genealogy of 'the subject' it was important, he argued, not to import contemporary understandings of persons as 'subjects' into a culture, historical period or investigative context in which they had no purchase and thus made no sense. While Hadot was well aware that a genealogy of 'the subject' might locate certain technical conditions for acquiring a consciousness of self in the spiritual exercises of later-Antiquity he was nonetheless certain that these exercises did not constitute persons as 'subjects' in the manner that Foucault seemed to be suggesting i.e. as Antique prototypes of a sort of modern self-generating 'aesthetics of existence'.

22

Homo clausus and the civilizing process
Norbert Elias

[. . .]

VIII

To understand the blockage which the predominant modes of thinking and feeling place in the way of the investigation of long-term changes of social structure and personality structure [. . .] it is not enough to trace the development of the image of men as societies, the image of society. It is also necessary to keep in mind the development of the image of men as individuals, the image of the personality. [. . .] [O]ne of the peculiarities of the traditional image of man is that people often speak and think of individuals and societies as if these were two phenomena existing separately – of which, moreover, one is often considered 'real' and the other 'unreal' – instead of two different aspects of the same human being.

This curious aberration of thinking, too, cannot be understood without a glance at its implicit ideological content. The splitting of the image of humanity into an image of man as individual and an image of men as societies has widely ramifying roots. One branch is a very characteristic split in the values and ideals encountered, on close inspection, in all the more developed nation-states, and perhaps most pronounced in nations with a strong liberal tradition. In the development of the value systems of all such nation-states, one finds, on the one hand, a strand which sees society as a whole, the nation, as the highest value; and, on the other, a strand which posits the wholly self-sufficient, free individual, the 'closed personality,' as the highest value. It is not always easy to harmonize

This chapter, which formed the introduction to the 1968 edition, is taken from *The Civilizing Process* (Oxford, Blackwell, 1978), pp. 221–63.

these two 'highest values' with one another. There are situations in which the two ideals are plainly irreconcilable. But usually this problem is not squarely faced. People talk with great warmth of the freedom and independence of the individual, and with equal warmth of the freedom and independence of their own nation. The first ideal arouses the expectation that the individual member of a nation-state, despite his community and interdependence with others, can reach his decisions in an entirely self-sufficient way, without regard to others; the second arouses the expectation – fulfilled particularly in war but often enough in peacetime, too – that the individual should and must subordinate everything belonging to him, even his life, to the survival of the 'social whole.'

This split in the ideals, this contradiction in the ethos by which people are brought up, finds expression in the theories of sociology. Some of these theories take as their starting point the independent, self-sufficient individual as the 'true' reality, and therefore as the true object of social science; others start with the independent social totality. Some theories attempt to harmonize the two conceptions, usually without indicating how it is possible to reconcile the idea of an absolutely independent and free individual with that of an equally independent and free 'social totality,' and often without clearly perceiving the problem. [. . .]

[. . .]

The image of the individual as an entirely free, independent being, a 'closed personality' who is 'inwardly' quite self-sufficient and separate from all other people, has behind it a long tradition in the development of European societies. In classical philosophy this figure comes onto the scene as the epistemological subject. In this role, as *homo philosophicus*, the individual gains knowledge of the world 'outside' him in a completely autonomous way. He does not need to learn, to take this knowledge from others. The fact that he came into the world as a child, the whole process of his development to adulthood and as an adult, is neglected as immaterial by this image of man. In the development of mankind it took many thousands of years for people to learn to understand the relations between natural events, the course of the stars, rain and sun, thunder and lightning, as manifestations of a blind, impersonal, purely mechanical and regular sequence of causal connections. But the 'closed personality' of *homo philosophicus* apparently perceives this mechanical and regular causal chain as an adult simply by opening his eyes, without needing to learn anything about it from others, and quite independently of the stage of knowledge reached by society. The process – the individual human being as a process in growing up, human beings together as a process in the development of mankind – is reduced in thought to a state. The individual opens his eyes as an adult and not only recognizes autonomously here and now, without learning from others, what all these objects are that he perceives; he not only knows immediately what he is to classify as animate and inanimate, as mineral, vegetable, or animal; but he also knows directly here and now that they are linked causally in accordance with natural laws. The question for philosophers is merely whether he gains this knowledge of causal connections here and now on the basis of his experience – whether, in other words, these connections are a property of the observable facts 'outside' him – or the connections are something rooted in the nature of human reason and superadded from 'inside' the human being to what flows into him from 'outside' through the sense organs. If we start from this image of man, from the *homo philosophicus* who was never a child and seemingly came into the world an adult, there is no way out of the epistemological impasse. Thought steers helplessly back and forth between the Scylla of positivism and the Charybdis of apriorism. It does so precisely because what is actually observable as a process, a development of the social macrocosm within which the development of the individual microcosm can also be observed, is reduced in thought to a state, an act of perception taking place here and now. We have here an example of how closely the inability to conceive long-term social processes (i.e., structured changes in the figurations formed by large numbers of interdependent human beings) or to understand the human beings forming such figurations is connected to a certain type of image of man and of self-perception. People to whom it seems self-evident that their own self (or their ego, or whatever else it may be called) exists, as it were, 'inside' them, isolated from all the other people and things 'outside,' have difficulty assigning significance to all those facts which indicate that individuals live from the first in interdependence with others. They have difficulty conceiving people as relatively but not absolutely autonomous and interdependent individuals forming changeable figurations with one another. Since the former self-perception seems self-evident to those subscribing to it, they cannot easily take account of facts which show that this kind of perception is itself limited to particular societies, that it comes into being in conjunction with certain kinds of interdependencies, of social bonds between people – in short, that it is a structural peculiarity of a specific stage in the development of civilization, corresponding to a specific stage of differentiation and individualization of human groups. If one grows up in the midst of such a group, one cannot easily imagine that there could be people who do not experience themselves in this way as entirely self-sufficient individuals cut off from all other beings and things. This kind of self-perception appears as obvious, a symptom of an eternal human state, simply the normal, natural, and universal self-perception of all human beings. The conception of the individual as *homo clausus*, a little world in himself who ultimately exists quite independently of the great world outside, determines the image of man in general. Every other human being is likewise seen as a *homo clausus*; his core, his being, his true self appears likewise as something divided within him by an invisible wall from everything outside, including every other human being.

But the nature of this wall itself is hardly ever considered and never properly explained. Is the body the vessel which holds the true self locked within it? Is the skin the frontier between 'inside' and 'outside'? What in

HOMO CLAUSUS AND THE CIVILIZING PROCESS

man is the capsule, and what the encapsulated? The experience of 'inside' and 'outside' seems so self-evident that such questions are scarcely ever posed; they seem to require no further examination. One is satisfied with the spatial metaphor of 'inside' and 'outside,' but one makes no serious attempt to locate the 'inner' in space; and although this omission to investigate one's own presuppositions is hardly appropriate to scientific procedure, this preconceived image of *homo clausus* commands the stage not only in society at large but also in the human sciences. Its derivatives include not only the traditional *homo philosophicus*, the image of man of classical epistemology, but also *homo oeconomicus*, *homo psychologicus*, *homo historicus*, and not least *homo sociologicus* in his present-day version. [. . .] As philosophers did before them, many sociological theorists today accept this self-perception, and the image of the individual corresponding to it, as the untested basis of their theories. They do not detach themselves from it in order to confront it and call its aptness into question. Consequently, this kind of self-perception and image of the individual often coexists unchanged with attempts to abolish the reduction to states. In Parsons, for example, the static image of the ego, the individual actor, the adult abstracted from the process of growing up, coexists unmediated with the psychoanalytical ideas that he has taken over in his theory – ideas which relate not to the state of adulthood but to the process of becoming adult, to the individual as an open process in indissoluble interdependence with other individuals. As a result, the ideas of social theorists constantly find themselves in blind alleys from which there seems no way out. The individual – or, more precisely, what the present concept of the individual refers to – appears again and again as something existing 'outside' society. What the concept of society refers to appears again and again as something existing outside and beyond individuals. One seems to have the choice only between theoretical approaches which present the individual as the truly existent beyond society, the truly 'real' (society being seen as an abstraction, something not truly existing), and other theoretical approaches which posit society as a 'system,' a 'social fact *sui generis*,' a reality of a peculiar type beyond individuals. At most one can – as is occasionally done in an apparent solution to the problem – juxtapose the two conceptions unconnectedly, that of the individual as *homo clausus*, as ego, as individual beyond society, and that of society as a system outside and beyond individuals. But the incompatibility of these two conceptions is not thereby disposed of. In order to pass beyond this dead end of sociology and the social sciences in general, it is necessary to make clear the inadequacy of both conceptions, that of the individual outside society and, equally, that of a society outside individuals. This is difficult as long as the sense of the encapsulation of the self within itself serves as the untested basis of the image of the individual, and as long as, in conjunction with this, the concepts 'individual' and 'society' are understood as if they related to unchanging states.

The conceptual trap in which one is continually being caught by these static notions of 'individual' and 'society' can only be prized open if, as is done here, these notions are developed further, in conjunction with empirical investigations, in such a way that the two concepts are made to refer to processes. But this development is initially blocked by the extraordinary conviction carried in European societies since roughly the Renaissance by the self-perception of human beings in terms of their own isolation, the severance of their own 'inside' from everything 'outside.' In Descartes the perception of the isolation of the individual, who finds himself confronted as a thinking ego within his own head by the entire external world, is somewhat weakened by the idea of God. In contemporary sociology the same basic experience finds theoretical expression in the acting ego, which finds itself confronted with people 'outside' as 'others.' Apart from Leibnizian monadology, there is in this philosophico-sociological tradition scarcely a single approach to the problem that sets out from the basis of a multiplicity of interdependent human beings. Leibniz, who did just that, only managed to do so by bringing his version of *homo clausus*, the 'windowless monads,' in relation to one another by a metaphysical construction. All the same, monadology represents an early advance in the direction of precisely the kind of model that is urgently in need of further development in sociology today. The decisive step Leibniz took was an act of self-distantiation, which enabled him to entertain the idea that one might experience oneself not as an 'ego' confronting all other people and things, but as a being among others. It was characteristic of the prevalent kind of experience in that whole period that the geocentric world-picture of the preceding age was superseded only in the area of inanimate nature by a world-picture demanding from the subject of experience a higher degree of self-detachment, a removal of oneself from the center. In men's reflection on themselves the geocentric world-picture was to a large extent preserved in the egocentric one that replaced it. At the center of the human universe, or so it appeared, stood each single human being as an individual completely independent of all others.

Nothing is more characteristic of the unquestioning way in which even today, in thinking about human beings, the separate individual is taken as the starting point than the fact that one does not speak of *homines sociologiae* or *oeconomiae* when talking of the image of man in the social sciences, but always of the image of the single human being, the *homo sociologicus* or *oeconomicus*. From this conceptual starting point, society presents itself finally as a collection of individuals completely independent of each other, whose true essence is locked within them and who therefore communicate only externally and from the surface. One must call on the help of a metaphysical solution, as Leibniz did, if, starting from windowless, closed, human and extrahuman monads, one is to justify the notion that interdependence and communication between them, or the perception by human beings of interdependence and communications, are possible. Whether we are dealing with human beings in their role as 'subject' confronting the 'object,' or in their role as 'individual' confronting 'society,' in both cases the problem is presented as if an adult human being, completely isolated and self-sufficient – that is, in a form reflecting the prevalent self-perception of people in the modern age crystallized in an objectifying concept – constitutes the frame of reference. What is discussed is his relation to something 'outside' himself conceived (like the isolated human being) as a state, to 'nature' or to 'society.' Does this something exist? Or is it only produced by a mental process, or at any rate founded primarily on a mental process? [. . .]

Let us try to make clear what the problem actually is that is being discussed here. We are not concerned with calling into doubt the authenticity of the self-perception that finds expression in the image of man as *homo clausus* and its many variations. The question is whether this self-perception, and the image of man in which it is usually crystallized quite spontaneously and without reflection, can serve as a reliable starting point for an attempt to gain adequate understanding of human beings – and therefore also of oneself – regardless of whether this attempt is philosophical or sociological. Is it justified – that is the question – to place at the foundation of philosophical theories of perception and knowledge, and of sociological and other theories in the human sciences, as a self-evident assumption incapable of further explanation, the sharp dividing line between what is 'inside' man and the 'external world,' a division which often appears directly given in self-awareness, and furthermore has put down deep roots in European intellectual and linguistic traditions, without a critical and systematic examination of its validity?

This conception has had, for a certain period of human development, an extraordinary persistence. It is found in the writings of all groups whose powers of reflection and whose self-awareness have reached the stage at which people are in a position not only to think but also to be conscious of themselves, and to reflect on themselves, as thinking beings. It is already found in Platonic philosophy and in a number of other schools of philosophy in antiquity. The idea of the 'self in a case,' as already mentioned, is one of the recurrent *leitmotifs* of modern philosophy, from the thinking subject of Descartes, Leibniz's windowless monads, and the Kantian subject of knowledge (who from his aprioristic shell can never quite break through to the 'thing in itself') to the more recent extension of the same basic idea of the entirely self-sufficient individual: beyond the perspective of thought and perception as reified into 'understanding' (*Verstand*) and 'reason' (*Vernunft*), to the whole 'being' of man, his 'existence' in the various versions of existentialist philosophy [. . .].

But one would gain only a very inadequate idea of the nature of this self-perception and this image of man if they were understood merely as ideas set forth in scholarly writings. The windowlessness of the monads, the problems surrounding *homo clausus*, which a man like Leibniz tries to make at least more bearable by a speculative solution showing the possibility of relationships between monads, is today accepted as self-evident not only by scholars. Expressions of this self-perception are found in a less reflected form in imaginative literature – for example, in Virginia Woolf's lament over the incommunicability of experience as the cause of human solitude. Its expression is found in the concept of 'alienation,' used more and more frequently within and outside literature in the most diverse variations in recent decades. It would be not uninteresting to ascertain more systematically whether and how far gradations and variations of this type of self-perception extend to the various elite groups and the broader strata of more developed societies. But the examples cited suffice to indicate how persistent and how much taken for granted in the societies of modern Europe is the feeling of people that their own 'self,' their 'true identity,' is something locked away 'inside' them, severed from all other people and things 'outside' – although, as has been mentioned, no one finds it particularly simple to show clearly where and what the tangible walls or barriers are which enclose this inner self as a vessel encloses its contents, and separate it from what is 'outside.' Are we here concerned, as it often appears, with an eternal, fundamental experience of all human beings accessible to no further explanation, or with a type of self-perception which is characteristic of a certain stage in the development of the figurations formed by people, and of the people forming these figurations? [. . .]

One can gain a clear idea relatively simply by first looking back at the change in people's self-perception that was influenced by the abandonment of the geocentric world-picture. Often this transition is presented simply as a revision and extension of knowledge about the movements of the stars. But it is obvious that this changed conception of the figurations of the stars would not have been possible had not the prevailing image of man been seriously shaken on its own account, had not people become capable of perceiving themselves in a different light than before. Of primary importance for human beings everywhere is a mode of experience by which they place themselves at the center of public events, not just as individuals but as groups. The geocentric world-picture is the expression of this spontaneous and unreflecting self-centeredness of men, which is still encountered unequivocally today in the ideas of people outside the realm of nature, e.g., in natiocentric sociological modes of thought or those centered on the isolated individual.

The geocentric experience is still accessible to everyone as a plane of perception even today. It merely does not constitute the dominant plane of perception in public thought. When we say, and indeed 'see,' that the sun rises in the east and goes down in the west, we spontaneously experience ourselves and the earth on which we live as the center of the cosmos, as the frame of reference for the movements of the stars. It was not simply new discoveries, a cumulative increase in knowledge about the objects of human reflection, that were needed to make possible the transition from a geocentric to a heliocentric world-picture. What was needed above all was an increased capacity in men for self-detachment in thought. Scientific modes of thought cannot be developed and become generally accepted unless people renounce their primary, unreflecting, and spontaneous attempt to understand all their experience in terms of its purpose and meaning for themselves. The development that led to more adequate knowledge and increasing control of nature was therefore, considered from one aspect, also a development toward greater self-control by men.

It is not possible to go into more detail here about the connections between the development of the scientific manner of acquiring knowledge of objects, on the one hand, and the development of new attitudes of men toward themselves, new personality structures, and especially shifts in the direction of greater affect control and self-detachment, on the other. Perhaps it will contribute to an understanding of these problems if one recalls the spontaneous, unreflecting self-centeredness of thought that can be observed at any time among children in our own society. A heightened control of the affects, developed in society and learned by the individual, and above all a heightened degree of autonomous affect control, was needed in order for the world-picture centered on the earth and the people living on it to be overcome by one which, like the heliocentric world-picture, agreed better with the observable facts but was at first far less satisfying emotionally; for it removed man from his position at the center of the universe and placed him on one of many planets circling about the center. The transition from an understanding of nature legitimized by a traditional faith to one based on scientific research, and the shift in the direction of greater affect control that this transition involved, thus represents one aspect of the civilizing process examined from other aspects in the following study.

But at that particular stage in the development of these more object-related than self-related conceptual instruments for exploring extra-human nature, it was apparently not possible to include in the investigation, and to reflect upon, this civilizational shift itself, the move toward stronger and more 'internalized' self-control that was taking place within man himself. What was happening to human beings as they increased their under-standing of nature remained at first inaccessible to scientific insight. It is not a little characteristic of this stage of self-consciousness that the classical theories of knowledge representing it are concerned far more with the problems of the object of knowledge than with the subject of knowledge, with object-perception than with self-perception. But if the latter is not included from the start in posing epistemological problems, then this very posing leads to an impasse of equally inadequate alternatives.

The development of the idea that the earth circles round the sun in a purely mechanical way in accordance with natural laws – that is, in a way not in the least determined by any purpose relating to mankind, and therefore no longer possessing any great emotional significance for men – presupposed and demanded at the same time a development in human beings themselves toward increased emotional control, a greater restraint of their spontaneous feeling that everything they experience and everything that concerns them takes its stamp from them, is the expression of an intention, a destiny, a purpose relating to themselves. Now, in the age that we call 'modern,' men reach a stage of self-detachment that enables them to conceive of natural processes as an autonomous sphere operating without intention or purpose or destiny in a purely mechanical or causal way, and having a meaning or purpose for themselves only if they are in a position, through objective knowledge, to control it and thereby give it a meaning and a purpose. But at this stage they are not yet able to detach themselves sufficiently from themselves to make their own self-detachment, their own affect restraint – in short, the conditions of their own role as the subject of the scientific understanding of nature – the object of knowledge and scientific enquiry.

Herein lies one of the keys to the question of why the problem of scientific knowledge took on the form of classical European epistemology familiar today. The detachment of the thinking subject from his objects in the act of cognitive thought, and the affective restraint that is demanded, did not appear to those thinking about it at this stage as an act of distancing but as a distance actually present, as an eternal condition of spatial separation between a mental apparatus apparently locked 'inside' man, an 'understanding' or 'reason,' and the objects 'outside' and divided from it by an invisible wall.

If we saw earlier how ideals can turn unawares in thought into something actually existing, how 'ought' becomes 'is,' we are here confronted with a reification of a different kind. The act of conceptual distancing from the objects of thought that any more emotionally controlled reflection involves – which scientific observations and thought demand in particular, and which at the same time makes them possible – appears to self-perception at this stage as a distance actually existing between the thinking subject and the objects of his thought. And the greater restraint of affect-charged impulses in the face of the objects of thought and observation, which accompanies every step toward increased conceptual distancing, appears here in people's self-perception as an actually existing cage which separates and excludes the 'self' or 'reason' or 'existence,' depending on the point of view, from the world 'outside' the individual.

[. . .]

That is the core of the structural change and the structural peculiarities of the individual which are reflected in self-perception, from about the Renaissance onward, in the notion of the individual 'ego' in its locked case, the 'self' divided by an invisible wall from what happens 'outside.' It is these civilizational self-controls, functioning in part automatically, that are now experienced in individual self-perception as a wall, either between 'subject' and 'object' or between one's own 'self' and other people ('society').

[. . .]

We thus come somewhat closer to the center of the structure of the individual personality underlying the self-experience of *homo clausus*. If we ask once again what really gives rise to this concept of the individual as encapsulated 'inside' himself, severed from everything existing outside him, and what the capsule and the encapsulated really stand for in human terms, we can now see the direction in which the answer must be sought. The firmer, more comprehensive and uniform restraint of the affects characteristic of this civilizational shift, together with the increased internal compulsions that, more implacably than before, prevent all spontaneous impulses from manifesting themselves directly and motorically in action, without the intervention of control mechanisms – these are what is experienced as the capsule, the invisible wall dividing the 'inner world' of the individual from the 'external world' or, in different versions, the subject of cognition from its object, the 'ego' from the 'other,' the 'individual' from 'society.' What is encapsulated are the restrained instinctual and affective impulses denied direct access to the motor apparatus. They appear in self-perception as what is hidden from all others, and often as the true self, the core of individuality. The term 'the inner man' is a convenient metaphor, but it is a metaphor that misleads.

There is good reason for saying that the human brain is situated within the skull and the heart within the rib cage. In these cases we can say clearly what is the container and what is contained, what is located within walls and what outside, and of what the dividing walls consist. But if the same figures of speech are applied to personality structures they become inappropriate. The relation of instinct controls to instinctive impulses, to mention only one example, is not a spatial relationship. The former do not have the form of a vessel containing the latter within it. There are schools of thought that consider the control mechanisms, conscience or reason, as more important, and there are others which attach greater importance to instinctual or emotional impulses. But if we are not disposed to argue about values, if we restrict our efforts to the investigation of what is, we find that there is no structural feature of man that justifies our calling one thing the core of man and another the shell. Strictly speaking, the whole complex of tensions, such as feeling and thought, or spontaneous behavior and controlled behavior, consists of human activities. If instead of the usual substance-concepts like 'feeling' and 'reason' we use activity-concepts, it is easier to understand that while the image of 'outside' and 'inside,' of the shell of a receptacle containing something inside it, is applicable to the physical aspects of a human being mentioned above, it cannot apply to the structure of the personality, to the living human being as a whole. On this level there is nothing that resembles a container – nothing that could justify metaphors like that of the 'inside' of a human being. The intuition of a wall, of something 'inside' man separated from the 'outside' world, however genuine it may be as an intuition, corresponds to nothing in man having the character of a real wall. One recalls that Goethe once expressed the idea that nature has neither core nor shell and that in her there is neither inside nor outside. This is true of human beings as well.

[. . .]

[. . .] So long as the concept of the individual is linked with the self-perception of the 'ego' in a closed case, we can hardly conceive 'society' as anything other than a collection of windowless monads. Concepts like 'social structure,' 'social process,' or 'social development' then appear at best as artificial products of sociologists, as 'ideal-typical' constructions needed by scientists to introduce some order, at least in thought, into what appears in reality to be a completely disordered and structureless accumulation of absolutely independent individual agents.

As can be seen, the actual state of affairs is the exact converse. The notion of individuals deciding, acting, and 'existing' in absolute independence of one another is an artificial product of men which is characteristic of a particular stage in the development of their self-perception. It rests partly on a confusion of ideals and facts, and partly on a reification of individual self-control mechanisms – of the severance of individual affective impulses from the motor apparatus, from the direct control of bodily movements and actions.

This self-perception in terms of one's own isolation, of the invisible wall dividing one's own 'inner' self from all the people and things 'outside,' takes on for a large number of people in the course of the modern age the same immediate force of conviction that the movement of the sun around an earth situated at the center of the cosmos possessed in the Middle Ages. Like the geocentric picture of the physical universe earlier, the egocentric image of the social universe is certainly capable of being conquered by a more realistic, if emotionally less appealing picture. The emotion may or may not remain: it is an open question how far the feeling of isolation and alienation is attributable to ineptitude and ignorance in the development of individual self-controls, and how far to structural characteristics of advanced societies. Just as the public predominance of emotionally less appealing images of a physical universe not centered on the earth did not entirely efface the more private self-centered experience of the sun as circling around the earth, the ascendancy of a more objective image of man in public thinking may not necessarily efface the more private ego-centered experience of an invisible wall dividing one's own 'inner world' from the world 'outside.' But it is certainly not impossible to dislodge this experience, and the image of man corresponding to it, from its self-evident acceptance in research in the human sciences. Here and in what follows one can see at least the beginnings of an image of man that agrees better with unhindered observations of human beings, and for this reason facilitates access to problems which, like those of the civilizing process or the state-building process, remain more or less inaccessible from the standpoint of the old image of man, or which, like the problem of the relation of individuals to society, continually give rise from that standpoint to unnecessarily complicated and never entirely convincing solutions.

The image of man as a 'closed personality' is here replaced by the image of man as an 'open personality' who possesses a greater or lesser degree of relative (but never absolute and total) autonomy vis-à-vis other people and who is, in fact, fundamentally oriented toward and dependent on other people throughout his life. The network of interdependencies among human beings is what binds them together. Such interdependencies are the nexus of what is here called the figuration, a structure of mutually oriented and dependent people. Since people are more or less dependent on each other first by nature and then through social learning, through education, socialization, and socially generated reciprocal needs, they exist, one might venture to say, only as pluralities, only in figurations. That is why, as was stated earlier, it is not particularly fruitful to conceive of men in the image of the individual man. It is more appropriate to envisage an image of numerous interdependent people forming figurations (i.e., groups or societies of different kinds) with each other. Seen from this basic standpoint, the rift in the traditional image of man disappears. The concept of the figuration has been introduced precisely because it expresses what we call 'society' more clearly and unambiguously than the existing conceptual tools of sociology, as neither an abstraction of attributes of individuals existing without a society, nor a 'system' or 'totality' beyond individuals, but the network of interdependencies formed by individuals. It is certainly quite possible to speak of a social system formed of individuals. But the undertones associated with the concept of the social system in contemporary sociology make such an expression seem forced. Furthermore, the concept of the system is prejudiced by the associated notion of immutability.

What is meant by the concept of the figuration can be conveniently explained by reference to social dances. They are, in fact, the simplest example that could be chosen. One should think of a mazurka, a minuet, a polonaise, a tango, or rock 'n'roll. The image of the mobile figurations of interdependent people on a dance floor perhaps makes it easier to imagine states, cities, families, and also capitalist, communist, and feudal systems as figurations. By using this concept we can eliminate the antithesis, resting finally on different values and ideals, immanent today in the use of the words 'individual' and 'society.' One can certainly speak of a dance in general, but no one will imagine a dance as a structure outside the individual or as a mere abstraction. The same dance figurations can certainly be danced by different people; but without a plurality of reciprocally oriented and dependent individuals, there is no dance. Like every other social figuration, a dance figuration is relatively independent of the specific individuals forming it here and now, but not of individuals as such. It would be absurd to say that dances are mental constructions abstracted from observations of individuals considered separately. The same applies to all other figurations. Just as the small dance figurations change – becoming now slower, now quicker – so too, gradually or more suddenly, do the large figurations which we call societies. The following study is concerned with such changes. Thus, the starting point of the study of the process of state formation is a figuration made up of numerous relatively small social units existing in free competition with one another. The investigation shows how and why this figuration changes. It demonstrates at the same time that there are explanations which do not have the character of causal explanations. For a change in a figuration is explained partly by the endogenous dynamic of the figuration itself, the immanent tendency of a figuration of freely competing units to form monopolies. The investigation therefore shows how in the course of centuries the original figuration changes into another, in which such great opportunities of monopoly power are linked with a single social position – kingship – that no occupant of any other social position within the network of interdependencies can compete with the monarch. At the same time, it indicates how the personality structures of human beings also change in conjunction with such figurational changes. [. . .]

23

The biographical illusion   **Pierre Bourdieu**

This chapter, originally published as 'L'illusion biographique', *Actes de la recherche en sciences sociales*, 62/3 (1986), pp. 69– 72, is taken from *Working Papers and Proceedings of the Centre for Psychosocial Studies*, ed. R.J. Parmentier and G. Urban (1987), pp. 1–7. It was translated by Yves Winkin and Wendy Leeds–Hurwitz.

'Life history' is one of those common-sense notions which has been smuggled into the learned universe, first with little noise among anthropologists, then more recently, and with a lot of noise, among sociologists. To speak of 'life history' implies the not insignificant presupposition that life is a history. As in Maupassant's title *Une Vie* (*A Life*), a life is inseparably the sum of the events of an individual existence seen as a history and the narrative of that history. That is precisely what common sense, or everyday language, tells us: life is like a path, a road, a track, with crossroads (Hercules between vice and virtue), pitfalls, even ambushes (Jules Romain speaks of successive ambushes of competitions and examinations). Life can also be seen as a progression, that is, a way that one is clearing and has yet to clear, a trip, a trajectory, a *cursus*, a passage, a voyage, a directed journey, a unidirectional and linear move ('mobility'), consisting of a beginning ('entering into life'), various stages, and an end, understood both as a termination and as a goal ('He will make his way,' meaning he will succeed, he will have a fine career). This way of looking at a life implies tacit acceptance of the philosophy of history as a series of historical events (*Geschichte*) which is implied in the philosophy of history as an historical narrative (*Historie*), or briefly, implied in a theory of the narrative. An historian's narrative is indiscernible from that of a novelist in this context, especially if the narration is biographical or autobiographical.

Without pretending to exhaustiveness, we can try to unravel some of the presuppositions of this theory. First, the fact that 'life' is a whole, a coherent and finalized whole, which can and must be seen as the unitary expression of a subjective and objective 'intention' of a project. In that respect, Sartre's notion of 'original project' simply states explicitly that which is implied in the expressions used in ordinary biographies ('already,' 'from now on,' 'since his earliest days,') or in 'life histories' ('always,' as in: 'I have always liked music'). This life is organized as a history, and unfolds according to a chronological order which is also a logical order, with a beginning, an origin (both in the sense of a starting point and of a principle, a *raison d'être*, a primal force), and a termination, which is also a goal.

The narrative, whether biographical or autobiographical, for example the discourse of the interviewee who 'opens up' to an interviewer, offers events which may not all or always unfold in their strict chronological succession (anybody who has ever collected life histories knows that informants constantly lose the thread of strict chronological order) but which nevertheless tend or pretend to get organized into sequences linked to each other on the basis of intelligible relationships. The subject and the object of the biography (the interviewer and interviewee) have in a sense the same interest in accepting the *postulate of the meaning* of narrated existence (and, implicitly, of all existence). So we may assume that the autobiographical narrative is always at least partially motivated by a concern to give meaning, to rationalize, to show the inherent logic, both for the past and for the future, to make consistent and constant, through the creation of intelligible relationships, like that of the cause (immediate or final) and effect between successive states, which are thus turned into *steps* of a necessary development. (And the more the interviewees have an interest, varying in relation to their social position and trajectory, in the biographical enterprise, the more do they have an interest in coherence and necessity.)[1] This inclination toward making oneself the ideologist of one's own life, through the selection of a few significant events with a view to elucidating an overall purpose, and through the creation of causal or final links between them which will make them coherent, is reinforced by the biographer who is naturally inclined, especially through his formation as a professional interpreter, to accept this artificial creation of meaning.

Significantly enough, the structure of the novel as a linear narrative was dropped at the time when the vision of life as an unfolding strip, both in terms of meaning and direction, was brought into question. This double break, symbolized by Faulkner's novel, *The Sound and the Fury*, is clearly expressed in the definition of life as anti-history that Shakespeare offers at the end of Macbeth: 'it is a tale told by an idiot, full of sound and fury, signifying nothing.'

To produce a life history or to consider life as a history, that is, as a coherent narrative of a significant and directed sequence of events, is perhaps to conform to a rhetorical illusion, to the common representation of existence that a whole literary tradition has always and still continues to reinforce. This is why it is logical to ask help from those who have had to break with this tradition on the very ground of its exemplary accomplishment. As Alain Robbe-Grillet indicates, 'The advent of the modern novel is precisely tied to this discovery: reality is discontinuous, formed of elements juxtaposed without reason; each of these elements is unique, and all the more difficult to grasp because more continue to appear, unpredictable, untimely, and at random.'[2]

The invention of a new mode of literary expression reveals *a contrario* the arbitrariness of the traditional representation of the discourse of the novel as a coherent and integrative history of the philosophy of existence which is implied by this rhetorical convention. Nothing necessitates the adoption of this philosophy of existence which, for some of its originators, is inseparable from this rhetorical revolution,[3] but in any case one cannot evade the question of the social mechanisms which favor or permit the ordinary experience of life as a unity and a totality. Indeed, how to answer within the limits of sociology the old empirical question on the existence of a self irreducible to the rhapsody of individual sensations? Without doubt one can find in the habitus the active principle, irreducible to passive perceptions, of the unification of the practices and of the representations (that is the historically constituted equivalent, hence, historically situated, of this self of which, according to Kant, one must postulate the existence in order to account for the synthesis of the various sensations given through intuition, and for the liaison of representations in a consciousness). But this practical identity reveals itself to intuition only in the inexhaustible series of its successive manifestations, in such a way that the only manner of apprehending it as such consists perhaps in attempting to recapture it in the unity of an integrative narrative (as allowed by the different, more or less institutionalized, forms of the 'speaking of oneself,' confidence, etc.).

The social world, which tends to identify normality with identity understood as the constancy to oneself of a responsible being that is predictable, or at least intelligible, in the way of a well-constructed history (as opposed to a history told by an idiot), has available all sorts of institutions of integration and unification of the self. The most evident of these institutions is of course the proper name, which as 'rigid designator,' to use Kripke's expression, 'designates the same object in every possible world,' that is concretely, in different states of the same social field (diachronic constancy) or in different fields at the same time (synchronic unity beyond the multiplicity of occupied positions).[4] And Ziff, who describes the proper name as 'a fixed point in a turning world,' is right to see 'baptismal rites' as the required way of assigning an identity.[5] Through this quite remarkable form of *nomination* constituted by the proper name, a constant and durable social identity is instituted which guarantees the identity of the biological individual in all possible fields where he appears as *agent*, that is in all his possible life histories. The proper name 'Marcel Dassault' is, along with the biological individuality for which it represents, the socially instituted form, that which assures constancy through time, and unity through the social spaces of the different social *agents* who are the manifestation of this individual in the different fields: the businessman, the publisher, the official, the film producer, etc. It is not by chance that the signature, *signum authenticum*, which authenticates the identity, is the legal condition of transfers from one field to another, that is from one agent to another, of properties held by the same instituted individual. As an institution, the proper name is independent of time and space and the variations according to time and place; in that way it offers to the designated individual, beyond all biological or social changes, the nominal constant, the identity in the sense of self-identity, *constantia sibi*, required by the social order. And one understands that in many social universes, the most sacred duties to oneself take the form of duties towards one's proper name (always to some extent also a common name, a *family name* made specific by a first name). The proper name is the visible affirmation of the identity of its bearer across time and social space, the basis of the unity of one's successive manifestations, and of the socially accepted possibilities of integrating these manifestations in official records, curriculum vitae, *cursus honorum*, police record, obituary, or biography, which constitute life as a finite sum through the verdict given in a temporary or final reckoning. 'Rigid designator,' the proper name is the form *par excellence* of the arbitrary imposition operated by the rites of institution, the attribution of a name and classification introduce clear-cut, absolute divisions, indifferent to circumstances and to individual accidents, amidst shifting biological and social realities. This is why the proper name cannot describe properties and conveys no information about that which it names; since what it designates is only a composite and disparate rhapsody of biological and social properties undergoing constant flux, all descriptions are valid only within the limits of a specific stage or place. In other words, it can only attest to the identity of the *personality*, as socially constituted individuality, at the price of an enormous abstraction. This is exemplified in the unusual usage that Proust made of the proper name preceded by the definite article ('the Swann of Buckingham Palace,' 'the then Albertine,' 'the rainy-day raincoated Albertine'), a complex figure through which are presented both the 'sudden revelation of a multiple fractured subject,' and the permanence beyond the plurality of worlds of the identity socially assigned by a proper name.[6]

So the proper name is the support (one would be tempted to say the substance) of social identity (what is called *l'état civil* in French), that is the support of the set of properties (nationality, sex, age, etc.) attached to persons to whom the civil law associates legal effects, which are *instituted* under the appearance of a mere record by the acts of social identity. The proper name is the product of the initial rite of institution which marks access to social existence. So the proper name is the true object of all successive rites of institution or nomination, through which the social identity is constructed. These acts of *attribution*, often public and cere-monial, are operated under the control and with the warrant of the State. There are also rigid designations (that is valid for all possible worlds) which develop a true *official description* of this kind of social essence, transcending historical fluctuations, which the social order institutes through the proper name. Indeed all these acts rest on the postulate of the constancy of the name, which is presupposed by all acts of nomination and more generally by all legal acts involving a long term future, be they *certificates* guaranteeing irreversibly a capacity (or an incapacity), contracts involving a distant future, like credit contracts or insurance policies, or penal sanctions (since any condemnation presupposes the affirmation of the identity of the one who committed the crime and received the punishment across time).[7]

All this leads us to believe that the life history draws closer to the official presentation of the official model of the self (identity card, civil record, curriculum vitae, official biography) and to the philosophy of identity which underlies it, as one draws closer to official interrogations in official inquiries – the limit of which is the judicial inquiry or police investigation – at the same time drawing away from the intimate exchanges between very close friends and from the logic of the secret which are current in these protected markets. The laws which govern the production of discourses in the relation between a habitus and a market apply to this particular form of expression which is the discourse on oneself; and the life history will vary, as much in its form as in its content, according to the social quality of the market on which it will be offered – the situation of the inquiry itself inevitably helping to determine the discourse recorded. But the proper object of this discourse, that is the *public* presentation, thus the officialization, of a *private* representation of one's life, implies an excess of constraints and specific censures (the legal sanctions against the usurpations of identity or the illegal wearing of medals represent the limit of this). And all this permits us to suppose that the laws of official biography will tend to impose themselves quite beyond official situations. This occurs through unconscious assumptions about the interview (like the concern for chronology, and all that which is inherent in the representation of life as history), and through the interview situation which, depending upon the objective distance between the interviewer and the interviewee and the ability of the interviewer to 'manipulate' this relationship, will move from this mild form of official interrogation (which is most often, without the knowledge of the sociologist, sociological inquiry), right to the secret, moving through the more or less conscious representation that the one queried will make of the situation of inquiry. This representation will be based on the interviewee's direct or indirect experience of equivalent situations (interview of a famous writer, or politician, examinations taken, etc.), and these will direct all his efforts to presentation of self, or rather, to production of self.

The critical analysis of the social processes, badly analyzed and badly mastered, that function without the researcher's awareness and with his complicity, in the construction of this kind of socially irreproachable artifact which is the 'life history,' and in particular in the privilege accorded to the longitudinal succession of constituent events of life considered as history in comparison with the social space in which they are carried out, is not an end in itself. It leads to constructing the notion of *trajectory* as a series of successively occupied positions by the same agent (or the same group) in a space which itself is constantly evolving and which is subject to incessant transformations. Trying to understand a life as a unique and self-sufficient series of successive events (sufficient unto itself), and without ties other than the association to a 'subject' whose constancy is probably just that of a proper name, is nearly as absurd as trying to make sense out of a subway route without taking into account the network structure, that is the matrix of objective relations between the different stations. The biographical events are defined as just so many *investments* and *moves* in social space, or more precisely, in the different successive states of the distribution structure of the different types of capital which are in play in the field considered. The understanding of movements leading from one position to another (from one professional post to another, from one publishing house to another, from one bishopric to another, etc.) is defined, from all the evidence, in the objective relation between the significance and the value of these positions within a directed space at the time they are considered. In other words, one can understand a trajectory (that is, the *social aging* which is independent of the biological aging although it inevitably accompanies it) only on condition of having previously constructed the successive states of the field through which the trajectory has progressed. Thus the collection of objective relations link the agent considered – at least in a certain number of pertinent states – to the collection of other agents engaged in the same field and facing the same realm of possibilities. This preliminary construction is also the condition of all rigorous evaluation of that which can be called the *social surface*, as rigorous description of the *personality* designated by the proper name, that is, the collections of positions simultaneously occupied at a given moment of time by a biological individual socially instituted, acting as support to a collection of attributes suitable for allowing him to intervene as an efficient agent in different fields.[8]

The necessity of this *detour* through the construction of space seems so evident as soon as it is stated – who would think to recall a trip without having an idea of the landscape in which it took place? – that one would have difficulty understanding why it is not imposed immediately on all researchers if one did not know that the individual, the person, the self ('the most irreplaceable of beings' as Gide used to say), towards which a socially reinforced narcissistic drive carries us, is also the seemingly most real of realities, the *ens realissimum*, immediately freed to our fascinated intuition, *intuitus personae*.

Notes

1   F. Muel-Dreyfus, *Le metier d'educateur* (Paris, Editions de Minuit, 1983).
2   A. Robbe-Grillet, *Le miroir qui revient* (Paris, Editions de Minuit, 1984), p. 208.
3   'All that which is real is just fragmentary, fleeting, useless, so accidental even, and so specific, that every event appears as gratuitous and all existence in the final analysis as

deprived of the least unifying signification' (Robbe-Grillet, *Le miroir*, p. 208).

4   S. Kripke, *Naming and Necessity* (Cambridge, MA, Harvard University Press, 1982), p. 48; also P. Engel, *Identité et référence* (Paris, Pens, 1985).

5   P. Ziff, *Semantic Analysis* (Ithaca, NY, Cornell University Press, 1960), pp. 102–4.

6   E. Nicole, 'Personnage et rhétorique du nom', *Poétique*, 46 (1981), pp. 200–16.

7   The strictly biological dimension of the individuality (that the civil status recognizes under the form of *description* and the identification photograph) has undergone variation according to time and place, that is, the social spaces make it a much less firm base than the pure nominal definition. On the variations of the bodily hexis according to social space, see S. Maresca, 'La représentation de la paysannerie: remarques ethnographiques sur le travail de représentation des dirigeants agricoles', *Actes de la recherche en sciences sociales*, 38 (May 1981), pp. 3–18.

8   The distinction between the concrete individual and the constructed individual, the efficient agent, goes hand in hand with the distinction between the agent, efficient in a field, and *personality*, as biological individuality socially instituted by nomination and bearer of properties and powers which assure him (in some cases) a *social surface*, namely, the capacity to exist as an agent in different fields. This gives rise to a number of problems normally ignored especially in statistical treatment: it is in this way, for example, that surveys of 'elites' will cause the question of a social surface to disappear in characterizing multiple position individuals by one of their properties considered dominant or determinant, thus placing the industrial manager who is also a publisher in the category of managers, etc. (In effect, this eliminates from the fields of cultural production all the producers whose principal activity is situated in other fields, allowing certain properties of the field to escape.)

24

A note on 'status'   **T.H. Marshall**

The purpose of this note [. . .] is to protest against the growing abuse of a potentially very valuable word. I say 'abuse' rather than 'misuse', because the latter would imply the breach of a linguistic canon, and I would not claim that any such canon exists today. But 'abuse' refers to mishandling of the kind that damages and eventually destroys. We can recognize it by its results, without having to lay down the law as to which usage is correct and which incorrect. If a word is being tossed around in such an irresponsible way that no consistent meaning remains to it and it is losing its value as a tool of exact thought, then obviously something is wrong.

The fault does not lie in the concept itself, for that is something with which we cannot dispense. It needs to be refined and sub-divided, but it cannot be abandoned. It has a part of special importance to play in social theory and that is why the abuse of the term, which threatens to make it unusable, is so serious. Status provides the link between the structural study of social systems and the psychological study of personality and motivation. [. . .]

[. . .] The basic unit of social systems, says [Talcott] Parsons, is the act. The next unit of higher order is the status-role. A person's status is 'his place in the relationship system considered as a structure, that is a patterned system of parts'. Thirdly, the actor himself is a unit of the social system. In this sense he is 'a composite bundle of statuses and roles. But this social actor must be distinguished from the personality as itself a system of action.'[1] Personality cannot be subsumed under status, but status is, as it were, the lowest *common* denominator in the analysis of both structure and personality. In the composite book, A *General Theory of Action*, Samuel A. Stouffer stresses this point of linkage, when he writes: 'One of the significant ideas in the system outlined in this volume is the

This chapter is taken from *Class, Citizenship and Social Development* (Chicago, University of Chicago Press, 1977), pp. 220–9.

concept of role. This is not a new concept, but its possible utility in unifying personality and societal theory has perhaps not before been seen so clearly.[2]

But Stouffer, in this context, refers to role rather than to status, and so does Henry A. Murray in a similar but more elaborate (and very confused) passage a few pages earlier in the same volume.[3] This fact may serve to introduce the first danger to which the term 'status' is exposed – the danger of being swallowed up by 'role' and then pocketed by those psychologists who regard 'role' as their private property. T.M. Newcomb is not one of these; he is scrupulously careful to retain the distinction between the structural and the personal. Using the word 'position' in lieu of 'status', he writes: 'The ways of behaving which are expected of any individual who occupies a certain position constitute the role associated with that position';[5] and then: 'roles and prescribed roles, therefore, are not concepts which refer to the actual behaviour of any given individual. Role behaviour, on the other hand, does refer to the actual behaviour of specific individuals as they take roles.'[6] And, very naturally, role behaviour, and the taking and playing of roles by individuals in certain circumstances is of the very greatest interest to social psychologists. There is consequently a tendency to forget the starting-point; 'role' comes to be used for 'role behaviour'; from this, which still relates to behaviour adjusted to a specific role, one can easily pass to the total behaviour of an individual while occupying a role. For example, if we consider the status of father, we can see three levels at which the term role might be applied: (1) the behaviour expected of fathers in that particular society; (2) the behaviour adopted by Mr X (consciously or unconsciously) in playing the role of father; (3) the total behaviour of Mr X in so far as it enters into his relationships as father. For instance, Mr X may have developed various oddities of behaviour before he married – personal peculiarities of speech, dress or manner, which persist and become for his children symbols of 'father' and important ingredients in the child–father situation. But such action is not part of the role nor of the role behaviour, and has no immediate reference to social structure. If, therefore, 'role' is carried off into this area of exploration of unique personality problems, and drags status with it, then status will lose its value as a bridge between social structure and personality studies, because it will have been wholly uprooted from the soil of structure.

Although confusion between role, role behaviour and total behaviour is clearly to be condemned, it is possible to make a case for the merging of status with role. It will be remembered that Linton, to whom most writers refer as the author of the modern terminology, said that role 'represents the dynamic aspect of a status' and that the distinction was 'only of academic interest'.[7] And Parsons, as we have seen, links the two with a hyphen. The main argument for the merger is that a status, conceived as a position in a social system, can be imagined only in terms of relationships, and the substance of social relationships is expected behaviour – or in the famous words of Max Weber (Parsons' translation) a 'social relationship thus consists entirely and exclusively in the existence of a probability that there will be, in some meaningfully understandable sense, a course of social action'.[8] It can be argued, therefore, that if the dynamic aspect of status is removed, nothing is left except a fallacious conception of a position in a social system as a static objective thing. Certainly the temptation to fallacious reification is present; but it is present whenever one thinks about social structure at all, and it should be possible to resist it. Status leans towards structural analysis and a high level of abstraction, and role towards individual behaviour and concrete situations. If this is kept clear, then 'role' can, with appropriate qualifying adjectives, be used in the study of unique personality problems, provided it keeps a firm grasp of the hand of status, which must remain planted on the other side of the fence. Briefly put, status emphasizes the position, as conceived by the group or society that sustains it, and role emphasizes the person who occupies the position. Status emphasizes the fact that expectations (of a normative kind) exist in the relevant social groups, while role emphasizes the items which make up the behaviour that is expected. Status is your idea of the plant whose seeds you are sowing, and role is the picture on the seed-packets.

It must be admitted that the apparent need for both terms is sometimes due to slovenly thinking. We may say, for instance, that we know what a policeman is (status), but have a very imperfect idea of what he does (role). This distinction is not legitimate because status should be as precise a concept as role. It should embrace all that distinguishes the position as an element in social structure, whether the facts are known to the general public or not. The slovenly use described above will, if permitted, lead to a concept of status as the meaning attached to a position by other members of the society in general; this is then translated into something like 'the popular assessment' of the position, and soon 'status' is (as we shall see) hopelessly confused with 'social status', 'rank' and 'rating'.

What has just been said does not imply that 'status' cannot be used at different levels of generalization, and therefore with differing completeness of attributes or contents. For instance, we may discuss the status of father in the upper middle classes of twentieth-century England, or we may speak of father-status as something found in all human societies. In the latter case the breadth of generalization is made possible by the paucity of attributes included in the definition of the concept. But at each level of generalization there is a role corresponding to the status. However, because (as noted above) role leans towards individual behaviour and concrete situations, we may find ourselves saying, for example, that 'the father-status is found in both societies X and Y, but the father-role is different in the two'. But if the latter part of the sentence is true, then the father-status, at the more restricted level of generalization, must also differ.

Undoubtedly the retention of the two concepts has its disadvantages. But the advantages are considerable and, I think, outweigh them. I have already spoken of the major advantage, that 'status' is less likely than 'role' to become detached from the structural side of the picture and carried off into the territory of personality-studies. Another advantage is that the use of the two terms enables us to distinguish between role and one of the meanings of function. Because status stands as a link between structure and the individual, therefore it has two dynamic aspects, one relating to structure and the other to the individual. The function of a status is the part it plays in the system of social structure, its role is the action on the part of its individual occupant which enables this function to be performed. The distinction is important, and is missed by Murray in the passage referred to above, where he first identifies 'group' with 'social system' and 'role' with 'function', and then refers to respiration and excretion as roles of the 'self-and-body', and to hierarchical organization and the recruitment and training of new members as 'social roles' of the group.[9] The retention of 'status', and the attachment of 'role' firmly to it, might help to prevent confusions of this kind.

Let us, then, retain the concept of status to denote a position in a social system. Parsons calls it 'a place in the relationship system'; Linton, after using a similar phrase, adds that it is 'simply a collection of rights and duties'.[10] This suggests my second point, that the popular emphasis on role and expected behaviour (without it being specified who 'expects') has caused one of the earliest uses of the word 'status' to fall gradually into disuse. I refer to the lawyer's use, illustrated by Maine's famous dictum about the movement of progressive societies 'from Status to Contract'.[11] The most positive rejection of this use comes from Benoît-Smullyan who calls it 'an older usage' which is 'no longer popular', – and is 'defective' because it presupposes a complex society.[12] Why a usage should be rejected because it is old, or deemed defective because it applies to relatively complex societies, is not clear. In reality the usage is valuable, and even necessary. C.K. Allen defines status as 'the condition of belonging to a particular class of persons to whom the law assigns peculiar legal capacities or incapacities, or both'.[13] The concept is a legal one, and sociologists are quite right to extend it, but the extension need not cause us to abandon the older meaning or even to lose sight of the significant difference between it and the extended meaning. The extension from legally established capacities and incapacities to socially recognized rights and duties and so to socially expected behaviour within the frame of specified relationships is perfectly natural and proper. But the concept of legal status need not be discarded, nor the distinction between it and what sociologists mean by plain 'status' ignored. It is a matter of very great importance to know whether the power of an upper class is based on legally enforceable rights or not, and whether labourers have the legal status of slaves or not. It is impossible to make comparative studies of the family if one does not pay attention to the shifting borderline between the legal rights and the socially approved and expected conduct of the husband–father or the wife–mother. Let us, then, retain the 'older usage', but bow to necessity and attach the adjective 'legal' to the noun 'status' when we wish to make use of it.

My third and last point relates to the confusion between status on the one hand and social status and ranking on the other. 'Status', as used by Linton, Parsons and others, has no direct or necessary reference to position on a scale or in a hierarchy. It embraces all relationships, not only those of superiority and inferiority. But 'social status' is now in general use to denote position in the hierarchy of social prestige. It is in effect very nearly what Linton meant by 'the status' of an individual (as distinct from 'a status' occupied by many individuals) and he described it as 'the sum total of all the statuses which he occupies'.[14] The hypothesis that there is a 'general status' which is the sum total of all special statuses was investigated by Hyman, whose results appeared to support it.[15] I find it impossible to do the required sum. How do you add together, for instance, doctor, father, councillor, wicket-keeper, church warden and husband to get a unitary result? But, although these statuses cannot be added up, they all contribute to the determination of social status, which is the position of the individual (envisaged in his totality) within the community (conceived as a social whole). Functional specialization is here pushed into the background, and it is not unreasonable to regard the superiority–inferiority dimension as entitled to appropriate to itself the use of the status concept in this setting.

But this annexation of 'social status' by the prestige scale should leave 'status' unaffected. Unfortunately this has not been the case. We can again refer to Benoît-Smullyan who states categorically that status means position in a hierarchy – economic, political or prestige.[16] And when M. Sherif cites and accepts this view without realizing that it diverges sharply from that of Linton (which he also professes to accept, though the passage he quotes from Linton as an explanation of status is in fact a comment on ascription), the results are disastrous.[17] For Sherif places the main emphasis on the hierarchical positions within groups, such as trade unions, gangs, professional bodies, universities, etc., and therefore ignores the primary concept of status as the fact of membership itself. The distinction (in England) between Harley Street specialist and country general practitioner is important, though not only in terms of hierarchy. But we must not ignore the status significance of the broader categories of professional man and doctor (which may include elements of legal status), again not only in terms of hierarchy. Then, having given this slant to the argument, and pointed out that 'the scale of status positions is a stimulus for the would-be member', Sherif proceeds to consider the relative roles attached to the statuses of father and mother. But obviously this is not a question simply of position in a hierarchy, and we can hardly imagine an individual being stimulated by status aspirations to become a father rather than a mother.

H.H. Hyman, in his important study of the psychology of status, defined status as 'the position of an individual relative to other individuals', but confined his investigation to the particular relationship of higher and lower on a scale. And when a girl's rating of her attractiveness on a scale of, say, one to ten is described as 'subjective status', it is obvious that we have moved a long way from the concept as used by Linton and Parsons. In fact it becomes clear that 'position relative to other individuals' implies only comparison, whereas 'place in the relationship system' implies interaction.

The conclusion to this note is bound to be unsatisfactory. For comparison is important as well as interaction, and hierarchical structure is not only of interest in the case of total communities to which the term 'social status' can be applied, and, though the distinction between legal and social rights is a necessary one, we must not sacrifice equally necessary distinctions in order to find words in which to speak of it. Our terminology is in a tangle, and it will take time to straighten it out. My own preference is for the retention of the term 'status' as used by Linton and Parsons, that is without any necessary reference to hierarchical position. The chief objection is that the hierarchical connotation is already so firmly attached to the word that it may be impossible to detach it. But against this are the arguments that, if we keep it, we can (1) also keep 'legal status' and go on discussing Maine's dictum; (2) retain the marriage of status and role, which may save 'role' from going to the bad from the sociologists' point of view. If we follow Newcomb and replace 'status' by 'position', I fear that the concept will lose its power and value. I would accept 'social status' for hierarchical position in a total community – but only in a community. And I would confine it to positions that are largely unstructured. Structured hierarchical positions are better referred to as 'ranks'. And 'rank' can also be used with reference to associations – e.g., army, civil service, university, etc. The chief difficulty is to find a word for hierarchical positions which are not sufficiently structured to be called ranks and which exist within associations (which precludes the use of 'social status'). I might say of a man: 'He likes his job, but is worried by his status.' Status here is local to the organization, and is not his social status, though it may influence and be influenced by it. It is not wholly structured as a position in an establishment, but includes elements of prestige, which are rather fluid. Society today is full of people who worry about their status in this sense, in the office or the village or the club and so forth. Personally, I should prefer the word 'standing' in order to preserve the more precise and technical sense of status. And where no more is meant than comparative value in terms of some allegedly measurable attribute such as intelligence or good looks or skill at tennis, I should say 'rating'.

Let us take, as a summary example, a university librarian or senior administrative officer such as registrar or bursar. His *status* differs from that of a professor, because his *role* and the *functions* of his post differ from those of a professor. But his university *rank* may be the same. He may, however, have a lower *social status* in the community at large than most professors (perhaps because of his family origins), and a rather low *rating* for intelligence or general culture or social graces. In consequence of all these factors his *standing* in the university is not quite what he would like it to be.

But I have no wish to impose a terminology on anyone. The main point is to agree as to the concepts we wish to use and the nature of the distinction between them. If we can do that, then perhaps we shall eventually agree about their names.

Notes

1   Talcott Parsons, *The Social System* (Glencoe, IL, The Free Press, 1951), pp. 24–6.
2   Samuel A. Stouffer, in *A General Theory of Action*, p. 480.
3   Henry A. Murray, in *A General Theory of Action*, p. 450.
5   T.M. Newcomb *Social Psychology*, p. 280.
6   Ibid., p. 330. The opposite view is taken by Kingsley Davis who defines role as 'the manner in which an individual actually carries out the requirements of his position', and claims (wrongly, as I believe) that in this he is following Linton ('A conceptual analysis of stratification', *American Sociological Review*, 7 (June 1942), p. 311). Marion Levy, in *The Structure of Society*, p. 158, maintains that this definition is accepted, not only by Linton, but also by Parsons. This is definitely not the case. Levy proposes to replace the terms 'status' and 'role', as allegedly used by Linton and Parsons, by 'ideal role' and 'actual role', but this would be clumsy and confusing.
7   R. Linton, *The Study of Man*, p. 114.
8   R. Linton, *The Theory of Social and Economic Organization*, p. 107.
9   Murray, in *A General Theory of Action*, p. 450.
10 Linton, op. cit., p. 113.
11 H.S. Maine, *Ancient Law* (1878), p. 170.
12 A. Benoît-Smullyan: 'Status, status types and status interrelations', *American Sociological Review*, 9 (April 1944) pp. 461.
13 C.K. Allen, *Legal Duties and Other Essays in Jurisprudence*, p. 42.
14 Linton, op. cit., p. 113.
15 H.H. Hyman: 'The psychology of status', *Archives of Psychology*, 269 (1942).
16 Benoît-Smullyan, 'Status, status-types and status interrelations', pp. 151–2.
17 M. Sherif, *An Outline of Social Psychology*, p. 297.

25

Identity, Genealogy, History   **Nikolas Rose**

[. . .]

Dimensions of our 'relation to ourselves'

A genealogy of subjectification is a genealogy of what one might term, following Michel Foucault, 'our relation to ourselves'.[1] Its field of investigation comprises the kinds of attention that humans have directed towards themselves and others in different places, spaces and times. To put this rather more grandly, one might say that this was a genealogy of 'being's relation to itself' and the technical forms that this has assumed. The human being, that is to say, is that kind of creature whose ontology is historical. And the history of human being, therefore, requires an investigation of the intellectual and practical techniques that have comprised the instruments through which being has historically constituted itself: it is a matter of analysing 'the problematizations through which being offers itself to be, necessarily, thought – and the practices on the basis of which these problematizations are formed' (Foucault, 1986a: 11; Jambet, 1992). The focus of such a genealogy, therefore, is not 'the historical construction of the self' but the history of *the relations* which human beings have established with themselves. These relations are constructed and historical, but they are not to be understood by locating them in some amorphous domain of culture. On the contrary, they are addressed from the perspective of 'government' (Foucault, 1991; cf. Burchell et al., 1991). Our relation with ourselves, that is to say, has assumed the form it has because it has been the object of a whole variety of more or less rationalized schemes, which have sought to shape our ways of understanding and enacting our existence as human

This chapter is taken from *Questions of Cultural Identity*, ed. S. Hall and P. du Gay (London, Sage, 1996), pp. 128–50.

beings in the name of certain objectives – manliness, femininity, honour, modesty, propriety, civility, discipline, distinction, efficiency, harmony, fulfilment, virtue, pleasure – the list is as diverse and heterogeneous as it is interminable.

One of the reasons for stressing this point is to distinguish my approach from a number of recent analyses that have, explicitly or implicitly, viewed changing forms of subjectivity or identity as consequences of wider social and cultural transformations – modernity, late modernity, the risk society (Bauman, 1991; Giddens, 1991; Beck, 1992; Lash and Friedman, 1992). Of course, this work continues a long tradition of narratives, stretching back at least to Jacob Burckhardt, that have written histories of the rise of the individual as a consequence of a general social transformation from tradition to modernity, feudalism to capitalism, *Gemeinschaft* to *Gesellschaft*, mechanical to organic solidarity and so forth (Burckhardt, 1990). These kinds of analysis regard changes in the ways in which human beings understand and act upon themselves as the outcome of 'more fundamental' historical events located elsewhere – in production regimes, in technological change, in alterations in demography or family forms, in 'culture'. No doubt events in each of these areas have significance in relation to the problem of subjectification. But however significant they may be, it is important to insist that such changes do not transform ways of being human by virtue of some 'experience' that they produce. Changing relations of subjectification, I want to argue, cannot be established by derivation or interpretation of other cultural or social forms. To explicitly or implicitly assume that they can is to presume the *continuity* of human beings as the subjects of history, essentially equipped with the capacity for endowing meaning (Dean, 1994). But the ways in which humans 'give meaning to experience' have their own history. Devices of 'meaning production' – grids of visualization, vocabularies, norms and systems of judgement – *produce* experience; they are not themselves *produced by* experience (Joyce, 1994). These intellectual techniques do not come ready made, they have to be invented, refined and stabilized, they have to be disseminated and implanted in different ways in different practices – schools, families, streets, workplaces, courtrooms. If we use the term 'subjectification' to designate all those heterogeneous processes and practices by means of which human beings come to relate to themselves and others as subjects of a certain type, then subjectification has its own history. And the history of subjectification is more practical, more technical and less unified than sociological accounts allow.

Thus a genealogy of subjectification would focus directly upon the *practices* within which human beings have been located in particular 'regimes of the person'. This would not be a continuous history of the self, but rather an account of the diversity of languages of 'personhood' that have taken shape – character, personality, identity, reputation, honour, citizen, individual, normal, lunatic, patient, client, husband, mother, daughter . . . – and the norms, techniques and relations of authority within which these have circulated in legal, domestic, industrial and other practices for acting upon the conduct of persons. Such an investigation might proceed along a number of linked pathways.

Problematizations

Where, how and by whom are aspects of the human being rendered problematic, according to what systems of judgement and in relation to what concerns? [. . .] [I]n the genealogy of subjectification, pride of place is not occupied by the philosophers reflecting in their studies on the nature of the person, the will, the conscience, morality and the like, but in the mundane practices where conduct has become problematic to others or the self, and in the mundane texts and programmes – on asylum management, medical treatment of women, advisable regimes of child-rearing, new ideas in workplace management, improving one's self-esteem – seeking to render these problems intelligible and, at the same time, manageable.[2]

Technologies

What means have been invented to govern the human being, to shape or fashion conduct in desired directions, and how have programmes sought to embody these in certain technical forms? The notion of technology may seem antithetical to the domain of human being, such that claims about the inappropriate technologization of humanity form the basis of many a critique. However, our very experience of ourselves as certain sorts of persons – creatures of freedom, of liberty, of personal powers, of self-realization – is the outcome of a range of human technologies, technologies that take modes of being human as their object.[3] Technology, here, refers to any assembly structured by a practical rationality governed by a more or less conscious goal. Human technologies are hybrid assemblages of knowledges, instruments, persons, systems of judgement, buildings and spaces, under-pinned at the programmatic level by certain presuppositions about, and objectives for, human beings. One can regard the school, the prison, the asylum as examples of one species of such technologies, those which Foucault termed disciplinary and which operate in terms of a detailed structuring of space, time and relations amongst individuals, through pro-cedures of hierarchical observation and normalizing judgement, through attempts to enfold these judgements into the procedures and judgements which the individual utilizes in order to conduct their own conduct (Foucault, 1977; cf. Markus, 1993 for an examination of the spatial form of such assemblies). [. . .]

Authorities

Who is accorded or claims the capacity to speak truthfully about humans, their nature and their problems, and what characterizes the truths about persons that are accorded such authority? Through which apparatuses are such authorities authorized – universities, the legal apparatus, churches, politics? To what extent does the authority of authority depend upon a claim to a positive knowledge, to wisdom and virtue, to experience and practical judgement, to the capacity to resolve conflicts? How are authorities themselves governed – by legal codes, by the market, by the protocols of bureaucracy, by professional ethics? And what then is the relation between authorities and those who are subject to them – priest/parishioner, doctor/patient, manager/employee, therapist/patient . . .? This focus upon authorities (rather than 'power'), upon all the diverse persons, things, devices, associations, modes of thought, types of judgement that seek, claim, acquire or are accorded authority, and upon the diversity of ways in which authority is authorized again seems to me to be a distinctive feature of this kind of investigation.

Teleologies

What forms of life are the aims, ideals or exemplars for these different practices for working upon persons: the professional persona exercising a vocation with wisdom and dispassion; the manly warrior pursuing a life of honour through a calculated risking of the body; the responsible father living a life of prudence and moderation; the labourer accepting his or her lot with a docility grounded in a belief in the inviolability of authority or a reward in a life to come; the good wife fulfilling her domestic duties with quiet efficiency and self-effacement; the entrepreneurial individual striving after secular improvements in 'quality of life'; the passionate lover skilled in the arts of pleasure . . .? What codes of knowledge support these ideals, and to what ethical valorization are they tied? Against those who suggest that a single model of the person comes to prominence in any specific culture, it is important to stress the heterogeneity and specificity of the ideals or model of personhood deployed in different practices, and the ways in which they are articulated in relation to specific problems and solutions concerning human conduct. It is only from this perspective, I think, that one can identify the peculiarity of those programmatic attempts to install a single model of the individual as the ethical ideal across a range of different sites and practices. For example, the Puritan sects discussed by Weber were unusual in their attempts to ensure that the mode of individual comportment in terms of sobriety, duty, modesty, self and so forth applied to practices as diverse as the enjoyment of popular entertainment, labour and comportment within the home. [. . .] But unification of subjectification has to be seen as an objective of particular programmes, or a presupposition of particular styles of thinking, not a feature of human cultures.

Strategies

How are these procedures for regulating the capacities of persons linked into wider moral, social or political objectives concerning the undesirable and desirable features of populations, workforce, family, society, etc.? Of particular significance here are the divisions and relations established between modalities for the government of conduct accorded the status of 'political', and those enacted through forms of authority and apparatus deemed non-political – whether these be the technical knowledge of experts, the judicial knowledge of the courts, the organizational knowledge of managers or the 'natural' knowledges of the family and the mother. [. . .]

The government of others and the government of oneself

Each of these directions for investigation is inspired, in large measure, by the writings of Michel Foucault. In particular, of course, they arise from Foucault's suggestions concerning a genealogy of the arts of government – where government is conceived of, most generally, as encompassing all those more or less rationalized programmes and strategies for 'the conduct of conduct' – and his conception of governmentality – which refers to the emergence of political rationalities, or mentalities of rule, where rule becomes a matter of the calculated management of the affairs of each and of all in order to achieve certain desirable objectives (Foucault, 1991; see the discussion of the notion of government in Gordon, 1991). Government, here, does not indicate a theory, but rather a certain perspective from which one might make intelligible the diversity of attempts by authorities of different sorts to act upon the actions of others in relation to objectives of national prosperity, harmony, virtue, productivity, social order, discipline, emancipation, self-realization and so forth. And this perspective is significant also because it directs our attention to the ways in which strategies for the conduct of conduct so frequently operate through trying to shape what Foucault also termed 'technologies of the self' – 'self-steering mechanisms', or the ways in which individuals experience, understand, judge and conduct themselves (Foucault, 1986a,b, 1988). Technologies of the self take the form of the elaboration of certain techniques for the conduct of one's relation with oneself, for example requiring one to relate to oneself epistemologically (know yourself), despotically (master yourself) or in other ways (care for yourself). They are embodied in particular technical practices (confession, diary writing, group discussion, the twelve-steps programme of Alcoholics Anonymous). And they are always practised under the actual or imagined authority of some system of truth and of some authoritative individual, whether these be theological and priestly, psychological and therapeutic or disciplinary and tutelary.

A number of issues arise from these considerations.

The first concerns the issue of ethics itself. In his later writings, Foucault utilized the notion of 'ethics' as a general designation for his investigations into the genealogy of our present forms of 'concern' for the self (Foucault, 1979, 1986a,b; cf. Minson, 1993). Ethical practices, for Foucault, were distinguished from the domain of morality, in that moral systems are, by and large, systems of injunction and interdiction – thou shalt do this or thou shalt not do that – and are most frequently articulated in relation to some relatively formalized code. Ethics, on the other hand, refers to the domain of practical advice as to how one should concern oneself with oneself, make oneself the subject of solicitude and attention, conduct oneself in the world of one's everyday existence. Different cultural periods, Foucault argued, differed in the respective weight that their practices for the regulation of conduct placed upon codified moral injunctions and the practical repertoires of ethical advice. However, one might undertake a genealogy of our contemporary ethical regime which, Foucault suggested, encouraged human beings to relate to themselves as the subject of a 'sexuality', and were enjoined to 'know themselves' through a hermeneutics of the self, to explore, discover, reveal and live in the light of the desires that comprised one's truth. Such a genealogy would disturb the appearance of enlightenment which clothed such a regime, by exploring the way in which certain forms of spiritual practice which could be found in Greek, Roman and early Christian ethics had become incorporated into priestly power, and later into the practices of the educational, medical and psychological type (Foucault, 1986a: 11).

Clearly the approach I have outlined above has derived much from Foucault's arguments on these issues. However, I would wish to develop this argument in a number of respects. First, as has been pointed out elsewhere, the notion of 'techniques of the self' can be somewhat misleading. The self does not form the transhistorical object of techniques for being human but only one way in which humans have been enjoined to understand and relate to themselves (Hadot, 1992). In different practices, these relations are cast in terms of individuality, character, constitution, reputation, personality and the like which are neither merely *different versions* of a self, nor do they *sum into* a self. Further, the extent to which our contemporary relation to ourselves – inwardness, self-exploration, self-fulfilment and the like – does indeed take the issue of sexuality and desire as its fulcrum must remain an open question for historical investigation. Elsewhere I have suggested that the self, itself, has become the object of valorization, a regime of subjectification in which desire has become freed from its dependence upon the law of an inner sexuality and been transformed into a variety of passions to discover and realize the identity of the self itself (Rose, 1989).

Further, I would suggest, one needs to extend an analysis of the relations between government and subjectification beyond the field of ethics, if by that one means all those styles of relating to oneself that are structured by the divisions of truth and falsity, the permitted and the forbidden. One needs to examine, also, the government of this relation along some other axes.

One of these axes concerns the attempt to inculcate a certain relation to oneself through transformations in 'mentalities' or what one might term 'intellectual techniques' – reading, memory, writing, numeracy and so forth (see, for some powerful examples, Goody and Watt, 1963; Eisenstein, 1979). [. . .]

A second axis would concern corporealities or body techniques. Of course, anthropologists and others have remarked upon the cultural shaping of bodies – comportment, expression of emotion and the like as they differ from culture to culture, and within cultures between genders, ages, status groups and the like. Marcel Mauss provides the classic account of the ways in which the body, as a technical instrument, is organized differently in different cultures – different ways of walking, sitting, digging, marching and so forth (Mauss, 1979; cf. Bourdieu, 1977). However, a genealogy of subjectification is not concerned with the general problem of the cultural relativity of bodily capacities, but with the ways in which different corporeal regimes have been devised and implanted in rationalized attempts to enjoin a particular relation to the self and to others. Norbert Elias has given many powerful examples of the ways in which explicit codes of bodily conduct – manners, etiquette and the self-monitoring of bodily functions and actions – were enjoined upon individuals in different positions within the apparatus of the court (Elias, 1983; cf. Elias, 1978; Osborne, 1996). Foucault's own studies of the asylum and the prison explore programmes in which the disciplining of the body of the pathological individual not only involved the catching up of that body within an external regime of hierarchical surveillance and normalizing judgement, and the imbrication of the body in a molecular regime governing movement in time and space, but also sought to enjoin an internal relation between the pathological individual and his or her body, in which bodily comportment would both manifest and maintain a certain disciplined mastery exercised by the person over themselves (Foucault, 1967, 1977; see also Smith, 1992 for a history of the notion of 'inhibition' and its relation to the manifestation of steadfastness and self-mastery through the exercise of control over the body). [. . .] Historians of gender have begun to analyse the ways in which the appropriate performance of sexual identity has historically been linked to the inculcation of certain regimes of the body (Butler, 1990). Certain ways of holding oneself, walking, running, holding the head and positioning the limbs, are not merely culturally relative or acquired through gender socialization, but are regimes of the body which seek to subjectify in terms of a certain truth of gender, inscribing a particular relation to oneself in a corporeal regime: prescribed, rationalized and taught in manuals of advice etiquette and manners, and enjoined by sanctions as well as seductions.

These comments should indicate something of the heterogeneity of the links between the government of others and the government of the self. It is important to stress two further aspects of this heterogeneity. The first concerns the diversity of modes in which a certain relation to oneself is enjoined. There is a temptation to stress the elements of self-mastery and restrictions over one's desires and instincts that are entailed in many regimes of subjectification – the injunction to control or civilize an inner nature that is excessive. [. . .] But there are many other modes in which this relation to oneself can be established and, even within the exercise of mastery, a variety of configurations through which one can be encouraged to master oneself. To master one's will in the service of character by the inculcation of habits and rituals of self-denial, prudence and foresight, for example, is different from mastering one's desire by bringing its roots to awareness through a reflexive hermeneutics in order to free oneself from the self-destructive consequences of repression, projection and identification.

Further, the very form of the relation can vary. It can be one of knowledge, as in the injunction to know oneself, which Foucault traces back to the Christian confession and forward to the techniques of psychotherapeutics: here the codes of knowledge are inevitably supplied not by pure introspection but by rendering one's introspection in a particular vocabulary of feelings, beliefs, passions, desires, values or whatever and according to a particular explanatory code derived from some source of authority. Or it can be one of concern and solicitude, as in contemporary projects for the care of the self in which the self is to be nurtured, projected, safeguarded by regimes of diet, stress minimization and self-esteem. Equally, the relation to authority can vary. [. . .]

As will be evident from the above discussion, whilst the relations to oneself enjoined at any one historical moment may resemble one another in various ways – for example the Victorian notion of character was widely dispersed across many different practices – the extent to which this is the case is a matter for empirical investigation. It is not a matter, therefore, of narrating a general history of the idea of the person or self, but of tracing the technical forms accorded to the relation to oneself in various practices – legal, military, industrial, familial, economic. And even within any practice, heterogeneity must be assumed to be more common than homogeneity – consider, for example, the very different configurations of personhood in the legal apparatus at any one moment – the difference between the notion of status and reputation as it functioned in civil proceedings in the nineteenth century and the simultaneous elaboration of a new relation to the law-breaker as a pathological personality in the criminal courts and the prison system (Pasquino, 1991).

[. . .]

Let me return to the issue of the diversity of regimes of subjectification. A further dimension of heterogeneity arises from the fact that ways of governing others are linked not only to the subjectification of the governed, but also to the subjectification of those who would govern conduct. Thus Foucault argues that the problematization of sex between men for the Greeks was linked to the demand that one who would exercise authority over others should first be able to exercise dominion over his own passions and appetites – for only if one was not a slave to oneself was one competent to exercise authority over others (Foucault, 1988: 6–7; cf. Minson, 1993: 20–1). Peter Brown points to the work required of a young man of the privileged classes in the Roman Empire of the second century, who was advised to remove from himself all aspects of 'softness' and 'womanishness' – in his gait, in his rhythms of speech, in his self-control – in order to manifest himself as capable of exercising authority over others (Brown, 1989: 11). Gerhard Oestreich suggests that the revival of Stoic ethics in seventeenth- and eighteenth-century Europe was a response to the criticism of authority as ossified and corrupt: the virtues of love, trust, reputation, gentleness, spiritual powers, respect for justice and the like were to become the means for authorities to renew themselves (Oestreich, 1982: 87). Stephan Collini has described the novel ways in which the Victorian intellectual classes problematized themselves in terms of such qualities as steadfastness and altruism: they interrogated themselves in terms of a constant anxiety about and infirmity of the will, and found, in certain forms of social and philanthropic work, an antidote to self-doubt (Collini, 1991, discussed in Osborne, 1996). [. . .]

From this perspective, it is no longer surprising that human beings often find themselves resisting the forms of personhood that they are enjoined to adopt. 'Resistance' – if by that one means opposition to a particular regime for the conduct of one's conduct – requires no theory of agency. It needs no account of the inherent forces within each human being that love liberty, seek to enhance their own powers or capacities, or strive for emancipation, that are prior to and in conflict with the demands of civilization and discipline. One no more needs a theory of agency to account for resistance than one needs an epistemology to account for the production of truth effects. Human beings are not the unified subjects of some coherent regime of domination that produces persons in the form in which it dreams. On the contrary, they live their lives in a constant movement across different practices that address them in different ways. Within these different practices, persons are addressed as different sorts of human being, presupposed to be different sorts of human being, acted upon as if they were different sorts of human being. Techniques of relating to oneself as a subject of unique capacities worthy of respect run up against practices of relating to oneself as the target of discipline, duty and docility. The humanist demand that one decipher oneself in terms of the authenticity of one's actions runs up against the political or institutional demand that one abides by the collective responsibility of organizational decision-making even when one is personally opposed to it. The ethical demand to suffer one's sorrows in silence and find a way of 'going on' is deemed problematic from the perspective of a passional ethic that obliges the person to disclose themselves in terms of a particular vocabulary of emotions and feelings.

Thus the existence of contestation, conflict and opposition in practices which conduct the conduct of persons is no surprise and requires no appeal to the particular qualities of human agency – except in the minimal sense that human being, like all else, exceeds all attempts to think it, simply because, whilst it is necessarily thought it does not exist in the form of thought.[4] Thus, in any one site or locale, humans turn programmes intended for one end to the service of others. One way of relating to oneself comes into conflict with others. For example, psychologists, management reformers, unions and workers have turned the vocabulary of humanistic psychology to account in a criticism of practices of management based upon a psycho-physiological or disciplinary understanding of persons. Reformers of the practices of welfare and medicine have, over the last two decades, turned the notion that human beings are subjects of rights against practices that presuppose human beings as the subjects of care. Out of this complex and contested field of oppositions, alliances and disparities of regimes of subjectification come accusations of inhumanity, criticisms, demands for reform, alternative programmes and the invention of new regimes of subjectification.

To designate some dimensions of these conflicts 'resistance' is itself perspectival: it can only ever be a matter of judgement. It is fruitless to complain, here, that such a perspective gives one no place to stand in the making of ethical critique and in the evaluation of ethical positions – the history of all those attempts to ground ethics that do appeal to some transcendental guarantor is plain enough – they cannot close conflicts over regimes of the person, but simply occupy one more position within the field of contestation (MacIntyre, 1981).

Folds in the soul

But the question may be asked: are not the kinds of phenomena that I have been discussing of interest precisely *because* they produce us as human beings with a certain kind of subjectivity? This is certainly the path followed by many who have investigated these issues, from Norbert Elias to contemporary feminist theorists who rely upon psychoanalysis to ground an account of the ways in which certain practices of the self become inscribed within the body and soul of the gendered subject (e.g. Butler, 1993; Probyn, 1993). For some, this path is advocated unproblematically. Elias, for example, did not doubt that human beings were the type of creatures inhabited by a psychoanalytic psychodynamics, and that this would provide the material basis for the inscription of civility into the soul of the social subject (Elias, 1978). I have already suggested that such a view is paradoxical, for it requires us to adopt a particular way of understanding the human being – that carved out at the end of the nineteenth century – as the basis for an investigation of the historicity of being human. For many others, this pathway is required if one is to avoid representing the human being as merely the passive and interminably malleable object of historical processes, if one is to have an account of agency and of resistance, and if one is to be able to find a place to stand in order to evaluate one regime of personhood over and above another (for one example of this argument, see Fraser, 1989). I have suggested that no such theory is required to account for conflict and contestation, and the stable ethical ground apparently provided by any given theory of the nature of human beings is illusory – one has no choice but to enter into a debate which cannot be closed by appeal to the nature of the human being as a subject of rights, of freedom, of autonomy or whatever. Is it possible, then, that one might write a genealogy of subjectification without a metapsychology? I think it is.

Such a genealogy, I suggest, requires only a minimal, weak or thin conception of the human material on which history writes (Patton, 1994). We are not concerned here with the social or historical construction of 'the person' or with the narration of the birth of modern 'self-identity'. Our concern is with the diversity of strategies and tactics of subjectification that have taken place and been deployed in diverse practices at different moments and in relation to different classifications and differentiations of persons. The human being, here, is not an entity with a history, but the target of a multiplicity of types of work, more like a latitude or a longitude at which different vectors of different speeds intersect. The 'interiority' which so many feel compelled to diagnose is not that of a psychological system, but of a discontinuous surface, a kind of infolding of exteriority.

[. . .]

Within a genealogy of subjectification, that which would be infolded would be anything that can acquire authority: injunctions, advice, techniques, little habits of thought and emotion, an array of routines and norms of being human – the instruments through which being constitutes itself in different practices and relations. These infoldings are partially stabilized to the extent that human beings have come to imagine themselves as the subjects of a biography, to utilize certain 'arts of memory' in order to render this biography stable, to employ certain vocabularies and explanations to make this intelligible to themselves. However, this exposes the limits of the metaphor of the fold. For the lines of these folds do not run through a domain coterminous with the fleshly bounds of the human individual. Human being is emplaced, enacted through a regime of devices, gazes, techniques which extend beyond the limits of the flesh into spaces and assemblies. Memory of one's biography is not a simple psychological capacity, but is organized through rituals of storytelling, supported by artefacts such as photograph albums and so forth. The regimes of bureaucracy are not merely ethical procedures infolded into the soul, but occupy a matrix of offices, files, typewriters, habits of time-keeping, conversational repertoires, techniques of notation. The regimes of passion are not merely affective folds in the soul, but are enacted in certain secluded or valorized spaces, through sensualized equipment of beds, drapes and silks, routines of dressing and undressing, aestheticized devices for providing music and light, regimes of partitioning of time and so forth (Ranum, 1989).

We might thus counterpose a *spatialization* of being to the narrativization of being undertaken by sociologists and philosophers of modernity and postmodernity. That is to say, we need to render being intelligible in terms of the localization of routines, habits and techniques within specific domains of action and value: libraries and studies, bedrooms and bathhouses, courtrooms and schoolrooms, consulting rooms and museum galleries, markets and department stores. The five volumes of *The History of Private Life* compiled under the general editorship of Philippe Ariès and George Duby provide a wealth of examples of the way in which novel human capacities such as styles of writing or sexuality depend upon and give rise to particular forms of spatial organization of the human habitat (Veyne, 1987; Duby, 1988; Chartier, 1989; Perrot, 1990; Prost and Vincent 1991). However, there is nothing privileged about what has come to be termed 'private life' for the emplacement of regimes of subjectification – it is in the factory as much as the kitchen, in the military as much as the study, in the office as much as the bedroom, that the modern subject has been required to identify his or her subjectivity. To the apparent linearity, unidirectionality and irreversibility of time, we can counterpose the multiplicity of places, planes and practices. And in each of these spaces, repertoires of conduct are activated that are not bounded by the enclosure formed by the human skin or carried in a stable form in the interior of an individual: they are rather webs of tension across a space that accord human beings capacities and powers to the extent that they catch them up in hybrid assemblages of knowledges, instruments, vocabularies, systems of judgement and technical artefacts. [. . .]

Notes

1   It is important to understand this in the *reflexive*, rather than the substantive mode. In what follows, the phrase always designates this relation, and implies no substantive 'self' as the object of that relation.

2   Of course, this is to overstate the case. One needs to look, on the one hand, at the ways in which philosophical reflections have themselves been organized around problems of pathology – think of the functioning of the image of the statue deprived of all sensory inputs in sensationalist philosophers such as Condillac – and also of the ways in which philosophy is animated by and articulated with, problems of the government of conduct (on Condillac, see Rose, 1985; on Locke, see Tully, 1993; on Kant, see Hunter, 1994).

3   Similar arguments about the necessity for analysing 'the self' as technological have been made in a number of quarters recently. See especially the discussion in Elspeth Probyn's recent book (Probyn, 1993). Precisely what is meant by 'technological' in this context is, however, less clear. As I suggest later, an analysis of the technological forms of subjectification needs to develop in terms of the relation between technologies for the government of conduct and the intellectual, corporeal and ethical devices that structure being's relation to itself at different moments and sites. I develop this argument further in Rose (1996).

4   This is not the place to argue this point, so let me just assert that only rationalists, or believers in God, imagine that 'reality' exists in the discursive forms available to thought. This is not a question to be addressed by reviving the old debates on the distinction between knowledge of the 'natural' and 'social' worlds – it is merely to accept that this must be the case unless one believes in some transcendental power that has so shaped human thought that it is homologous with that which it thinks of. Nor is it to rehearse the old problem of epistemology, which poses an ineffable divide between

thought and its object and then perplexes itself as to how one can 'represent' the other. Rather, perhaps one might say that thought makes up the real, but not as a 'realization' of thought.

References

Bauman, Z. (1991) *Modernity and Ambivalence*. Cambridge: Polity Press.

Beck, U. (1992) *Risk Society: towards a New Modernity*. London: Sage.

Bourdieu, P. (1977) *Outline of a Theory of Practice*, trans. R. Nice. New York: Cambridge University Press.

Brown, P. (1989) *The Body and Society*. London: Faber and Faber.

Burchell, G., Gordon, C. and Miller, P. (1991) *The Foucault Effect: Studies in Governmentality*. Hemel Hempstead: Harvester Wheatsheaf.

Burckhardt, J. (1990) *The Civilization of the Renaissance in Italy* (1860), trans. S.G.C. Middlemore. London: Penguin.

Butler, J. (1990) *Gender Trouble: Feminism and the Subversion of Identity*. London: Routledge.

Butler, J. (1993) *Bodies that Matter: on the Discursive Limits of 'Sex'*. London: Routledge.

Chartier, R. (ed.) (1989) *A History of Private Life, Vol. 3: Passions of the Renaissance*, trans. Arthur Goldhammer. Cambridge, MA: Belknap Press of Harvard University Press.

Collini, S. (1991) *Public Moralists: Political Thought and Intellectual Life in Britain 1850–1930*. Oxford: Oxford University Press.

Dean, M. (1994) '"A social structure of many souls": moral regulation, government and self-formation', *Canadian Journal of Sociology*, 19: 145–68.

Duby, G. (ed.) (1988) *A History of Private Life, Vol. 2: Revelations of the Medieval World*, trans. Arthur Goldhammer. Cambridge, MA: Belknap Press of Harvard University Press.

Eisenstein, E.L. (1979) *The Printing Press as an Agent of Change*. Cambridge: Cambridge University Press.

Elias, N. (1978) *The Civilizing Process, Vol. 1: The History of Manners*, trans. Edmund Jephcott. Oxford: Basil Blackwell.

Elias, N. (1983) *The Court Society*, trans. E. Jephcott. Oxford: Basil Blackwell.

Foucault, M. (1967) *Madness and Civilization: a History of Insanity in the Age of Reason*. London: Tavistock.

Foucault, M. (1977) *Discipline and Punish: the Birth of the Prison*. London: Allen Lane.

Foucault, M. (1979) *The History of Sexuality, Vol. 1: The Will to Truth*. London: Allen Lane.

Foucault, M. (1986a) *The Care of the Self: the History of Sexuality, Vol. 3*, trans. R. Hurley. New York: Pantheon.

Foucault, M. (1986b) 'On the genealogy of ethics: an overview of work in progress', in P. Rabinow (ed.), *The Foucault Reader*. Harmondsworth: Penguin. pp. 340–72.

Foucault, M. (1988) 'Technologies of the self', in L.H. Martin, H. Gutman and P.H. Hutton (eds), *Technologies of the Self*. London: Tavistock. pp. 16–49.

Foucault, M. (1991) 'Governmentality', in G. Burchell, C. Gordon and P. Miller (eds), *The Foucault Effect: Studies in Governmentality*. Hemel Hempstead: Harvester Wheatsheaf. pp. 87–104.

Fraser, N. (1989) 'Foucault on modern power: empirical insights and normative confusions', in *Unruly Practices*. Minneapolis, MN: University of Minnesota Press.

Giddens, A. (1991) *Modernity and Self-identity: Self and Society in the Late Modern Age*. Cambridge: Polity Press.

Goody, J. and Watt, I. (1963) 'The consequences of literacy', *Comparative Studies in Society and History*, 5. Reprinted in J. Goody (ed.), *Literacy in Traditional Societies*. Cambridge: Cambridge University Press, 1975. pp. 27–84.

Gordon, C. (1991) 'Introduction', in G. Burchell, C. Gordon and P. Miller (eds), *The Foucault Effect: Studies in Governmentality*. Hemel Hempstead: Harvester Wheatsheaf. pp. 1–51.

Hadot, P. (1992) 'Reflections on the notion of "the cultivation of the self"', in T.J. Armstrong (ed.), *Michel Foucault, Philosopher*. Hemel Hempstead: Harvester Wheatsheaf. pp. 225–32.

Hunter, I. (1994) *Rethinking the School: Subjectivity, Bureaucracy, Criticism*. St Leonards, Australia: Allen and Unwin.

Jambet, C. (1992) 'The constitution of the subject and spiritual practice', in T.J. Armstrong (ed.), *Michel Foucault, Philosopher*. Hemel Hempstead: Harvester Wheatsheaf. pp. 233–47.

Joyce, P. (1994) *Democratic Subjects: the Self and the Social in Nineteenth Century England*. Cambridge: Cambridge University Press.

Lash, S. and Friedman, J. (eds) (1992) *Modernity and Identity*. Oxford: Basil Blackwell.

MacIntyre, A. (1981) *After Virtue: a Study in Moral Theory*. London: Duckworth.

Markus, T.A. (1993) *Buildings and Power: Freedom and Control in the Origin of Modern Building Types*. London: Routledge.

Mauss, M. (1979) 'Body techniques', in *Psychology and Sociology: Essays*. London: Routledge and Kegan Paul.

Minson, J.P. (1993) *Questions of Conduct*. London: Macmillan.

Oestreich, G. (1982) *Neo-Stoicism and the Early Modern State*. Cambridge: Cambridge University Press.

Osborne, T. (1996) 'Constructionism, authority and the ethical life', in I. Velody and R. Williams (eds), *Social Constructionism*. London: Sage.

Pasquino, P. (1991) 'Criminology: the birth of a special knowledge', in G. Burchell, C. Gordon and P. Miller (eds), *The Foucault Effect: Studies in Governmentality*. Hemel Hempstead: Harvester. pp. 235–50.

Patton, P. (1994) 'Foucault's subject of power', *Political Theory Newsletter*, 6(1): 60–71.

Perrot, M. (ed.) (1990) *A History of Private Life, Vol. 4: From the Fires of Revolution to the Great War*, trans. Arthur Goldhammer. Cambridge, MA: Belknap Press of Harvard University Press.

Probyn, E. (1993) *Sexing the Self: Gendered Positions in Cultural Studies*. London: Routledge.

Prost, A. and Vincent, G. (eds) (1991) *A History of Private Life, Vol. 5: Riddles of Identity in Modern Times*, trans. Arthur Goldhammer. Cambridge, MA: Belknap Press of Harvard University Press.

Ranum, O. (1989) 'The refuges of intimacy', in R. Chartier (ed.), *A History of Private Life, Vol. 3: Passions of the Renaissance*, trans. Arthur Goldhammer. Cambridge, MA: Belknap Press of Harvard University Press. pp. 207–63.

Rose, N. (1985) *The Psychological Complex: Psychology, Politics and Society in England 1869–1939*. London: Routledge and Kegan Paul.

Rose, N. (1989) *Governing the Soul: the Shaping of the Private Self*. London: Routledge.

Rose, N. (1996) *Inventing our Selves: Psychology, Power and Personhood*. New York: Cambridge University Press.

Smith, R. (1992) *Inhibition: History and Meaning in the Sciences of Mind and Brain*. Berkeley, CA: University of California Press.

Tully, J. (1993) 'Governing conduct', in *An Approach to Political Philosophy: Locke in Contexts*. Cambridge: Cambridge University Press.

Veyne, P. (ed.) (1987) *A History of Private Life, Vol. 1: From Pagan Rome to Byzantium*, trans. Arthur Goldhammer. Cambridge, MA: Belknap Press of Harvard University Press.

26

A category of the human mind: The notion
of person, the notion of self
Marcel Mauss

The subject:[1] the 'person' (*personne*)

My audience and readers will have to show great indulgence, for my
subject is really enormous, and in these fifty-five minutes I shall be able
only to give you some idea of how to treat it. It deals with nothing less
than how to explain to you the way in which one of the categories of the
human mind – one of those ideas we believe to be innate – originated
and slowly developed over many centuries and through numerous
vicissitudes, so that even today it is still imprecise, delicate and fragile,
one requiring further elaboration. This is the idea of 'person' (*personne*),
the idea of 'self' (*moi*). Each one of us finds it natural, clearly
determined in the depths of his consciousness, completely furnished with
the fundaments of the morality which flows from it. For this simplistic
view of its history and present value we must substitute a more precise
view.

[. . .]

[. . .] In the present short space of time, I shall conduct you, with
some daring and at inordinate speed, across the world and through time,
guiding you from Australia to our European societies, from extremely
ancient history to that of our own times. More extensive research studies
could be undertaken, each one of which could be gone into much more
deeply, but I can only claim to show you how such research might be
organised. What I intend to do is to provide you with a summary
catalogue of the forms that the notion has assumed at various times and
in various places, and to show you how it has ended up by taking on flesh
and blood, substance and form, an anatomical structure, right up to

This chapter,
originally published
in 1938, is taken
from *The Category
of Person*, ed. M.
Carrithers, S. Collins
and S. Lukes
(Cambridge,
Cambridge
University Press,
1985), pp. 1–25. It
was translated by
W.D. Halls.

modern times, when at last it has become clear and precise in our civil-isations (in our European ones, almost in our lifetime), but not yet in all of them. I can only rough out the beginnings of the sketch or the clay model. I am still far from having finished the whole block or carved the finished portrait.

Thus I shall not discuss the linguistic problem which, for the sake of completeness, should indeed be tackled. In no way do I maintain that there has ever been a tribe, a language, in which the term 'I', 'me' (*je*, *moi*) (you will note that we still decline it with two words) has never existed, or that it has not expressed something clearly represented. This is far from the case: as well as possessing the pronoun, a very large number of languages are conspicuous for their use of many 'positional' suffixes, which deal for the most part with the relationships existing in time and space between the speaker (the subject) and the object about which he is speaking. Here the 'self' (*moi*) is everywhere present, but is not expressed by 'me' (*moi*) or 'I' (*je*). However, in this vast domain of languages my scholarship is only mediocre. My investigation will concern solely law and morality.

Nor shall I speak to you of psychology, any more than I shall of linguistics. I shall leave aside everything which relates to the 'self' (*moi*), the conscious personality as such. Let me merely say that it is plain, particularly to us, that there has never existed a human being who has not been aware, not only of his body, but also at the same time of his individuality, both spiritual and physical. The psychology of this awareness has made immense strides over the last century, for almost a hundred years. [. . .]

My subject is entirely different, and independent of this. It is one relating to social history. Over the centuries, in numerous societies, how has it slowly evolved – not the sense of 'self' (*moi*) – but the notion or concept that men in different ages have formed of it? What I wish to show you is the succession of forms that this concept has taken on in the life of men in different societies, according to their systems of law, religion, customs, social structures and mentality.

One thing may alert you to the drift of my exposition: I shall show you how recent is the word 'self' (*moi*), used philosophically; how recent 'the category of "self"' (*moi*), 'the cult of the "self"' (*moi*) (its aberration); and how recent even 'the respect of "self"' (*moi*), in particular the respect of others (its normal state).

Let us therefore draw up a classification. Making no claim to reconstitute a general history from pre-historical times to the present day, let us first study some of the forms assumed by the notion of 'self' (*moi*). We shall then launch into historical times with the Greeks and work out from there some definite linkages. Beforehand, with no other concern save that of logic, we will make an excursion into that kind of museum of facts (I dislike the word 'survivals', when it is used for institutions still active and proliferating) which ethnography affords us.

The 'role' (*personnage*), and the place of the 'person' (*personne*)

The Pueblos

Let us start with the fact that has been the point of departure for all this research. I borrow it from the Pueblo Indians, the Zuñi – or more accurately from those of the Pueblo of Zuñi, so admirably studied by Frank Hamilton Cushing (who was fully initiated into the Pueblo), and by Mathilda Cox Stevenson and her husband for a great number of years. Their work has been criticised, but I believe it to be reliable and, in any case, unique. It is true that there is nothing 'very primitive' about things. The 'Cities of Cibola' were once converted to Christianity and have preserved their baptismal registers. Yet, at the same time they have practised their ancient laws and religions – almost in the 'aboriginal state', if one may say so: this was roughly that of their predecessors, the cliff dwellers and the inhabitants of the 'mesa' as far as Mexico. In their material civilisation and social constitution they were, and have remained, very comparable to the Mexicans and to the most civilised Indians of the two Americas. 'Mexico, that Pueblo', writes admirably the great L.H. Morgan, who was so unfairly treated, and yet the founder of our disciplines.[2]

The document below is by Frank Hamilton Cushing,[3] an author much criticised, even by his colleagues at the Bureau of American Ethnology. Yet, knowing his published work and having considered very carefully what has appeared on the Zuñi and the Pueblo in general, strengthened also by what I believe I know about a large number of American societies, I persist in considering him one of the best portrayers of societies of all time.

If you will allow me, I will pass over everything concerning the orientation and distribution of the characters (*personnages*) in the ritual, although this has very great importance, to which we have already drawn attention elsewhere. But I cannot omit two points: *The existence of a limited number of forenames in each clan; and the definition of the exact role played by each one in the 'cast-list' of the clan, and expressed by that name.*

> In each clan is to be found a set of names called the names of childhood. These names are more of titles than of cognomens. They are determined upon by sociologic and divinistic modes, and are bestowed in childhood as the 'verity names' or titles of the children to whom given. But this body of names relating to any one totem – for instance, to one of the beast totems – will not be the name of the totem beast itself, but will be names both of the totem in its various conditions and of various parts of the totem, or of its functions, or of its attributes, actual or mythical. Now these parts of functions, or attributes of the parts or functions, are subdivided also in a six-fold manner, so that the name relating to one member of the totem – for example, like the

MARCEL MAUSS

right arm or leg of the animal thereof – would correspond to the north, and would be the first in honor in a clan (not itself of the northern group); then the name relating to another member – say to the left leg or arm and its powers, etc. – would pertain to the west and would be second in honor; and another member – say the right foot – to the south and would be third in honor; and of another member – say the left foot – to the east and would be fourth in honor; to another – say the head – to the upper regions and would be fifth in honor; and another – say the tail – to the lower region and would be sixth in honor; while the heart or the navel and center of the being would be first as well as last in honor. The studies of Major Powell among the Maskoki and other tribes have made it very clear that kinship terms, so called, among other Indian tribes (and the rule will apply no less or perhaps even more strictly to the Zuñis) are rather devices for determining relative rank or authority as signified by relative age, as elder or younger, of the person addressed or spoken of by the term of relationship. So that it is quite impossible for a Zuñi speaking to another to say simply brother; it is always necessary to say elder brother or younger brother, by which the speaker himself affirms his relative age or rank; also it is customary for one clansman to address another clansman by the same kinship name of brother-elder or brother-younger, uncle or nephew, etc.; but according as the clan of the one addressed ranks higher or lower than the clan of the one using the term of address, the word-symbol for elder or younger relationship must be used.

With such a system of arrangement as all this may be seen to be, with such a facile device for symbolizing the arrangement (not only according to number of the regions and their subdivisions in their relative succession and the succession of their elements and seasons, but also in colours attributed to them, etc.) and, finally, with such an arrangement of names correspondingly classified and of terms of relationship significant of rank rather than of consanguinal connection, mistake in the order of a ceremonial, a procession or a council is simply impossible, and the people employing such devices may be said to have written and to be writing their statutes and laws in all their daily relationships and utterances.

Thus, on the one hand, the clan is conceived of as being made up of a *certain number of persons*, in reality of 'characters' (*personnages*). On the other hand, the role of all of them is really to act out, each insofar as it concerns him, the prefigured totality of the life of the clan.

So much for persons and the clan. The 'fraternities' are even more complicated. Among the Pueblo of Zuñi, and clearly among the others too – the Pueblos of Sia and Tusayan, in the Hopi tribe, those of Walpi and Mishongnovi – the names do not merely correspond to the organisation of the clan, its processions and ceremonies, whether private or public. They correspond principally to ranks in the fraternities, in what the original terminology of Powell and the Bureau of American Ethnology designated 'Fraternities', viz., 'Secret Societies', which we might very exactly compare to the Colleges of the Roman Religion. There were preparations in secret, and numerous solemn rituals reserved for the Society of the Men (Kaka or Koko, Koyemshi, etc.), but also public demonstrations – almost theatrical performances – and, especially at Zuñi, and above all among the Hopi, mask dances, particularly those of the Katchina. These were visits of spirits, represented by their delegates upon earth, who bore their titles. All this, which has now become a spectacle for tourists, was still very much alive less than fifty years ago, and is so even today.

[. . .]

Moreover, let us add that these lives of individuals, the driving force of clans and of the societies superimposed upon them, not only sustain the life of things and of the gods, but the 'propriety' of things. They not only sustain the life of men, both here and in the after-life, but also the rebirth of individuals (men), sole heirs of those that bear their forenames (the reincarnation of women is a completely different matter). Thus, in short, you will understand that with the Pueblo we already see a notion of the 'person' (*personne*) or individual, absorbed in his clan, but already detached from it in the ceremonial by the mask, his title, his rank, his role, his survival and his reappearance on earth in one of his descendants endowed with the same status, forenames, titles, rights and functions.

The American North-West

If I had time, another group of American tribes would well deserve in this study a detailed analysis of the same facts. These are the tribes of the American North-West – and it is to the great credit of your Royal Anthropological Institute and the British Association to have instigated a complete analysis of their institutions. This was begun by Dawson, the great geologist, and so magnificently continued, if not completed, by the great works of Boas and his Indian assistants, Hunt and Tate, and by those of Sapir, Swanton and Barbeau, etc.

Here also is posed, in different terms but ones identical in nature and function, the same problem – that of the name, the social position and the legal and religious 'birthright' of every free man, and even more so, of every noble and prince.

I shall take as a starting-point the best known of these important societies, the Kwakiutl, and confine myself only to some broad facts.

One word of caution: just as with the Pueblos, so also with the Indians of the North-West, we must not think of anything in any way primitive. [. . .]

[. . .] [T]he Kwakiutl, installed in their settlements a whole social and religious system where, in a vast exchange of rights, goods and services, property, dances, ceremonies, privileges and ranks, persons as well as groups give satisfaction to one another. We see very clearly how, from classes and clans, 'human persons' adjust to one another and how, from these, the gestures of the actors in a drama fit together. Here *all* the actors are theoretically the sum total of *all* free men. But this time the drama is more than an aesthetic performance. It is religious, and at the same time it is cosmic, mythological, social and personal.

Firstly, as with the Zuñi, every individual in each clan has a name, even two names, for each season, one profane (summer) (WiXsa), and one sacred (winter) (LaXsa). These names are distributed between the various families, the 'Secret Societies' and the clans cooperating in the rituals, occasions when chiefs and families confront each other in innumerable and interminable *potlatch*,[4] about which I have attempted elsewhere to give some idea. Each clan has two complete sets of its proper names, or rather its forenames, the one commonly known, the other secret, but which itself is not simple. This is because the forename, actually of the noble, changes with his age and the functions he fulfils as a consequence of that age.[5] As is said in an oration, made, it is true, about the clan of the Eagles, i.e. about a kind of privileged group among privileged clans:

> For that they do not change their names starts from (the time) when long ago // Ō᷄ᶜ maxt!ālaLē᷄ᶜ, the ancestor of the numaym G ̄ıg ̄ılgam of the / Q!ōmoyâ'yē, made the seats of the Eagles; and those went down to the / numayms. And the name-keeper Wīltsē᷄ᶜstala says, / 'Now our chiefs have been given everything, and I will go right down (according to the order of rank).' / Thus he says, when he gives out the property; for I will just name the names // of one of the head chiefs of the numayms of the / Kwakiutl tribes. They never change their names from the beginning, / when the first human beings existed in the world; for names can not go out / of the family of the head chiefs of the numayms, only to the eldest one / of the children of the head chief.//[6]

What is at stake in all this is thus more than the prestige and the authority of the chief and the clan. It is the very existence of both of these and of the ancestors reincarnated in their rightful successors, who live again in the bodies of those who bear their names, whose perpetuation is assured by the ritual in each of its phases. The perpetuation of things and spirits is only guaranteed by the perpetuating of the names of individuals, of persons. These last only act in their titular capacity and, conversely, are responsible for their whole clan, their families and their tribes. For instance, from conquest in war are acquired: a rank, a power, a religious and aesthetic function, dancing and demoniacal possession, *paraphernalia*, and copper objects in the form of buckler shields – real *crown* shapes in copper, important currency for present and future *potlatch*: it suffices to kill the one possessing them, or to seize from him one of the trappings of ritual, robes or masks, so as to inherit his names, his goods, his obligations, his ancestors, his 'person' (*personne*), in the fullest sense of the word.[7] In this way ranks, goods, personal rights, and things, as well as their particular spirit, are acquired.

This huge masquerade in its entirety, this whole drama, this complicated ballet of ecstatic states, concerns as much the past as the future, becomes a test for its performer, and proof of the presence within him of the *naualaku*, an element of an impersonal force, or of the ancestor, or of the personal god, in any case of the superhuman power, spiritual and ultimate. The *potlatch* of victory, of the copper won by conquest, correspond to the impeccable dance, to a successful state of possession.

There is no time left to develop all these subjects. Almost from an anecdotal viewpoint, I would like to draw your attention to an institution, an object commonly found from the Nootka right up to the Tlingit of North Alaska. This is the use of those remarkable shutter masks, which are double and even triple, which open up to reveal the two or three creatures (totems placed one upon the other) personified by the wearer of the mask.[8] You can see some very fine examples of them in the British Museum. And all those celebrated totem poles, those soapstone pipes, etc., all those objects which have become rubbishy goods designed for the tourists brought there by train or on cruises – all these may be analysed in the same way. A pipe I believe to be Haida in origin, one to which I have hardly given any attention, in point of fact represents a young initiate in his pointed headdress, presented by his spirit father, likewise behatted, bearing the grampus. Beneath the one initiated, to whom they are subordinate in descending order: a frog – doubtless his mother – and a crow, doubtless his maternal grandfather.

[. . .]

Moreover, it is very remarkable that among the Kwakiutl (and their nearest kin, the Heiltsuk, the Bellacoola, etc.) every stage of life is named, personified by a fresh name, a fresh title, whether as a child, an adolescent or an adult, both male and female. Thus one may possess a name as a warrior (naturally this does not apply to women), as a prince or princess, as a chief or a female chieftain. There is a name for the feast that men and women give, and for the particular ceremonial that belongs to them, for their age of retirement, their name in the society of seals (those retired: no states of ecstacy or possession, no responsibilities, no gains, save those arising from past memories). Finally is named *their* 'secret society', in which they are protagonists (a bear – frequent among women, who are represented in it by their menfolk or their sons – wolves, Hamatse [cannibals], etc.). Names are also given to: the chief's house, with its roofs, posts, doors, ornamentation, beams, openings, double-headed and double-faced snake, the ceremonial boat, the dogs. To the lists set out in the 'Ethnology of the Kwakiutl'[9] it must be added that the dishes, the forks, the copper objects, everything is emblazoned, endowed with life, forming part of the *persona* of the owner and of the *familia*, of the *res* of his clan.

We have singled out the Kwakiutl, and in general the peoples of the North-West, because they really do represent the extremes, an excessiveness which allows us better to perceive the facts than in those places where, although no less essential, they still remain small-scale and involuted. Yet we must understand that a large part of the Americans of the prairies, in particular the Sioux, possess institutions of this kind. Thus the Winnebago, who have been studied by our colleague Radin, have in point of fact these successions of forenames, which are determined by clans and families, who distribute them according to a certain order, but always following precisely a kind of logical distribution of attributes or powers and natures,[10] founded upon the myth of the origin of the clan, and legitimating the right of some person or another to assume the role.

Below is an example of this origin of the names of individuals which Radin gives in detail in his model autobiography of *Crashing Thunder*:

> Now in our clan whenever a child was to be named it was my father who did it. That right he now transmitted to my brother.
>
> Earthmaker, in the beginning, sent four men from above and when they came to this earth everything that happened to them was utilized in making proper names. This is what our father told us. As they had come from above so from that fact has originated a name Comes-from-above; and since they came like spirits we have a name Spirit-man. When they came, there was a drizzling rain and hence the names Walking-in-mist, Comes-in-mist, Drizzling-rain. It is said that when they came to Within-lake they alighted upon a small shrub and hence the name Bends-the-shrub; and since they alighted on an oak tree, the name Oak-tree. Since our ancestors came with the thunderbirds we have a name Thunderbird and since these are the animals who cause thunder, we have the name He-who-thunders. Similarly we have Walks-with-a-mighty-tread, Shakes-the-earth-down-with-his-face, Comes-with-wind-and-hail, Flashes-in-every-direction, Only-a-flash-of-lightning, Streak-of-lightning, Walks-in-the-clouds, He-who-has-long-wings, Strikes-the-tree.
>
> Now the thunderbirds come with terrible thunder-crashes. Everything on earth, animals, plants everything, is deluged with rain. Terrible thunder-crashes resound everywhere. From all this a name is derived and that is my name – Crashing-Thunder.[11]

Each one of the names of the thunder birds which divide up the different elements of the thunder totem is that of ancestors who are perpetually reincarnated. (We even have a story of two reincarnations.)[12] The men who reincarnate them are intermediaries between the totemic animal and the protecting spirit, and the things emblazoned and the rites of the clan or of the great 'medicines'. All these names and bequeathals of 'roles' (*personnalités*) are determined by revelations whose limits, indicated by his grandmother or the elders, are known to the beneficiary beforehand. We discover, if not the same facts, at least the same kind of facts, almost everywhere in America. We could continue this exposition for the world of the Iroquois and the Algonquin, etc.

[. . .] Here also the clan is in no way conceived to be entirely reduced to an impersonal, collective being, the totem, represented by the animal species and not by individuals – on the one hand men, on the other, animals.[13] Under its human aspect it is the fruit of the reincarnation of spirits that have migrated and are perpetually being reborn in the clan. (This is true for the Arunta, the Loritja and the Kakadu, etc.) Even among the Arunta and the Loritja, these spirits are reincarnated with very great precision at the third generation (grandfather-grandson) and at the fifth, where grandfather and great-great-grandson are homonyms. Here again it is the fruit of uterine descent crossed with male descent. We can, for example, study in the distribution of names by individuals, clans and exact matrimonial *category* (eight Arunta categories) the relationship of these names to the eternal ancestors, to the *ratapa*, in the form they take at the moment of conception, in the foetus and in the children that they bring to the light of day, and between the names of these *ratapa* and those of adults (which are, in particular, those of the functions fulfilled at clan and tribal cere-monies).[14] The art underlying all these kinds of distribution is not only to arrive at religion, but also to define the position of the individual in the rights he enjoys and his place in the tribe, as in its rites.

Moreover, if, for reasons that will immediately become apparent, I have spoken especially about societies with permanent masks (Zuñi, Kwakiutl), we must not forget that in Australia, as elsewhere, temporary masquerades are simply ceremonies with masks that are not permanent. In these men fashion for themselves a superimposed 'personality' (*personalité*), a true one in the case of ritual, a feigned one in the case of play-acting. Yet, as between the painting of the head and frequently of the body, and the wearing of a robe and a mask, there is only a difference in degree, and none in function. In both cases all has ended in the enraptured representation of the ancestor.

What is more, the presence or absence of the mask are more distin-guishing marks of a social, historical and cultural arbitrariness, so to speak, than basic traits. Thus the Kiwai, the Papuans of the Isle of Kiwai, possess admirable masks, even rivaling those of the Tlingit of North America, whilst their not very distant neighbours, the Marind-Anim, have scarcely more than one *single* mask, which is entirely simple, but enjoy admirable celebrations of fraternities and clans, of people decorated from top to toe, unrecognizable because of their adornment.

Let us conclude this first part of our demonstration. Plainly what emerges from it is that a whole immense group of societies have arrived at the notion of 'role' (*personnage*), of the role played by the individual in sacred dramas, just as he plays a role in family life. The function had already created the formula in very primitive societies and subsists in societies at the present day. Institutions like that of the 'retired', seals of the Kwakiutl, usages like that of the Arunta, who relegate to the people of no consequence he who can no longer dance, 'he who has lost his Kabara', are entirely typical.

[. . .]

Let us move on from the notion of 'role' (*personnage*) to the notion of 'person' (*personne*) and of 'self' (*moi*).

The Latin 'persona'

You all know how normal and classical is the notion of the Latin *persona*: a mask, a tragic mask, a ritual mask, and the ancestral mask. It dates back to the beginnings of Latin civilisation.

I have to show you how indeed the notion has become one shared also by us. The space, the time and the differences that separate that origin from this terminal point are considerable. Evolutions and revolutions pile up upon one another, this time in history, according to precise dates, for causes, plain to see, which we are about to describe. In one place this category of the mind has wavered, in another it has set down deep roots.

Even among the very great and ancient societies which first became conscious of it, two of them, so to speak, invented it, only to allow it to fade away almost irrevocably. All this occurred in the last centuries BC. The examples are edifying: they concern Brahamanic and Buddhist India, and ancient China.

India

India appears to me indeed to have been the most ancient of civilisations aware of the notion of the individual, of his consciousness – may I say, of the 'self' (*moi*). *Ahaṃkāra*, the 'creation of the "I"' (*je*), is the name of the individual consciousness; *aham* equals 'I' (*je*): it is the same Indo-European word as 'ego'. The word *ahaṃkāra* is clearly a technical word, invented by some school of wise seers, risen above all psychological illusions. The *sāṃkhya*, the school which in point of fact must have preceded Buddhism, maintains the composite character of things and minds (*sāṃkhya* actually means 'composition'), esteeming that the 'self' (*moi*) is the illusory thing. For its part, Buddhism, in a first phase of its history, laid down that it was a mere composite, capable of division and of being resolvable into the *skandha*, and sought after its annihilation in the monk.

The great Brahmanic schools of the Upanishads – assuredly predating the *sāṃkhya* itself, as well as the two orthodox forms of the Vedānta which follow them – all start from the maxim of the 'seers' (*voyants*), right up to the dialogue of Vishnu in the Bhagavad Gītā demonstrating the truth to Arjuna: *tat tvam asi*, which corresponds almost word for word to the English, 'that thou art' (the universe). Even the later Vedic ritual and the commentaries upon it were already imbued with these metaphysics.

China

About China I know only what Marcel Granet, my colleague and friend, has been kind enough to inform me. Even today nowhere is more account taken of the individual, and particularly of his social status, nowhere is he more rigorously categorized. What Granet's admirable studies reveal to us about ancient china is the strength and grandeur of institutions comparable to those of the American North-West. Birth-order, rank and the interplay of the social classes settle the names and life style of the individual, his 'face', as is still said, in terms that we are also beginning to employ. His individuality is his *ming*, his name. China has preserved these archaic notions, yet at the same time has removed from individuality every trace of its being eternal and indissoluble. The name, the *ming*, represents a collective noun, something springing from elsewhere: one's corresponding ancestor bore it, just as it will fall to the descendant of its present bearer. Whenever they have philosophized about it, whenever in certain metaphysical schools they have attempted to explain what it is, they have said of the individual that he is a composite, made up of *shen* and *kwei* – two other collective nouns – in this life. Taoism and Buddhism also went down this road, and the notion of the 'person' (*personne*) ceased to evolve.

Other nations have known or adopted ideas of the same kind. Those who have made of the human person a complete entity, independent of all others save God, are rare.

The most important were the Romans. In our view it was there, in Rome, that this latter idea was worked out.

The 'persona'

In contrast to the Hindus and the Chinese, the Romans, or perhaps rather the Latins, seem to be the people who in part established the notion of 'person' (*personne*), the designation for which has remained precisely the Latin word. From the very outset we are transported into the same systems of facts as those mentioned before, but already in a new form: the 'person' (*personne*) is more than an organisational fact, more than a name or a right to assume a role and a ritual mask. It is a basic fact of law. In law, according to the legal experts, there are only *personae*, *res* and *actiones*: this principle still regulates the divisions between our codes of law. Yet this outcome is the result of particular evolution in Roman law.

Somewhat rashly, this is the way I can envisage this state of affairs to have arisen.[15] It does seem that the original meaning of the word was exclusively that of 'mask'. Naturally the explanation of Latin etymologists, that *persona*, coming from *per/sonare*, is the mask through which (*per*) resounds the voice (of the actor) is a derivation invented afterwards – although we do distinguish between *persona* and *persona muta*, the silent role in drama and mime. In reality the word does not even seem to be from a sound Latin root. It is believed to be of Etruscan origin, like other nouns ending in '-na' (Porsenna, Caecina, etc.). Meiller and Ernout's *Dictionnaire Etymologique* compares it to a word, *farsu*, handed down in garbled form, and M. Benveniste informs me that it may come from a Greek borrowing made by the Etruscans, πρόσωπον ('perso'). Yet it is the case that materially even the institution of masks, and in particular of masks of ancestors, appears mainly to have had its home in Etruria. The Etruscans had a 'mask' civilization. There is no comparison between the masses of wooden masks and of those in terra cotta – the wax ones have vanished – the masses of effigies of sleeping or seated ancestors found in the excavations made of the vast Tyrrhenian kingdom, and those found at Rome, in the Latium, or in Greater Greece (Graecia Magna) – moreover, in my view, these are very frequently of Etruscan manufacture.

Yet if it is not the Latins who invented the word and the institutions, at least it was they who gave it the original meaning which has become our own. This was the process that occurred.

Firstly, among them are to be found definite traces of institutions of the same kind as ceremonies of clans, masks and paints with which the actors bedeck themselves according to the names they bear. At least one of the great rituals of earliest Rome corresponds exactly to the common type whose salient forms we have depicted. This is that of the *Hirpi Sorani*, the wolves of the Soracte (*Hirpi* is the name of the wolf in Samnite). Festus (93, 25) states: *Irpini appellati nomine lupi, quem irpum dicunt Samnites; eum enim ducem secuti agros occupavere.* ('They are called Irpini, the name of the wolf, which the Samnites call *irpus*; following a wolf they arrived at their later domain.')[16]

Members of the families who bore that title walked on burning coals at the sanctuary of the goddess Feronia, and enjoyed privileges, including exemption from taxation. Sir James Frazer already speculated that they were the remnants of an ancient clan, which had become a fraternity, bearing names, and wearing skins and masks. Yet there is something else: it seems that we are truly in the presence of the very myth of Rome. 'Acca Larentia', the old woman, the mother of the Lares, who was honoured at the Larentalia (December) is none other than the *indigitamentum*, the secret name of the Roman She-Wolf, the mother of Romulus and Remus (Ovid, *Fastes*, I, 55 ff).[17] A clan, dances, masks, a name, names, a ritual. I accept that the facts are divided somewhat into two elements: a fraternity which survives, and a myth which recounts what preceded the foundation of Rome itself. But the two parts form a complete whole. The study of other Roman *collegia* would permit other hypotheses. All in all, Samnites, Etruscans and Latins still lived in an environment we have just left, from *personae*, masks and names, and individual rights to rituals and privileges.

From this to the notion of 'person' (*personne*) but a single step needs to be taken. It was perhaps not taken immediately. I imagine that legends like that of the consul Brutus and his sons and the end of the right of the

THE NOTION OF 'PERSON', THE NOTION OF 'SELF'

pater to kill his sons, his *sui*, signify the acquisition of the *persona* by the sons, even while their father was still alive. I believe that the revolt of the Plebs, the right to full citizenship that, following upon the sons of senatorial families, was gained by all the plebeian members of the *gentes*, was decisive. All freemen of Rome were Roman citizens, all had a civil *persona*; some became religious *personae*; some masks, names and rituals remained attached to some privileged families of the religious *collegia*.

Yet another custom arrived at the same final state: that of forenames, surnames and pseudonyms (nicknames). The Roman citizen had a right to the *nomen*, the *praenomen* and the *cognomen* that his *gens* assigned to him. A forename, for example, might signify the birth-order of the ancestor who bore it: Primus, Secundus. The sacred name – *nomen, numen* – of the *gens*; the *cognomen*, the pseudonym (nickname) – not surname – such as Naso, Cicero, etc.[18] A senatus-consultus decision determined (clearly there must have been some abuses) that one had no right to borrow and adorn oneself with any other forename of any other *gens* than one's own. The *cognomen* followed a different historical course: it ended by confusing *cognomen*, the pseudonym that one might bear, with *imago*, the wax mask moulded upon the face, the πρόσωπον of the dead ancestor kept in the wings of the *aula* of the family house. For a long time the use of these masks and statues must have been reserved for patrician families, and in fact, even more so than in law, it does not appear to have spread very widely among the plebeians. It is rather usurpers and foreigners who adopt *cognomina* which did not belong to them. The very words *cognomen* and *imago* are, in a manner of speaking, indissolubly linked in formulas that were almost in current use. I give below one of the facts – in my view typical – which was my starting point for all this research, one which I found without even looking for it. It concerns a doubtful individual, Staienus, against whom Cicero is pleading on behalf of Cluentius. This is the scene. *Tum appelat hilari vultu hominem Bulbus, ut placidissime potest. 'Quid tu, inquit, Paete?' Hoc enim sibi Staienus cognomen ex imaginibus Aeliorum delegerat ne sese Ligurem fecisset, nationis magis quam generis uti cognomine videretur.*[19] Paetus is a *cognomen* of the Aelii, to which Staienus, a Ligurian, had no right, and which he usurped in order to conceal his nationality and to make believe that he was of an ancestry other than his own. Usurpation of 'person' (*personne*), fictitiousness of 'person' (*personne*), title and affiliation.

One of the finest documents, and among the most authentic, signed in the bronze by Claudius the emperor (just as the Tables of Ancyre of Augustus have come down to us), the Table of Lyons (AD 48) containing the imperial oration on the senatorial decision *de Jure honorum Gallis dando*, concedes to the young Gaulish senators freshly admitted to the Curia the right to the *imagines* and *cognomina* of their ancestors. Now they will have nothing more to regret. Such as Persicus, 'my dear friend' (who had been obliged to choose this foreign pseudonym [nickname] . . . lacking this senatorial decision) and who can now *inter imagines majorum suorum Allobrogici nomen legere* ('choose his name of Allobrogicus among the "images" of his ancestors').

To the very end the Roman Senate thought of itself as being made up of a determinate number of *patres* representing the 'persons' (*personnes*), the 'images' of their ancestors.

It is to the *persona* that is attributed the property of the *simulacra* and the *imagines*.[20]

Along with them the word *persona*, an artificial 'character' (*personnage*), the mask and role of comedy and tragedy, of trickery and hypocrisy – a stranger to the 'self' (*moi*) – continued on its way. Yet the personal nature of the law had been established,[21] and *persona* had also become synonymous with the true nature of the individual.[22]

Moreover, the right to the *persona* had been established. Only the slave is excluded from it. *Servus non habet personam*. He has no 'personality' (*personnalité*). He does not own his body, nor has he ancestors, name, *cognomen*, or personal belongings. Old Germanic law still distinguished him from the freeman, the *Leibeigen*, the owner of his body. But at the time when the laws of the Saxons and Swabians were drawn up, if the serfs did not possess their body, they already had a soul, which Christianity had given them.

But before turning to Christianity, we must trace back another source of enrichment, in which not only the Latins participated, but also their Greek collaborators, their teachers and interpreters. With Greek philosophers, and Roman nobles and legal experts it is altogether a different edifice that is erected.

The 'person' (*personne*): a moral fact

Let me make myself plain: I think that this effort, this step forward, came about above all with the help of the Stoics, whose voluntarist and personal ethics were able to enrich the Roman notion of the 'person' (*personne*), and was even enriched itself whilst enriching the law.[23] I believe, but unfortunately can only begin to prove it, that the influence of the Schools of Athens and Rhodes on the development of Latin moral thinking cannot be exaggerated, and, conversely, the influence of Roman actions and of the educational needs of young Romans on the Greek thinkers. Polybius and Cicero already attest to this, as do later Seneca, Marcus Aurelius and others.

The word πρόσωπον did indeed have the same meaning as *persona*, a mask. But it can then also signify the 'personage' (*personnage*) that each individual is and desires to be, his character (the two words are often linked), the true face. From the second century BC onwards it very quickly assumes the meaning of *persona*. Translating exactly and legally *persona*, it still retains the meaning of a superimposed image; for example, in the case of the figure at the prow of a boat (among the Celts, etc.). But it also signifies the human, even divine, 'personality' (*personnalité*). It all depends upon the context. The word πρόσωπον is extended to the individual, with his nature laid bare and every mask torn away, and, nevertheless, there is retained the sense of the artificial: the sense of what is the innermost nature of this 'person' (*personne*), and the sense of what is the 'role-player' (*personnage*).

Everything about the classical Latin and Greek Moralists (200 BC to AD 400) has a different ring to it. πρόσωπον is no longer only a *persona*, and – a matter of capital importance – to its juridical meaning is moreover added a moral one, a sense of being conscious, independent, autonomous, free and responsible. Moral conscience introduces consciousness into the juridical conception of law. To functions, honours, obligations and rights is added the conscious moral 'person' (*personne*). In this respect I am perhaps more venturesome, and yet more clear-cut than M. Brunschvicg, who, in his great work, *Le Progrès de la conscience*, has often touched upon these matters.[24] For me the words designating first consciousness and then psychological consciousness, the συνείδησις-τὸ συνειδός are really Stoic, seem technical and clearly translate *conscius, conscientia* in Roman law. We may even perceive, between the early phase of Stoicism and that of the Greco-Latin era, the progress and changes definitively accomplished by the age of Epictetus and Marcus Aurelius. In one of the original meanings of accomplice, 'he who has seen with one', σύνοιδε, as a witness, we have passed to the meaning of the 'consciousness of good and evil'. In current use in Latin, the word finally takes on this meaning with the Greeks, with Diodorus of Sicily, Lucian and Dionysus of Halycarnassus, and self-consciousness (*conscience de soi*) has become the attribute of the moral person. Epictetus still keeps the meaning of the two images which this civilisation had worked on, when he writes what Marcus Aurelius quotes, 'carve out your mask', put on your 'role' (*personnage*), your 'type', your 'character', when he suggested to him what has become with us the examination of conscience. Renan saw the importance of this moment in the life of the Mind.[25]

But the notion of 'person' (*personne*) still lacked any sure metaphysical foundation. This foundation it owes to Christianity.

The Christian 'person' (*personne*)

It is Christians who have made a metaphysical entity of the 'moral person' (*personne morale*), after they became aware of its religious power. Our own notion of the human person is still basically the Christian one. Here I need only follow the excellent book of Schlossman.[26] He clearly saw – after others, but better than they did – the transition from the notion of *persona*, of 'a man clad in a condition', to the notion of man, quite simply, that of the human 'person' (*personne*).

Moreover, the notion of a 'moral person' had become so clear that, from the very beginning of our era, and even earlier at Rome and throughout the Empire, it was applied to all non-real 'personalities' (*personnalités*) – what we still call by the term 'moral persons' ('legal entities'): corporations, religious foundations, etc., which have become 'persons' (*personnes*). The word πρόσωπον designated them right up to the New Laws and most recent Constitutions. A *universitas* is a 'collective person' (*une personne de personnes*), but like a city, like Rome, it is a 'thing', an entity. Indeed as Cicero (*De Officiis*, I, 34) says: *Magistratus gerit personam civitatis*. And von Carolsfeld compares and comments very aptly upon the Epistle to the Galatians, ch. 3, v. 28: 'You are, with respect to the one, neither Jew nor Greek, slave nor freeman, male nor female, for you are all one person, εἷς, in Christ Jesus.'

The question was raised regarding the unity of the 'person' (*personne*), and the unity of the Church, in relationship to the unity of God (εἷς). It was resolved after many discussions. It is the entire history of the Church that would have here to be retraced (cf. Suidas, s.v., and the passages of the celebrated Discourse upon the Epiphany by St Gregory of Nanzianzus, 39, 630,A).[27] It is the quarrel concerning the Trinity, the Monophysite dispute, which continued for a long while to exercise men's minds and which the Church resolved by taking refuge in the divine mystery, although however with decisive firmness and clarity: *Unitas in tres personas, una persona in duas naturas*, the Council of Nicea pronounced definitively. Unity of the three persons – of the Trinity – unity of the two natures of Christ. It is from the notion of the 'one' that the notion of the 'person' (*personne*) was created – I believe that it will long remain so – for the divine persons, but at the same time for the human person, substance and mode, body and soul, consciousness and act.[28]

I shall not comment further, or prolong this theological study. Cassiodorus ended by saying very precisely: *persona – substantia rationalis individua* (Psalmum VII). The person is a rational substance, indivisible and individual.[29]

It remained to make of this rational, individual substance what it is today, a consciousness and a category.

This was the work of a long study by philosophers, which I have only a few minutes left to describe.[30]

The 'person' (*personne*): a psychological being

Here I hope I may be forgiven if, summarising a certain amount of personal research and countless views the history of which might be traced back, I put forward more ideas than proofs.

However, the notion of the 'person' (*personne*) was still to undergo a further transformation to become what it has become over less than one and a half centuries, the 'category of "self"' (*moi*). Far from existing as the primordial innate idea, clearly engraved since Adam in the innermost depths of our being, it continues here slowly, and almost right up to our own time, to be built upon, to be made clearer and more specific, becoming identified with self-knowledge and the psychological consciousness.

All the long labours of the Church, of churches and theologians, of the Scholastic philosophers and the Renaissance philosophers – disturbed by the Reformation – even brought about some delay, setting up some obstacles to the creation of the idea that this time we believe to be clear. Up to the seventeenth and even up to the end of the eighteenth century, the mentality of our ancestors is obsessed with the question of knowing whether the individual soul is a substance, or supported by a substance: whether it is the nature of man, or whether it is only one of the two natures of man; whether it is one and indivisible, or divisible and separable; whether it is free, the absolute source of all action, or whether it is determined, fettered by other destinies, by predestination. Anxiously they wonder whence it came, who created it and who directs it. And in the arguments between sects, between coteries in both the great institutions of the Church and in the philosophical schools, we do hardly any better than the results achieved in the fourth century AD. Fortunately the Council of Trent put a stop to futile polemics regarding the personal creation of each individual soul.

Moreover, when we speak of the precise functions of the soul it is to thought, thought that is discursive, clear and deductive, that the Renaissance and Descartes address themselves in order to understand their nature. It is thought that contains the revolutionary *Cogito ergo sum*; this it is that constitutes Spinoza's opposition of the 'extension' to 'thought'.

Even Spinoza[31] continued to hold precisely the idea of Antiquity regarding the immortality of the soul. We know that he does not believe in the survival after death of any part of the soul other than that which is imbued with 'the intellectual love of God'. Basically he was reiterating Maimonides, who was repeating Aristotle (*De Anima*, 408, 6; cf. 430 a).[32] Only the noetic soul can be eternal, since the other two souls, the vegetative and the sensory, are necessarily linked to the body, and the energy of the body does not penetrate into the νοῦς. At the same time, by a natural opposition that Brunschvicg[33] has effectively highlighted, it is Spinoza who, better than Descartes, better than Leibnitz himself, because he posed above all else the ethical problem, has the soundest view of the relationships of the individual consciousness with things and with God.

It is elsewhere, and not among the Cartesians, but in other circles that the problem of the 'person' (*personne*) who is only consciousness has found its solution. We cannot exaggerate the importance of sectarian movements throughout the seventeenth and eighteenth centuries for the formation of political and philosophical thought. There it was that were posed the questions regarding individual liberty, regarding the individual conscience and the right to communicate directly with God, to be one's own priest, to have an inner God. The ideas of the Moravian Brothers, the Puritans, the Wesleyans and the Pietists are those which form the basis on which is established the notion: the 'person' (*personne*) equals the 'self' (*moi*); the 'self' (*moi*) equals consciousness, and is its primordial category.

All this does not go back very far. It was necessary to have Hume revolutionizing everything (following Berkeley, who had begun to do so) before one could say that in the soul there were only 'states of consciousness', 'perceptions'. Yet he ended up by hesitating when faced with the notion of 'self' (*moi*)[34] as the basic category of consciousness. The Scots adapted his ideas better.

Only with Kant does it take on precise form. Kant was a Pietist, a follower of Swedenborg, the pupil of Tetens, a feeble philosopher but a well-informed psychologist and theologian. He found the indivisible 'self' (*moi*) all around him. Kant posed the question, but did not resolve it, whether the 'self' (*moi*), *das Ich*, is a category.

The one who finally gave the answer that every act of consciousness was an act of the 'self' (*moi*), the one who founded all science and all action on the 'self' (*moi*), was Fichte. Kant had already made of the individual consciousness, the sacred character of the human person, the condition for Practical Reason. It was Fichte[35] who made of it as well the category of the 'self' (*moi*), the condition of consciousness and of science, of Pure Reason.

From that time onwards the revolution in mentalities was accomplished. Each of us has our 'self' (*moi*), an echo of the Declaration of the Rights of Man, which had predated both Kant and Fichte.

Conclusion

From a simple masquerade to the mask, from a 'role' (*personnage*) to a 'person' (*personne*), to a name, to an individual; from the latter to a being possessing metaphysical and moral value; from a moral consciousness to a sacred being; from the latter to a fundamental form of thought and action – the course is accomplished.

Who knows what progress the Understanding will yet make on this matter? We do not know what light will be thrown on these recent problems by psychology and sociology, both already well advanced, but which must be urged on even more.

Who knows even whether this 'category', which all of us here believe to be well founded, will always be recognised as such? It is formulated only for us, among us. Even its moral strength – the sacred character of the human 'person' (*personne*) – is questioned [. . .] in the countries where this principle was discovered. We have great possessions to defend. With us the idea could disappear. But let us refrain from moralising. [. . .]

Notes

Mauss's notes have been corrected and elaborated by Ben Brewster, in his translation of Mauss's essays, *Sociology and Psychology* (1979: Routledge and Kegan Paul, London), which we have largely followed in our presentation of the notes here.

1   Two theses of the Ecole des Hautes Etudes have already touched upon problems of this nature: Charles le Coeur, *Le Culte de la génération en Guinńee* (vol. 45 of the Bibliothèque de l'Ecole des Hautes Etudes, Sciences Religieuses); and V. Larock, *Essai sur la Valeur sacrée et la Valeur sociale des noms de personnes dans les Sociétes inférieures* (Paris, 1932).

2   On the respective dates of the different civilizations which have occupied this area of the 'basket people', the 'cliff dwellers', the people of the ruins of the 'mesa' and finally of the 'pueblo' (of square and circular shape), a good exposition of likely recent hypotheses is to be found in F.H.H. Roberts, 'The village of the great Kivas on the Zuñi reservation', *Bulletin of American Ethnology*, 111 (1932), pp. 23 ff. Also, by the same author, 'Early Pueblo ruins', *Bulletin of American Ethnology*, 90 (1930), p. 9.

3   Frank Hamilton Cushing (1896), 'Outlines of Zuñi creation myths', *13th Annual Report of the Bureau of American Ethnology to the Secretary of the Smithsonian Institution, 1891–2*, Washington, DC, pp. 371–2.

4   See also G. Davy, *Foi jurée* (Paris, 1922); Mauss, 'Essai sur le Don', *Année Sociologique*, 1923, where I was not able to emphasise, because it was outside my subject, the fact of the 'person' (*personne*), his rights, duties and religious powers, nor the succession of names, etc. Neither Davy nor I was able either to insist on the fact that the *potlatch* not only comprises 'exchanges' of men and women, inheritances, contracts, property, ritual services, and first, especially, dances and initiations – but also, ecstatic trances, states of possession by the eternal and reincarnate spirits. *Everything, even war and conflicts, takes place only between the bearers of these hereditary titles, who incarnate these souls.*

5   Franz Boas, 'Ethnography of the Kwakiutl based on data collected by George Hunt, *35th Annual Report of the Bureau of American Ethnology to the Secretary of the Smithsonian Institution, 1913–14*, Washington, DC, p. 431.

6   Ibid., p. 823.

7   The best general exposition of Boas is to be found in 'The social organisation and the secret societies of the Kwakiutl Indians', *Report of the US National Museum* (1895), pp. 396 ff. *See also* pp. 465, 505, and 658.

8   The last shutter opens to reveal if not his whole face, at least in any case his mouth, and most frequently his eyes and mouth (see Boas, 'Ethnology of the Kwakiutl', p. 628, fig. 195).

9   Ibid., pp. 792–801.

10   P. Radin, 'The Winnebago tribe', *37th Annual Report of the Bureau of American Ethnology to the Secretary of the Smithsonian Institution*, Washington, DC, V, p. 246, gives the names of the Buffalo clan and in the following pages those of the other clans. Note especially the distribution of the first four to six forenames for men, and those for women. See also other lists, dating from J.O. Dorsey's work.

11   Note also the same fact, set out differently, in Radin, 'The Winnebago tribe', p. 194.

12   P. Radin, *Crashing Thunder: the Autobiography of an American Indian* (New York, Appleton, 1926), p. 41.

13   Forms of totemism of this kind are to be found in French West Africa and in Nigeria, the number of manatees and crocodiles in such and such a backwater corresponding to the number of living people. Also probably elsewhere individual animals correspond to the number of individual men.

14   Concerning these three series of names, see the bottom of the five genealogical tables (Arunta), in Strehlow, *Aranda Stämme*, Vol. 5, Plates. One can follow with interest the case of the Jerrambas (the honey-ant) and the Malbankas (the bearers of the name of civilising hero who was the founder of the wild-cat clan), both of which occur several times in these entirely reliable genealogies.

15   The sociologist and historian of Roman law are still hampered by the fact that we have almost no authentic sources for the very earliest law: some fragments from the era of the Kings (Numa) and some pieces from the Law of the Twelve Tables, and then only facts written down very much later. Of the complete Roman law, we only begin to

have a certain idea by legal texts duly reported or discovered in the third and second centuries BC and even later. Yet we need to conceive of what was the past for the law and the City. Regarding the City and its earliest history, the books of M. Piganiol and M. Carcopino can be used.

16   A clear allusion to a wolf-totem form of the god of cereals (*Roggenwolf*: Germanic). The word 'hirpex' gave 'herse' (cf. 'Lupatum', Cf. Meillet and Ernout, *Dictionnaire Etymologique*).

17   Cf. the commentaries of Frazer, ad loc., cf. ibid., p. 453. Acca lamenting over the corpse of Remus killed by Romulus – the foundation of the Lemuria (the sinister feast of the Lemures, of the souls of the dead lying bleeding) – play of words upon *Remuria* and *Lemuria*.

18   We should develop further this problem of the relationships at Rome between the *persona* and the *imago*, and of the latter with the name: *nomen, praenomen, cognomen*. We have not sufficient time here. The 'person' (*personne*): this is '*conditio*', '*status*', '*munus*'. '*Conditio*' signifies rank (e.g., '*secunda persona Epaminondae*', 'the second person after Epaminondas'). '*Status*' is one's standing in civil life. '*Munus*' signifies one's responsibilities and honours in civil and military life. All this is determined by the name, which is itself determined by family place, class and birth. One should read in *Fastes*, in the translation and admirable commentary of Sir James Frazer, the passage in which the origin of the name of Augustus is dealt with (II, 1. 476; cf. 1, line 589), and why Octavius Augustus did not wish to take the name of Romulus, nor that of Quirinus ('*qui tenet hoc numen, Romulus ante fuit*') and took one which summed up the sacred character of all the others (cf. Frazer, ad loc., line 40). We find there the whole Roman theory regarding names. Likewise in Virgil: Marcellus, son of Augustus, is already named in limbo, where his 'father', Aeneas sees him. Here also should be added a consideration of '*titulus*', which is raised in this line. M. Ernout tells me that the word itself might well be of Etruscan origin. Likewise the grammatical notion of 'person' (*personne*) which we still use, '*persona*' (Greek πρόσωπον, grammarians), should be considered.

19   Cicero, Marcus Tullius (1927), *The Speeches, Pro lege Manilia, Pro Caecina, Pro Cluentio, Pro Rabirio perduellionis*, trans. H. Grose Hodge (London, Heinemann), pp. 296–7. ('Then Bulbus, with a smile on his face, approached Staienus and said in his most ingratiating manner: "Hullo, Paetus!" – for Staienus had adopted the surname of Paetus from the family tree of the Aelii for fear that if he styled himself Ligur, it would be thought that his surname came from his race and not his family'.)

20   Pliny, *Natural History*, 35, 43, *Iustiniani Digesta* 19.1.17 ff and Lucretius, 4, 296.

21   For further examples of the usurpation of '*praenomina*', cf. Suetonius, *Nero*, I.

22   Thus Cicero, in *Ad Atticum*, says '*naturam et personam mean*' and '*personam sceleris*' elsewhere.

23   To my knowledge the best book on Stoic ethics is still Adolf Bonhöffer, *Die Ethik des Stoikers Epictet* (Stuttgart, Ferdinand Enke, 1894).

24   M. Brunschvicg, *Le Progrès de la conscience* I, pp. 69 ff.

25   Joseph Ernest Renan, 'Examen de conscience philosophique', *Revue des Deux Mondes*, 94 (1889), pp. 721–37.

26   Siegmund Schlossman, *Persona und πρόσωπον, im Recht und im Christlichen Dogma* (Leipzig, 1906). M. Henri Lévy-Bruhl introduced it to me a long while ago and in so doing has made this whole demonstration easier. See also the first part of Vol. I of Ludwig Schnorr von Carolsfeld, *Geschichte der Juristischen Person* (Munich, C.H. Beck'sche Verlagsbuchhandlung, 1933).

27   Suidas (1935) *Suidae Lexicon* (edited by Ada Adler), vol. I (Leipzig, Teubner); Gregory of Nauzizanzus, Ἐις τὰ 'ἀγια φῶτα or Oratio in Sancta Lumine', *Patriologiae Cursus Completus, Series Graeca*, ed. J.-P. Migne (Paris, Petit-Moutrouge, 1858), V. 36, cols 335–60.

28   Cf. the notes of Schlossmann, *Persona und πρόσωπον*, p. 65, etc.

29   Cf. the *Concursus* of Rusticus. Magnus Aurelius Cassiodorus Senator, 'Exposito

Psalmorum I-LXX', *Magni Aurelii Cassiodore Senatoris Opera*, para, II, I, *Corpus Christianorum Series Latina* (Brepols, Turnbolt, 1958).

30   Regarding this history, this revolution in the notion of unity, there might be a lot more to say here. Cf. especially the second volume of Brunschvicg, *Progrès de la conscience*.

31   *Ethics*, Part V, Proposition XL, corollary, Pr. XXIII and scholia, in conjunction with Pr. XXXIX and scholia, Pr. XXXVIII and scholia, Pr. XXIX and Pr. XXI. The notion of intellectual love comes from Leo Hebraeus, the Florentine Platonist.

32   *Generation of Animals*, trans. A.L. Peck (London, Heinemann/Harvard University Press), II, 3, p. 736b.

33   Brunschvicg, *Progrès de la conscience*, I, p. 182 ff.

34   M. Blondel reminds me of the relevance of the notes of Hume, where the latter poses the question of the relationship between 'consciousness and self' (*conscience – moi*). See *Treatise of Human Nature (Of Personal Identity)*.

35   J.G. Fichte, *Die Tatsachen des Bewusstseins* (Winter lecture course, 1810–11). A very fine and very brief summary is to be found in Xavier Léon, *Fichte et son temps* (1927), III. pp. 161–9.

27

The profession and vocation of politics   **Max Weber**

[. . .]

What kinds of inner joy does politics have to offer, and what kinds of personal qualifications does it presuppose in anyone turning to this career?

Well, first of all, it confers a feeling of power. The professional politician can have a sense of rising above everyday existence, even in what is formally a modest position, through knowing that he exercises influence on people, shares power over them, but above all from the knowledge that he holds in his hands some vital strand of historically important events. But the question facing such a person is which qualities will enable him to do justice to this power (however narrowly circumscribed it may actually be in any particular case), and thus to the responsibility it imposes on him. This takes us into the area of ethical questions, for to ask what kind of a human being one must be in order to have the right to seize the spokes of the wheel of history is to pose an ethical question.

One can say that three qualities are pre-eminently decisive for a politician: passion, a sense of responsibility, judgement. Passion in the sense of *concern for the thing itself* (*Sachlichkeit*), the passionate commitment to a 'cause' (*Sache*), to the god or demon[1] who commands that cause. Not in the sense of that inner attitude which my late friend Georg Simmel was wont to describe as 'sterile excitement'.[2] This is characteristic of a particular type of intellectual (especially Russian intellectuals, but of course not all of them!), and also plays such a large part amongst our own intellectuals at this carnival which is being graced with the proud name of a 'revolution'; it is the 'romanticism of the intellectually interesting', directed into the void and lacking all objective (*sachlich*) sense of responsibility. Simply to feel passion, however genuinely, is not sufficient to make a politician unless, in the form of service to a 'cause', *responsibility* for that

This chapter, originally given as a lecture and published in 1919, is taken from *Weber: Political Writings*, ed. P. Lassman and R. Speirs (Cambridge, Cambridge University Press, 1994), pp. 309–69.

cause becomes the decisive lode-star of all action. This requires (and this is the decisive psychological quality of the politician) *judgement*, the ability to maintain one's inner composure and calm while being receptive to realities, in other words *distance* from things and people. A 'lack of distance', in and of itself, is one of the deadly sins for any politician and it is one of those qualities which will condemn our future intellectuals to political incompetence if they cultivate it. For the problem is precisely this: how are hot passion and cool judgement to be forced together in a single soul? Politics is an activity conducted with the head, not with other parts of the body or soul. Yet if politics is to be genuinely human action, rather than some frivolous intellectual game, dedication to it can only be generated and sustained by passion. Only if one accustoms oneself to distance, in every sense of the word, can one achieve that powerful control over the soul which distinguishes the passionate politician from the mere 'sterile excitement' of the political amateur. The 'strength' of a political 'personality' means, first and foremost, the possession of these qualities.

Every day and every hour, therefore, the politician has to overcome a quite trivial, all-too-human enemy which threatens him from within: common *vanity*, the mortal enemy of all dedication to a cause and of all distance – in this case, of distance to oneself.

Vanity is a very widespread quality, and perhaps no one is completely free of it. In academic and scholarly circles it is a kind of occupational disease. In the case of the scholar, however, unattractive though this quality may be, it is relatively harmless in the sense that it does not, as a rule, interfere with the pursuit of knowledge. Things are quite different in the case of the politician. The ambition for *power* is an inevitable means (*Mittel*) with which he works. 'The instinct for power', as it is commonly called, is thus indeed one of his normal qualities. The sin against the holy spirit of his profession begins where this striving for power becomes detached from the task in hand (*unsachlich*) and becomes a matter of purely personal self-intoxication instead of being placed entirely at the service of the 'cause'. For there are ultimately just two deadly sins in the area of politics: a lack of objectivity and – often, although not always, identical with it – a lack of responsibility. Vanity, the need to thrust one's person as far as possible into the foreground, is what leads the politician most strongly into the temptation of committing one or other (or both) of these sins, particularly as the demagogue is forced to count on making an 'impact', and for this reason is always in danger both of becoming a play-actor and of taking the responsibility for his actions too lightly and being concerned only with the 'impression' he is making. His lack of objectivity tempts him to strive for the glittering appearance of power rather than its reality, while his irresponsibility tempts him to enjoy power for its own sake, without any substantive purpose. For although, or rather precisely *because*, power is the inevitable means of all politics, and the ambition for power therefore one of its driving forces, there is no more pernicious distortion of political energy than when the parvenu boasts of his power and vainly mirrors himself in the feeling of power – or indeed any and every worship of power for its own sake. The mere 'power politician', a type whom an energetically promoted cult is seeking to glorify here in Germany as elsewhere, may give the impression of strength, but in fact his actions merely lead into emptiness and absurdity. On this point the critics of 'power politics' are quite correct. The sudden inner collapse of typical representatives of this outlook (*Gesinnung*) has shown us just how much inner weakness and ineffectuality are concealed behind this grandiose but empty pose. It stems from a most wretched and superficial lack of concern for the *meaning* of human action, a blasé attitude that knows nothing of the tragedy in which all action, but quite particularly political action, is in truth enmeshed.

It is certainly true, and it is a fundamental fact of history (for which no more detailed explanation can be offered here), that the eventual outcome of political action frequently, indeed regularly, stands in a quite inadequate, even paradoxical relation to its original, intended meaning and purpose (*Sinn*). That does not mean, however, that this meaning and purpose, service to a *cause*, can be dispensed with if action is to have any firm inner support. The *nature* of the cause the politician seeks to serve by striving for and using power is a question of faith. He can serve a national goal or the whole of humanity, or social and ethical goals, or goals which are cultural, inner-worldly or religious; he may be sustained by a strong faith in 'progress' (however this is understood), or he may coolly reject this kind of faith; he can claim to be the servant of an 'idea' or, rejecting on principle any such aspirations, he may claim to serve external goals of everyday life – but some kind of belief must always be *present*. Otherwise (and there can be no denying this) even political achievements which, outwardly, are supremely successful will be cursed with the nullity of all mortal undertakings.

Having said this, we have already broached the last problem which concerns us this evening, the problem of the ethos of politics as a 'cause' (*Sache*). What vocation can politics *per se*, quite independently of its goals, fulfil within the overall moral economy of our conduct of life? Where is what one might call the ethical home of politics? At this point, admittedly, ultimate *Weltanschauungen* collide, and one has eventually to *choose* between them. The problem has recently been re-opened for discussion (in a quite wrong-headed fashion in my view), so let us approach it resolutely.

Let us begin by freeing the problem from a quite trivial falsification. In the first place, ethics can appear in a morally quite calamitous role. Let us look at some examples. You will rarely find a man whose love has turned from one woman to another who does not feel the need to legitimate this fact to himself by saying, 'She did not deserve my love', or, 'She disappointed me', or by offering some other such 'reasons'. This is a profoundly unchivalrous attitude, for, in addition to the simple fate of his ceasing to love her, which the woman must endure, it invents for itself a 'legitimacy' that allows the man to lay claim to a 'right' while attempting to burden her not only with misfortune but also with being in the wrong. The successful rival in love behaves in exactly the same way: the other man must be of lesser worth, otherwise he would not have been defeated. The same thing happens after any victorious war, when the victor will of course assert, with ignoble self-righteousness, 'I won because I was in the right.' Or when the horrors of war cause a man to suffer a psychological breakdown, instead of simply saying, 'It was all just too much for me', he now feels the need to justify his war-weariness by substituting the feeling, 'I couldn't bear the experience because I was obliged to fight for a morally bad cause.' The same applies to those defeated in war. Instead of searching, like an old woman, for the 'guilty party' after the war (when it was in fact the structure of society that produced the war), anyone with a manly, unsentimental bearing would say to the enemy, 'We lost the war – you won it. The matter is now settled. Now let us discuss what conclusions are to be drawn in the light of the *substantive (sachlichen)* interests involved and – this is the main thing – in the light of the responsibility for the *future* which the victor in particular must bear.' Anything else lacks dignity and will have dire consequences. A nation will forgive damage to its interests, but not injury to its honour, and certainly not when this is done in a spirit of priggish self-righteousness. Every new document which may emerge decades afterwards will stir up the undignified squabble, all the hatred and anger, once again, whereas the war ought at least to be buried *morally* when it comes to an end. That is only possible through a sober, matter-of-fact approach (*Sachlichkeit*) and chivalry, and, above all, it is only possible where there is *dignity*. But it can never be made possible by an 'ethic' which in fact entails indignity for both sides. Instead of dealing with what concerns the politician (the future and our responsibility for it), such an 'ethical' approach concerns itself with politically sterile (because unresolvable) questions of past guilt. *This*, if anything, is what constitutes political guilt. What is more, in this process people lose sight of the inevitable falsification of the whole problem by very material interests – the interests of the victor in maximising the gain (whether moral or material), and the hopes of the defeated that they will negotiate advantages by confessing their guilt. If anything is '*common*' (*gemein*)[3] it is this, and it is the consequence of using 'ethics' as a means of 'being in the right'.

What, then, is the real relationship between *ethics* and *politics*? Have they nothing at all to do with one another, as has sometimes been said? Or is the opposite true, namely that political action is subject to 'the same' ethic as every other form of activity? At times people have believed that these two possibilities were mutually exclusive alternatives, and that either the one or the other was correct. But is it in fact true that any ethic in the world could establish substantially *identical* commandments applicable to all relationships, whether erotic, business, family or official, to one's relations with one's wife, greengrocer, son, competitor, with a friend or an accused man? Can the fact that politics operates with a quite specific means, namely power, backed up by the use of *violence*, really be a matter of such indifference as far as the ethical demands placed on politics are concerned? Have we not seen that the Bolshevik and Spartacist[4] ideologues, precisely because they use this political instrument, bring about exactly the *same* results as any militarist dictator? What, apart from the identity of the holders of power (and their amateurism) distinguishes the rule of the Workers' and Soldiers' Councils from the rule of any wielder of power under the old regime? What distinguishes the polemics directed by most exponents of the supposedly new ethics at the opponents they criticise from the polemics of any other demagogues? Their noble intentions, some will say. Very well. But the question under discussion here is the means, and their enemies lay just as much claim to noble ultimate aims, and do so with complete subjective sincerity. 'All they that take the sword shall perish with the sword',[5] and fighting is fighting everywhere. What about the ethics of the *Sermon on the Mount* then? The Sermon on the Mount, by which we mean the absolute ethics of the Gospel, is something far more serious than those who are so fond of citing its commandments today believe. It is not to be taken frivolously. What has been said about causality in science also applies to this ethic, namely that it is not a hired cab which one may stop at will and climb into or out of as one sees fit. Rather, the meaning of the sermon (if it is not to be reduced to banality) is precisely this: we must accept it in its entirety *or* leave it entirely alone. Hence the case of the rich young man: 'he went away sorrowful, for he had great possessions.'[6] The commandment of the Gospel is unconditional and unambiguous – 'give all that thou hast' – *everything*, absolutely. The politician will say that this is an excessive and socially meaningless demand if it is not made to apply to *everybody*, which means taxation, expropriation by taxation, confiscation, in other words, coercion and order applied to *all*. The ethical commandment disregards such questions *completely* – that is its essence. The same applies to the injunction to 'turn the other cheek!' – unconditionally, without asking by what right the other person has struck you. An ethic of indignity, except for a saint. This is the heart of the matter: it is necessary to be a saint in *all* things, or at least one must want to be one, one must live like Jesus, the Apostles, Saint Francis and men of that kind; *then* this type of ethic becomes meaningful and expresses a kind of dignity. *But not otherwise.* For while it is a consequence of the unworldly ethic of love to say, 'resist not evil with force',[7] the politician is governed by the contrary maxim, namely, 'You *shall* resist evil with force, for if you do not, you are *responsible* for the spread of evil.' Anyone seeking to act in accordance with the ethic of the Gospel should not go on strike, since strikes are a form of coercion; instead he should join an unaffiliated trade union. Above all, he should not talk of 'revolution', for that ethic surely does not teach that civil war of all things is the only legitimate form of war. The pacifist whose actions are guided by the Gospel will refuse weapons or throw them away, as we Germans were recommended to do, so that we might fulfil our ethical duty to end the war, and thus to end all war. The politician will say that the only sure means of discrediting war for the *foreseeable* future would have been peace on the basis of the *status quo*. Then the people of all nations would have asked what the point of the war was. It would have been reduced to absurdity, which is not now possible. For the war will have proved to be politically profitable for the victors, or at least for some of them. The responsibility for this outcome lies with the behaviour which made it quite impossible for us to resist. What will now happen – once the phase of exhaustion has passed – is, that *peace, not war, will have been discredited* – and this will be the result of absolute ethics.

Finally, there is the duty to be truthful. For the ethic of absolute principles this is an unconditional duty.[8] Hence it was concluded that all documents should be published, especially those which placed a burden of guilt on our country, and that a confession of guilt should be made on the basis of these documents – unilaterally, unconditionally, regardless of the consequences. The politician will take the view that the upshot of this will not serve the cause of truth, but rather that truth will certainly be obscured by the misuse of the documents and by the passions they unleash. He will take the view that the only productive approach would be a systematic, comprehensive investigation, conducted by disinterested parties; any other way of proceeding could have consequences for the nation which could not be repaired in decades. 'Consequences', however, are no *concern* of absolutist ethics.

That is the crucial point. We have to understand that ethically oriented activity can follow two fundamentally different, irreconcilably opposed maxims. It can follow the 'ethic of principled conviction' (*Gesinnung*) or the 'ethic of responsibility'. It is not that the ethic of conviction is identical with irresponsibility, nor that the ethic of responsibility means the absence of principled conviction – there is of course no question of that. But there is a profound opposition between acting by the maxim of the ethic of conviction (putting it in religious terms: 'The Christian does what is right and places the outcome in God's hands'),[9] and acting by the maxim of the ethic of responsibility, which means that one must answer for the (foreseeable) *consequences* of one's actions. A syndicalist who is committed to the ethics of conviction might be fully aware that the likely consequences of his actions will be, say, increased chances for the forces of reaction, increased oppression of his own class, a brake on the rise of his class. But none of this will make the slightest impression on him. If evil consequences flow from an action done out of pure conviction, this type of person holds the world, not the doer, responsible, or the stupidity of others, or the will of God who made them thus. A man who subscribes to the ethic of responsibility, by contrast, will make allowances for precisely these everyday shortcomings in people. He has no right, as Fichte correctly observed,[10] to presuppose goodness and perfection in human beings. He does not feel that he can shuffle off the consequences of his own actions, as far as he could foresee them, and place the burden on the shoulders of others. He will say, 'These consequences are to be attributed to my actions.' The person who subscribes to the ethic of conviction feels 'responsible' only for ensuring that the flame of pure conviction (for example, the flame of protest against the injustice of the social order) is never extinguished. To kindle that flame again and again is the purpose of his actions, actions which, judged from the point of view of their possible success, are utterly irrational, and which can and are only intended to have exemplary value.

Yet we have still not reached the end of the problem. No ethics in the world can get round the fact that the achievement of 'good' ends is in many cases tied to the necessity of employing morally suspect or at least morally dangerous means, and that one must reckon with the possibility or even likelihood of evil side-effects. Nor can any ethic in the world determine when and to what extent the ethically good end 'sanctifies' the ethically dangerous means and side-effects.

The decisive means of politics is the use of violence. Just how great are the ramifications of the ethical tension between ends and means in politics can be seen in the case of the revolutionary socialists (the Zimmerwald faction).[11] Even during the war, as is generally known, they espoused a principle which one might characterise thus: 'If the choice lies between a few more years of war, followed by a revolution, and peace now but no revolution, we choose a few more years of war.' If then asked what this revolution might achieve, any scientifically trained socialist would have replied that there could be no question of a transition to an economy deserving the name 'socialist' as *he* understood the term. Rather, a bourgeois economy would arise again which would have shed only its feudal elements and the remnants of dynasticism. For this modest result they would accept 'a few more years of war'! In this instance it could well be said that even a person of very firm socialist convictions might reject the end if these are the means it demands. But this is precisely how things stand with Bolshevism and Spartacism and indeed every type of revolutionary socialism. Hence it is of course utterly ridiculous for such people to condemn *morally* the 'politicians of violence' of the old regime for using precisely the same means as they are prepared to use (no matter how justified they may be in rejecting the *aims* of the other side).

It seems that the ethics of conviction is bound to founder hopelessly on this problem of how the end is to sanctify the means. Indeed the only position it can logically take is to *reject any* action which employs morally dangerous means. Logically. In the real world, admittedly, we repeatedly see the proponent of the 'ethics of conviction' suddenly turning into a chiliastic prophet. Those who have been preaching 'love against force' one minute, for example, issue a call to force the next; they call for one *last* act of force to create the situation in which *all* violence will have been destroyed for ever – just like our military leaders who said to the soldiers before every attack that this would be the last, that it would bring victory and then peace. The man who espouses an ethic of conviction cannot bear the ethical irrationality of the world. He is a cosmic-ethical 'rationalist'.

Those of you who know their Dostoyevsky will recall the scene with the Grand Inquisitor, where the problem is dissected very acutely.[12] It is not possible to unite the ethic of conviction with the ethic of responsibility, nor can one issue an ethical decree determining which end shall sanctify *which* means, if indeed any concession at all is to be made to this principle.

My colleague, F.W. Foerster,[13] a man I hold in the highest personal esteem because of the undoubted integrity of his convictions (although I reject him unreservedly as a politician), thinks that he can get round the difficulty in his book with the simple thesis that only good can flow from good, only evil from evil. Were this so, the whole, complex problem would admittedly not exist. Yet it is astonishing that such a thesis could still see the light of day 2,500 years after the Upanishads were composed. Not just the entire course of world history, but any unbiased examination of daily experience, proclaims the opposite. The development of all the religions in the world rests, after all, on the fact that the opposite is true. The age-old problem of theodicy is, after all, the question of how a power which is said to be both all-powerful and benevolent can possibly have created such an irrational world of undeserved suffering, unpunished injustice and incorrigible stupidity. Either that power is not all-powerful or it is not benevolent – or quite other principles of compensation and retribution govern life, principles which we may be able to interpret metaphysically or which will for ever elude our interpretation. This problem, the experience of the irrationality of the world, was, after all, the driving force behind all religious development. The Indian doctrine of *karma*, Persian dualism, original sin, predestination and the concept of the *deus absconditus*, all these notions have grown out of precisely this experience. The early Christians too knew very well that the world was governed by demons, that anyone who gets involved with politics, which is to say with the means of power and violence, is making a pact with diabolical powers, and that it does *not* hold true of his actions that only good can come of good and only evil from evil, but rather that the opposite is often the case. Anyone who fails to see this is indeed a child in political matters.

Religious ethics have adopted various strategies to come to terms with the fact that we are placed in various orders of life, each of which is subject to different laws. Hellenic polytheism sacrificed to Aphrodite and also to Hera, to Dionysos as well as to Apollo, knowing that these gods were often in conflict with one another. The Hindu order of life made each of the various occupations subject to a particular ethical law, a *dharma*, and forever divided them one from another into castes, setting them in a rigid hierarchy of rank from which there was no escape for the individual born into a particular caste, except through reincarnation in the next life; the different occupations were thereby placed at varying distances from the highest religious goods of salvation. Hinduism was therefore able to elaborate the *dharma* for each caste, from the ascetics and Brahmins down to the rogues and whores, according to the immanent and particular laws governing each occupation, including war and politics. How war is fitted into the totality of the orders of life can be found in the *Bhagavad Gita*, in the discussion between Krishna and Arduna. 'Do what is necessary', which means whatever 'work' is imposed as a duty by the *dharma* of the warrior caste and its rules, whatever is objectively necessary in relation to the purpose of war. According to this belief, acting thus is not injurious to religious salvation; indeed it serves this end. Admission to Indra's heaven had always been assured to the Indian warrior who died a hero's death just as certainly as Valhalla was to the Germanic warrior. But the former would have scorned Nirvana just as surely as the latter would have scorned the paradise of Christianity with its choirs of angels. This specialisation of ethics made it possible for Indian ethics to treat the regal art of politics quite without reservation or scruple, following the peculiar laws of politics alone, indeed intensifying them radically. Truly radical 'Machiavellianism', in the popular sense of the word, finds its classic expression in Indian literature in the *Kautaliya Artha-Sastra* (composed long before Christianity, allegedly in the time of Chandragupta), in comparison with which Machiavelli's *Principe* is harmless. In Catholic ethics, to which Professor Foerster is otherwise sympathetic, the *consilia evangelica* are, as is generally known, a special ethic for those gifted with the charisma of holy life. Here, alongside the monk, who may spill no blood nor seek material gain, there stand the pious knight and the burgher, the first of whom may do the former, while the second may do the latter. The gradations in this ethic and its integration within an organic doctrine of salvation are less consistent than in India, as was bound to be the case, given the assumptions of the Christian faith. Because the world was corrupted by original sin, it was possible to build violence relatively easily into ethics as a means of chastising sin and heretics who endangered the soul. But the unworldly demands of the Sermon on the Mount, which represent a pure ethics of conviction, and the absolute demand for religious natural justice founded on the Sermon, have retained their revolutionary force and come to the fore with elemental power in almost every period of social upheaval. In particular they created the radical pacifist sects, one of which experimented in Pennsylvania with a state that abjured force in its relations with other states. The outcome of the experiment was tragic, however, inasmuch as the Quakers could not take up arms on behalf of their own ideals at the outbreak of the War of Independence, although this was fought on behalf of those very ideals. Normal Protestantism, by contrast, legitimated the state absolutely (and thus its means, violence) as a divine institution, and gave its blessing to the legitimate authoritarian state in particular. Luther relieved the individual of ethical responsibility for war and placed it on the shoulders of authority, asserting that no guilt could ever be involved in obeying authority in matters other than faith. Calvinism in its turn recognised as a matter of principle the use of force as a means to defend the faith, in other words religious war, which, in Islam, was a vital element in religion from the very beginning. Plainly, the problem of political ethics is *not* just one that has been thrown up by the modern lack of faith engendered by the cult of the hero during the Renaissance. All religions have grappled with it, and with very varying degrees of success; in view of what has been said above, things could not have been otherwise. The specific means of *legitimate violence per se* in the hands of human associations is what gives all the ethical problems of politics their particular character.

Anyone who makes a pact with the means of violence, for whatever purpose – and every politician does this – is at the mercy of its specific consequences. This applies particularly to the man fighting for a belief, whether religious or revolutionary. Let us simply take the present as an example. Anyone wishing to establish absolute justice on earth by *force* needs a following in order to do so, a human 'apparatus'. He must promise these people the necessary inner and outward prizes – rewards in heaven or on earth – because the apparatus will not function otherwise. Under the conditions of modern class-warfare the inner rewards are the satisfaction of hatred and revenge, of *ressentiment* and the need for the pseudo-ethical feeling of being in the right, the desire to slander one's opponents and make heretics of them. The outward rewards are adventure, victory, booty, power and prebends. The success of the leader is entirely dependent on the functioning of his apparatus. He is therefore dependent on *its* motives, not his own. He is dependent also on the possibility of providing those prizes *permanently* to his following, the Red Guard, the informers, the agitators he needs. Given these conditions of his activity, what he actually achieves does not, therefore, lie in his own hands but is, rather, prescribed for him by the, in ethical terms, predominantly base or common (*gemein*) motives prompting the actions of his following. He can only keep control of his following as long as a sincere belief in his person and his cause inspires at least some of the group, probably never in this life even the majority of them. Not only is this faith, even when held with subjective sincerity, in many cases merely the ethical 'legitimation' of the craving for revenge, power, booty and prebends (and let no one try to persuade us differently, for the materialist interpretation of history is not a cab which may be boarded at will, and it makes no exceptions for the bearers of revolutions!), but the emotionalism of revolution is then followed by a return to traditional, *everyday existence*, the hero of the faith disappears, and so, above all, does the faith itself, or it becomes (even more effectively) a part of the conventional rhetoric used by political philistines and technicians. This development comes about particularly quickly in a war of faith, because these are usually conducted or inspired by genuine *leaders*, prophets of revolution. For it is one of the conditions of success in this, as in any apparatus subordinate to a leader, that things must be emptied and made into matters-of-fact (*Versachlichung*), and the following must undergo spiritual proletarianisation, in order to achieve 'discipline'. This is why the following of a man fighting for a faith, when it begins to rule, tends to decline particularly easily into a quite ordinary stratum of prebendaries.

Anyone wishing to practise politics of any kind, and especially anyone who wishes to make a profession of politics, has to be conscious of these ethical paradoxes and of his responsibility for what may become of *himself* under pressure from them. He is becoming involved, I repeat, with the diabolical powers that lurk in all violence. The great virtuosi of unworldly goodness and love for mankind, whether they came from Nazareth or Assisi or from the palaces of Indian kings, did not employ the means of politics, force. Their kingdom was 'not of this world' and yet they worked, and work still, in this world, and the figures of Platon Karatayev[14] and Dostoyevsky's saints are still the closest imitations of their lives. Anyone seeking to save his own soul and the souls of others does not take the path of politics in order to reach his goal, for politics has quite different tasks, namely those which can only be achieved by force. The genius – or demon – of politics lives in a state of inner tension with the god of love, and even with the Christian God as manifested in the institution of the church, a tension that may erupt at any moment into irresolvable conflict. Even in the days of church rule people were aware of this. Again and again the interdict was imposed on Florence (something which represented at the time a far greater power over men and the salvation of their souls than what Fichte has called the 'cold approbation' of Kant's ethical judgement),[15] and yet the citizens of Florence fought against the Holy See. Machiavelli had such situations in mind when, in a beautiful passage in his Florentine histories (if my memory does not deceive me),[16] he has one of his heroes praise those citizens who placed the greatness of their native city above the salvation of their souls.

To see the problem in its current guise, replace the terms 'native city' or 'Fatherland' (which may not strike everyone as an unambiguous value at present) with 'the future of socialism' or even 'the achievement of international peace'. The 'salvation of the soul' is endangered by each of these, whenever men strive to attain them by *political* activity, employing the means of violence and acting on the basis of an ethic of responsibility. Yet if the soul's salvation is pursued in a war of faith fought purely out of an ethic of conviction, it may be damaged and discredited for generations to come, because responsibility for the *consequences* is lacking. In such circumstances those engaged in action remain unaware of the diabolical powers at work. They are inexorable, bringing about the consequences of their actions, including consequences for their inner being, to which they will fall helpless victims if they remain blind to them. 'The devil is old, so become old if you want to understand him'[17] – the saying does not refer to one's age measured in years. I too have never allowed myself to be outdone in debate simply because of a date on a birth certificate; equally, the mere fact that someone is twenty whereas I am over fifty does not persuade me that this in itself is an achievement before which I must expire in awe. What matters is not age but the trained ability to look at the realities of life with an unsparing gaze, to bear these realities and be a match for them inwardly.

For truly, although politics is something done with the head, it is certainly not something done with the head *alone*. On this point the conviction-moralists are entirely correct. But whether one *ought* to act on the basis of an ethics of conviction or one of responsibility, and *when* one should do the one or the other, these are not things about which one can give instructions to anybody. There is just one thing one can say in these times of excitement – *not*, you believe, a 'sterile' form of excitement (although excitement is not always the same as true passion) – if, *suddenly*, conviction-politicians spring up all around, proclaiming, 'The world is stupid and base (*gemein*), not I. Responsibility for the consequences does not fall on me but on the others, in whose service I work and whose stupidity or baseness I shall eradicate', then I say plainly that I want to know how much *inner weight* is carried by this ethic of conviction. For it is my impression that, in nine cases out of ten, I am dealing with windbags, people who are intoxicated with romantic sensations but who do not truly feel what they are taking upon themselves. Such conduct holds little human interest for me and it most certainly does not shake me to the core. On the other hand it is immensely moving when a mature person (whether old or young) who feels with his whole soul the responsibility he bears for the real consequences of his actions, and who acts on the basis of an ethics of responsibility, says at some point, 'Here I stand, I can do no other.'[18] That is something genuinely human and profoundly moving. For it must be *possible* for *each* of us to find ourselves in such a situation at some point if we are not inwardly dead. In this respect, the ethics of conviction and the ethics of responsibility are not absolute opposites. They are complementary to one another, and only in combination do they produce the true human being who is *capable* of having a 'vocation for politics'.

And now, ladies and gentlemen, let us return to these questions *ten years* from now. If by that time, as I am bound to fear will be the case, an age of reaction has set in for a whole series of reasons, and little has been realised of all those things which many of you and (as I freely admit) I too have wished and hoped for – perhaps not exactly none of them but apparently only very little (this is very likely, but it will not break my spirit, although I confess that it is an inward burden) – then I would very much like to see what has become of those of you – what has 'become' of you in the innermost sense of the word – who at present feel themselves genuinely to be 'politicians of conviction' and who share in the intoxication (*Rausch*)[19] which this revolution signifies, It would be fine indeed if Shakespeare's Sonnet 102 fitted the situation:

> Our love was new, and then but in the spring,
> When I was wont to greet it with my lays;
> As Philomel in summer's front doth sing,
> And stops her pipe in growth of riper days.

But that is not how things are. What lies immediately ahead of us is not the flowering of summer but a polar night of icy darkness and hardness, no matter which group wins the outward victory now. For, where there is nothing, not only has the Kaiser lost his rights but so too has the proletarian. When this night slowly begins to recede, which of those people will still be alive whose early summer seems now to have flowered so profusely? And what will have become of you all inwardly? Embitterment or philistinism, sheer, dull acceptance of the world and of your job (*Beruf*) – or the third, and not the least common possibility, a mystical flight from the world on the part of those with the gift for it or – a frequent and pernicious variant – on the part of those who force themselves into such an attitude because it is fashionable. In every such case I will draw the conclusion that they were *not* inwardly a match for their own actions, *nor* were they a match for the world as it really is, nor for their daily existence. Objectively and actually, they did not have the vocation they thought they had for politics in the innermost sense of the word. They would have done better to cultivate plain and simple brotherliness with other individuals, and, for the rest, to have worked soberly (*sachlich*) at their daily tasks.

Politics means slow, strong drilling through hard boards, with a combination of passion and a sense of judgement. It is of course entirely correct, and a fact confirmed by all historical experience, that what is possible would never have been achieved if, in this world, people had not repeatedly reached for the impossible. But the person who can do this must be a leader; not only that, he must, in a very simple sense of the word, be a hero. And even those who are neither of these things must, even now, put on the armour of that steadfastness of heart which can withstand even the defeat of all hopes, for otherwise they will not even be capable of achieving what is possible today. Only someone who is certain that he will not be broken when the world, seen from his point of view, is too stupid or too base for what he wants to offer it, and who is certain that he will be able to say 'Nevertheless' in spite of everything – only someone like this has a 'vocation' for politics.

Notes

1   In this instance Weber is using *Dämon* in the same sense as the English 'demon'; elsewhere he uses it without the sense of moral evil.

2   This use of *Aufgeregtheit* as a derogatory term for revolutionary fervour was prefigured in Goethe's fragmentary satire on the consequences of the French Revolution, *Die Aufgeregten*.

3   For Nietzsche, as for Weber, *gemein* ('common', 'base', 'contemptible') was the antithesis of *vornehm* ('distinguished', 'noble'). Weber's objection to the (mis-)use of 'ethics' to prove one is 'in the right' echoes Nietzschean scepticism about the 'moral interpretation of phenomena'.

4   The Spartakus League, led by Karl Liebknecht, was formed in 1916–17. A left socialist group opposed to war, it adopted the name of the Communist Party of Germany in December 1918.

5   Matthew 26: 52.

6   Matthew 19: 22.

7   Matthew 5: 39: 'That ye resist not evil: but whosoever shall smite thee on thy right cheek, turn to him the other also.'

8   Kant's attempt to found ethics on the 'categorical imperative' led him to argue that there was an absolute obligation to tell the truth, even where to do so might lead to the loss of human life. See, for example, *The Metaphysics of Morals*, ed. M. Gregor (Cambridge, 1991), pp. 225–7. Kant's was one of the most influential voices arguing for 'anti-consequentialism' in ethics in Germany.

9   Although an exact source for these words (used on several occasions by Weber) has not been traced, the editors of the new *Gesamtausgabe* believe they allude to a passage in Luther's lectures on *Genesis*, 'Fac tuum officium, et eventum Deo permitte', *D. Martin Luthers Werke. Kritische Gesamtausgabe*, vol. 44 (Weimar, 1915), p. 78.

10   Fichte quotes such sentiments from Machiavelli's *Discourses* in 'Über Macchiavelli (sic!) als Schriftsteller', *Johann Gottlieb Fichtes nachgelassene Werke*, vol. 3 (Bonn, 1856), p. 420.

11   In September 1915 a group of radical socialists held a conference in Zimmerwald (near Berne) with the aim of founding a new (Third) International. Despite further conferences in 1916 and 1917, they could not achieve unity.

12   F. Dostoyevsky, *The Brothers Karamazov*, book 5, ch. 5.

13   F.W. Foerster (1869–1966) was a leading spokesman of the Society for Ethical Culture. His *Staatsbürgerliche Erziehung* (1910) ('Education for Citizenship', reprinted under the title *Politische Ethik und politische Pädagogik*) was a popular expression of the ideas of this movement for social reform.

14   Platon Karatayev is a character in Tolstoy's *War and Peace*.

15   'Das System der Sittenlehre nach den Principien der Wissenschaftslehre', *Johann Gottlieb Fichtes sämmtliche Werke*, vol. 4 (Berlin, 1845) p. 167.

16   The reference is to Machiavelli, *Florentine Histories*, book 3, ch. 7, p. 114: 'so much more did those citizens esteem their fatherland than their souls' (in the translation by L.F. Banfield and H.C. Mansfield, Princeton, 1988).

17   Goethe, *Faust*, Part II, lines 6817–18.

18   Luther is reported to have said this at the Diet of Worms in 1521.

19   In criticising the *Rausch* ('intoxication') of revolutionary enthusiasm, Weber is striking at the ready welcome given to the 'Dionysian' aspects of Nietzsche's thought by many German intellectuals at the time.

28

Introduction to 'The Use of Pleasure'
Michel Foucault

Modifications

This series of studies [. . .] was intended to be neither a history of sexual
behaviors nor a history of representations, but a history of 'sexuality' – the
quotation marks have a certain importance. My aim was not to write a
history of sexual behaviors and practices, tracing their successive forms,
their evolution, and their dissemination; nor was it to analyze the scientific,
religious, or philosophical ideas through which these behaviors have been
represented. I wanted first to dwell on that quite recent and banal notion of
'sexuality': to stand detached from it, bracketing its familiarity, in order to
analyze the theoretical and practical context with which it has been
associated. The term itself did not appear until the beginning of the nineteenth century, a fact that should be neither underestimated nor over-
interpreted. It does point to something other than a simple recasting of
vocabulary, but obviously it does not mark the sudden emergence of that
to which 'sexuality' refers. The use of the word was established in connection with other phenomena: the development of diverse fields of
knowledge (embracing the biological mechanisms of reproduction as well
as the individual or social variants of behavior); the establishment of a set
of rules and norms – in part traditional, in part new – which found
support in religious, judicial, pedagogical, and medical institutions; and
changes in the way individuals were led to assign meaning and value to
their conduct, their duties, their pleasures, their feelings and sensations,
their dreams. In short, it was a matter of seeing how an 'experience' came
to be constituted in modern Western societies, an experience that caused
individuals to recognize themselves as subjects of a 'sexuality,' which was
accessible to very diverse fields of knowledge and linked to a system of

This chapter is
taken from *The Use
of Pleasure*
(Harmondsworth,
Penguin, 1987),
chapters 1–3. It was
first published in
France as *L'Usage
des plaisirs* in 1984.

rules and constraints. What I planned, therefore, was a history of the experience of sexuality, where experience is understood as the correlation between fields of knowledge, types of normativity, and forms of subjectivity in a particular culture.

To speak of sexuality in this way, I had to break with a conception that was rather common. Sexuality was conceived of as a constant. The hypothesis was that where it was manifested in historically singular forms, this was through various mechanisms of repression to which it was bound to be subjected in every society. What this amounted to, in effect, was that desire and the subject of desire were withdrawn from the historical field, and interdiction as a general form was made to account for anything historical in sexuality. But rejection of this hypothesis was not sufficient by itself. To speak of 'sexuality' as a historically singular experience also presupposed the availability of tools capable of analyzing the peculiar characteristics and interrelations of the three axes that constitute it: (1) the formation of sciences (*savoirs*) that refer to it, (2) the systems of power that regulate its practice, (3) the forms within which individuals are able, are obliged, to recognize themselves as subjects of this sexuality. Now, as to the first two points, the work I had undertaken previously – having to do first with medicine and psychiatry, and then with punitive power and disciplinary practices – provided me with the tools I needed. The analysis of discursive practices made it possible to trace the formation of disciplines (*savoirs*) while escaping the dilemma of science versus ideology. And the analysis of power relations and their technologies made it possible to view them as open strategies, while escaping the alternative of a power conceived of as domination or exposed as a simulacrum.

But when I came to study the modes according to which individuals are given to recognize themselves as sexual subjects, the problems were much greater. At the time the notion of desire, or of the desiring subject, constituted if not a theory, then at least a generally accepted theoretical theme. This very acceptance was odd: it was this same theme, in fact, or variations thereof, that was found not only at the very center of the traditional theory, but also in the conceptions that sought to detach themselves from it. It was this theme, too, that appeared to have been inherited, in the nineteenth and twentieth centuries, from a long Christian tradition. While the experience of sexuality, as a singular historical figure, is perhaps quite distinct from the Christian experience of the 'flesh,' both appear nonetheless to be dominated by the principle of 'desiring man.' In any case, it seemed to me that one could not very well analyze the formation and development of the experience of sexuality from the eighteenth century onward, without doing a historical and critical study dealing with desire and the desiring subject. In other words, without undertaking a 'genealogy.' This does not mean that I proposed to write a history of the successive conceptions of desire, of concupiscence, or of libido, but rather to analyze the practices by which individuals were led to focus their attention on themselves, to decipher, recognize, and acknowledge themselves as subjects of desire, bringing into play between themselves and themselves a certain relationship that allows them to discover, in desire, the truth of their being, be it natural or fallen. In short, with this genealogy the idea was to investigate how individuals were led to practice, on themselves and on others, a hermeneutics of desire, a hermeneutics of which their sexual behavior was doubtless the occasion, but certainly not the exclusive domain. Thus, in order to understand how the modern individual could experience himself as a subject of a 'sexuality,' it was essential first to determine how, for centuries, Western man had been brought to recognize himself as a subject of desire.

A theoretical shift had seemed necessary in order to analyze what was often designated as the advancement of learning; it led me to examine the forms of discursive practices that articulated the human sciences. A theoretical shift had also been required in order to analyze what is often described as the manifestations of 'power'; it led me to examine, rather, the manifold relations, the open strategies, and the rational techniques that articulate the exercise of powers. It appeared that I now had to undertake a third shift, in order to analyze what is termed 'the subject.' It seemed appropriate to look for the forms and modalities of the relation to self by which the individual constitutes and recognizes himself *qua* subject. After first studying the games of truth (*jeux de verité*) in their interplay with one another, as exemplified by certain empirical sciences in the seventeenth and eighteenth centuries, and then studying their interaction with power relations, as exemplified by punitive practices – I felt obliged to study the games of truth in the relationship of self with self and the forming of oneself as a subject, taking as my domain of reference and field of investigation what might be called 'the history of desiring man.'

But it was clear that to undertake this genealogy would carry me far from my original project. I had to choose: either stick to the plan I had set, supplementing it with a brief historical survey of the theme of desire, or reorganize the whole study around the slow formation, in antiquity, of a hermeneutics of the self. I opted for the latter, reasoning that, after all, what I have held to, what I have tried to maintain for many years, is the effort to isolate some of the elements that might be useful for a history of truth. Not a history that would be concerned with what might be true in the fields of learning, but an analysis of the 'games of truth,' the games of truth and error through which being is historically constituted as experience; that is, as something that can and must be thought. What are the games of truth by which man proposes to think his own nature when he perceives himself to be mad; when he considers himself to be ill; when he conceives of himself as a living, speaking, laboring being; when he judges and punishes himself as a criminal? What were the games of truth by which human beings came to see themselves as desiring individuals? It seemed to me that by framing the question in this way, and by attempting to develop it for a period that was rather far from the horizons with which I was familiar, I would be going more closely into the inquiry that I have long been committed to – even if this approach were to demand a few years of additional work. [. . .]

[. . .]

The studies that follow [in *The Use of Pleasure*], like the others I have done previously, are studies of 'history' by reason of the domain they deal with and the references they appeal to; but they are not the work of a 'historian.' Which does not mean that they summarize or synthesize work done by others. Considered from the standpoint of their 'pragmatics,' they are the record of a long and tentative exercise that needed to be revised and corrected again and again. It was a philosophical exercise. The object was to learn to what extent the effort to think one's own history can free thought from what it silently thinks, and so enable it to think differently.

[. . .]

It seemed that by starting from the modern era, and proceeding back through Christianity to antiquity, one would not be able to avoid raising a question that was at the same time very simple and very general: why is sexual conduct, why are the activities and pleasures that attach to it, an object of moral solicitude? Why this ethical concern – which, at certain times, in certain societies and groups, appears more important than the moral attention that is focused on other, likewise essential, areas of individual or collective life, such as alimentary behaviors or the fulfillment of civic duties? A reply comes to mind immediately, I know: they have been the object of fundamental interdictions, and transgressing the latter is considered a serious offense. But this is to make an answer of the question itself; and further, it shows a failure to recognize that the ethical concern over sexual conduct is not, in its intensity or its forms, always directly tied to the system of interdictions. It is often the case that the moral solicitude is strong precisely where there is neither obligation nor prohibition. In other words, the interdiction is one thing, the moral problematization is another. It seemed to me, therefore, that the question that ought to guide my inquiry was the following: how, why, and in what forms was sexuality constituted as a moral domain? Why this ethical concern that was so persistent despite its varying forms and intensity? Why this 'problematization?' But, after all, this was the proper task of a history of thought, as against a history of behaviors or representations: to define the conditions in which human beings 'problematize' what they are, what they do, and the world in which they live.

But in raising this very general question, and in directing it to Greek and Greco-Roman culture, it occurred to me that this problematization was linked to a group of practices that have been of unquestionable importance in our societies: I am referring to what might be called the 'arts of existence.' What I mean by the phrase are those intentional and voluntary actions by which men not only set themselves rules of conduct, but also seek to transform themselves, to change themselves in their singular being, and to make their life into an *oeuvre* that carries certain aesthetic values and meets certain stylistic criteria. These 'arts of existence,' these 'techniques of the self,' no doubt lost some of their importance and autonomy when they were assimilated into the exercise of priestly power in early Christianity, and later, into educative, medical, and psychological types of practices. Still, I thought that the long history of these aesthetics of existence and these technologies of the self remained to be done, or resumed. It has been a long time now since Burckhardt pointed out their significance for the epoch of the Renaissance, but their perpetuation, their history, and their development do not end there.[1] In any case, it seemed to me that the study of the problematization of sexual behavior in antiquity could be regarded as a chapter – one of the first chapters – of that general history of the 'techniques of the self.'

There is irony in those efforts one makes to alter one's way of looking at things, to change the boundaries of what one knows and to venture out a ways from there. Did mine actually result in a different way of thinking? Perhaps at most they made it possible to go back through what I was already thinking, to think it differently, and to see what I had done from a new vantage point and in a clearer light. Sure of having traveled far, one finds that one is looking down on oneself from above. The journey rejuvenates things, and ages the relationship with oneself. I seem to have gained a better perspective on the way I worked – gropingly, and by means of different or successive fragments – on this project, whose goal is a history of truth. It was a matter of analyzing, not behaviors or ideas, nor societies and their 'ideologies,' but the *problematizations* through which being offers itself to be, necessarily, thought – and the *practices* on the basis of which these problematizations are formed. The archaeological dimension of the analysis made it possible to examine the forms themselves; its genealogical dimension enabled me to analyze their formation out of the practices and the modifications undergone by the latter. There was the problematization of madness and illness arising out of social and medical practices, and defining a certain pattern of 'normalization'; a problematization of life, language, and labor in discursive practices that conformed to certain 'epistemic' rules; and a problematization of crime and criminal behavior emerging from certain punitive practices conforming to a 'disciplinary' model. And now I would like to show how, in classical antiquity, sexual activity and sexual pleasures were problematized through practices of the self, bringing into play the criteria of an 'aesthetics of existence.'

These, then, are the reasons that led me to recenter my entire study on the genealogy of desiring man, from classical antiquity through the first centuries of Christianity. The documents I will refer to are for the most part 'prescriptive' texts – that is, texts whose main object, whatever their form (speech, dialogue, treatise, collection of precepts, etc.) is to suggest rules of conduct. I will appeal to the theoretical texts on the doctrine of pleasures and passions only to look for clarifications. The domain I will be analyzing is made up of texts written for the purpose of offering rules, opinions, and advice on how to behave as one should: 'practical' texts, which are themselves objects of a 'practice' in that they were designed to be read, learned, reflected upon, and tested out, and they were intended to constitute the eventual framework of everyday conduct. These texts thus served as functional devices that would enable individuals to question their own conduct, to watch over and give shape to it, and to shape themselves as ethical subjects; in short, their function was 'etho-poetic,' to transpose a word found in Plutarch.

But since this analysis of desiring man is situated at the point where an archaeology of problematizations and a genealogy of practices of the self intersect, I would like to explain how I was led, through certain paradoxes and difficulties, to substitute a history of ethical problematizations based on practices of the self, for a history of systems of morality based, hypothetically, on interdictions. [. . .]

[. . .]

Morality and practice of the self

By 'morality,' one means a set of values and rules of action that are recommended to individuals through the intermediary of various prescriptive agencies such as the family (in one of its roles), educational institutions, churches, and so forth. It is sometimes the case that these rules and values are plainly set forth in a coherent doctrine and an explicit teaching. But it also happens that they are transmitted in a diffuse manner, so that, far from constituting a systematic ensemble, they form a complex interplay of elements that counterbalance and correct one another, and cancel each other out on certain points, thus providing for compromises or loopholes. With these qualifications taken into account, we can call this prescriptive ensemble a 'moral code.' But 'morality' also refers to the real behavior of individuals in relation to the rules and values that are recommended to them: the word thus designates the manner in which they comply more or less fully with a standard of conduct, the manner in which they obey or resist an interdiction or a prescription; the manner in which they respect or disregard a set of values. In studying this aspect of morality, one must determine how and with what margins of variation or transgression individuals or groups conduct themselves in reference to a prescriptive system that is explicitly or implicitly operative in their culture, and of which they are more or less aware. We can call this level of phenomena 'the morality of behaviors.'

There is more. For a rule of conduct is one thing; the conduct that may be measured by this rule is another. But another thing still is the manner in which one ought to 'conduct oneself' – that is, the manner in which one ought to form oneself as an ethical subject acting in reference to the prescriptive elements that make up the code. Given a code of actions, and with regard to a specific type of actions (which can be defined by their degree of conformity with or divergence from the code), there are different ways to 'conduct oneself' morally, different ways for the acting individual to operate, not just as an agent, but as an ethical subject of this action. Take, for example, a code of sexual prescriptions enjoining the two marital partners to practice a strict and symmetrical conjugal fidelity, always with a view to procreation; there will be many ways, even within such a rigid frame, to practice that austerity, many ways to 'be faithful.' These differences can bear on several points worth considering.

They concern what might be called the *determination of the ethical substance*; that is, the way in which the individual has to constitute this or that part of himself as the prime material of his moral conduct. Thus, one can relate the crucial aspects of the practice of fidelity to the strict observance of interdictions and obligations in the very acts one accomplishes. But one can also make the essence of fidelity consist in the mastery of desires, in the fervent combat one directs against them, in the strength with which one is able to resist temptations: what makes up the content of fidelity in this case is that vigilance and that struggle. In these conditions, the contradictory movements of the soul – much more than the carrying out of the acts themselves – will be the prime material of moral practice. Alternatively, one can have it consist in the intensity, continuity, and reciprocity of feelings that are experienced *vis-à-vis* the partner, and in the quality of the relationship that permanently binds the two spouses.

The differences can also have to do with the *mode of subjection* (*mode d'assujettissement*); that is, with the way in which the individual establishes his relation to the rule and recognizes himself as obliged to put it into practice. One can, for example, practice conjugal fidelity and comply with the precept that imposes it, because one acknowledges oneself to be a member of the group that accepts it, declares adherence to it out loud, and silently preserves it as a custom. But one can practice it, too, because one regards oneself as an heir to a spiritual tradition that one has the responsibility of maintaining or reviving; one can also practice fidelity in response to an appeal, by offering oneself as an example, or by seeking to give one's personal life a form that answers to criteria of brilliance, beauty, nobility, or perfection.

There are also possible differences in the forms of *elaboration*, of *ethical work* (*travail éthique*) that one performs on oneself, not only in order to bring one's conduct into compliance with a given rule, but to attempt to transform oneself into the ethical subject of one's behavior. Thus, sexual austerity can be practiced through a long effort of learning, memorization, and assimilation of a systematic ensemble of precepts, and through a regular checking of conduct aimed at measuring the exactness with which one is applying these rules. It can be practiced in the form of a sudden, all-embracing, and definitive renunciation of pleasures; it can also be practiced in the form of a relentless combat whose vicissitudes – including momentary setbacks – can have meaning and value in themselves; and it can be practiced through a decipherment as painstaking, continuous, and detailed as possible, of the movements of desire in all its hidden forms, including the most obscure.

Other differences, finally, concern what might be called the *telos* of the ethical subject: an action is not only moral in itself, in its singularity; it is also moral in its circumstantial integration and by virtue of the place it occupies in a pattern of conduct. It is an element and an aspect of this conduct, and it marks a stage in its life, a possible advance in its continuity. A moral action tends toward its own accomplishment; but it also aims beyond the latter, to the establishing of a moral conduct that commits an individual, not only to other actions always in conformity with values and rules, but to a certain mode of being, a mode of being characteristic of the ethical subject. Many differences are possible here as well: conjugal fidelity can be associated with a moral conduct that aspires to an ever more complete mastery of the self; it can be a moral conduct that manifests a sudden and radical detachment *vis-à-vis* the world; it may strain toward a perfect tranquillity of soul, a total insensitivity to the agitations of the passions, or toward a purification that will ensure salvation after death and blissful immortality.

In short, for an action to be 'moral,' it must not be reducible to an act or a series of acts conforming to a rule, a law, or a value. Of course all moral action involves a relationship with the reality in which it is carried out, and a relationship with the self. The latter is not simply 'self-awareness' but self-formation as an 'ethical subject,' a process in which the individual delimits that part of himself that will form the object of his moral practice, defines his position relative to the precept he will follow, and decides on a certain mode of being that will serve as his moral goal. And this requires him to act upon himself, to monitor, test, improve, and transform himself. There is no specific moral action that does not refer to a unified moral conduct; no moral conduct that does not call for the forming of oneself as an ethical subject; and no forming of the ethical subject without 'modes of subjectivation' and an 'ascetics' or 'practices of the self' that support them. Moral action is indissociable from these forms of self-activity, and they do not differ any less from one morality to another than do the systems of values, rules, and interdictions.

These distinctions are bound to have effects that are not confined to theory. They also have consequences for historical analysis. Anyone who wishes to study the history of a 'morality' has to take into account the different realities that are covered by the term. A history of 'moral behaviors' would study the extent to which actions of certain individuals or groups are consistent with the rules and values that are prescribed for them by various agencies. A history of 'codes' would analyze the different systems of rules and values that are operative in a given society or group, the agencies or mechanisms of constraint that enforce them, the forms they take in their multifariousness, their divergences and their contra-dictions. And finally, a history of the way in which individuals are urged to constitute themselves as subjects of moral conduct would be concerned with the models proposed for setting up and developing relationships with the self, for self-reflection, self-knowledge, self-examination, for the decipherment of the self by oneself, for the transformations that one seeks to accomplish with oneself as object. This last is what might be called a history of 'ethics' and 'ascetics,' understood as a history of the forms of moral subjectivation and of the practices of self that are meant to ensure it.

If it is true, in fact, that every morality, in the broad sense, comprises the two elements I have just mentioned: codes of behavior and forms of subjectivation; if it is true that they can never be entirely dissociated, though they may develop in relative independence from one another – then we should not be surprised to find that in certain moralities the main emphasis is placed on the code, on its systematicity, its richness, its capacity to adjust to every possible case and to embrace every area of behavior. With moralities of this type, the important thing is to focus on the instances of authority that enforce the code, that require it to be learned and observed, that penalize infractions; in these conditions, the subjectivation occurs basically in a quasi-juridical form, where the ethical subject refers his conduct to a law, or set of laws, to which he must submit at the risk of committing offenses that may make him liable to punishment. It would be quite incorrect to reduce Christian morality – one probably should say 'Christian moralities' – to such a model; and yet it may not be wrong to think that the organization of the penitential system at the beginning of the thirteenth century, and its development up to the eve of the Reformation, brought about a very strong 'juridification' – more precisely, a very strong 'codification' – of the moral experience. It was against this codification that many spiritual movements reacted before the Reformation.

On the other hand, it is easy to conceive of moralities in which the strong and dynamic element is to be sought in the forms of subjectivation and the practices of the self. In this case, the system of codes and rules of behavior may be rather rudimentary. Their exact observance may be relatively unimportant, at least compared with what is required of the individual in the relationship he has with himself, in his different actions, thoughts, and feelings as he endeavors to form himself as an ethical subject. Here the emphasis is on the forms of relations with the self, on the methods and techniques by which he works them out, on the exercises by which he makes of himself an object to be known, and on the practices that enable him to transform his own mode of being. These 'ethics-oriented' moralities (which do not necessarily correspond to those involving 'ascetic denial') have been very important in Christianity, functioning alongside the 'code-oriented' moralities. Between the two types there have been, at different times, juxtapositions, rivalries and conflicts, and compromises.

Now, it seems clear, from a first approach at least, that moral conceptions in Greek and Greco-Roman antiquity were much more oriented toward practices of the self and the question of *askēsis* than toward codifications of conducts and the strict definition of what is permitted and what is forbidden. If exception is made of the *Republic* and the *Laws*, one finds very few references to the principle of a code that would define in detail the right conduct to maintain, few references to the need for an authority charged with seeing to its application, few references to the possibility of punishments that would sanction infractions. Although the necessity of respecting the law and the customs – the *nomoi* – was very often underscored, more important than the content of the law and its conditions of application was the attitude that caused one to respect them. The accent was placed on the relationship with the self that enabled a person to keep from being carried away by the appetites and pleasures, to maintain a mastery and superiority over them, to keep his senses in a state of tranquillity, to remain free from interior bondage to the passions, and to achieve a mode of being that could be defined by the full enjoyment of oneself, or the perfect supremacy of oneself over oneself.

This explains the choice of method I have kept to throughout this study on the sexual morality of pagan and Christian antiquity; that is, I had to keep in mind the distinction between the code elements of a morality and the elements of ascesis, neglecting neither their coexistence, their interrelations, their relative autonomy, nor their possible differences of emphasis. I had to take into account everything, in these moralities, that seemed to have to do with the privileged status of the practices of the self and the interest that may have been accorded them; with the effort that was made to develop them, perfect them, and teach them; and with the debate that went on concerning them. Consequently, the question that is so often raised regarding the continuity (or break) between the philosophical moralities of antiquity and Christian morality had to be reformulated; instead of asking what were the code elements that Christianity may have borrowed from ancient thought, and what were those that it added in its own right, in order to define what was permitted and what forbidden within a sexuality assumed to be constant, it seemed more pertinent to ask how, given the continuity, transfer, or modification of codes, the forms of self-relationship (and the practices of the self that were associated with them) were defined, modified, recast, and diversified.

I am not supposing that the codes are unimportant. But one notices that they ultimately revolve around a rather small number of rather simple principles: perhaps men are not much more inventive when it comes to interdictions than they are when it comes to pleasures. Their stability is also rather remarkable; the notable proliferation of codifications (concerning permitted or forbidden places, partners, and acts) occurred rather late in Christianity. On the other hand, it appears – at any rate this is the hypothesis I would like to explore here – that there is a whole rich and complex field of historicity in the way the individual is summoned to recognize himself as an ethical subject of sexual conduct. This will be a matter of seeing how that subjectivation was defined and transformed, from classical Greek thought up to the formulation of the Christian doctrine and pastoral ministry regarding the flesh. [. . .]

MICHEL FOUCAULT

Note

1   It is not quite correct to imply that since Burckhardt the study of these arts and this aesthetics of existence has been completely neglected. One thinks of Benjamin's study on Baudelaire. There is also an interesting analysis in Stephen Greenblatt's recent book, *Renaissance Self-fashioning* (1980).

29

Reflections on the idea of the 'cultivation of the self'
Pierre Hadot

In his preface to *The Use of Pleasure*, as well as in a chapter of *The Care of the Self*,[1] Michel Foucault made mention of my article 'Exercices spirituels', the first version of which dates back to 1976.[2] Foucault seems to have been particularly interested by the following points, which I developed in this article: the description of ancient philosophy as an art, style, or way of life; the attempt I made to explain how modern philosophy had forgotten this tradition, and had become an almost entirely theoretical discourse; and the idea I sketched out in the article, and have developed more fully [in *Philosophy as a Way of Life*], that Christianity had taken over as its own certain techniques of spiritual exercises, as they had already been practiced in antiquity.

Here, I should like to offer a few remarks with a view to delineating the differences of interpretation, and in the last analysis of philosophical choice, which separate us, above and beyond our points of agreement. These differences could have provided the substance for a dialogue between us, which, unfortunately, was interrupted all too soon by Foucault's premature death.

In *The Care of the Self*, Foucault meticulously describes what he terms the 'practices of the self' (*pratiques de soi*), recommended in antiquity by Stoic philosophers. These include the care of one's self, which can only be carried out under the direction of a spiritual guide; the attention paid to the body and the soul which the 'care of the self' implies; exercises of abstinence; examination of the conscience; the filtering of representations; and, finally, the conversion toward and possession of the self. M. Foucault conceives of these practices as 'arts of existence' and 'techniques of the self.'

It is quite true that, in this connection, the ancients did speak of an 'art of living.' It seems to me, however, that the description M. Foucault

This chapter is taken from *Philosophy as a Way of Life* (Oxford, Blackwell, 1995), pp. 206–13.

gives of what I had termed 'spiritual exercises,' and which he prefers to call 'techniques of the self,' is precisely focused far too much on the 'self,' or at least on a specific conception of the self.

In particular, Foucault presents Greco-Roman ethics as an ethics of the pleasure one takes in oneself: 'Access to the self is liable to replace this kind of violent, uncertain, and temporary pleasures with a form of pleasure one takes in oneself, serenely and forever.'[3] To illustrate his point, Foucault cites Seneca's twenty-third Letter, where he speaks of the joy one can find within oneself, and specifically within the best portion of oneself. In fact, however, I must say that there is a great deal of inexactitude in this way of presenting the matter. In Letter 23, Seneca explicitly opposes *voluptas* and *gaudium* – pleasure and joy – and one cannot, therefore, speak of 'another form of pleasure,' as does Foucault (*Care of the Self*, p. 83) when talking about joy. This is not just a quibble over words, although the Stoics did attach a great deal of importance to words, and carefully distinguished between *hedone* – 'pleasure' – and *eupatheia* – 'joy'.[4] No, this is no mere question of vocabulary. If the Stoics insist on the word *gaudium*/'joy,' it is precisely because they refuse to introduce the principle of pleasure into moral life. For them, happiness does not consist in pleasure, but in virtue itself, which is its own reward. Long before Kant, the Stoics strove jealously to preserve the purity of intention of the moral consciousness.

Secondly and most importantly, it is not the case that the Stoic finds his joy in his 'self;' rather, as Seneca says, he finds it 'in the best portion of the self,' in 'the true good.'[5] Joy is to be found 'in the conscience turned towards the good; in intentions which have no other object than virtue; in just actions.'[6] Joy can be found in what Seneca calls 'perfect reason'[7] (that is to say, in divine reason)[8] since for him, human reason is nothing other than reason capable of being made perfect. The 'best portion of oneself,' then, is, in the last analysis, a transcendent self. Seneca does not find his joy in 'Seneca,' but by transcending 'Seneca'; by discovering that there is within him – within all human beings, that is, and within the cosmos itself – a reason which is a part of universal reason.

In fact, the goal of Stoic exercises is to go beyond the self, and think and act in unison with universal reason. The three exercises described by Marcus Aurelius,[9] following Epictetus, are highly significant in this regard. [. . .] [T]hey are as follows:

1 to judge objectively, in accordance with inner reason;
2 to act in accordance with the reason which all human beings have in common; and
3 to accept the destiny imposed upon us by cosmic reason. For the Stoics, there is only one single reason at work here, and this reason is man's true self.

I can well understand Foucault's motives for giving short shrift to these aspects, of which he was perfectly aware. His description of the practices of the self – like, moreover, my description of spiritual exercises – is not merely an historical study, but rather a tacit attempt to offer contemporary mankind a model of life, which Foucault calls 'an aesthetics of existence.' Now, according to a more or less universal tendency of modern thought, which is perhaps more instinctive than reflective, the ideas of 'universal reason' and 'universal nature' do not have much meaning any more. It was therefore convenient to 'bracket' them.

For the moment, then, let us say that, from an historical point of view, it seems difficult to accept that the philosophical practice of the Stoics and Platonists was nothing but a relationship to one's self, a culture of the self, or a pleasure taken in oneself. The psychic content of these exercises seems to me to be something else entirely. In my view, the feeling of belonging to a whole is an essential element: belonging, that is, both to the whole constituted by the human community, and to that constituted by the cosmic whole. Seneca sums it up in four words: *Toti se inserens mundo*,[10] 'Plunging oneself into the totality of the world.' In his admirable *Anthropologie philosophique*,[11] Groethuysen pointed out the importance of this fundamental point. Such a cosmic perspective radically transforms the feeling one has of oneself.

Oddly, Foucault does not have much to say about the Epicureans. This is all the more surprising in that Epicurean ethics is, in a sense, an ethics without norms. It is an autonomous ethics, for it cannot found itself upon nature, which according to its views is the product of chance. It would seem, therefore, to be an ethics perfectly suited to the modern mentality. Perhaps the reason for this silence is to be found in the fact that it is rather difficult to integrate Epicurean hedonism into the overall schema of the use of pleasures proposed by M. Foucault. Be this as it may, the Epicureans did make use of spiritual exercises, for instance the examination of conscience. As we have said, however, these practices are not based on the norms of nature or universal reason, because for the Epicureans the formation of the world is the result of mere chance. Nevertheless, here again, this spiritual exercise cannot be defined simply as culture of the self, a relationship of the self to the self, or pleasure that can be found in one's own self. The Epicurean was not afraid to admit that he needed other things besides himself in order to satisfy his desires and to experience pleasure. He needed bodily nourishment and the pleasures of love, but he also required a physical theory of the universe, in order to eliminate the fear of the gods and of death. He needed the company of the other members of the Epicurean school, so that he could find happiness in mutual affection. Finally, he needed the imaginative contemplation of an infinite number of universes in the infinite void, in order to experience what Lucretius calls *divina voluptas et horror*. Metrodorus, a disciple of Epicurus, gives a good account of the Epicurean sage's immersion in the cosmos: 'Remember that, although born mortal with a limited life-span, you have risen in thought as far as the eternity and infinity of things, and that you have seen everything that has been, and everything that shall be.'[12] In Epicureanism, there is an extraordinary reversal of perspective. Precisely because existence seems to the Epicurean to be pure chance, inexorably unique, he greets life like a kind of miracle, a gratuitous, unexpected gift of nature, and existence for him is a wonderful celebration.

Let us consider another example to illustrate the differences between our interpretations of the 'care of the self.' In an interesting article entitled 'Écriture de soi,'[13] M. Foucault took as his point of departure a remarkable text concerning the therapeutic value of writing, which I had studied in *Exercices spirituels*. According to this text, St Antony used to advise his disciples to write down their actions and the emotions of their souls, as if they were going to make them known to others. 'Let writing take the place of the eyes of other people,' Antony used to say. This anecdote leads M. Foucault to reflect on the various forms adopted in antiquity by what he calls the 'writing of the self.' In particular, he examines the literary genre of *hypomnemata*, which one could translate as 'spiritual notebooks,' in which one writes down other people's thoughts, which may serve for the edification of the person writing them down. Foucault describes the goal of this exercise in the following terms: the point is to 'capture what-has-already-been-said [*capter le déjà-dit*],' and to 'collect what one may have heard or read, with a view to nothing less than the constitution of the self.'[14] He then asks himself, 'How can we be placed in the presence of our selves with the help of ageless discourses, picked-up from any old place?' And he replies as follows: 'this exercise was supposed to allow one to turn back towards the past. The contribution of the *hypomnemata* is one of the means by which one detaches the soul from worries about the future, in order to inflect it towards meditation on the past.' Both in Epicurean and in Stoic ethics, Foucault thinks he perceives the refusal of a mental attitude directed toward the future, and the tendency to accord a positive value to the possession of a past which one can enjoy autonomously and without worries.

It seems to me that this is a mistaken interpretation. It is true that the Epicureans – and *only* the Epicureans – did consider the memory of pleasant moments in the past as one of the principal sources of pleasure, but this has nothing to do with the meditation on 'what-has-already-been-said' practiced in *hypomnemata*. Rather, Stoics and Epicureans had in common an attitude which consisted in liberating oneself not only from worries about the future, but also from the burden of the past, in order to concentrate on the present moment; in order either to enjoy it, or to act within it. From this point of view, neither the Stoics nor even the Epicureans accorded a positive value to the past. The fundamental philosophic attitude consisted in *living in the present*, and in possessing not the past, but the present. That the Epicureans also attached a great deal of importance to the thoughts formulated by their predecessors is a wholly different matter. But although *hypomnemata* deal with what has already been said, they do not deal with just anything 'already said,' the only merit of which would be that it is a part of the past. Rather, it is because one recognizes in

THE 'CULTIVATION OF THE SELF'

this 'thing already said' – which usually consisted in the dogmas of the school's founding members – that which reason itself has to say *to the present*. It is because one recognizes, in the dogmas of Epicurus or Chrysippus, an *ever-present* value, precisely because they are the very expression of reason. In other words, when one writes or notes something down, it is not an alien thought one is making one's own. Rather, one is utilizing formulae considered as apt to actualize what is already present within the reason of the person writing, and bring it to life.

According to M. Foucault, this method made a deliberate attempt to be eclectic, and therefore implied a personal choice; this then explains the 'constitution of the self.'

> Writing as a personal exercise, done by oneself and for oneself, is an art of disparate truth; more precisely, it is a way of combining the traditional authority of what has already been said, with the singularity of the truth which asserts itself in it, and the particularity of the circumstances which determine its utilization.

In fact, however, personal choice is not to be found in eclecticism, at least for the Stoics and Epicureans. Eclecticism is only used for converting beginners. At that stage, anything goes. For instance, Foucault finds an example of eclecticism in the *Letters to Lucilius*, in which the Stoic Seneca quotes sayings of Epicurus. The goal of these letters, however, is to convert Lucilius, and to cause him to begin to lead a moral life. The utilization of Epicurus appears only in the first letters, and soon disappears.[15] On the contrary, personal choice in fact intervenes only when one adheres exclusively to a precise form of life, be it Stoicism or Epicureanism, considered as in conformity with reason. It is only in the New Academy – in the person of Cicero, for instance – that a personal choice is made according to what reason considers as most likely at a given moment.

It is thus not the case, as Foucault maintains,[16] that the individual forges a spiritual identity for himself by writing down and re-reading disparate thoughts. In the first place, as we have seen, these thoughts are not disparate, but chosen because of their coherence. Secondly, and most importantly, the point is not to forge oneself a spiritual identity by writing, but rather to liberate oneself from one's individuality, in order to raise oneself up to universality. It is thus incorrect to speak of 'writing of the self': not only is it not the case that one 'writes oneself,' but what is more, it is not the case that writing constitutes the self. Writing, like the other spiritual exercises, *changes the level of the self*, and universalizes it. The miracle of this exercise, carried out in solitude, is that it allows its practitioner to accede to the universality of reason within the confines of space and time.

For the monk Antony, the therapeutic value of writing consisted precisely in its universalizing power. Writing, says Antony, takes the place of other people's eyes. A person writing feels he is being watched; he is no longer alone, but is a part of the silently present human community. When one formulates one's personal acts in writing, one is taken up by the machinery of reason, logic, and universality. What was confused and subjective becomes thereby objective.

To summarize: what Foucault calls 'practices of the self' do indeed correspond, for the Platonists as well as for the Stoics, to a movement of conversion toward the self. One frees oneself from exteriority, from personal attachment to exterior objects, and from the pleasures they may provide. One observes oneself, to determine whether one has made progress in this exercise. One seeks to be one's own master, to possess oneself, and find one's happiness in freedom and inner independence. I concur on all these points. I do think, however, that this movement of interiorization is inseparably linked to another movement, whereby one rises to a higher psychic level, at which one encounters another kind of exteriorization, another relationship with 'the exterior.' This is a new way of being-in-the-world, which consists in becoming aware of oneself as a part of nature, and a portion of universal reason. At this point, one no longer lives in the usual, conventional human world, but in the world of nature. One is then practicing 'physics' as a spiritual exercise.

In this way, one identifies oneself with an 'Other': nature, or universal reason, as it is present within each individual. This implies a radical transformation of perspective, and contains a universalist, cosmic dimension, upon which, it seems to me, M. Foucault did not sufficiently insist. Interiorization is a going beyond oneself; it is universalization.

The preceding remarks are not intended to be relevant only to an historical analysis of ancient philosophy. They are also an attempt at defining an ethical model which modern man can discover in antiquity. What I am afraid of is that, by focusing his interpretation too exclusively on the culture of the self, the care of the self, and conversion toward the self – more generally, by defining his ethical model as an aesthetics of existence – M. Foucault is propounding a culture of the self which is *too* aesthetic. In other words, this may be a new form of dandyism, late twentieth-century style. This, however, deserves a more attentive study than I am able to devote to it here. Personally, I believe firmly – albeit perhaps naïvely – that it is possible for modern man to live, not as a sage (*sophos*) – most of the ancients did not hold this to be possible – but as a practitioner of the ever-fragile *exercise* of wisdom. This can be attempted, starting out from the lived experience of the concrete, living, and perceiving subject, under the triple form defined, as we saw above, by Marcus Aurelius:

1   as an effort to practice objectivity of judgment;
2   as an effort to live according to justice, in the service of the human community; and
3   as an effort to become aware of our situation as a part of the universe. Such an exercise of wisdom will thus be an attempt to render oneself open to the universal.

More specifically, I think modern man can practice the spiritual exercises of antiquity, at the same time separating them from the philosophical or mythic discourse which came along with them. The same spiritual exercise can, in fact, be justified by extremely diverse philosophical discourses. These latter are nothing but clumsy attempts, coming after the fact, to describe and justify inner experiences whose existential density is not, in the last analysis, susceptible of any attempt at theorization or systematization. Stoics and Epicureans, for example – for completely different reasons – urged their disciples to concentrate their attention on the present moment, and free themselves from worries about the future as well as the burden of the past. Whoever concretely practices this exercise, however, sees the universe with new eyes, as if he were seeing it for the first time. In the enjoyment of the pure present, he discovers the mystery and splendor of existence. At such moments, as Nietzsche said, we say yes 'not only to ourselves, but to all existence.'[17] It is therefore not necessary, in order to practice these exercises, to believe in the Stoics' nature or universal reason. Rather, as one practices them, one lives concretely according to reason. In the words of Marcus Aurelius: 'Although everything happens at random, don't you, too, act at random.'[18] In this way, we can accede concretely to the universality of the cosmic perspective, and the wonderful mystery of the presence of the universe.

Notes

1 M. Foucault, *The Care of the Self: History of Sexuality*, vol. 3, trans. Robert Hurley (New York 1986). [*Translator's note*: references are to the French edition, *Le Souci de soi* (Paris, 1984).]

2 P. Hadot, 'Exercices spirituels', *Annuaire de la 5ᵉ Section de l'École pratique des Hautes Études* (1975–6).

3 Foucault, *Souci*, pp. 83–4.

4 We find this distinction again in Plotinus and in Bergson, the latter linking together joy and creation; cf. Henri Bergson, *L'Energie spirituelle*, 14th edn (Paris, 1930), p. 24.

5 Seneca, *Letters*, 23, 6.

6 Ibid., 23, 7.

7 Ibid., 124, 23.

8 Ibid., 92, 27.

9 Marcus Aurelius, *Meditations*, 7, 54; 9, 6; 8, 7.

10 Seneca, *Letters* 46, 6.

11 B. Groethuysen, *Anthropologie philosophique* (Paris, 1952, repr. 1980), p. 80.

12 Cf. above.

13 M. Foucault, 'L'écriture de soi', *Corps écrit*, 5 (1983), pp. 3–23.

14 Foucault, 'L'écriture de soi', p. 8.

15 Cf. P. Hadot, 'Épicure et l'enseignement philosophique héllenique et romain', in *Actes du VIIIe Congrès Budé* (Paris, 1969), p. 351.

16 Foucault, 'L'écriture de soi', pp. 11–13.

17 [567]

18 Marcus Aurelius, *Meditations*, 10, 28, 3.

30

Persons and personae   **Amélie Oksenberg Rorty**

Forced options are usually false options.

Will there be an entry for *persons* in the great concordance that replaces an ontological table of contents? If so, it would have to be a very complex set of multiple listings, with cross-referenced entries that allow individuals or classes – families, corporations, fetuses, the legally disenfranchised – to qualify as persons by some criteria, not by others. With so complex a system of cross-classification, it does not matter whether we deny that there is a single concept of persons, or recognize that the diversity of criteria for its attribution allows individuals and classes to qualify as persons on radically different grounds. The difficult cases are, of course, practical cases where the legal and sociopolitical treatment of individuals and classes are affected by their classification. The criteria for persons are coordinate with, rather than foundational for, a range of normative political principles, and the criteria for personal identity express rather than provide the grounds for legal principles. Neither can provide a foundational justification for the other, and both are primarily expressed and articulated in the details of the particular practices that serve as their context.

The class of persons and the criteria for their identity are defined by reference to a range of activities that are regarded, often unselfconsciously, as centrally and normatively important to a culture, a historical period, or an investigative context. [. . .] Practical and political considerations are brought into play even when – as is the case in the abortion controversy – 'the' concept of person is adjusted to conform to theological doctrine or to the wide-ranging implications of scientific discoveries.

The modern Western conception of persons derives many of its characterizations – that persons are reflective responsible agents – from Augustine. But his account appears within a theological frame that defines the primary concerns and tasks of the post-Adamic condition. Augustine held that our basic activities are directed toward integrating the divided and corrupt psyche of the natural, fallen condition, so that we can freely consent to being the agents of God's purposes. Augustine used his analysis of the doctrine of the Trinity – his account of how the three persons of the divinity form a single substantial unity – to explain how persons can be simple unified agents despite the diversity, and sometimes the conflicts, among their faculties and powers. His discussions are constrained by the normative requirements set by biblical texts and orthodox doctrine. But his account of persons as agents directed toward integration and salvation is also indebted to Platonic accounts of the soul's erotic attraction to the form of the Good and to legal and dramatic conceptions of *personae* as agents responsible for the unfolding of events.

When political activity is regarded as the privileged, primary activity, the political definition of persons is detached from the theological context in which it had been developed. Conceptions of persons and their powers are reoriented: philosophic interest shifts from political to legal and to social and communitarian issues. Focusing on the source and grounds for the political contract, Hobbes concentrates on the capacities for prudential, rational choice; Locke locates the legal conditions for personal liability and responsibility in the continuity of memory; Hume analyzes the relation between the self-interested passions and those actuated by the sentiment of justice; Rousseau attempts to reconcile the tensions between individual autonomy and the social formation of character. Kant argues that the possibility of morality depends on the capacity of persons to treat one another with respect, as rational agents, members of the kingdom of ends. Theories of political and social persons focus on issues of equality and rights, and on the social formation and transformation of natural psychological processes.

Some of the apparently intractable debates about persons occur when the concerns of one context are imported to another, in the premature interest of constructing a unified theory, or as a rhetorical move in a political polemic. The appearance of forced options often arises from a misguided attempt to derive decisions from 'the' (illicitly decontextualized) concept of a person. When there are repetitive irresolvable debates about the primacy of competing concepts of persons – as there are, for instance, in the controversies over the justifiability of abortion – the first move should be to formulate the issues that lie behind the dispute, specifying the distinctive sources and contexts of conflicting intuitions. Apparently irreconcilable opponents are often interested in different issues, asking different questions, each assuming that the answer to one question determines the answer to the others. In the case of the abortion issue, for instance, apparently conflicting intuitions on the primacy of theological, biological, or sociopolitical criteria for personal identity might be reconciled by regionalizing their respective dominance. Even if a particular sectarian theology classifies the fetus as a person, nothing follows about the propriety of importing that particular theological conception to legal and political contexts. However detailed and articulated it may be, a theological doctrine does not, by itself, establish the propriety of its dominance in a nontheocratic legal system. The criteria for biological and legal individuation need not coincide; nor need those for theological and social identification.

Concerns about how such a strongly contextualist approach identifies entities across contexts are deflected by refusing to provide a general answer. Since questions and contexts are particular all the way up and all the way down, such questions are given their sense and direction by the particular context in which they arise. The question 'How are contexts identified and individuated?' is answered by the counter-question, 'Which contexts?'[1]

Note

1   An analogy might be helpful: because maps are constructed for specific purposes (to chart mountain passes, or to facilitate navigation, for example), it is sometimes difficult to identify topographical locations across maps. The system of latitudinal and longitudinal designations serves the purpose for which it was constructed: to permit the identification or projection of geographical locations across maps. That system of coordination is constructed from a perspective that is independent of any particular terrestrial map; but it is nevertheless still a particular perspective, selected to serve a particular function. It cannot, for example, be used to resolve disputes about the relative merits of various definitions of absolute space.

misrecognition, 48, 52
  and ideology, 32
morality
  Christian, 341–2, 370, 371
  history of, and moral behaviours, 369–70
  and practices of self, 367–71, 373–9
mother, 22, 52, 63, 72
  body of, 72
  breast/object relations, 130–1, 132–5, 137, 156–7
  and desire, 54–5
  good-enough, 156, 157, 158
  mirror role of, 22, 52, 144–9
  oedipal model, 231, 232, 235–40
  rage against, 134–5, 224–5
mourning
  classic theories of, 268–70
  development of contemporary theory, 128, 270–3
  psychotherapy as social control, 273–5
mutual trust, 263–4

Name of the Father, 55
names
  at each stage of life, 333
  Australian tribal culture, 335
  forenames, 333–4, 339
  fraternity, 330–1, 338
  kinship, 330
  profane and sacred, 332
  proper, 301–3, 334
  pseudonyms (nicknames), 339–40
  representing collective noun, 337
  and role in clan, 329–30
  secret, 332, 333
  surnames, 339
narcissism, 138, 222–3
  characteristics, 223–7
  and oedipal model, 232, 233, 234, 236, 244
  primary, secondary and pathological, 223
  social influences on, 227–9
neuroses, 203, 227–8
nursing service study, 163, 179–81
  defensive techniques, 166–73, 178–9
  nature of anxiety, 164–6
  social defense system, 173–9

object love, 235–6, 238
object relations, 130–43, 144–6
  and narcissism, 222–3
  rage against absent or lost objects, 192, 224–5
  schizoid, 137–9, 188–91, 192
  see also transitional objects/phenomena

Oedipal crisis, 21
oedipal model
  father, 231, 232, 233–5, 237–8, 241–2, 244, 245
  mother, 231, 232, 235–40
  new, 244–5
  polarity principle, 240–4
  and subjectivity, 22–3
Oedipus, 100
Oedipus complex, 56, 80
omnipotence phantasies
  in infancy, 134, 164, 234–5
  in narcissism, 224, 225, 226
Osbourne, P., 22, 23
Other, 13, 17, 19, 22, 35, 53, 54, 56, 61, 62, 79, 83, 95, 96, 97, 99, 100, 101, 112, 378
  Absent One, 79, 82, 83
  castration, 83, 85
  and 'I', 41, 109
  race issues, 95–6, 99–101, 206
Oudart, J.-P., 76–7, 79, 82

paranoia, 131, 137
paranoid-schizoid position, 131
  and depressive position, 139–41
Parkes, C.M., 268, 270–1
Parsons, T., 306, 307
paternal law, 54
paternal metaphor, 55, 100–1
patriarchy, 11, 12
Pêcheux, M., 20
performativity, 10, 13, 15, 26, 28, 108
  and gender, 109
  as power, 108
  and power, 116
'persona', 336–40
personal pronouns see 'I'
personal satisfactions, deprivation in nursing service, 177–9
'persons', 327–8
  Christian, 341–2
  moral fact, 340–1
  options in conceptualization of, 380–2
  psychological being, 342–4
  'role' and place of, 329–36
phallic monism, theory of, 238–9
phallus, 55, 56–8, 59, 62, 63, 64–5
  castration, 56
  symbolic, 57, 58
phantasy
  infant, 133, 134–5, 137, 164, 234–5
  narcissistic, 224, 225, 226
  situations and objective reality, 165, 179
Platonists, 375, 378

self
  -actualization, 253, 254
  care of, 376
  consciousness of, 40–1
  constitution of, 377
  ethics of pleasure one takes in, 374
  false, in therapy, 275
  -formation as ethical subject, 369
  government of others and, 317–22
  and 'I', 328
  -identity, history and modernity, 251–5
  -image and internalized image, 225
  as internally referential, 255
  knowledge of, 320
  -mastery, 319–20
  -perception, 291–2, 294, 296
  production of, 26
  reflexivity of, 252–3, 262
  'relation to ourselves', 313–17
  'techniques of', 318, 365–6, 370, 373–4
  'technologies of', 317
  -therapy, 248–51, 252, 255–6, 262–3, 274
  trajectory of, 252, 255
  see also practices of self
semiotic, 72, 73
semiotic chora, 70
  normative, 27
Seneca, 374, 377
'sex', 102
  discursively constructed, 27
  and identification, 28
sexual anxiety and racism, 206–12
sexual difference, 11, 28, 57, 61, 115
sexual difference and language, 53, 57–8,
    59–60, 61
sexual identity, 56, 57
sexuality, 13, 21, 53, 56, 58, 102, 362–4,
    365, 366
  of children, 103
  and concept of drive, 53–4
  deployment of, 104–6
  and desire, 53
  and power relations, 102–6, 116
  and unconscious, 51, 62–5
shared histories, 264
shot/reverse shot formations, 12, 77–9, 81–3
sign and language, 87, 88–9
signifiance, 62, 70, 71
signifying practice, 69
signifying systems, 70, 71–2, 73
Silverman, K., 12, 76–86
social aging, 304
social class
  dynamics of capitalism, 197
  of teachers and children, 195, 196

social control, psychotherapy as, 273–5
social defense system in nursing service,
    173–9
social influences on narcissism, 227–9
social space, 303–4
social status, 310, 311
socialization of procreative behaviour, 103
socially instituted identity, 301–3
society and individuals ('inside/outside'),
    286–91, 292, 294, 295–8
Souter, J., 29
spatialization of being, 323–4
speech-act theory, 13
speech acts, 40
spiritual exercises of antiquity, 373–9
spiritual notebooks, 376
splitting, 52
  in connection with projection and
    introjection, 133–7, 138–9
  dream analysis, 141–2
  individuals and society ('inside/outside'),
    286–91, 292, 294, 295–8
  nursing service study, 166, 170, 177
  postcolonial subject, 95–6, 99–101
  and racism, 188–94
  schizoid object relations, 132–3, 137–9
squiggle method, 125, 160
status
  dynamic aspects of, 308, 309
  as 'position' in social system, 307–8, 309,
    311
  social, 310, 311
  subjective, 310–11
  vs. role, 307, 308–9, 311
Stoics, 374, 375, 376, 377, 378, 379
subject, 37
  produced in language, 43, 52, 97
  as product of discourse, 109
  subject-of-language approach, 3, 9–13, 29
subject of ideology, 11
subjectification, 16, 24, 26
  changing relations of, 314
  diversity of regimes, 320–2
  see also genealogies, of subjectification
subjectivity
  linguistic basis of, 40–3
  and Oedipus crisis, 22–3
superego, 233–4
surnames, 339
'suture', 10, 12, 17, 19, 29, 76, 77, 78, 80,
    81, 82, 85
  cinematic model, 77–85
symbolic, 64, 72, 73, 76, 79, 80, 97
symbolic consciousness, 97–8
symbolic order, 18, 52, 54, 55, 56, 59, 63

symbolisation, 52, 59, 63, 64, 165
symbolism and transitional objects, 154–5

'techniques of self', 318, 365–6, 370, 373–4
technologies
   in genealogies of subjectification, 315
   of self, 10, 26, 27, 317
teleologies in genealogies of subjectification,
      316
telos of ethical subject, 369
'tenses', 42–3
theological definition of persons, 343–4,
      381–2
time, control of, 253
trajectory of self, 252, 255
transitional objects/phenomena, 125, 152–3,
      157–8
   characteristics, 155
   first possession, 150–5
   psychopathology manifested in area of,
      159–61
   and symbolism, 154–5
   vs. internal object, 155

unconscious, 20, 21, 51, 58, 112
   in psychoanalysis, 222
   and sexuality, 51, 62–5
   see also collective unconscious; phantasy
universality, 377, 378, 379

Veith, I., 228
violence, 351–3, 354

Weber, M., 281–2, 348–61
'windowless monads', 290, 291–2, 296
Winnicott, D.W., 52, 123, 124–5, 144–9,
      150–62
women, 59, 60–5
   in Lacanian theory, 60, 61, 62, 63, 64, 65,
      66
women's bodies, 27–8
   hysterization of, 102–3
   as language, 63
writing, therapeutic value of, 249–50, 253,
      376, 377–8